UNLIKELY

Unlikely History

The Changing German-Jewish Symbiosis, 1945–2000

EDITED BY

Leslie Morris
and Jack Zipes

palgrave

UNLIKELY HISTORY
Copyright © Leslie Morris and Jack Zipes, 2002.
All rights reserved. No part of this book may be used or reproduced in any manner whatsoever without written permission except in the case of brief quotations embodied in critical articles or reviews.

First published 2002 by PALGRAVE™
175 Fifth Avenue, New York, N.Y. 10010 and
Houndmills, Basingstoke, Hampshire, England RG21 6XS.
Companies and representatives throughout the world.

PALGRAVE is the new global publishing imprint of St. Martin's Press LLC Scholarly and Reference Division and Palgrave Publishers Ltd. (formerly Macmillan Press Ltd.).

ISBN 0–312–29389–5 (hardback)
ISBN 0–312–29390–9 (paperback)

Library of Congress Cataloging-in-Publication Data
Unlikely history : the changing German-Jewish symbiosis, 1945–2000 / edited by Leslie Morris and Jack Zipes.
   p. cm.
   Includes bibliographical references and index.
   ISBN 0–312–29390–9 (alk. paper) – ISBN 0–312–29389–5
   1. Jews—Germany—History—1945—Congresses.   2. Holocaust survivors—Germany—History—Congresses.   3. Jews—Germany—Intellectual life—Congresses.   4. Jews—Germany—Public opinion—Congresses.   5. Public opinion—Germany—Congresses.   6. Holocaust, Jewish (1939–1945)—Germany—Influence—Congresses.   7. Germany—Ethnic relations—Congresses.

DS135.G332 U55   2002
943'.004924—dc21

2001046161

Design by Letra Libre, Inc.

First edition: February 2002
10   9   8   7   6   5   4   3   2   1

Printed in the United States of America.

CONTENTS

Contributors   vii

Preface   German and Jewish Obsession   xi
                Leslie Morris and Jack Zipes

The Debate

One   Encounters Across the Void:
           Rethinking Approaches to German-Jewish Symbioses   3
               Karen Remmler

Two   The Rift and Not the Symbiosis   31
               Katja Behrens

Social and Historical Background

Three   The Transformation of the German-Jewish Community   49
               Michael Brenner

Four   Home and Displacement in a City of Bordercrossers:
           Jews in Berlin 1945–1948   63
               Atina Grossmann

Five   Jewish Existence in Germany from the
           Perspective of the Non-Jewish Majority:
           Daily Life between Anti-Semitism and Philo-Semitism   101
               Wolfgang Benz

Six   Austrian Exceptionalism: Haider,
           the European Union, the Austrian Past
           and Present: An Inimical World for the Jews   119
               Andrei S. Markovits

Seven   Anti-Semitism in East Germany, 1952–1953:
         Denial to the End   141
           Mario Kessler

Eight   Reading "Between the Lines":
         Daniel Libeskind's Berlin Jewish Museum
         and the Shattered Symbiosis   155
           Noah Isenberg

                    Cultural Relations

Nine   The Critical Embracement of Germany:
         Hans Mayer and Marcel Reich-Ranicki   183
           Jack Zipes

Ten   Return to Germany:
         German-Jewish Authors Seeking Address   203
           Pascale R. Bos

Eleven   The Janus-Faced Jew: Nathan and Shylock
         on the Postwar German Stage   233
           Anat Feinberg

Twelve   Fritz Kortner's Last Illusion   251
           Robert Shandley

Thirteen Comic Vision and "Negative Symbiosis"
         in Maxim Biller's *Harlem Holocaust* and
         Rafael Seligmann's *Der Musterjude*   263
           Rita Bashaw

Fourteen German and Austrian Jewish Women's
         Writing at the Millennium   277
           Dagmar Lorenz

Fifteen Postmemory, Postmemoir   291
           Leslie Morris

Bibliography   307
Index   327

CONTRIBUTORS

RITA BASHAW is currently a graduate student in the Department of German, Scandinavian, and Dutch at the University of Minnesota. She has recently completed her Ph.D. dissertation entitled *Witz at Work: Comic Cognition and the Grotesque in Works by Hilsenrath, Lind, and Tabori.*

KATJA BEHRENS is a translator, novelist, and short-story writer. From 1973 to 1978 she was active as an editor in the Limus and Luchterhand publishing houses, while also writing stories and working on a novel. With the publication of *Die weiße Frau* in 1978, a collection of short stories, she resigned from her editorial position and began her career as a freelance writer. Earlier that year Ms. Behrens had won the esteemed Ingeborg Bachmann award. Her second collection of stories *Jonas* (1981) won the Thaddäus Troll Prize for authors in 1982. Since that time Ms. Behrens has produced a collection of short stories, *Salomo und die anderen* (1993) as well as three novels, *Die dreizehnte Fee* (1983), *Die Vagantin* (1997), and *Zorro—Im Jahr des Pferdes* (1999). In addition, she has written radio plays and edited anthologies of letters such as *Frauenbriefe der Romantik* (1983). She has won such honors as the Villa Massimo Fellowship in 1986 and a literary sabbatical sponsored by German television (ZDF) and the city of Mainz in 1992. At various times she has also taught at Washington University (1986) and Dartmouth College (1991) in the United States and currently lives in Darmstadt.

WOLFGANG BENZ is Director of the Center for Research on Anti-Semitism at the Technical University of Berlin. He is also the co-editor of two important scholarly journals, *Dachauer Hefte* and *Zeitschrift für Geschichtswissenschaft*. His scholarship has focused largely on racism, prejudice, and genocide, and he has published numerous books dealing with anti-Semitism and the Holocaust. Among his publications are: *Die Juden in Deutschland, 1933–1945* (1988), *Das Exil der kleinen Leute* (1991), *Antisemitismus in Deutschland* (1995), *Der Holocaust* (1995), *Feindbild und Vorurteil: Beiträge über Ausgrenzung und Verfolgung* (1996), and *Deutschland 1945–1949* (1998).

PASCALE BOS is Assistant Professor of Dutch and German at the University of Texas, Austin, and has published several articles dealing with German-Jewish topics, gender, and Dutch literature. She is currently working on a study of German-Jewish Holocaust literature.

MICHAEL BRENNER is Professor of Jewish History and Culture at the University of Munich. He previously taught at Brandeis University and Indiana University. Among his publications are: *The Renaissance of Jewish Culture in Weimar Germany* (1996) and *After the Holocaust: Rebuilding Jewish Lives in Post-War Germany* (1997). He is also coauthor and coeditor of the four-volume *German-Jewish History in Modern Times* (1997–98).

ANAT FEINBERG is a Professor at the University for Jewish Studies at Heidelberg, where she teaches courses on Hebrew and Jewish literature with a specialty in theater. Among her important publications are: *Wiedergutmachung im Programm: Jüdisches Schicksal im deutschen Nachkriegsdrama* (1988), *Kultur in Israel* (1993), *Wüstenwind auf der Allee. Zeitgenössische israelische Autoren blicken auf Deutschland* (1998), and *Embodied Memory: The Theatre of George Tabori* (1999). She has also published three novels in Hebrew.

ATINA GROSSMANN is Professor of History at Cooper Union, where she focuses on twentieth- century German history. She has coedited *When Biology Became Destiny: Women in Weimar and Nazi Germany* (1984) and published *Reforming Sex: The German Movement for Birth Control and Abortion Reform, 1920–1950* (1995). She is currently working on *Victim, Victors, and Survivors: Germans, Allies, and Jews in Occupied Germany 1945–1949* (forthcoming).

NOAH ISENBERG is Associate Professor of German Studies at Wesleyan University and the author of *Between Redemption and Doom: The Strains of German-Jewish Modernism* (1999). He is currently at work on a new book, *Perennial Detour: The Cinema of Edgar G. Ulmer,* which focuses on the career of the Austrian-born filmmaker. His translation of *The Face of Eastern Jewry* by Arnold Zweig is forthcoming from the University of California Press.

MARIO KESSLER is currently a Research Fellow at the Center for Contemporary Historical Research at the University of Potsdam. His book publications include: *Antisemitismus, Zionismus and Sozialismus: Internationale Arbeiterbewegung und jüdische Frage im 20. Jahrhundert* (1993), *Zionismus und internationale Arbeiterbewegung 1897–1933* (1994), *Die SED und die Juden: Zwischen Repression und Toleranz. Politische Entwicklungen bis 1967* (1995), *Heroische Illusion und Stalin-Terror: Beiträge zur Kommunismus-Forschung*

(1999), and *Exilerfahrung in Wissenschaft und Politik: Remigrierte Historiker in der frühen DDR* (2001).

DAGMAR LORENZ is Professor of German at the University of Illinois at Chicago and is currently editor of the *German Quarterly.* In 2000 she was elected vice president of the International Association for Germanic Studies (IVG) and serves on the program committees of the Modern Language Association and the German Studies Association. Her research has dealt primarily with German literature and culture since 1800 with a focus on Austrian and German-Jewish literary and cultural issues and Holocaust studies. Among her numerous publications are: *Holocaust-Diskurse in deutscher Sprache aus der Sicht der Verfolgten* (1992), *Insiders and Outsiders: Jewish and Gentile Culture in Germany and Austria* (1994), *Jewish Women Writers* (1997), *Keepers of the Motherland: German Texts by Jewish Women writers* (1997), *Transforming the Center, Eroding the Margins: Essays on Ethnic and Cultural Boundaries in German-Speaking Countries* (1998), and *Contemporary Jewish Writing in Austria* (1999).

ANDREI MARKOVITS is Professor of Politics in the Department of Germanic Languages and Literatures at the University of Michigan. He was the founder and remains the editor of *German Politics and Society.* Markovits's scholarship and teaching has focused on numerous aspects of German and Austrian politics as well as European social democracy, new social movements, labor unions, and political scandals. He has also published extensively on German-Jewish relations, anti- Semitism, and anti-Americanism in Europe. Among his publications are: *The German Left: Red, Green and Beyond* (1993), *The German Predicament: Memory and Power in the New Europe* (1997), and *Offside: Soccer and American Exceptionalism* (2001).

LESLIE MORRIS is Assistant Professor of German at the University of Minnesota. She is the author of a forthcoming book on history and memory in Ingeborg Bachmann's poetry and is coediting with Karen Remmler a volume on contemporary Jewish writing in Germany with the University of Nebraska Press. She has written articles on the poetics of exile, diaspora, translation, and the border, and on artistic and theoretical approaches to memory and the Holocaust. She is currently working on a book on elegy and postmemory in German, American, and French poetry.

KAREN REMMLER is Associate Professor of German Studies at Mount Holyoke College and is currently the codirector of the Harriet L. and Paul M. Weissman Center for Leadership. She has coedited *Reemerging Jewish Culture in Germany: Life and Literature since 1989* (1994) with Sander

Gilman and has published *Waking the Dead: Correspondences between Walter Benjamin's Concept of Remembrance and Ingeborg Bachmann's Ways of Dying* (1996). She is currently finishing an anthology (with Leslie Morris) of contemporary Jewish writing in Germany and continuing research on a book project entitled "Proper Burial: Sites of Memory and Identity in Post-Wall Berlin."

ROBERT R. SHANDLEY is Assistant Professor of German at Texas A & M University. He has recently completed a book entitled *Rubble Films: Cinema in the Shadow of the Third Reich* (2001). He is also editor of *Unwilling Germans?: The Goldhagen Debate* (1998).

JACK ZIPES is Professor of German and Director of the Center for German and European Studies at the University of Minnesota. He has written numerous articles on twentieth-century German literature, politics, and theater, and his numerous book publications include *Germans and Jews since the Holocaust* (1986), edited with Anson Rabinbach; *Fairy Tales and Fables from Weimar Days* (1989); *The Operated Jew: Two Tales of Anti-Semitism* (1991); and the *Yale Companion to Jewish Writing and Thought in German Culture, 1096–1996* (1997), edited with Sander Gilman.

GERMAN AND JEWISH OBSESSION

L E S L I E   M O R R I S   A N D   J A C K   Z I P E S

For the past 20 years there has been a plethora of conferences, books, and special issues of journals about Germans, Jews, and the Holocaust in North America and Europe.[1] More recently there have been four controversial studies—Peter Novick's *The Holocaust in American Life* (1999), Tim Cole's *Selling the Holocaust: From Auschwitz to Schindler: How History Is Bought, Packaged, and Sold* (1999), Hilene Flanzbaum's edited work, *The Americanization of the Holocaust* (1999), and Norman Finkelstein's *The Holocaust Industry: Reflections on the Exploitation of Jewish Suffering* (2000)—that question how the Holocaust has been exploited by Jews, Germans, and Americans alike for political reasons. Some critics, such as Novick, even argue that American Jews have more invested in recalling the Shoah and memorializing it than the German Jews. For the most part, the focus of all the conferences and works has been on the Holocaust, and one could argue that this focus must by necessity stamp any writing on Germans and Jews. Yet, this emphasis on the Holocaust often conceals the astonishing transformation of the relations between Germans and Jews since 1945.

Our book, *Unlikely History: The Changing German-Jewish Symbiosis, 1945–2000,* which originated at a conference held at the University of Minnesota in May 2000, proposes to explore the changing relations between Jews and Germans in Germany 45 years after the defeat of Nazism. Within the last 20 years there has been a kind of renascence of Jewish culture in Germany and numerous studies that deal with the social, cultural, and political relations between Jews and Germans since the Holocaust. In fact, the Jewish population in Germany today continues to increase, and Jews apparently can integrate themselves in German society to the degree that they wish without fear of a recurrence of Nazism or marginalization. Yet, accompanying this reemerging Jewish presence in Germany in the past years, there has also been a tendency toward nostalgic memorialization of past Jewish life, of Jewish absence. Furthermore, the question of what constitutes "minority" experience in Germany has become increasingly complex and is no longer polarized between "German" and "Jew" but rather broadened to nonwestern "foreigners" living in Germany.

It seems that Dan Diner's declaration of a negative symbiosis between Germans and Jews that may have been true during the first 30 years following the Holocaust may no longer be true. Certainly, the relations between Jews and Germans since 1945 keep undergoing major shifts. Our book seeks to understand how these relations are remembered and recorded by Jews and Germans both inside and outside Germany since 1945. Some of the questions and topics that the essays in the book examine are: How were the early relations between Jews and Germans established in the period of 1945 to 1950? How have Jews played a role in the development of a democratic republic in both the West and the East? What were the differences between Jewish-German relations in the West and East and are these differences manifested today? How have Germans and Jews dealt with anti-Semitism and philo-Semitism? Is there a difference between Jewish and German historical perspectives on German postwar history? How have writers, artists, and filmmakers reflected upon Jewish-German relations since 1945? What does the "Jewish renascence" mean in the "new" German Republic? Whose memory plays a role in recording the symbiosis, especially the symbiosis before and after the Holocaust?

Although the memory of the Holocaust in all its aspects is a determining factor in the way Germans and Jews relate to one another, the focus of our book is on the postwar years 1945 to 2000 and the changing relations between Germans and Jews. In this respect, it is impossible to investigate the German-Jewish symbiosis today without dealing with the Holocaust. Even here, however, the essays tend to concentrate on shifts and problems that shed new light on the manner in which Jews and Germans have encountered their "checkered" history up to the present.

Our conference on "The Changing German-Jewish Symbiosis, 1945–2000" at the University of Minnesota in May of 2000 was held with the hope that we might be able to open areas of discussion about German-Jewish relations that had been somehow obfuscated by the waves of other conferences and studies. Our goal was to make a modest contribution to understanding those cultural and social elements that have historically bound and continue to bind Germans and Jews to one another. It often seems that we are witnessing a manifold obsession today: Germans fascinated by the meaning of the Holocaust and their ugly past, and Jews fascinated by Germans and the German fascination in all things Jewish that appears at times to be determined by Germans. All of this mutual "fascination" has occurred during the postwar years when notions of Jewish and German identity have undergone constant change, which has affected the German-Jewish symbiosis—if there is such a thing as symbiosis.

In many ways, the trace of the symbiosis—that is, the historical discourse about the symbiosis and the challenge to the very concept in recent years—has been maintained in imaginative writing that seeks to explore the contours, however mythical and fictive, of the German-Jewish symbiosis. For instance, the German-Jewish writer Barbara Honigmann, in a 1992 essay entitled "Selbstporträt als Jüdin" ["Self-portrait of a Jewish Woman"] captures the contradictions and complexities of the "symbiosis" as the "inability to come free of one another," explaining: "Germans and the Jews had now become a pair in Auschwitz, whom even death could not separate." [2] In her keynote address at the Minnesota Forum, the novelist Katja Behrens affirmed both the fragility and the persistence of the symbiosis as she noted the instability of what she terms the "rift" between German and Jew: "This rift between us, the progeny of both sides, is an unstable thing. It isn't always the same size. Sometimes it closes and becomes a hairline crack, a fracture you can forget, then it suddenly yawns wide and becomes unbridgeable."

In her book, *Jews in Germany after the Holocaust: Memory, Identity and Jewish-German Relations* (1997), based on interviews she conducted mainly in Frankfurt in 1984 and updated through 1994, Lynn Rappaport writes, "The Jewish perception of Germans is a selective one. . . . Through the lens of Jewish experience, Germany is not recorded as a democratized, reconstructed Federal Republic. Instead, one predominant meaning for Jews of living in Germany is to live in the land of the murderers. The term murderer refers to the categorical nature of Germans, not to a particular individual. This categorical nature and the traits that Jews focus on to devalue Germans enable them to better differentiate themselves from Germans as a distinct ethnic identity." [3]

Germany as land of the murderers has been a major marker for Jews living in Germany in the history of the relations between Germans and Jews since 1945. There are, of course, many other markers, those signs and events that Jews living in Germany have used and continue to use to mark themselves off from Germans and that, in some instances, are used self-reflexively by Germans in their search for self-understanding: the Eichmann Trial of 1961 to 1962; the 1964 to 1965 Auschwitz trials in Frankfurt am Main; Peter Weiss's play *The Investigation* (1966); the Six-Day War in 1967; the desecrations of Jewish cemeteries during the 1970s; Beate Klarsfeld's slapping of Chancellor Georg Kiesinger in 1972; the telecast of the American *Holocaust* film in 1979; the Heimat series of the 1980s; the Fassbinder scandal of 1985 concerning his alleged anti-Semitic play, *Der Müll, die Stadt und der Tod* [The Garbage, the City and Death]; the Bitburg commemoration of SS soldiers by Reagan and Kohl in 1985; the Historians' Debate of the 1980s concerning German normalcy, November 9, 1989; the transformation of the Jewish mourning for *Kristallnacht* into a celebration of German unity; the insult to Ignaz Bubis, president of the Central Committee of Jews, by the mayor of Rostock in 1991; the Walser affair in October 1998, which led to a debate about the necessity of memorializing the Holocaust; and the controversy over Bubis's burial site in 1999. These are just a few of the public events and displays that are transformed into markers by Jews in Germany to distinguish themselves from Germans. They are sometimes made more significant for one group than the other, but for the Jews, they are markers of fear and recollection, fear that the Germans might revert to barbarianism, recollection that the past cannot be forgotten. Just as Germans developed a fascination for Jews after the Holocaust that has constantly changed but essentially fetishizes the Jew as the exotic and mysterious other, the Jews have been obsessed with Germans as murderers or potential murderers.

It would be foolish and misleading to think that this obsession overwhelms the lives of Jews living in Germany and that all Jews live with the obsessive guilt that they are living in the land of their murderers. Too much has changed in Germany. As Micha Brumlik has pointed out in a recent book, *Zuhause, keine Heimat? Junge Juden und ihre Zukunft in Deutschland* [*Home, No Homeland? Young Jews and their Future in Germany,* 1998], there have been significant demographic and generational shifts since 1990 that are bringing about clear shifts in the attitudes of Jews, particularly those of the third generation. "If everything is not deceptive, the significance of the Holocaust—although it is continually mentioned and regarded as a burden—for a course of self-understanding and way of life is declining, the significance of family, profession, and religion is growing, while the question about the political placement as citizen in the future Germany of the Berlin Republic appears to be curiously blurred. Much differently than in previous years, the catastrophe of the Jewish people no longer appears to directly stamp the life projects [of the third generation], rather it appears as a theme that is to be faced as part of an arduous process of self-understanding." [4]

Brumlik stresses that it is difficult to discern definite trends among Jews in the new Federal Republic of Germany, and clearly with the large immigration of Russian Jews to Germany it is more than ever almost impossible to define what constitutes Jewishness for Jews in Germany. The common denominator that was clearly outlined by the title of Henryk Broder and Michael Lang's 1979 book, *Fremd in eigenem Land* [Alien in One's Own Country], no longer holds true: Jews no longer feel as alienated in Germany as they used to feel. Yet, the obsession with Germany as a national body with an ugly past is still important for the conflicting manner in which Jews continually define themselves. If there is a difference in Jewish self-definition vis-à-vis Germany since 1990, it can be seen in the conflicting positions that the Jews assume not within a Jewish community but within the German public sphere to which they lay claim, whether they speak within Germany or whether they speak from emigration. Self-critically, Jewish writers of different generations question how they reflect upon Germany for their own self-definition, and they ponder their obsession with the German past while making real-life choices in the present and for the future. If there is a shift in attitudes and perspectives in Jewish self-awareness since the unification of Germany, it appears that Jews are coping more with the German within themselves, not so much to demarcate themselves from Germany but to psychologically (and perhaps politically) cope with those contradictions that forge their identities. At the same time, Germans cannot operate without the Jew within them, that is, without constant reminders that their identity may be tied to the Nazi past, and in this regard the relationship between Jews and Germans in the postwar period has shifted from what Gershom Scholem called a one-sided monologue to a dialogue about guilt and working through guilt and a reevaluation of German culture.

The essays in this volume seek to explain, in strikingly different forms, the vicissitudes of what one could call, with greater or lesser certainty and comfort, the "German-Jewish symbiosis." As all of the essays presented here suggest, the legacy of this term is not unproblematic: evoked at times in the past to draw attention to the "grandeur that was Germany"—a grandeur that encompassed the Jewish contribution to German culture—the term itself has assumed, in recent years, an epigone dimension, a linguistic marker to something now tragically lost. By reinvestigating this heavily charged term, the essays in this volume provide new perspectives on the relationships between Germans and Jews, indeed, between Germanness and Jewishness and the developments of German and Jewish culture since 1945.

Preface

1. For example, see *The German Quarterly* 73 (2000), which features articles by Dagmar Lorenz, Sander Gilman, Matti Bunzl, Helgra Kraft, Esther Parada, and Norma Claire Moruzzi that grew out of an international symposium entitled "Politics, Memory and Representation: Post-Shoah Jewish Culture in German-Speaking Countries," held at the University of Illinois in Chicago in November 1998; and *New German Critique* 80 (Spring-Summer 2000), a special issue on the Holocaust, which contains essays by Saul Friedländer, Michael Naumann, David Bathrick, and Omer Bartov that were first presented as papers at the conference on "Germany, Jews, and the Future of Memory" at Princeton University, April 15–19, 1999.

2. "Selbstporträt als Jüdin" in *Damals, Dann und Danach* (Munich: Hanser, 1999), 16.
3. Lynn Rappaport, *Jews in Germany after the Holocaust: Memory, Identity and Jewish-German Relations* (Cambridge: Cambridge University Press, 1997), 81–82.
4. Micha Brumlik, ed. *Zuhause, keine Heimat? Junge Juden und ihre Zukunft in Deutschland* (Gerlingen: Bleicher, 1998), 18.

THE DEBATE

CHAPTER ONE

ENCOUNTERS ACROSS THE VOID

Rethinking Approaches to German-Jewish Symbioses

KAREN REMMLER

In one of the discussions at a conference on the changing German-Jewish symbiosis, a participant wondered if the discourse on this topic had become so self-referential as to be stuck in a rut.[1] Indeed, the presentations at the conference and the essays in this volume refer to the same anecdotes and public incidents that describe the fraught relations between Germans and Jews in postwar and post-Wall Germany. As fraught as the relations are, scholars and writers often end their descriptions and analyses of postwar German-Jewish identities on a note of cautious optimism. This optimism is based in part on entrenched notions of what constitutes the German-Jewish symbiosis even as many scholars agree on the ambiguity and ambivalence attached to the concept. We need to deepen the study of this troubled symbiosis by paying more attention to the conceptualization of the symbiosis as it emerges in interdisciplinary studies, in intertextual correspondences, and in recent theoretical debates about (West) German–(East) German relations in the aftermath of unification. In this essay, I present four approaches to the study of the German-Jewish relations in order to rethink and redirect the growing field of German-Jewish Studies.

First, I argue for a deeper understanding of the methodological divide between historians and literary scholars that defines the parameters for studying German-Jewish symbioses. The essays in this volume embody this divide, even as they work to cross it. On one side of the divide stand the scholars who study German-Jewish relations as they manifest themselves in history and everyday lives of self-identified German Jews. On the other side are those who study the relationship as an expression of language—not necessarily separate from the lived lives of German Jews, but embedded in literature, in poetry, in art, and in memoirs that defy the division between reality and imagination, and between history and representation. On both sides of the divide, scholars are alert to the ambiguity and inadequacy of the term "symbiosis" and of the heterogeneity of the markers "German" and "Jewish." I will explore how the contributors to this volume address this ambiguity.

A second argument for expanding the study of German-Jewish studies lies in the study of intertextual correspondences that often constitute the meaning of German-Jewish symbiosis. Instead of focusing only on correspondences between Germans and Jews, scholars may discover an equally complex and fruitful interchange in the observations of non-Germans and non-Jews who have created encounters among Germans, Jews, and others in their writing. Encounters between Germans and Jews often require the written page, and often, a third interlocutor. As a scholar and teacher of German-Jewish relations, I am often struck by the desire in the scholarly literature on symbiosis to find a language beyond taboo and elegy in which Germans and Jews might confront one another in a more or less "normal" sphere. In this sphere, affinities and antipathies between Germans and Jews would occupy a discursive space not possible in actual physical spaces. It is this desire for correspondence that I will pursue as my second point of inquiry. The term "correspondence" is intentionally ambiguous. I am concerned here with actual correspondences, as in dialogue or letters, and with searching for those correspondences that draw on affinities. A dialogue between Germans and Jews often fails face-to-face. Intertextual correspondences can substitute for such failed face-to-face encounters, even in texts by non-Germans and non-Jews. I will argue that Jorge Semprun's novel/memoir *Literature or Life* creates space for such an encounter.

My third argument concerns correspondences between the research on German-Jewish symbioses and new theoretical approaches to cosmopolitanism. I offer a double criticism here. Locating the discourse about the symbiosis in the broader context of postcolonial theory and newer works on cosmopolitanism would widen the scope of present studies on German-Jewish relations. Scholars engaged in German-Jewish studies often refer to the figure of the German Jew as embodying a cosmopolitan stance without clear reference to the abundant postcolonial and post-Enlightenment studies of cosmopolitanism from Plato through Kant and up to the present. On the other hand, theorists of the new cosmopolitanism need to be more attentive to the silence about the pejorative and anti-Semitic associations of the term "cosmopolitan." Even as an explicit reference to the German Jew as the cosmopolitan par excellence may have been missing, the German Jew stands for a cosmopolitan figure based on constructions dating from the Weimar Republic. At the same time, those who use the concept of cosmopolitanism as a construct to resolve the tension between particularist movements and the desire for universal values, evade the older pejorative connotation of cosmopolitanism with Jews.[2] Above I suggested that we expand a study of correspondences to include textual encounters orchestrated by non-Germans and non-Jews. Now I propose that we expand the scope of German-Jewish studies to include an analysis of the transformation of "cosmopolitanism" from an anti-Semitic euphemism into a term embraced by theorists critical of Eurocentric appropriations.

The debate about a new German-Jewish symbiosis does not take place in a void, even if the void is the favorite metaphor to describe the relations. The current revitalization of the concept of cosmopolitanism is a case in point. Here, Edward Said's practice of tracing the correspondences between intellectual exiles (in particular, Adorno) is another point of entry for grasping how the German-Jewish symbiosis is part of a larger global context. The status of the German Jew as the cosmopolitan par excellence obscures the shifts in meaning that have been both politically charged and over generalized. The recuperation of the term cosmopolitanism and its relation to universalism has coincided with a silence about the pejorative coupling of the term with anti-Semitism and anti-Communism. In the growing literature on the new cosmopolitanism, this usage of the term is rarely analyzed.

Finally, we need to pay more attention to how the German-German (negative) symbiosis and Germany's national project to integrate itself into the European community play out in contemporary approaches to German-Jewish relations. Often, the supposed essential cosmopolitan existence of the German Jew implicit in some of the discussions about present-day German-Jewish symbioses displaces the failure of the symbiosis for providing a model for an enlightened German national understanding.[3] The striking absence of references to the larger context in which troubled attempts to unify German-German sensibilities and cultures have led to displaced anger toward those deemed "non-German" is a case in point. The imaginary presence of German-Jewish symbioses has become an unspoken measure by which to test the success or failure of Germany's national project of democratization with open-mindedness toward strangers. I will argue that the desire to revive a German-Jewish symbiosis expressed by some of the scholars represented in this volume coincides with the desire of some German public figures to reinstate a cosmopolitan notion of *German* identity. This identity is often based on a nostalgic reference to the cosmopolitan German-Jewish models of the Weimar Republic. In my reading of a speech by Michael Naumann, Germany's Minister of Culture, I will argue that models for a cosmopolitan—and thus a more democratic—German republic are based in part on a longing for a revival of German-Jewish symbioses, and at the same time, a longing among Germans to mourn their own.[4]

The Divide

The essays in this volume on the so-called German-Jewish symbiosis often stumble across the divide between methodologies that focus on historical and sociological data and those that rely on textual artifacts and metaphor for insights into the meaning of encounters between Germans and Jews. Much of the tension surrounding discussions about the German-Jewish symbiosis as an actual state as opposed to an imagined condition is produced in part by our sometimes drastically different approaches to the problem and different assessments of what constitutes such a symbiosis, real or imagined. At times, the articles in this volume have crossed the divide between different modes of inquiry—one historical, one textual (and I define textual broadly here). Instead of evaluating the approaches per se, I would like to suggest that we try to engage in a productive dialogue across disciplinary divides without losing sight of the professional and personal attachments some, if not all, of us have to getting it right. I do not wish to produce an artificial or comfortable synthesis among the various stances, nor do I wish to have a last or even parting word. Rather, I hope to raise some provocative theses, some of which are quite preliminary and speculative.

The importance of this volume on German-Jewish symbioses after the Shoah does not lie in having found the definitive answers to the question of what constitutes the symbiosis once and for all. Rather, the essays increase our awareness of the slippage that occurs whenever we try to speak of the relations between Germans and Jews, while at the same time recognizing the fallacy of "the" Germans and "the" Jews. The difficulty of talking about "the" Germans or "the" Jews needs to be addressed more fully. At the same time, we need to question why discussions about the German-Jewish symbiosis usually revolve around the role of German Jews rather than a closer examination of the growing heterogeneity within German and Jewish categories of identity.

Predictably, scholars engaged in the debates about German-Jewish symbioses agree that the word "symbiosis" is hopelessly inadequate and perhaps outdated, perhaps more imaginary than real, perhaps history and no longer experience. We seem to be trapped in that discursive space between antipathy and affinity, a tension that, as Jack Zipes suggests in his discussion of Marcel Reich-Ranicki and Hans Mayer, can be as fruitful as it is painful.[5] To what extent do scholars in German-Jewish studies create a self-referential, self-fulfilling discourse that ignores the larger context in which German-Jewish symbioses arise and/or recede? More work needs to be done on teasing out the changing notions of German identities or the German-German negative symbiosis and how our focus on entrenched notions of German-Jewish relations, however negative or conflicted, ignores the actual political movements and cultural production in Germany.

Most of the essays in this volume note the rift in the symbiosis under question. Katja Behrens's essay exemplifies and echoes the sentiments of other contemporary Jewish writers writing in Germany.[6] Behrens's essay provides example after example of the ever-present rift between Jews and Germans in Germany. The narrative of her encounters with non-Jewish Germans provides evidence of both latent and overt anti-Semitism, and a non-Jewish fascination for things Jewish. The "layers of snow" about which Behrens writes and the "silence in the noise of ritualized commemorative activities," are contested in part by Michael Brenner's call for a less monolithic approach to understanding present-day relations between Germans and Jews. In his essay "The Transformation of the German-Jewish Community," Brenner suggests that the epilogues to the German-Jewish symbiosis may not just be epilogues, but rather the development of a history of Jews in Germany that has taken root. He asks us to rethink this history and to recognize the heterogeneity of the community, not least since the influx of Jews from the former Soviet Union. Even though there can be no "normal" relation, there can be one less overshadowed by the Shoah and more focused on the present and the future.

The haunting memories of the Weimar Republic are evoked in Atina Grossmann's essay as well. "A City of Bordercrossers: Jews in Occupied Berlin, 1945–1949" takes us through a fascinating landscape of rubble, a multicultural Berlin from 1945 to 1948, in which heterogeneous groups of Germans, Jews, Americans, Soviets, and others interacted. Some of the same conflicts within the reemerging Jewish community of today prevailed in this brief period before the two Germanys were established. Debates abounded about the definition of Jewish identity, relations to Germans, naming the Jewish community, and, perhaps most saliently, in the debates about how to build memorials. Two strands in her article deserve further discussion: the references to the cachet of the Weimar Republic and the subsequent squelching of this tradition (both artistic and political) by the Cold War and, especially in the Soviet Union, against what was deemed cosmopolitan—usually in association with Jews. The Weimar Republic continues to be the reference point for many nostalgic desires for a return to a culturally diverse and international German culture, much of which once had been produced by assimilated Jews.

As Noah Isenberg points out in his critical account of Daniel Libeskind's Jewish Museum, "[a]s we know, in the early decades of the twentieth century, German Jews managed to make their mark in nearly all branches of Berlin life: science, literature, politics, commerce and the arts.

Indeed, these were the much-celebrated (and vilified) years of the cosmopolitan city, now memorialized and preserved in scholarly and popular literature, as well as in recent Museum exhibitions" ("Reading 'Between the Lines': Daniel Libeskind's Berlin Jewish Museum and the Shattered Symbiosis," 155–179). The particular cosmopolitan flavor of the Republic that Isenberg alludes to is often directly or subtly connected to the presence of German Jews. This points to a deeper phenomenon that is related to a strange, uncanny and contradictory movement within Germany to reconnect with German roots. On the one hand, Germans seek ways to find pride in their national heritage, however tainted it may be by National Socialism. These movements are sometimes nationalistic, sometimes folkloric, and often attached to local customs and legends, in short, a return to regionalism in the form of dress, food, and dialect. Simultaneously there is a desire to recreate a cosmopolitan culture, which would embrace certain values (not unlike the *Wertecanon* [a canon of values] from which Andrei Markovits writes in his essay in this volume) from the supposed beginning of emancipation in the Enlightenment to the ideals of *Bildung* in the nineteenth century without the fatal imbrications with myth from which Adorno and Horkheimer wrote in the *Dialectic of Enlightenment.* There is a refashioning in the public sphere to imagine the best of German history by referring to the Weimar Republic while alluding to the presence of German-Jewish culture today.

What role does the construct of a German-Jewish symbiosis conjured from the memory of the Weimar Republic play in defining German-Jewish symbioses in the present? How does one describe the symbiosis without relying on the figure of the assimilated German Jew? Often, the divide in disciplinary methodologies manifests itself in the absence of adequate theorizing about German identities. Instead, it seems that evidence of the symbiosis resides within the individual psyches of German Jews, not in the spaces of encounter between Germans and Jews.

Encounters of the Textual Kind

I propose that a dialogue between Germans and Jews (keeping in mind the complexity of their definition) often receives too little attention in discussions of the present-day symbiosis. What of those encounters between Germans and Jews that fail face-to-face? Instead, intertextual correspondences create the space of encounter even in texts by non-Germans and non-Jews, who are observers of the rift, about which Behrens writes so eloquently in "The Rift and Not the Symbiosis."[7]

One such observer of the rift, Jorge Semprun, remembers his survival in Buchenwald by retrospectively creating encounters between lived experience and the "artifice" necessary to write it down.[8] Semprun was born in 1923 in Madrid, the son of a diplomat for the Spanish Republic. After the defeat of the Republican government by Franco, Semprun emigrated to France and eventually joined the French resistance. In 1943 he was arrested and transported to Buchenwald. He survived and later became Spain's minister of culture from 1988–1991. In his memoir, *Écriture ou la vie* [Literature or Life], Semprun describes conversations with other prisoners and their desperate recognition that what they have to tell is too unbelievable to be written down or spoken. "How do you tell such an unlikely truth, how do you foster the imagination of the unimaginable, if not by elaborating, by reworking reality, by putting it in perspective? With a bit of artifice, then!" (124). Another former prisoner responds:

> "I imagine there'll be a flood of accounts," he continues. "Their value will depend on the worth of the witness, his insight, his judgment. . . . And then there will be documents. . . . Later, historians will collect, classify, analyze this material, drawing on it for scholarly works. . . . Everything will be said, put on record. . . . Everything in these books will be true. . . . except that they won't contain the essential truth, which no historical reconstruction will ever be able to grasp, no matter how thorough and all-inclusive it may be."
> (124–25)

Semprun's novel is an extraordinary account of the intersection of literature and survival in memory. The narrator remembers incident after incident as they arise in memory, not as they occurred in time. In one scene, the narrator describes the excruciating dilemma of shooting a German soldier who is singing *La Paloma*. This song triggers a childhood memory for the narrator, a fighter in the resistance movement against the Nazi occupiers in France. Eventually, he is able to kill the soldier after a brief moment of paralysis. His comrade Julien, a young Burgundian, startled by the narrator's hesitation to shoot, fires shots at the soldier with him. The account is followed by a confession by Semprun's authorial voice. In a previous version of the same incident in a largely unknown short novel, *L'Évanouissement* [The Disappearance], his companion is not Julien, but rather Hans Freiburg, a fictionalized Jewish character. Semprun explains his invention of his "Jewish friend" Hans:

> We invented Hans . . . as the image of ourselves: the purest image, the one closest to our dreams. He wound up German because we were internationalists: we weren't aiming at the foreigner in each German soldier we cut down in ambush, but at the most blatant and murderous essence of our own bourgeoisie, in other words, of those class structures we wanted to change in our own society. He turned out to be Jewish because we wanted to liquidate all

oppression and because the Jew—even passive, even resigned—was the intolerable embodiment of the oppressed. (36–37)

Ironically, the invention of the German Jew in the first version humanizes the German soldier. It is not he the narrator and Hans finally shoot, but the "murderous essence" that he represents. In the second version, the artifice of the fictionalized Jew is no longer needed because this passage is embedded in an encounter with a dying Jewish survivor of Buchenwald, who is chanting the prayer for the dead in Yiddish. Semprun, as narrator, responds to the dying man, whose face he associates with the face of the crucified Jesus (31), by singing a line or two of *La Paloma,* thus triggering the memory of the scene in which he shoots the German soldier. The presence of the dying Jew in the text negates the necessity of creating a fictionalized Jewish presence to alleviate the paralysis of shooting another human being, German or otherwise.

The act of writing that which can not be told without artifice is the leitmotif in Semprun's accounts. He can only write about what happened by imposing artifice upon reality through memory. Similarly, he reenacts the life-saving force of the poetry he reads throughout his imprisonment and after, by commenting on the elusiveness and form of remembrance. His rendition of the past relies on "[t]he other kind of understanding, the essential truth of the experience, can not be imparted. . . . Or should I say, it can be imparted only through literary writing. . . . Through artifice of a work of art, of course" (125).

Poetry and its ability to provide hope in the utter horror of the camps leads the narrator to contemplate one of the most difficult and excruciating German-Jewish relationships—that between Heidegger and Celan. Upon opening a volume of poetry by Celan, Semprun happens on the poem "Todtnauberg." Celan's poem is the only trace of his fateful meeting with Heidegger after the war.[9] Semprun assumes that the poem is the only trace left of the conversation between Celan and Heidegger "in the latter's cabin hideaway in the Black Forest" (288–89). What Paul Celan wanted from Martin Heidegger, "was a clear statement of his position on Nazism. And on the extermination of the Jewish people in Hitler's camps, specifically. As you doubtless also recall, Celan was unsuccessful. He found only that silence some have tried to fill with empty chatter [*Gerede*] or to erase from memory: Heidegger's definitive silence on the question of German culpability" (289). Semprun quotes the poem in its original German:

> die in das Buch
> —wessen Namen nahms auf
> vor dem meinen?—
> die in dies Buch

geschriebene Zeile von
einer Hoffnung, heute,
auf eines Denkenden
kommendes
Wort
im Herzen . . .

[Hope for a heartfelt word from the philosopher. About what, this hope for word, spoken from the heart? About the subject of their conversation, which has just ended, probably. Which had just ended in the silence of the heart. (289–90)]

Semprun's narrator contemplates the state of German language; a language of barked SS commands, and sees the language of Celan, Kafka, Benjamin, Freud, Canetti, and Husserl, "of so many other Jewish intellectuals who created the grandeur and richness of German culture during the 1930s" as a language of subversion and as "the universal affirmation of critical reason" (290). Semprun ends his excursion into the relationship between Heidegger and Celan by noting that Celan drowned himself in the Seine. "No heartfelt word had held him back" (291). Writers such as Semprun and poets such as Ingeborg Bachmann understood the desire to retrieve this subversive language from the ashes of the German language that many German Jews wrote. Semprun's reading of Celan's disappointment at Heidegger's refusal to show any remorse for his stance during the early years of the Third Reich points to the impossibility of reconciling the rift in the symbiosis, but it also records a faint semblance of hope.[10]

Is it the absence of the German-Jewish symbiosis that conjures up the hope for a presence of a space, even imaginary, in which the impossible and thus failed work of a symbiosis can take place? How can a word of reconciliation be spoken, the word that Libeskind refers to in his discussion of Schoenberg's opera *Moses and Aron* (64)? Or the word that Celan sought from Heidegger, evoked in Semprun's novel *Literature or Life?* Or the word that Marcel Reich-Ranicki wished he had spoken to Bachmann before she died?[11] In his memoir *Mein Leben* he describes his encounter at the Gruppe 47 and his regret about not telling Bachmann how much he admired a number of her poems.

> When Ingeborg Bachmann died on October 16, 1973 [*sic*] under circumstances still not fully revealed, I was asked to write an obituary. I ended the obituary with the confession that I considered a number of poems from her collection *Die gestundete Zeit* and *Anrufung des Großen Bären* to be some of the most beautiful poems written in German in this century. I asked myself, filled with guilt, why I had not told Bachmann this while she was still alive.[12]

Is the symbiosis only possible in its afterlife, on paper, in the text, not in the flesh? Can there be a shared space "in the presence of the other"? Do Germans and Jews live bound by the silence of the dead, whose words only begin to speak when the physical encounter is no longer possible? Is the imaginary space the only possible space where that face-to-face encounter can take place; the not-in-different encounter with the other as Emmanuel Levinas has suggested? Can a face-to-face encounter between a German and Jew, one of the most ultimate encounters of difference, of the rift from which Behrens speaks, take place in the presence of the other?

Sigrid Weigel, in her book *Ingeborg Bachmann. Hinterlassenschaften unter Wahrung des Briefgeheimnisses* [Ingeborg Bachmann: Legacies Protected by the Privacy of the Post], takes up this question in her exacting analysis of the literary correspondences between Bachmann and Celan. Whereas Celan hoped in vain for a word from Heidegger, Bachmann responded to Celan by acknowledging hope's existence. Weigel's reading of the intertextual dialogue between Celan and Bachmann focuses on the single words from Celan's poems that reappear in Bachmann's poetry and references to Celan in her Frankfurter Lecture in December, 1959 (427). Bachmann speaks the word that Celan sought from Heidegger; a word that gestures toward a common hope across the divide of the Shoah and the void:

> This word [*unverloren* (not lost)] becomes a linguistic topos for a poetic language of hope for both authors. This hope is only possible with the knowledge of its loss, of the simultaneity therefore of radical disillusionment and the hope for salvation, that—in the tradition of Walter Benjamin—is characteristic for both writers.[13]

The loss is the driving force behind a simultaneous sense of "radical disillusionment" and "hope for salvation." That which is *unverloren* can be found in the language that Weigel uncovers in other fragments of the correspondences between Celan and Bachmann, a correspondence that was by no means continuous (452).

As I reflect upon the essays in this volume, I am struck by the desire to create a space for this shared hope of an encounter that would embody a future, even as we repeatedly question the feasibility of a common ground upon which to build this hope. In her essay "Postmemory, Postmemoir," Leslie Morris moves us beyond the narrow confines of the German-Jewish realm, which is itself hardly confined to German-speaking borders if we note the history of exile, particularly in the United States. On the one hand, those who write memoirs write of the impossibility of narrative and memory. On the other hand, they invent modes of writing and of collecting that disrupt traditional notions of narrative, history, and memory. Unlike most of the other contributors to this volume, Morris refers to a postsymbiotic relationship between Germans and Jews. Such a relationship is not an illusion per se, but rather points to the context in which the writing of this relationship remains overshadowed by the Shoah, itself no longer a firsthand experience, but one imagined and represented in a culture that has become saturated in postmemory and postmemoir. Instead of considering the movement away from constant reference to the Shoah, Morris reminds us of its ever-present presence, even in those locations and in those lives where it did not take place. She explores the "echoes and traces, as they emerge in text, of the myth of a German-Jewish symbiosis in American Jewish memoir writing." That is, she is less interested in the actual vicissitudes of the so-called symbiosis as in the traces it leaves behind.

As Noah Isenberg remarks in his discussion of the Jewish Museum in Berlin, the traces are both crucial and self-referential. Libeskind asks us to note how contemporary life and Jewish absence intermesh. Most importantly, as Isenberg notes, Libeskind quotes from Schoenberg's *Moses and Aron*, "O word, thou word, that I lack. The word that does not become deed." The word remains in the void, unspoken like the word that Celan desires from Heidegger, that Heidegger never utters. Without this word, the void cannot be filled and the symbiosis remains imaginary. Libeskind's Jewish Museum represents that space of material reality constituting an act both recalling silence and providing glimpses beyond this silence. Libeskind's design speaks across the void and is embodied in architecture: a space both memorial and enlightening, uncommon in Berlin where the histories, experiences, and memories of all humanity manage to traverse the void without repressing it. In Libeskind's own words:

> The museum for such a place as Berlin should not only be for the citizens of the present, but should be accessible, let's say imaginatively or metaphysically, to citizens of the past and of the future, a place for all citizens, a place to confirm a common heritage. Since they are Berliners, were Berliners, and will be Berliners, they should also find in it a shared hope, which is created in individual desire. To this end I saw that the museum form needed to be rethought, in order to encourage public participation. Thus, the extension to the Berlin Museum, with its special function of housing the Jewish museum, is an attempt to give voice to a common fate, common to Jews, to non-Jews, to Berliners, to non-Berliners, to those who live abroad and those who live at home, those in exile, and those in the wilderness, the ordered and disordered, the chosen and not chosen, the vocal and the silent. . . . I thought therefore that this "void" which runs centrally through the contemporary culture of Berlin should be made visible, accessible. (65–66)[14]

The void can not correspond to a rebuilding of Jewish presence. It is its absence that the museum signifies. As fragmented as those pieces might be, the

museum is as much a plea for the development of future connections between Jews and Germans in Berlin as it is a record of the void. Its present
function, as a receptacle for those seeking a memorial to the dead of the
Shoah, has fashioned it into a memorial site, because that is the expectation
with which people enter it. Libeskind, of course intended this, but not to the
exclusion of giving visitors glimpses into the present-day and the future. It is
through the jaggedly shaped windows that the visitors can gaze onto the
Berlin Museum, onto the surrounding buildings, and onto swatches of sky
and of grass, keeping the perspective outward as much as the Holocaust tower
in the museum turns one inward. The imposing upon the space to recall the
loss of many spaces once occupied and shared by Germans and Jews breaks
down the demand for the same space. Isenberg notes in his contribution to
this volume that the Jewish museum deromanticizes the semblance of the
symbiosis, which is not seen as a continuity but rather as a flash, a temporary
or very personal moment in the lives of some Jews and perhaps some Germans. The dilemma is to depict the intersection of German and Jewish histories as occupying both the same space and separate space.

The remembrance of the failed correspondences between Germans and
Jews can provide a model for thinking about German-Jewish relations in
terms of *Eingedenken,* that by now familiar mode of Benjaminian commemorative insight that is born through the recognition of the dialectical
images of forgotten moments of rapprochement. Actual encounters often
obscure the deeper lines of communication and correspondence that Weigel,
for example, documents in her book on Bachmann. Encounters may need
the presence of traces to be recalled. Semprun's memoir, like Libeskind's Jewish Museum, captures the flash of an encounter that can only take place in
a space of language that couples "radical disillusion" with "the hope for salvation." We may need to further study the relations between German Jews
and Germans that have been recorded and that belong to some of the most
moving and crucial correspondences of our time: Hannah Arendt and Karl
Jaspers, Heidegger and Celan, Bachmann and Celan. Symbiosis through
correspondences—at times successful, but rarely continuous—would record
the attempts to break the silence and yet to preserve it, and to distinguish
between the silences—those that remember the essential experience and
those that further erase it from memory.

It is exactly this form of writing—literature or life—that embodies the
dilemma of incorporating artifice into the canon of writing about the Shoah.
Artifice by those who have gone through the traumatic event, do not speak
for the dead, but rather create a textual space in which the dead may speak.
They take on a presence, even as their agency has been obliterated forever.
Their presence in imagination is what makes the artifice desirable. The authorship does matter, however. Non-Jews, such as Semprun, have lived the

experience. They can write from the vantage point of distance. Yet, they know to what their Jewish counterparts were subjected. They are witnesses, and without them a great deal of memory would be lost.

Thus, many memoirs, as Leslie Morris has pointed out, are not historical accounts, but rather narratives about the vicissitudes of remembering and often genuine, if misguided, attempts to empathize with the victims. The process becomes unhinged, however, when the distinction between the subjects blurs as was the case with Wilkomirski's (Dossecker's) *Fragments* or Helen Demidenko's *The Hand that Signed the Paper* as Morris discusses. Does the fictional nature of the piece diminish its impact? No. It does demand that we continue to search the depths of language for a possibility to speak the memory of the Shoah without firsthand knowledge of it, while distinguishing between the imagination and memory of witnesses and that of those who were not present at the traumatic event.

Fictional accounts can become a record of a trespass upon the landscape of the survivors and their descendants—an identification that counters Emmanuel Levinas's dictum that the *I* must be there for the other, even as he remains different." The relationship with the other is not an idyllic and harmonious relationship of communion, or a sympathy through which we put ourselves in the other's place; we recognize the other as resembling us, but exterior to us; the relationship with the other is a relationship with a Mystery" (*Time and the Other*, 75). Even as Levinas alludes to the transcendental notion of otherness in the exteriority of the experience, his notion of a confrontation with an other is a useful paradigm to imagine the correspondences between Germans and German Jews that take place in intertextual spaces.

Immediately, one and the other is one *facing* the other.

> It is myself for the other. . . . to be non-in-different to the other. . . . Difference—a non-in-difference in which the other—though absolutely other, "more other," so to speak, than are the individuals with respect to one another within the "same species" from which the *I* has freed itself—in which the other "regards" me, not in order to "perceive" me, but in "concerning me" in "mattering" to me as someone for whom I am answerable."[15]

It is the answerability, the imperative to respond that connotes the encounters between Germans and German Jews.

At the end of her essay, Morris proposes a new symbiosis, "not between Germans and Jews, but between American Jews and Germans." I can vouch for this growing presence not just in literature but in encounters between the third-generation Jews and Germans in the United States, often the students in courses that I teach on this subject. The American Jews in the class feel they must reach out to the Germans. In one instance a Jewish student comforts an older German woman who is auditing the class when she breaks down and tells her story—her father was a Nazi, but he hid a Jewish friend. After the war he is imprisoned by the Soviets and her family must leave their home to move with other westward-bound German refugees. The student comforts her by saying that he holds no malice toward her or her father. If he had lived in Germany under the Nazis and had not been a Jew, he is not sure that he would not have become a Nazi. Thus an encounter in the aftermath of the Shoah works both ways. In another instance, two students, one German American and the other Jewish American, who have been at odds throughout the course, each claiming that they cannot overcome their emotional aversion to the other, end up reading Goldhagen's *Hitler's Willing Executioners* together and writing:

> It is fittingly ironic that we find ourselves, as a German and a Jew respectively, in a position of engaging in a dialogue on the nature of the Holocaust. . . . It is perhaps from these attempts at dialogue, and not necessarily from their conclusions themselves, that we begin to come to terms with the component of the Holocaust's legacy which affects not only Germans and Jews, but the global community at large. While it might be presumptuous of us to imply that we are contributing to the "legendary" German-Jewish symbiosis, it is nevertheless noteworthy that we are engaged in a not-so-illusory mutually beneficial relationship, each becoming richer for the other's contributions.[16]

Cosmopolitanism in Theory and Practice

If those encounters depicted above can take place outside the borders of Germany, what can one say about the encounters within Germany's borders? Can we even confine German-Jewish studies to these borders, when other global contingencies influence the relations between Germans and others on a larger scale? Any current study of contemporary German-Jewish symbioses would benefit by an examination of other discourses on cosmopolitanism. It is time to place our discussions within the broader context of mass globalization and a return to the ideal of cosmopolitanism, sometimes now a veiled philo-Semitic identification with the emancipatory ideas of the *Bildungsbürgertum*. How can we talk of Jewishness and Germanness, when the terms are no longer embedded in fixed identities or national borders? As the world moves away from national markers on one level, the diasporic existence becomes the norm, epitomized by the intellectual exile. The so-called symbiosis might be measured not through the physical presence of living Jews in Germany (if we ever agreed upon how to count them), nor even through representations and images produced by

Jews for Jews, by Jews for Germans, by Germans for Jews, or by Germans for Germans. We might speak of the so-called symbiosis in cultural geographic terms. Who occupies which public spaces in Germany? Where are the sites marked Jewish, either physically or symbolically and what function do they fulfill? Are there German-Jewish spaces? Is it desirable to speak of Jewish spaces? Or might it make more sense to explore the permeability of borders and of barriers as Germany itself both disintegrates into regional enclaves and melds into Europe? Is the attempt to establish a presence of Jews in Germany a nostalgic reflex by Germans and/or Jews? Or do we need to look elsewhere for the remnants and possible emergence of German and Jewish rapport?

In the remaining pages of my essay, I will argue that a strong desire within the German political sphere for a return of a *German* cosmopolitanism coincides with the wresting away of the term from its derogatory usage by anti-Semites and anti-Communists to one that is an alternative to the negative aspects of globalization and of nationalistic movements.[17] The desire for a cosmopolitan cultural realm in Germany, I argue, expresses itself in the public sphere through a longing for a return of a German-Jewish symbiosis to mark a cosmopolitan state of being.

More recently, such encounters have been nourished by a valorization of an implicit, but an untested notion of cosmopolitan existence associated with German-Jewish experience in the Weimar Republic. Even as many scholars note the metamorphosis of the term from antiquity to the present from an ideal of "universal citizenship" to "a strategic bargain with universalism," there is a noticeable silence about the intersection of European nationalism and the vilification of Jews as "cosmopolites."[18]

In the immediate aftermath of unification, Germany became obsessed with two opposing desires: 1) to establish an ethnic national identity free of the taint of the Nazi past, but decidedly based on German blood and 2) to establish a civic nationalism that would "normalize" Germany in the eyes of the world. The foremost thinker on the subject of cosmopolitanism as an alternative to nationalism and to narrow definitions of identity is Edward Said, a Palestinian Arab educated in the West. His critique aims to imagine forms of coexistence that allow for difference without exclusion. Joan Cocks has cogently defined Said's brand of new cosmopolitanism:

> Against the traditional cosmopolitanism, Said attests that a "contrapuntal" perspective on any individual's part does not come from shedding the particular and parochial for a god's-eye stance. That perspective is the consequence instead of beginning located in one place and then another, and achieving through that double location a clarity about home and inherited identity as things that are shaping but not fatally determining.[19]

Consequently, a nostalgic turn to the supposed German-Jewish symbiosis of the Weimar Republic obscures the development of a cosmopolitanism that grows out of the specific exile experience, which has become the norm in the post-Shoah era. According to Michael Geyer, this existence is marked by "incommensurability of simultaneous man-made life-worlds of utter privilege, wealth, and consumption, and death-worlds of utter degradation, starvation, and brutal annihilation . . ." (670).

In his article, "Germany, or, The Twentieth Century as History," Geyer, like Said, reads Adorno's experience of exile as a cipher for marking the dialectical images of history from which Walter Benjamin wrote. These images of destruction and buried hope are visible, if faintly, in the blinding light of moments of danger.[20] To understand current discussions of what constitutes a binding cosmopolitan way of being, one must make sense of how the Enlightenment has been gleaned for its shortcomings, but also for its virtues. Even as Adorno and Horkheimer noted "how enlightenment emerged from myth, how it remains entangled in myth, and how it reverts to myth," their work remains "[l]ike Homer's epic, . . . a sustained and painful effort to find a way home after slaughter. It is a book of mourning that retains, if faintly, a reflection of hope" (668). Geyer notes how German-Jewish exiles like Adorno, even as they are part of the world that has waged the destruction, are the keepers of memories who have contributed to a postnational cosmopolitan mixture of humanism and efficiency in West Germany's society. Even as German-Jewish culture no longer exists, their work remains as a "palpable testimony of an absence" (669). Despite the destruction, thinkers like Horkheimer and Adorno, as Geyer writes, did not "lose hope in the possibility of enlightenment—not as relentless progress toward a perfect world but as infinite struggle for public-mindedness as the source of all liberty" (672).

Like Geyer, Said has recalled how a cosmopolitan stance can rekindle hope for the Enlightenment project, of which the fateful imbrication with myth has placed it repeatedly in critical light. But it is a more hopeful dialectic of Enlightenment that we can turn to, a hope that Zipes also expresses in his portrayal of Hans Mayer and Marcel Reich-Ranicki, two German Jews who revived a critical approach to German literature and culture after the war and had a major impact on postwar notions of Germanness.[21]

The desire to claim a reemergence of the German-Jewish symbiosis should be extended beyond German borders in order to examine the relationship in a more multivalenced and multifaceted light. The importance of exile for telling German history, as Geyer has explicated, on the one hand, and a growing interest among Jews for reconnecting or even creating a new practice of Judaism, on the other hand, is cognizant of both the imperative to remember, and the demand to act in the present. Even as Said acknowledges the misery of those exiled, he sees them as border crossers who break down barriers of thought and experience. Even as we remain cautious about seeing any benefit in what Said calls "the rich art forged out of the exile experience," the very space occupied by the exile may provide a chance for a "scrupulous subjectivity."[22] Said attributes this form of subjectivity to Adorno, who for him embodied a nonindulgent form of exile. Said's model provides a form to rethink the imaginary relations between Jews and Germans by looking outside that relation to those who observe and forge symbiotic forms of intellectual exchange, though, granted, almost always predicated on metaphor. It is the intertextual correspondences that make us take note and help us move beyond simple dichotomies and definitions of cosmopolitanism. Said offers a case in point when he quotes Eric Auerbach, the literary scholar who spent the war years in exile in Turkey, quoting Hugo St. Victor, a twelfth-century monk from Saxony:

> It is, therefore, a source of great virtue for the practiced mind to learn, bit by bit, first to change about invisible and transitory things, so that afterwards it may be able to leave them behind altogether. The man who finds his homeland sweet is still a tender beginner; he to whom every soil is as his native one is already strong, but he is perfect to whom the entire world is as a foreign land. The tender soul has fixed his love on one spot in the world; the strong man has extended his love to all places; the perfect man has extinguished his. (365)

Thus, as Said explicates, the "strong" or "perfect" man can only achieve "independence and detachment by *working through* attachments, not by rejecting them. Exile is predicated on the existence of, love for, and bond with, one's native place" (366). In some respects, German Jews, even as their numbers dwindle, have become a metaphoric medium to store [*aufheben*] the desire and hope for a nomadic, decentered, *contrapuntal* existence, thus providing a semblance of a possible world beyond exclusion (366). Are German Jews, then, the saviors of the faith in that aspect of the Enlightenment that went so wrong?

In a talk on the "Berlin Republic" at Mount Holyoke College, Michael Naumann, Germany's former minister of culture and media, began his remarks by quoting the late *FAZ* publicist Johannes Gross, who said that "the Berlin Republic meant a return to European normality."[23] Naumann's talk considers strategies for giving the new Berlin Republic an impetus to recognize its role within Europe instead of withdrawing into regionalist movements or political apathy. Quoting Crosby, Stills & Nash, Naumann wonders if Germany "has a code that you can live by," a line he returns to at the end of his speech:

> We are so free at the end of the century to let a new history begin, a history that does look to the future—no longer driven by old guilt, but by a new and

keen creativity. We could begin our talk with ourselves about the code to live by, about how we can save the European idea of the Republic, the social state based on the rule of law, the tension between art and the world by drawing them, for instance, into a digital capitalism.

For Naumann, the "code to live by," at least in the new old capital, Berlin, can be found in the opportunity to cast the controversial Holocaust Memorial as a "symbolic pivotal symbol between the past and the present and the future." According to Naumann, the memorial will not only "keep alive the memory of the most monstrous genocide in history," but also become "a painful document within the foundations of our [German] democracy only after the rupture of civilization that was Auschwitz. . . ." Naumann reiterates throughout his speech that overcoming the "excesses of exclusion" must be one of the primary goals of the new Republic. All must be invited to participate in the democratic process, a difficult task in light of the unification malaise facing Berlin ten years after a more euphoric start. Naumann finds the source of the energy to carry the Berlin Republic into the future in the words of Walther Rathenau. Without first naming his source, Naumann quotes the words of the Weimar Republic's German-Jewish Minister of State Rathenau, calling him the "spiritual godfather" of the new Republic. By quoting Rathenau, who was murdered by right-wing nationalists in 1922, Naumann expresses the desire that the new Republic will become a polity that "serves the commonwealth more charitably in times of restriction than in former times of surplus," a direct quote from Rathenau's charter for the Weimar Republic. Naumann's model for a "code to live by" is both forward looking and based on the vision of a self-identified German-Jewish "plutocrat" who understood that the success of the Weimar Republic depended on the inclusion of the people in the political process.

> The economy is not a private matter but a community matter, not an end in itself but a means towards the absolute, not a right but a responsibility. . . . We have no reason to replace competition with police-run bureaucracy in accordance with a crack formula for socialism, but once again we are being pointed in the direction of a reformation which will build a new realm of social freedom on the basis of fairer consumption, more equal distribution of wealth and greater prosperity of the state.

Naumann, I argue, expressed a desire for a more just, socially aware, and cosmopolitan Berlin, if not Germany. Thus, he chooses Rathenau as the "spiritual godfather" because he "embodied the unity of intellect, industry, and republican politics." Via Rathenau, the new republic will hark back to the best of the Weimar Republic, but at the same time the "murder" will occupy the same space. Again a dialogue between a German and a German Jew takes place in an intertextual realm, an attempt to claim a heritage for Germany that was forged out of a faith in the presence of a German-Jewish symbiosis, even as its precariousness was accentuated in the killing of one of its most supportive proponents. The success of a pluralistic, open-minded, and fair Germany will depend on a strong political movement against xenophobia and against the two-thirds society in which the bottom one-third remain out of work. The relevance of Naumann's speech for a discussion about German-Jewish symbioses lies in the reference to Rathenau, whose tragic death calls attention to how a cosmopolitan Germany can only be imagined through the inclusion of German-Jewish history, culture, and presence. And yet Germany's quest for "normal" nation status involves much more than nostalgic yearnings for a return of leaders bearing the qualities that Rathenau embodied. It also depends upon the ability to open up dialogues among its minority population in addition to claiming "normalcy" through its good work commemorating the victims of the Shoah.

The indirect and direct references to retrieving a cosmopolitan past embodied by the memory of *assimilated* German Jews, are all the more intriguing because this phenomenon has not received much attention in many of the discussions about present-day German-Jewish symbioses. The attempt by some Germans to recover an international, cosmopolitan tradition by harking back to German-Jewish tradition as an integral part of *German,* not just German-Jewish history, counters a more nationalistic movement among some Germans to revive traditional customs and traditions that hark back to a notion of German *heimat.* This revival, which I would argue includes an appropriation of klezmer music and Yiddish theater as an ersatz for German folk culture, expresses a German desire to return to a pre-Shoah period in which a mythic cosmopolitanism coincided with a particularly unstable brand of democratic civic society. It is exactly the instability of the relation between cultures that constitute German folk identity and a German-Jewish culture that was perceived to be cosmopolitan "and" German. That is, while Nazi propagandists were blaming Jews for corrupting the German soul and body politic, Germans were identifying on some level with a culture that included an openness to otherness, though the otherness was more a mode of entertainment and exoticism than a part of everyday life. That is, the underlying, unspoken desire by Naumann and, I would suggest, by other prominent voices in present-day Germany, is to reinstate a form of imagined cosmopolitanism that would return Germany to a sense of "normalcy" it most likely never enjoyed. At the same time, there is an attempt to save a remnant of German-Jewish culture that might give present-day Germany a second chance to redeem itself; that is, to share a sense of "inwardly directed (German) nationalism," a form of nationalism shared with other nations less troubled by a perpetrator legacy.[24] We might recall that Michael Wolffsohn, whose words I quote here, was born in 1947 in Tel Aviv and has been living in Germany since 1954. Wolffsohn is presently a professor of modern history at the University of the German Armed Forces in Munich. "My very own personal microcosm has always been a part of the political macrocosm of the times, and this is how a living fossil emerged, a German-Jewish patriot" (126). Wolffsohn continues:

> In other words, the kind of patriotism I am talking about here is nationalism in the very literal sense of the word (*natur sum*). And this nationalism is something quite natural. But—it is a form of nationalism which is *inwardly* directed, a reflection of something on the inside within the soul. It is not aimed at anything or anyone. It is not pointed outward, much less *against* anything on the outside. (129)

We all know how conflicted these statements are, particularly given the role Wolffsohn has played in helping to "normalize" German-Jewish relations. I would like to suggest that the filtering of this nonexclusionary and controversial stance outlined by Wolffsohn is itself a projection for which he has unwittingly served as a screen for some Germans seeking a possibility to be German and proud without being accused of forgetting the Shoah. Are German Jews the only Germans who manage to conjure up such images of a cosmopolitan and open German nation? Does this imply that Germans need the (imaginary) presence of German Jews (not Russian Jews, not Israeli Jews, not even American Jews) in order to be cosmopolitan?

German Identities in the German-Jewish Symbioses

I have noted the correspondences that conjure up images of German-Jewish relations that have provided evidence against symbiosis, even as they have hoped to emulate such a possibility beyond German-Jewish relations. What are we missing when we concentrate solely on German-Jewish relations and overlook the centrality of German-German relations for defining Germany's present? If there is a similar nostalgic shift among third-generation Germans and Jews to recreate a community, it remains separate precisely because Germans and Jews can never share the same spaces of memory. The debates about who owns which memorial space are a case in point and the continued controversy over the building of the Holocaust Memorial in the center of Berlin is clearly a sign that consensus does not exist in either group. And what of German-German relations? Might we speak of a German-German negative symbiosis that has resulted in recriminations and very little direct and unbiased investigation of the German Democratic Republic's Stalinist past and anti-Semitism in the GDR? Might we compare this to a parallel movement among young Germans who refuse to let their lives be determined by the Shoah and who identify as Europeans and form allegiances with non-Germans? And how do Jews remain more and more in their symbolic mode: as an alibi for those less willing to examine a German-German past for which the recovering of Jewish history becomes a screen for facing German history?

Here, too, German-Jewish history has become a cipher, a way of avoiding inner German relations. After unification, many unemployed historians, mostly from former East Germany, applied for funding to engage in work creation projects [*Arbeitbeschaffungsmaßnahmen*] in order to research and document the history of Jews in Berlin. In the *Scheunenviertel* alone, 30 such projects were in progress in 1994.[25] They ranged from the history of Jewish rag pickers to the architecture of formerly owned Jewish homes. Is this just another example of how some Germans need the imaginary Jew to veil confrontations with their own histories? The almost voyeuristic interest in things Jewish in the public sphere outweighs the actual Jewish presence, and the promotion of Jewish film festivals, klezmer music, and Talmud reading groups is not dissimilar from the phenomena in which oral traditions of dying cultures are recorded by anthropologists, who register lost tradition permanently and then mediate this tradition back to the younger generation of a tribe. At times, things Jewish appear to be an ersatz folk culture for some Germans, or at the very least, an attempt to be cosmopolitan. They associate that lifestyle and worldview with German-Jewish tradition (often mistakenly associated with romanticized versions of Eastern European Jewish culture).

Concomitant with the movement among Jews to define themselves in the present, instead of being determined by the legacy of the Shoah and the imperative to remember, a similar movement has been afoot among young Germans as well. At the very least, German unification brought about a desire among second-generation Germans to mourn their own—even as they busily mourned Jews and other victims murdered, maimed, and made to disappear by the Nazis and their accomplices. That is, there has been a spade of literature and historical writing on the experience of Germans during the Nazi period and World War II, which is not part of a strictly defined perpetrator legacy. Even as Germans mourned their own at home, in the private sphere and the semiprivate sphere of churches and village cemeteries, works such as Kempowski's *Das Echolot* and Inge Müller's poetry are part of a perhaps overdue and understandable trend to publicly (through text) mourn the German victims of the Second World War, the civilians buried in cellars after bombing raids, and even the so-called semiwilling soldiers who died fighting on the Eastern front, particularly in former Stalingrad.[26] In the last decade, more and more Germans have come forth to bear witness to *German* experiences during the war or to write about this period secondhand. This parallels an explosion of memorial building dedicated to Jewish victims of the Shoah. Even beyond Germany's borders, the lives of Germans during the war and the impact of the war on their subsequent lives and memories has captured the imagination of, for example, U.S. audiences. The popularity of Ursula Hegi's *Stones From the River* and the English translation of Bernard Schlink's novel, *The Reader,* are a case in point.[27] The displacement of the desire to mourn one's own onto the commemorative activities dedicated to the Jewish victims of the Shoah has, to some extent, become replaced by a direct mourning of one's own. Now Germans can mourn their own, because that mourning, too, has become imaginary, just as the remembrance of the Shoah has entered the realm of representation. And here, too, an uncanny slippage occurs between fiction and reality—two realms already unstable and permeable, as Leslie Morris has suggested in her article on postmemory in this volume. Consciousness in the public realm about the history of a so-called German-Jewish symbiosis may be diminishing in importance because German Jews and their other European counterparts are developing a broader identity. At the same time, Germans (and I am speaking here of white, Christian Germans for the most part) are also developing an identity based on an alliance with other Europeans, not on their inherited responsibility for remembering and studying the crimes of their ancestors. Some German's desire for a proper burial for their dead killed in the war represents a desire for closure that can never be achieved in the name of the Jewish victims, and which may represent a projected desire for symbiosis between the dead. I will commemorate your dead, says the German to the Jew, now let me commemorate my own. The problem here becomes clear in an excerpt in Esther Dischereit's novel, *Joëmis Tisch* [Joëmi's Table], in which a German character asks her Jewish friend to find the remains of her husband, a fallen *Wehrmacht* soldier in France.[28] When the Jewish narrator returns, not having found the grave, a symbolic grave is erected for the fallen German soldier and a proper burial ensues. The Jewish figure laments: "Imagine, if she would ask Frau Steder [the German woman] to go with her to her father's or her brother's mass grave in order to search . . ." (109). The dead victims of the Shoah leave no traces (another reason why the traces are so often invented), whereas the dead Germans are more apt to remain as scattered bones, now in the process of being gathered, identified, and properly buried.[29] Ironically, the various memorial sites dedicated to the Jewish victims that abound in Berlin and elsewhere in Germany have often become unconscious vehicles for Germans to mourn their own—to mourn the loss of innocence, as it were, and to mourn the burden of being the ones responsible for the utter destruction of another people.

The program description of the conference that generated this volume notes a renascence of Jewish culture in Germany that coincides with a "nostalgic memorialization of past Jewish life, of Jewish absence" and hopes that the conference will raise the question of how the increasingly complex constituting of "minority" experience in Germany no longer allows for a polarization between "German" and "Jew." A further analysis of the impact of other "foreign" bodies in Germany is in order. The articles in this volume, for the most part, have not even begun to consider the complexity of relationships that are no longer dichotomous—since the rubric "German-Jewish" itself has become imaginary and mythic. How does the presence of non-white, non-Christian Germans; German Turks or Turkish Germans; Afro-Germans; political and economic refugees; and Germans who are not western, and identify with the nonwestern, non-capitalistic legacy of the GDR contribute to a more complex attempt to trace German-Jewish relations? Leslie Adelson has called for a deeper understanding of how the "touching tales" of Germans, Turks, and Jews has affected both present-day relations among these supposedly homogenous groups and each other and the metaphoric discourse about otherness in unified Germany. The status of other is by no means static. It may be that Jews themselves live lives that have very little semblance to their symbolic meaning within German culture, though I would argue that writers, intellectuals, and others are heavily invested in questioning and transforming that symbolic meaning.

Despite all the talk about difference, about metaphor, and about text, scholars in the field of German-Jewish studies are still facing the dilemma of how to describe the way that a changing German-Jewish symbiosis might operate in the flesh. We have not agreed to agree about the very presence or possibility of a symbiosis in the first place. What remains? A reading of the Jewish philosopher Emmanuel Levinas directs our attention to a possible signpost out of the impasse. In his writing on the subject of the other, Levinas suggests that an ethically sound relation between two individuals cannot ignore the collectivizing context in which they encounter one another nor can the relations between the I and the other be constituted in a process of identification. As Gershom Scholem has argued, a dialogue, to be genuine, must include a mutual desire to participate in the dialogue. According to Scholem, Jews sought out the dialogue with Germans, but the attempt was not mutual. Today, I would argue, Germans are seeking a dialogue with the Jews, whereas Jews are ambivalent about whether or not to accommodate this plea from Germans. A dialogue or encounter between an I who can only engage with an other by identifying does more harm than good. Levinas writes about the image of the face, best translated in German as *Antlitz,* in French as *visage.*[30] The face is the most masked attribute of the human being and at the same time the most revealing (eyes). How might one encounter another human being face-to-face? This would not consist of Germans appropriating the supposed culture of the other (klezmer music, conversion, and so on) but rather of a form of empathy that would recognize the difference of the other and take responsibility for that person's well being, while acknowledging the impossibility of becoming the other.

> Responsibility for the Other, for the naked face of the first individual to come along. A responsibility that goes beyond what I may or may not have done to the Other or whatever acts I may or may not have committed, as if I were devoted to the other man before being devoted to myself. . . . A guiltless responsibility, whereby I am none the less open to an accusation of which no alibi, spatial or temporal, could clear me.[31]

Yet, what good is such a relationship if it continues to be based on the crime that has inextricably bound the Jew and the German, as much as it has manifest the void and the divide, metaphors that many survivors employ as well for the deep and common memories that clash? It is good precisely because it recalls the void, while building bridges across it.

I have suggested different approaches to analyzing German-Jewish symbioses that might help us build those bridges as scholars in German-Jewish studies. In addition to conceptualizing the terms that we use within a broader theoretical and cultural context, I look forward to studies that take not only German-Jewish, German, or Jewish identities and lives into account, but that also recognize that these lives exist in larger global contexts and relations. The failed peace process in the Middle East is perhaps the most tragic recent reminder of the importance of widening our scope of present-day German-Jewish relations within and beyond Germany's borders.

Notes

1. The conference, "The Changing German-Jewish Symbiosis," took place on May 3–6, 2000, at the University of Minnesota. This essay grew out of the concluding remarks that I delivered at the conference on May 6. Unless otherwise noted, translations from German to English are my own. I would like to thank Joan Cocks, Leslie Morris, and Gail Hornstein for their helpful comments on previous drafts of this essay.
2. For an overview of current debates on the meaning and application of cosmopolitan ideals from antiquity to the present, see Pheng Cheah and Bruce Robbins, eds., *Cosmopolitics. Thinking and Feeling beyond the Nation* (Minneapolis: University Press of Minnesota, 1998).
3. Among the works on this topic see Cheah and Robbins, *Cosmopolitics* and *Constellations* 7:1 (March 2000).

4. This is echoed in Zipes's essay in this volume, pp. 183–202, "The Critical Embracement of Germany: Hans Mayer and Marcel Reich-Ranicki," which discusses the centrality of Marcel Reich-Ranicki and Hans Mayer for producing *German* culture in postwar Germany.

5. See Zipes, pp. 183–202, "The Critical Embracement of Germany."

6. For example, see Rita Bashaw's essay in this volume, "Comic Vision and 'Negative Symbiosis' in Maxim Biller's *Harlem Holocaust* and Rafael Seligmann's *Der Musterjude.*" A forthcoming anthology of writing by contemporary German-Jewish writers includes a number of texts that further support Behrens's perspective. See Leslie Morris and Karen Remmler, eds. *Jewish Writing in Germany* (Lincoln: University of Nebraska Press, 2002). For a quick overview of the skepticism expressed by Jews living in Germany, see Elena Lappin, ed., *Jewish Voices, German Words: Growing up Jewish in Postwar Germany & Austria* trans. Krishna Winston (New Haven: Catbird Press, 1994), and Susan Stern, ed., *Speaking Out: Jewish Voices from United Germany* (Chicago: edition q, 1995).

7. See Behrens's essay in this volume, "The Rift and Not the Symbiosis."

8. Jorge Semprun, *Literature or Life,* trans. Linda Coverdale (New York: Viking, 1997).

9. For an account of Celan's visit to Heidegger's home in the mountains, see John Felstiner, *Paul Celan: Poet, Survivor, Jew* (New Haven: Yale University Press, 1995), 244–47.

10. This encounter has been the focus of numerous studies of Celan and, more recently, served as the basis for a parody by Elfriede Jelinek. See Jelinek, *Totenauberg: ein Stück* (Reinbek bei Hamburg: Rowohlt, 1991). John Felsteiner's superb biography of Celan, *Paul Celan: Poet, Survivor, Jew,* refers to a number of these studies (no. 10, 334–35).

11. Marcel Reich-Ranicki, *Mein Leben* (Stuttgart: Deutsche Verlags-Anstalt, 1999).

12. "Als Ingeborg Bachmann am 16. Oktober 1973 unter nie ganz geklärten Umständen starb, bat man mich einen Nachruf zu schreiben. Er endete mit dem Bekenntnis, daß ich einige Gedichte aus ihren Sammlungen 'Die gestundete Zeit' und 'Anrufung des Großen Bären' zu den schönsten zähle, die in diesem Jahrhundert in deutscher Sprache geschrieben wurden. Ich fragte mich, schuldbewußt, warum ich dies ihr, Ingeborg Bachmann, nie gesagt hatte" Reich-Ranicki, *Mein Leben,* 417.

13. "Dieses Wort ['unverloren'] wird für beide Autoren zum sprachlichen Topos für eine poetische Sprache der Hoffnung, die erst vom Ort eines Wissens um das Verlorensein aus möglich ist, für jene Gleichzeitigkeit also von radikaler Desillusionierung und Erlösungshoffnung, die—In der Tradition Benjamins—für beider Literatur kennzeichend ist." In Sigrid Weigel, *Ingeborg Bachmann. Hinterlassenschaften unter Wahrung des Briefgeheimnisses.* (Vienna: Paul Zsolnay, 1999), 426.

14. This quotation is taken from a transcript of a talk at Hannover University on December 5, 1989. The transcript is published in Daniel Libeskind, *Erweiterung des Berlin Museums mit Abteilung Jüdisches Museum* [Extension

to the Berlin Museum with Jewish Museum Department], ed. Kristin Feireiss (Berlin: Ernst & Sohn, 1992).

15. Emanuel Levinas, *Outside the Subject* (Stanford: Stanford University Press, 1994). This quotation is taken from "The Rights of Man and the Rights of the Other," 124.

16. I gratefully acknowledge permission from Marcus Klebe and Daniel Sahlein to quote from their seminar paper for German 43, Amherst College (Spring 1995), 3.

17. The theoretical literature on cosmopolitanism has increased recently. See *Constellations* 7.1 (March 2000) and Cheah and Robbins, *Cosmopolitics.*

18. In his essay "The Varieties of Cosmopolitan Experience," Scott L. Malcomson reviews the historical trajectory of the usage of the term cosmopolitan (Cheah and Robbins, *Cosmopolitics,* 233–34).

19. Joan Cocks, "A New Cosmopolitanism? V. S. Naipaul and Edward Said," *Constellations* 7.1 (March 2000): 57.

20. Michael Geyer's article appears in *The South Atlantic Quarterly* 96, no.4 (Fall 1997). His discussion of Adorno's *The Dialectic of Enlightenment* is particularly poignant for the discussion here. See 667–72.

21. See Zipes's essay in this volume, "The Critical Embracement of Germany."

22. See Edward Said, "Reflections on Exile," *Out There: Marginalization and Contemporary Cultures,* ed. Russel Feguson, Martha Gever, Trinh T. Minh-ha, and Cornel West (Cambridge, MA: MIT University Press, 1990), 365. Compare Said, "Intellectual Exile: Expatriates and Marginals," in which Said calls Adorno the "quintessential intellectual," in *Representations of the Intellectual* (New York: Pantheon Books, 1994), 55.

23. Naumann's talk (in English) at Mount Holyoke was based on an earlier talk (in German) from November 17, 1999. Staatsminister Michael Naumann, "Auf dem Weg in die Berliner Republik" Gesellschaftspoltisches Forum der Privaten Banken Berlin. The quotations here are from the videotape of the talk delivered on April 18, 2000 at Mount Holyoke College, South Hadley, Massachusetts.

24. Michael Wolffsohn, "Plea for an Inwardly Directed Nationalism" (Stern, *Speaking Out,* 126).

25. This is based on my observations at a meeting in Berlin to exchange ideas about such projects that took place in 1994.

26. Walter Kempowsk, *Das Echolot: Ein kollektives Tagebuch, Januar und Februar 1943* (Munich: A. Knaus, 1993); and Inge Müller, *Irgendewo; noch einmal möcht ich sehn. Lyrik, Prosa, Tagebücher. Mit Beiträgen zu ihrem Werk,* ed. Ines Geipel (Berlin: Aufbau, 1996).

27. Ursula Hegi, *Stones from the River* (New York: Poseidon Press, 1994); and Bernard Schlink, *The Reader,* trans. Carol Brown Janeway (New York: Pantheon Books, 1997).

28. Esther Dischereit, *Joëmis Tisch* (Frankfurt am Main: Suhrkamp, 1988).

29. The excavation and reburial of the bones of German soldiers is being funded by the German War Veteran's Association in former battlegrounds outside

Berlin and outside the former Stalingrad.

30. For a more in-depth discussion of this phenomenon, especially as it pertains to video testimonies by Holocaust survivors, see my article "Im Anlitz des Anderen: Video- Interviews von Überlebenden der Shoah," *Verfolgung und Erinnerung,* ed. Cathy Gelbin and Eva Lezzi (Potsdam: Moses Mendelssohn Zentrum, 1998): 119–34.

31. "Ethics as First Philosophy," in *The Levinas Reader,* ed. Sean Hand (Oxford: Blackwell, 1989), 83.

CHAPTER TWO

The Rift and Not the Symbiosis

K A T J A   B E H R E N S

[This is the entire text of the keynote address for The Minnesota Forum on German Culture: The Changing German/Jewish Symbiosis 1945–2000 conference, held at the University of Minnesota, May 3–6, 2000]

When the past finally caught up with Tinchen Tannenbaum, 35 years had passed, years that she had taken the precaution of spending in bed. She lived in an old people's home; peace reigned in Germany; and it was for her ears alone that the SA marched past the building. But she could not be persuaded of the truth of that. She heard what she heard: And when Tinchen Tannenbaum's blood spurts from the knife, it'll be a better life. She was ignorant of the fact that she had changed the words of the song, which actually goes: And when the blood of the Jews spurts from the knife. . . . She had obviously taken that very personally then, and now she was once more waiting to be taken away, a fate that she had again and again escaped—with a lot of luck—at that time, a time she never spoke about. In a psychiatric clinic she returned to the present. She shared the room with a one-legged old woman who called herself "Frau Müller from the Eastern Territories." Hardly had Mother and I entered the room than she would make a peremptory motion summoning us to her side: "Just come over here!" And when we ignored her because we already knew what was coming, she became imperious: "Come here, I say!" And when we ignored that too, the old woman pointed her finger accusingly at us: "What are you doing here? You don't belong here!" And when we then left the room with Tinchen she called after us indignantly: "Are those German folk?"

Frau Müller from the Eastern Territories had apparently heard nothing about the German-Jewish symbiosis, though she had immediately "recognized" us; she was not, however, what you call an educated woman, and her ignorance is no proof of this symbiosis not having existed. It was, of course, the so-called educated classes who—after 1945 in particular—liked to refer to the German-Jewish symbiosis that had supposedly existed before 1933, as if what then happened had been a bolt from the blue, just like that, without any menacing clouds. A past transfigured does tend to make memory, and consequently life in the present, more bearable.

When requested to contribute to a *Festschrift* for Margarete Susman on her ninetieth birthday, a contribution that according to the invitation was to be "understood not only as a tribute but as a document of an basically indestructible German-Jewish dialogue," Gershom Scholem wrote in 1962:

> The allegedly indestructible spiritual community of the German and the Jewish natures always only existed—as long as these two natures did in fact cooperate—on the part of the chorus of Jewish voices and was, on the level of historical reality, never anything but a fiction. . . . I dispute that there has ever been such a German-Jewish dialogue in any genuine sense as a historical phenomenon. It takes two to create a dialogue, two who listen to each other, who are prepared to become aware of the other, both what he is and what he represents, and reply to him. . . . Certainly, the Jews endeavored to enter into a dialog with the Germans, . . . demanding, imploring and beseeching, both crawling on their knees and defiant, ranging through the whole diapason of heart-stirring dignity and godforsaken lack of dignity; and today, now the symphony is over, it may be time to study its motives and attempt a critique of its tones. Nobody, including those who have comprehended the hopelessness of this cry into the void from the beginning, will disparage its passionate intensity and the notes of hope and grief resonating in it. . . . In all of this I can see no sign of a dialogue.[1]

After 1945 Hannah Arendt coined the term "negative symbiosis," which Dan Diner adopted in his 1988 essay entitled "Negative Symbiosis—Germans and Jews after Auschwitz": "Since Auschwitz it has indeed been possible to speak of a German-Jewish symbiosis—but of a negative one. For both Germans and for Jews the result of mass extermination has become the basis of how they see themselves, a kind of opposed reciprocity they have in common, willy-nilly."[2]

The term "negative symbiosis" was used by Hannah Arendt (in a letter to Karl Jaspers) in the year 1946, at a time, namely, when she was still able to believe that "the Germans," too, could not free themselves from what had occurred. At that time she apparently considered it unimaginable that they could just carry on as usual. Four years later, after her visit to Germany in the winter of 1949 to 1950, there was no more talk of symbiotic entangle-ment: "If one observes the Germans stumbling busily through the ruins of their thousand-year history with only a shrug of the shoulders to spare for the destroyed landmarks or how they resent one reminding them of the atrocities that haunt the entire rest of the world, then one grasps that busi-ness as usual has become their principal weapon for warding off reality."

"Let's leave the past in peace" was the motto, the length and breadth of the country. I still remember it well. Or, even then: "There must be an end of it at last." There were the references to the highways that Hitler had—after all—built, there were the indignant assertions that it had only been four million, not six, and there was the litany: "We didn't know anything." Margaret Bourke-White, in Germany as the *Life* correspondent in 1945 stated, "We all got to hear these words so often and so monotonously that they seemed to us like a German national anthem." I recall yet a second sen-tence that occasionally followed the first: "And if we had said something we would have ended up in the concentration camp (too)."

The rest was silence. Germany in the snow, buried under a thick layer of snow that swallows all sounds, so that there prevails that special silence Büch-ner means in having his character Lenz say: "Can't you hear the terrible voice screaming around the whole horizon and which is usually called silence?"

"Let's leave the past in peace," said my former homeroom teacher when I visited him in order to dig up some signs of the past. It was the beginning of the 1990s, and he quoted his former teacher, who had shown him the way after the war: "Now we have to look ahead."

My former teacher still teaches at the same school. Gray-haired, other-wise quite unchanged. I had rung him up, as I said, to see what I could dig up. I was prepared to have to go into long explanations, but he remembered me at once. And that may indicate that there's something in Dan Diner's theory about negative symbiosis.

He stood there at the door. I saw the outstretched hand, and it was just the same as it used to be. It was only at a second glance that I realized some-thing had changed. There was no finger pointing at me, only the question as to whether I had found the way without any trouble, not a single sneer-ing remark about my nose.

He sat opposite me in waistcoat and slippers. Waistcoat and slippers did-n't go with the dash with which he rattled off the number of his *Volkssturm* battalion. I quoted Faulkner: "The past isn't over; it isn't even past."

He threw me out. I was glad to go. The apartment was petty bourgeois, the air bad, and I'd gotten what I wanted: had thawed off the snow in one place and seen: what was underneath was amazingly well preserved. Like the Ötzi. (I don't know if you know who the Ötzi is. The Ötzi is a man who died millennia ago in the Ötztaler Alps, whose cadaver was recently found in the ice, still clothed and so well preserved that a lot of conclusions can be drawn about the way people lived in those days.) So I left my former tormentor's apartment not as the victor but as one who had gained something: I had confronted him as an equal and no longer as the powerless child. "Being completely powerless," Jan Philipp Reemtsma writes in his book *In the Cellar,* "One is alive but no longer there." One could also say: whoever feels completely powerless. . . . With us powerlessness is a family feeling, and I had visited the man in order to get rid of that feeling with all its concomitant feelings like fear, shame, and suppressed rage, and to be there in Reemtsma's sense. This, too, may indicate that the theory of negative symbiosis is not altogether wrong.

Visiting my former teacher was of course only one of many attempts to achieve the state of "being-there."

In the 1960s I left for Israel. I thought I could somehow undo Mother's remaining in Germany and cringing, and my inherited feeling of powerlessness. I thought I could make up for lost leaving, on behalf of all those who stayed, on their behalf and retrospectively, for it was no longer necessary, at least not necessary for survival. Mother got a so-called reparation pension, even if her eyes were still fixed on the ground, forget about the upright carriage, her head was lowered to the end, deeper and deeper, whether it was for shame about her nose or shame at having survived remained her secret. She died emaciated, starved away, as if she came from one of those camps she had never been in. Later I learned that there is a term for what she had felt without being aware of it: survivor's guilt. I also learned that it is the downtrodden who are ashamed afterwards and not those who tread them down.

At the beginning of the 1980s I began to tackle the problem of my family history. I wrote a story, "Emigrated to the Interior." And even while I was writing, I was tormented by the question: Am I going to show this to my mother? Do I read it to her? She was almost blind. She couldn't read any more, and I thought I had the choice. On the one hand, I knew that I had broken a family taboo, was a traitress who publicly blurts out nosehood. So at the very least I owed Mother a confession of my "treason"; on the other hand I wanted to spare her. Pangs of conscience. Guilty feelings. Guiltladen if I don't tell her, guiltladen if I tell her. I decided to say nothing.

The text appeared in the *Frankfurter Allgemeine Zeitung.* When I visited my mother she already knew it. Her neighbor had read it to her.

She was very sore at me. She said: "You had to drag all that out into the open." I justified myself. Reminded her that she had brought me up as a Jewish girl, not as a believer but as one who knows what side she's on. She said: "You know the neighbors don't know anything about the reparations pension. They're always cursing about reparations anyway." Between us there opened a gulf that was normally between us and the others. The last thing she said on the subject was: "One just doesn't like to blare out that one belongs to a despised race." To quote Jan Philipp Reemtsma once again in this context: "It may be that being overpowered is always accompanied by feelings of shame. . . . Being overpowered makes you small, reduces you, puts you at others' mercy. . . . What's more, one always believes one is partly to blame for it." Reemtsma goes on: "Nonetheless the punishment is of great importance for the victim. Not because it satisfies the need for revenge, because it usually doesn't. But because the punishment demonstrates society's solidarity with the victim. The punishment excludes the culprit, thus including the victim."

But how do things look as far as the punishment of the culprits is concerned? The writer and historian Joseph Wulf came to Germany after two years in Auschwitz. In 1974 he took his own life in Berlin. Two months before his death he wrote to his son: "I have published eighteen books on the Third Reich and none of it has had any effect. With the Germans you can document a case until you're blue in the face, there can be the most democratic government in Bonn—and the mass murderers walk about in liberty, they've got their cottage and grow flowers." Twenty years later Peter Finkelgruen wrote in his book *House Germany or the Story of an Unexpiated Murder* about the SS-overseer Anton Malloth, who had killed his grandfather in Terezín in full view of witnesses still alive today. The book also referred to the fact that the District Attorney responsible for the case, Klaus Schacht, had refused to institute legal proceedings against Malloth, who had already been convicted of murder (and sentenced in his absence in Czechoslovakia). In his review of *House Germany* Ralph Giordano wrote in the *Frankfurter Rundschau:* "The finding is as follows: there is only *one* interest of the lawyers dealing with the case: to prevent any proceedings against Anton Malloth." Thereupon preliminary proceedings were instigated against Ralph Giordano for "libel and defamation of character to the detriment of the District Attorney Klaus Schacht." The prosecuting attorney's office in Frankfurt brought charges against Giordano. There was a solidarity campaign by fellow writers that some joined and many didn't. At any rate Schacht had to withdraw charges and Giordano was not convicted. The murderer Anton Malloth, however, is still living undisturbed in a German old people's home. One of many. And if Eichmann hadn't been abducted back then, he would presumably also have been permitted to enjoy the natural course of his life. It was the prosecuting attorney Fritz Bauer—utterly isolated among his colleagues— who had learned of Eichmann's whereabouts and gave the Israeli authorities the tip-off, well knowing that the German authorities would take no steps and that Eichmann would even most probably be warned. So Eichmann was abducted by the Israeli secret service, as though it had been the Israelis' business to punish the mass murderer. If the "negative symbiosis" really existed and had the murder "become the basis of how the Germans see themselves," then it would have been the Germans' job. But that is unthinkable. I still have a vivid memory of the indignation of a publisher's reader with whom I was acquainted. His outrage was not aimed at Eichmann's crimes. He was indignant (like many others at the time) about the abduction. "Even if he did wrong," said the reader, "no one has the right to disregard the law." In all seriousness the reader insisted on the law. He did not speak of brother Eichmann. That was the Jew Heinar Kipphardt. The reader had grown up and been brought up in the Nazi period and had learned what all his generation had learned: treat 'em rough, make 'em tough. So neither compassion nor dismay nor shame nor horror, not to mention mourning.

Of course there have always been "discussions." Before and after the Eichmann abduction. About the *Holocaust* series. About Fassbinder's play *Garbage, the City and Death*. About the so-called Holocaust Memorial (for over ten years). But these discussions shouldn't actually have taken place. There was nothing to discuss. These discussions amid the monstrous silence were an expression of the "inability to mourn," and they were attempts to ward off guilt, not only by the generation of perpetrators and their fellow travelers but by their descendants.

The "complicity of the generations" was, for instance, also effective among the members of the generation of 1968, who on the one hand took their unforthcoming parents to task, but on the other furiously took sides against Israel in the Six Day War, which was only ostensibly a question of the oppression of the Palestinians but in reality an opportunity to see "the Jews" as culprits, thus relativizing the burden of German guilt. The complicity of the generations is to a large extent active in the realm of the unconscious, and that makes it so hard to get hold of. When, for example, in the middle of the 1960s the publicist Manfred Schlösser asked Gershom Scholem and others for a contribution to a *Festschrift* on the occasion of Margarete Susman's birthday and wished it to be seen "not only as a tribute, but as a document of an a basically indestructible German-Jewish dialogue," then that is tantamount to a downright denial: one year previously Schlösser had edited a volume of Margarete Susman's essays, and one is justified in assuming that he was familiar with her "The Book of Job and the Fate of the Jewish People," in which you may read:

> And the answer to the question as to whether it was chance that this inhumanity issued from this people in particular is a definite No: the characteristics that . . . led down into this abyss can be traced in German history, in German intellectual culture, in the German cast of mind. But yes, this is immediately accompanied by the question: Didn't we, the German Jews, participate in this culture and this character? Didn't we also live in that country and

bear its vicissitudes, think its thoughts? Don't we speak its language? Did we not receive in the German language all that we know and are ourselves? It was not voluntarily but artificially, violently and with the most depraved means that we had to be singled out and expelled from this people. We had to tear ourselves apart in order not to be Germans any more, and we did it. Did we then formerly fail to see the Germans as they became through and because of the medium of what we regarded as characteristically German? Or only through a closely woven enchanted veil? How is it then that we recognized them nevertheless when it came to it? We recognized them as in the old Chinese folk-tale the peasant, setting his cherished neighbor behind him on his horse for protection against a terrible monster and then looking round, suddenly recognizes the monster itself and falls unconscious from the horse.

When Manfred Schlösser wants to make a *Festschrift* for Margarete Susman the document of "a basically indestructible dialogue," the Ötzi appears, meaning: There was the good will of one who tries to avoid complicity with his fathers and yet evades the reality of what happened and its consequences. The Ötzi appears, you can look at him, and, well, it's bearable. But when the snow falls and the silence is deafening, it's something else again. I am among friends. One word recalling persecution and expulsion and already silence takes over, an embarrassed silence among people who only just now were close to me, a silence that tells me: oops, you've put your foot in it. In the stillness the rift between us becomes palpable.

This rift between us, the progeny of both sides, is an unstable thing. It isn't always the same size. Sometimes it closes and becomes a hairline crack, a fracture you can forget, then it suddenly yawns wide and becomes unbridgeable.

It's a mild evening in Italy. We are both scholarship holders of the Villa Massimo, a German church musician and I. We are sitting over wine and olives, talking about music.

"To get somewhere in music," the German church musician says, "you have to be either Jewish or gay." I can hardly believe my ears. "Sure," he says. "They're all ensconced in there, occupying the key positions." I protest to him that it's impossible because they were all killed. He insists: "Not at all. They fix one another up with the good positions." A few glasses of wine and the Ötzi is exposed. Not a pleasant sight, but you know at once: That's the Ötzi, an old acquaintance in the meantime, one who turns up pretty frequently.

Recently I met someone from the old days, a friend of my husband's. We talked about the past. I hadn't known that he had volunteered for military service as a fifteen-year-old. He hadn't known that my mother was a Jew.

"What?" he cried in a tone of incredulous amazement. "That charming woman!" As if to say it was impossible that such a charming woman could be something so abominable as a Jew.

For the duration of a sentence the thaw was on, meaning that little Dietrich was speaking out of the mouth of the grown man, who is now seventy and was not my friend.

My friends are good friends. We have a lot in common, read the same books, speak the same language, share political views. We understand one another, and then the Gulf War is on and suddenly we don't understand one another any more. Words like gas oven, gas heating, gas bill make me start. I have difficulty breathing. I telephone my Israeli friends, who have insulated a room in their apartment and take along a gas mask when they go out. I tell my German friends that and think it ought to get to them as it does to me. German gas. "Yes but," they say and don't understand that I don't want to go to Bonn to demonstrate for peace. "The gas," I say. "The gas." And they say: "But Israel has the atomic bomb." They say they are for all suffering human beings, the Iraqi population, millions of dead people. They say, it has to stop, at once. And I watch the rift between them and me, that mere hairline crack, get wider. "Israel has made mistakes," they say. "The Palestinians," they say. "Of course it's clear that you are bound to see it differently." They are generously forbearing with me, my German friends. They don't resent my failure to stand up for peace as usual. They make clear that the gas that concerns me doesn't concern them. "Of course it's awful, the thing about the gas, but—." And already they've made their getaway. It's not their business. The crack widens and becomes a rift when they proceed to count the Israelis' mistakes. Only then does their breath become irregular, does outrage enter their voices. Just now we were so close, and now the gulf between us seems to me unbridgeable. As if we lived forever on two separate continents. As if I were not a German as well. German passport, German language, German heritage. Part of this legacy is that I escaped the German gas. And when I ring my Israeli friends up they ask why we are not demonstrating against the armaments industry. "You Germans," they say, for I am "the German" to them.

There it is again, the crack, that is not only a mobile thing but pops up in very different places. In his book *The Erlking's Realm* Peter Finkelgruen tells how his grandmother, who had survived Auschwitz and taken him to Israel, was beaten up because she had spoken German. The *Jekkes* (as the German Jews were called) were not particularly popular in Israel. They were regarded as pedantic and arrogant, typically German. Only the Germans regarded their German Jews as un-German. "Let's not delude ourselves," wrote the writer and journalist Moritz Goldstein, long before he left Germany in 1933. "We Jews may have for ourselves the impression that we speak as Germans to Germans—we do have that impression. But as utterly German as we may feel ourselves, the others feel us to be quite un-German."

That hasn't really changed much up to the present day. The word *un-German* has gone out of fashion, people now say our Jewish fellow citizens, but when the weekly newspaper *Die Woche* carried out a poll in the middle of the 1990s on the subject of the nationality of the president of the National Council of the Jews in Germany, Ignatz Bubis, born in Dresden in 1927 and resident in Frankfurt am Main, as many as 22 percent of the German respondents thought he was Israeli, 32 percent were don't knows and less than half, 43 percent, considered their Jewish fellow citizen to be a German.

So it is the rift, the gulf, the dichotomy, and not the symbiosis—which would mean that Jews and Germans related to each other as a whole. The majority of Germans have managed to evade the matter, and individual Jews have found an island on which they can live. Thus the German literary critic Marcel Reich-Ranicki has made himself more or less comfortable on his island of literature. You may know that Reich-Ranicki is generally labeled as "the pope of German literature." As far as I know he has never objected to that, but this man who grew up in Berlin and has been living in Germany again since 1958 objects violently to being regarded as a German: "You cannot consider me a German. I'm not a German. Don't make me into a German. I'm a citizen of the Federal Republic: no question and with pleasure. I like this state, in spite of everything. I am a German literary critic, I write in German, I belong to German literature and culture, but I'm not a German and will never be one."

Another great literary critic, Hans Mayer, puts it less ebulliently but even more skeptically: "Do I feel myself to be a German, after all that has happened? What remains is skepticism about all possibilities of the complete emancipation of the Jews on German ground. There are hardly any more Jews in this country and the generation of fervent followers of their Führer will die out very soon. Nevertheless there are once more Nazis among the younger generation. The Jewish dead are reviled; the German judges go out of their way to confirm the legality of the new Nazi party. There is still a certain amount of affluence. But what will happen if a crisis really occurs and there is a renewal of the old blindness? There are many instances in both Jewish and German history of what it might be like then."

Every Jew in Germany knows it, that treading-on-thin-ice and asking: Will it hold? And what's underneath? Forget the Ötzi. He's dead. They got him out of the ice and put him in a museum. But what about the thing the Ötzi was used to stand for metaphorically here? How alive is that? What forces are keeping it at bay? When and under what circumstances might it break out (again)?

On the one hand, the fears, on the other, the defense against feelings of guilt. To what extent the progeny of the perpetrators are conflicted is demonstrated by what happened to the author Aliana Brodmann-Menkes, born in Munich and living in Boston. The Ellermann publishing company had asked her to write a children's book version of "The Story of the Figs," a tale from the Talmud. When the book was ready the author dedicated it to her grandparents, murdered in a concentration camp. The publisher took exception to the word "murdered." There was a long correspondence about the wording of the dedication. Aliana Brodmann-Menkes was requested to tone down the word "murdered." Finally she was told to dispense with the dedication altogether. She withdrew the manuscript. The book appeared in print nevertheless—without the dedication. That is to say, on the one hand, the publisher had asked a Jewish author for a specifically Jewish story, and on the other hand, the publisher couldn't bear to have a displeasing fact from Jewish history actually named. This occurrence reminds me of the sentence current among Jewish intellectuals: The Germans will never forgive the Jews Auschwitz.

So there it is: on the one hand, the defenses against feelings of guilt, on the other, the fears of the survivors, arduously kept down, and the insecurity of their progeny (living in Germany). I think of my friend Jehuda and his daughter. Jehuda was the only survivor of a large family that had lived in Netra, a little village in the north of Hesse, for generations. There one was accustomed to what one called *bekowede rischess.* That means something like "respectable anti-Semitism" and refers to the usual nastiness towards the Jews. One had learned to live with it; one didn't take it personally; it had always been like that. Jehuda was the only one in his family who noticed that something else had taken the place of *bekowede rischess.* In vain he attempted to persuade his parents and siblings to emigrate to Israel. Finally he went alone, and so he was the only one who survived. At the beginning of the 1950s he returned to Germany, married a woman who wasn't a Jew, and had children with her. He came back to Germany because he couldn't think of himself outside of German culture. He collected pictures by German painters, put on home concerts at which Germans and Jews got together and had his little private symbiosis with his "pet goy." He had his breakdowns and outbreaks, but he slept well and could more or less keep his anxieties under control. His daughter, however, was only able to find peace after she had become a strict orthodox Jew, who follows all the rules and prohibitions with which she did not grow up. In these shackles, which her father would probably not have accepted and which her mother suffers in silence, she finds urgently needed security.

I myself sought security in writing and, apparently paradoxically, found it in very close contact with what is hidden under the surface. I say apparently paradoxically because it's obvious that murder threats frighten one. Of course they do. But uncertainty, not knowing what is concealed behind the silence is even more frightening.

It started like this. After writing a series of "Jewish stories" dealing with the ways in which the past lives on in the present, I heard of Arthur Mayer, the first doctor in the place I lived in at that time.

Arthur Mayer's death in Auschwitz had not been cleared up. There was a well-hidden stone memorial outside the town. The older inhabitants told me that he had been very popular. "I knew him well, he treated me when I was a child," people said before I talked about writing about him. All of them, even the old Nazis, expressed their esteem, a good doctor, very popular, and then something broke off: silence set in.

Arthur Mayer had not been taken away in Seeheim. He had fled to Alsace, his wife's native country, in 1934, then later to Lyon, where after the invasion of the German troops he was recognized by a man from Seeheim, handed over to the Gestapo, and taken to Auschwitz with his wife and mother-in-law. So the silence had nothing to do with any direct participation by the population of Seeheim in his arrest.

I inquired about Arthur Mayer for a whole year and yet only found out from the documents relating to him preserved in Auschwitz that he was an unusually small man and had a command of several languages. The longer I researched the more clearly the rift became apparent, the chasm into which Arthur Mayer had disappeared. He and the other murdered Jews from the town. One—a man—declared to me as cool as you please, "nothing happened to the Jews of Seeheim, believe me"; another, a woman, a former neighbor of Arthur Mayer who hadn't forgotten how he lovingly cared for her dying mother, said she had heard he had died in Auschwitz of homesickness and replied to my incredulous inquiry that she'd been told that by a Jew, as though that were the definitive proof of the truth of the statement. Not one of the many people I spoke to expressed grief or pain or was aghast about what had happened, not even those who as local historians had concerned themselves with the fate of the local Jews. "What?" exclaimed a retired teacher and local historian, "Arthur Mayer, he was in Auschwitz? I thought he was in France and was done in by the Gestapo." Done in. No mourning, no memorial plaque on his house or on the former synagogue. "That was a good doctor, he was very popular." And then it started: the anonymous letters, the phone calls, the murder threats, obviously instigated by those who had spoken of the good doctor.

In Seeheim there were a number of local historians who had taken on the subject of the Jews and whose competition with one another was marked by genuine hatred. One of them, at the same time a Christian Democrat town councillor, had won the tussle: Only he was permitted to evaluate the Jewish registers. Only he knew which houses owned by Jews had gone to whom and at what price. The others complained that he had "the Jewish monopoly" and called him "the king of the Jews." He was working on a documentary about the Jews of Seeheim. The local authority had allocated a generous sum of money to him for that purpose, which I disturbed by my appearance and my questions. The guy was afraid of the competition. And he was afraid that "something would come out." He didn't say: "Let's leave the past in peace." He said: "Let's leave the lid on." This was how the exhibition about the Jews of Seeheim that he arranged was designed. It made the impression that at some time some disaster had befallen the Jews, like some Indio people whose buildings have been discovered in the jungle, the silent witnesses of a lofty civilization that has inexplicably disappeared. But the man was particularly proud of his "Jewish friends all over the world" and considered that it redounded to his special credit that he had "seen Auschwitz twice." Thus the rift became visible not only in silence but occasionally in words: as if Auschwitz were a sight to be seen like Cologne Cathedral or the Empire State Building. Decades before I asked about Arthur Mayer the then attorney general, Fritz Bauer, said: "The air would be cleared if only a human word were uttered at last—it hasn't been and it won't be any more."

Of course, at the time when I was writing about Arthur Mayer I had already long known of the uncanny secret continuity between the pre-1945 and the post-1945 periods, but it was only this experience that made it clear to me that it was not a matter of individual cases. Since then I have regarded the theory of "negative symbiosis" as wishful thinking, Jewish wishful thinking. On the level of politics it looks as if the extermination of the Jews were "the basis of how the Germans see themselves," but there are hardly any traces of this in the German public at large. Even a half-century afterwards repression and denial are still predominant.

Finally, two more examples of what I call the uncanny secret continuity:

Before 1945, Karl Korn, the longtime editor of the review section of the postwar *Frankfurter Allgemeine Zeitung,* held the same position at *Das Reich,* the newspaper for the "discriminating" readers of the Nazi era. Its circulation was around a half-million. One of the things you could read in it went as follows: "The Jews wanted their war and now they have got it. But for them the prophecy is coming true, the prophecy uttered by the Führer in the German Reichstag on the 30th of January 1939 that if international finance Jewry should succeed in plunging the nations into a world war once again, the result would not be the Bolshevization of the earth, and thus the victory of Jewry, but the annihilation of the Jewish race in Europe. We are experiencing the fulfillment of this prophecy, and Jewry is thus befallen by a destiny that is admittedly hard but more than deserved; pity or even regret are completely uncalled-for." Joseph Goebbels, November 16, 1941.

After 1945 it was then said that *Das Reich* had been the paper of the "inner emigration," of the decent, "unpolitical" reviewers, a legend in the dissemination of which at least those who had written for *Das Reich* were interested, not least the former review section editor, who had for instance reviewed the film *Jud Süß* as follows:

> "Then the Jew begins to lodge himself in the host body of the Reich. He acts out his lust for power, suppressed for centuries, and takes revenge for more than a millennium of the curse upon his race. . . . How the dark-eyed, smooth, slim man shaves off the curls of his beard and lusts after the blonde woman, how he swallows humiliations by the duke and straight away bounces back again, how he chalks up triumphs and, now he has sufficient power and knows he is firmly in the saddle, threatens brutally, how he looks cruelly into his adversaries' eyes, approaches them physically and makes them feel the hatred of ancient vindictiveness." (Karl Korn, on September 29, 1940.) A few years later he was, as I said, the editor of the review section of the *Frankfurter Allgemeine Zeitung,* which at that time advertised with the slogan: "There's always a good head behind it."

Karl Korn, one of many who managed the seamless transition from the one to the other. Of course, that gives rise to the question as to whether the transition was really so seamless as it appeared, or whether the fracture was only adroitly glued and then not taken cognizance of thanks to a silent agreement by those indirectly and directly involved. So let us speak of the return of the repressed: when Ingrid Bacher said in the 1990s at the height of the conflict about the merging of the two German PEN-centers: "We have a rift in our PEN," she meant the rift of that time, which the glue could no longer hold together, the rift that had arisen at the much-cited "New starting point," which in reality never existed. And now, a half-century afterward it could be watched as it became visible.

As I said, the dispute was about the merging of the West and East German PENs. It was known that several members of the East-PEN had spied on and informed on their writer colleagues. Some of the informed-on had been in prison; others had been expatriated and were in the meantime members of the West-PEN. The East-PEN, however, refused to expel those known as informers on the basis of records. In the West-PEN there was one group that declined a merger under these circumstances—one reason being that they felt they could not expect their colleagues who had been expatriated from the GDR to sit in an association with those who had deceived and betrayed them—and another group that pled for "generosity," one argument being: "I don't know what *I* would have done." And again the phrase "emigration in the sun" made the rounds—this time it was the writers who stayed in the GDR who reproached their colleagues who had moved to the West, either voluntarily or against their will, with having had a good time in the "Californian sun" while they who stayed at home had had a much tougher time. The phrase about the "Californian sun" referred directly to the émigrés of the Nazi period, about whom Gottfried Benn wrote at that time (in a letter of March 19, 1945): "If someone wants to discuss and judge Germany he has to have stayed here." The returned émigrés were by no means welcome. Alfred Döblin, in February 1946 said: "And when I came back I . . . didn't come back."

So we have, on the one side, the generous ones, the goodies who took sides for the weak, who did not want to be judgmental or self-righteous, and, on the other, the grudge-bearers, who were also described as the "stick-in-yesterday's-muds" (an expression hitherto applied to incorrigible Nazis). Suddenly the victims of persecution like Rainer Kunze, Sarah Kirsch, and the now late Jürgen Fuchs, probably dead of the after-effects of the X-rays to which he was exposed in prison, were left looking like kill-joys. They and about fifty others resigned from PEN.

At the annual conference in Mainz in 1997 the lawyer Uwe Wesel then spoke in favor of generosity, in the following words: "Adenauer did after all go all out for integration. In 1950 he had an expertise prepared on the question of pardoning—in whatever form or whether it was at all possible—all the Nazi criminals who were sentenced between 1945 and 1949, most of them were, partly they were sentenced by the Allies . . . what he did was called a pardon-fever, you know. . . . He said to himself: we've got a new start, we have to build up a democracy, and then it's not possible, we can't do that, by excluding an extraordinarily great number of people from the very beginning. That's why he passed that law more or less allowing the old Nazis the right to be reinstated in public service. . . . In spite of—or perhaps, precisely, because of Adenauer's integration policy we have managed to make the Federal Republic what it is today: a relatively stable democracy. In all these debates about amnesty, in my experience, rational arguments don't cut any ice. Usually the situation is that the ones are hard and the others are soft. One can also say: the ones are generous and the others are not generous. It's a question of pre-formed behavioral patterns. . . . The sentence 'We are a nation of the perpetrators, not of the victims' is basically right: we deal with the perpetrators with the goal of reintegrating them. In fact our society does not relate to the victims, that is true, but it does not exempt us from a certain responsibility towards the perpetrators. If I punish a perpetrator, I do not thereby help the victim, not at all. I grew up in Berlin, with the trials, that's why I am for amnesty, I don't want to talk about it any more. I will only repeat once more: I plead for generosity towards the perpetrators."

It should be added that with the sentence "We are a nation of the perpetrators, not of the victims," Wesel had picked up an interruption by Ralph Giordano, not without putting Giordano down with bland arrogance: "Mr. Giordano, you are always so excited."

And so it is the rift and not the symbiosis. And if you ask me now why I live in Germany in spite of everything, I can only say that I feel like little Kohn sitting in the train, looking out of the window and commencing to lament at every station they reach: "Oy vey, oy Gevalt, wie ist mir?" The train stops frequently and little Kohn's cries become louder and louder every time. Finally one of his fellow travelers asks him what's wrong. And little Kohn roars: "I'm sitting in the wrong train! Every station that comes, I'm sitting wronger and wronger!"

Translation: M. J. Walker 1999

Notes

1. Gershom Scholem, "Against the Myth of the German-Jewish Dialogue," in *On Jews and Judaism: Selected Essays* (New York: Schocken, 1976), 63.
2. Dan Diner, "Negative Symbiose," *Babylon* 1 (1986): 9.

SOCIAL AND HISTORICAL BACKGROUND

CHAPTER THREE

THE TRANSFORMATION OF THE GERMAN-JEWISH COMMUNITY

MICHAEL BRENNER

The changes in the German-Jewish community in recent years can perhaps best be illustrated by a personal recollection. When I left the small Bavarian town of Weiden in the early 1980s, I was the last student to have enrolled in the obligatory Jewish religion lessons. My religion teacher, who taught one or two students at a time in a handful of towns near the Czech border, was also the *ba'al tefilah,* the person to lead the three or four annual prayer services that were held in this dwindling Jewish community of 30 souls. By the late 1980s I heard that preparations were underway to combine the holiday prayer services with those of another small Jewish community in the region. Even on the holiest day of the year, Yom Kippur, it grew increasingly difficult to find the necessary quorum of ten men [*minyan*].

When I visited my home town a few years ago, 40 children, ranging in age from 6 to 17 years of age, were enrolled in weekly Jewish religion classes in Weiden, which today counts about 350 Jews, ten times as many as in 1990 and twice as many as in the 1920s. The newly employed teacher had no time to serve other communities, since he also arranges the regular Shabbat services on a biweekly basis and instructs the new adult members in basic tenets of Judaism. For this purpose he requires an interpreter, because 80 percent of the community members are Russian Jews who have arrived within the last 20 months. In 1997 the first rabbi ever employed by the Jewish community of Weiden was inaugurated—a German-born Conservative rabbi who had most recently served in São Paulo, Brazil. Although he has by now left the town of barely 50,000 inhabitants, the Jewish community, which faced extinction only a few years ago, is still expanding.

In larger cities the situation is different only in proportion. In Berlin, where the Jewish community has doubled in recent years, a second Jewish elementary school and the first Jewish high school in postwar Germany were opened a few years ago. The five official synagogues of the Jewish community are no longer the exclusive sites for Jewish prayer. Today a separatist Orthodox congregation, *Adass Jissroel*, exists, and there is an egalitarian prayer service. The secular *Jüdischer Kulturverein* is a meeting place mainly for former East German and Russian Jews. In Düsseldorf the Jewish population grew from 1,500 in 1989 to over 4,000 a decade later. As a result, the *Jitzchak Rabin School* makes the city on the Rhine the fourth in Germany, after Berlin, Frankfurt, and Munich, to have a Jewish day school. Oldenburg's new Jewish community, established in the early 1990s, is the first in postwar Germany to employ a woman rabbi. In the small region of Baden in the southwest of Germany, four new Jewish communities were founded in the 1990s. The number of Jews in Baden tripled in the first half of the 1990s.[1]

Epilogue or New Beginning?

Before I return to the present situation, let us look at the historical questions of postwar Jewish settlement in Germany. When the concentration camps on German soil were liberated in April and May of 1945, the Allied armies encountered only a few surviving Jews. Many of them were too sick and too weak to recover and died shortly after liberation. The official number of Jewish displaced persons (DPs) in Germany in September 1945, according to statistics prepared by the UNRRA (United Nations Relief and Rehabilitation Agency), was 53,322. They constituted only a small minority of a total of several million DPs in postwar Germany. In contrast to those Eastern European refugees, whom the Nazis had brought to Germany by force and who expressed their desire to return to their home countries, the vast majority of the Jewish DPs opposed any plans of resettling in their countries of origin, mainly Poland, Hungary, Romania and the Soviet Union. Jewish culture had been destroyed in these Eastern European countries, and a new wave of anti-Semitism awaited those Jewish survivors who had been liberated from the camps in Eastern Europe. The anti-Jewish atrocities after the Holocaust culminated in the pogrom of Kielce, where more than 40 Jews were killed on July 4, 1946. The renewed anti-Semitism led to a mass flight of Jewish survivors from Eastern Europe. While the ultimate destinations of most of those refugees were Palestine and the United States, occupied Germany became their immediate shelter.[2]

It is one of the ironies of history that Germany, whose death machine the Jews had just escaped, became a center for Jewish life in postwar Europe. The number of Jewish DPs in the American Zone of Germany alone increased from 39,902 in January of 1946 to 145,735 in December of the same year.[3] Some areas of Germany that Hitler did not have to make *juden-rein*, because Jews had never lived there, were now populated by several hundreds or thousands of Jews. The numbers of the Jewish population in such unlikely Bavarian places as Feldafing, Föhrenwald, Pocking, and Landsberg came close to that of the prewar centers of Jewish life in Bavaria, such as Munich and Nuremberg. Bavaria was one of the very few places in Europe where the Jewish population one year after the Holocaust was higher than at any time before. To be sure, this phenomenon was a temporary one, but during their stay in Germany, the Jewish DPs developed a wide-ranging network of religious, social, and cultural institutions. Of the approximately 250,000 Jewish DPs who went through Germany in the postwar years, about ten percent remained in the newly founded German states after these states had been established in 1949.

The Eastern European DPs were the largest and most prominent group of Jews living in Germany immediately after the war. However, they were not alone. At the same time, there existed a small group of German Jews who had survived the Nazi terror within Germany itself. Approximately 15,000 German Jews were liberated in 1945, some of whom had been in hiding, while others were in concentration camps. Most of them had had only very loose contacts with the Jewish communities before 1933, and a high percentage of them had survived only because they had been protected to a certain degree by a non-Jewish spouse or parent. More than two-thirds of the 7,000 members of the Berlin Jewish community of 1946 were intermarried or children of mixed marriages. In some smaller communities all of the members were either married to non-Jews or were Jews only according to Nazi definitions of Jewishness. The years of persecution, however, had strengthened the Jewish consciousness of many of the German-Jewish survivors. These people, whose knowledge of Judaism and experience in Jewish organizations were very weak, were now confronted with the difficult task of organizing some form of Jewish life upon the ruins of formerly flourishing Jewish communities.

A considerable number of Jewish communities were officially established as early as 1945. The Jewish community of Cologne resumed its activities in April 1945,[4] before the end of the war. By 1948, more than 100 Jewish communities had been founded, and a total of some 20,000 German Jews were registered in the reestablished communities in 1948. Thus two distinct groups of Jews living in Germany developed after 1945: a large number of Eastern European DPs who came to Germany more or less by chance, many of whom again lived in camps and expressed their wish to leave the country as soon as possible, and a small group of German Jews, most of whom had been highly assimilated into and connected with their German surroundings because of their non-Jewish spouses or parents.

The principal question that divided Eastern European and German Jewish Holocaust survivors in postwar Germany was whether to stay or to leave. The officially expressed attitudes of the two groups concerning this question differed substantially. On the one hand, the Jewish DP organizations regarded their stay on unholy German earth as a short interlude before emigration to the Jewish state that was to be established in Palestine and that needed their support. On the other hand, the German-Jewish organizations expressed their willingness to help in the process of the foundation of a new Germany with democratic structures.

It is not the task of the historian to analyze the reasons why Jews stayed or settled in the postwar Germanies. There was always more than one reason. Some Jews were just not able to move to a foreign place and learn a new language after all that they had been through; others had found non-Jewish German partners; others had established themselves economically; and, finally, there were those German Jews who returned immediately after the war to help build a new and democratic Germany. These political idealists could be found more frequently in the East, where the more prominent Jews lived in the first postwar years: the writer Arnold Zweig returned from Palestine, Anna Seghers from Mexico, and quite a few leading Communist politicians were at least of Jewish descent. In absolute numbers, however, the Jewish presence in East Germany was almost negligible, especially after many Jews had left in the tumultuous weeks of anti-Semitic propaganda in the late Stalinist years of 1952 to 1953. This wave of emigration left only about 1,500 Jews, most of whom were elderly, in the Jewish communities of East Germany, a number that was further reduced to 350 by the late 1980s.[5]

German-Jewish Identities

When the umbrella organization of German-Jewish communities was founded in 1950, it deliberately called itself the Central Council of Jews in Germany, which stood in clear contrast to the pre-1933 Central Association of German Citizens of the Jewish Faith and also the Reich Association of German Jews, established in 1933. This change of name bears witness to the widespread notion expressed by Rabbi Leo Baeck and others that German Jewry as we knew it had come to its end with the Shoah. Those who remained in Germany or came to Germany after 1945 were Jews in Germany—Jews who had ended up in Germany by accident. Although some German Jews emphasized the continuity of Jewish life in their old home, the majority indeed regarded their stay on German soil as unconnected to previous German-Jewish life. The same held true for the many different groups of Jewish immigrants who settled in Germany after the 1950s. Local Jewish history and tradition are, therefore, often unknown to the postwar Jewish population in

German cities today, or at best remained secondary to the memory of the Eastern European *shtetl* and to a deep attachment toward Israel.

The transformation of German Jewry started, at least in the larger communities, already in the late 1970s and 1980s, when the first generation of Jews born in postwar Germany realized and admitted that not only they themselves but their children, too, would probably stay on what the survivors had considered cursed soil. For decades Jews in postwar Germany had lived "with their bags packed." By the late 1970s most of them were already unpacked. The Jewish communities no longer considered themselves "liquidation communities," but began to plan for their future. In 1979, the *Hochschule für Jüdische Studien,* a new university for Jewish studies, opened its doors in Heidelberg to educate a new religious leadership for German-speaking Jewry. In the 1980s the religious landscape changed as liberal initiatives spread through the major cities and thus challenged the mainly Orthodox-run communities. Public appearances and street demonstrations by German Jews on the occasion of the attempted performance of Rainer Werner Fassbinder's allegedly anti-Semitic play "Garbage, the City and Death" in Frankfurt or at the Kohl-Reagan visit to Bitburg signified a new self-confidence.

All these changes would have been merely cosmetic if the demographics had not also changed. In 1989, the official number of Jews in Germany was given as 27,711, more or less the same number as during the preceding 30 years. Despite natural population decline and one of the highest intermarriage rates, the numbers of the postwar German-Jewish community had always remained constant due to a trickling immigration. In the 1950s there were returnees from Israel and South America, in 1956 and 1968 Polish Jews arrived, and, in the 1970s, Iranian Jews settled mainly in Hamburg, Israelis moved to all major cities, and some Russian Jews had already ended up in Berlin and a few other places. However, by the late 1980s there were no signs whatsoever that this situation would change dramatically.

Russians, Germans, Jews

November 9, which once had signified the downfall of German and European Jewry, received an additional meaning not only in German history, but also in German-Jewish history in 1989. When the Berlin wall came down, the doors were not only opened to hundreds of thousands of East Germans from the former GDR and to ethnic Germans from the former Soviet Union but also to more unlikely candidates of immigration. With the rise of anti-Semitic rhetoric and action, political instability, and economic depression, the Jews of the former Soviet Union began to look for a new home. Most of them found it in the Jewish homeland, while others came to what is still perceived in many ways as the *Goldene Medine*. But not all Russian, Ukrainian, and Baltic Jews were ready to move to a country threatened by war and internal tension, and not all were able to receive immigrant visas to the United States. Those who were willing to leave but did not want to go to Israel and could not go to the United States had one other option: to stay in Europe and settle in the recently reunified Germany. Why Germany? Germany was the only country in the world besides Israel that could not say no to Jews knocking at its gates. Considering itself the legal heir of Nazi Germany and anxious to confront its own past, the German government was always eager to preserve and protect its tiny Jewish community. Postwar democratic Germany has always been judged, among other things, by its behavior towards the Jews. In the case of former Soviet Jews, however, Germany's "right" choice was not simple. Israel was not happy to see its potential new citizens go to the "worst of all diasporas." Israel's President Ezer Weizmann reiterated this position during his state visit to Bonn in January 1996 by publicly claiming that he could not understand how Jews could live in Germany today.[6]

Despite Israeli criticism and despite the fact that Germany is officially a nonimmigrant country, it opened its doors to Jewish immigrants and has been trying to integrate them with relatively few bureaucratic procedures. There was a general agreement that Germany could absorb up to 10,000 Jewish refugees annually without, however, enforcing the limitation of this number. In 1990, the first year of substantial immigration, 8,000 Jews arrived from the former Soviet Union; in 1991 another 8,000; in 1992, 4,000; in 1993 the number rose to almost 15,000. This number is negligible compared to more than one million asylum seekers, mainly from Third World countries, and over one million ethnic Germans from the former Soviet Union who entered Germany during the same years. In terms of the Jewish exodus from the former Soviet Union the emigrants to Germany constituted about ten percent of all Jewish emigrants in 1994 and much less in the years before. The numbers of emigrants going to Israel and the United States were much higher, although the gap has closed somewhat in recent years.[7]

The situation in 1990 may be summarized as follows: The tiny Jewish community was faced with serious demographic problems but had started a process of cultural revitalization and religious diversification. At the same time the fascination with anything Jewish combined with serious attempts by Germans to face their own past, producing what one might call a "non-Jewish Jewish culture." In this situation the immigration of Jews from Eastern Europe was welcomed by different parties for different reasons: by the Jewish communities because it was their only chance to survive as a community; by German intellectuals because they saw in the immigration not only an act of restitution but also the chance to create a more authentic Jewish culture; and, finally, by the German government, which could demonstrate its favorable position toward the Jews by granting them asylum and ultimately even citizenship.

There were still the potential new German Jews, of course. What would make any Jew want to immigrate to Germany? Seen from a psychological perspective, the immigrants' choice may indeed sound awkward. To go to the country that was responsible for the near extermination of European Jewry, often for their own parents' and grandparents' deaths, does not sound like a natural choice. However, many of those who come to Germany do so for substantive reasons.[8] One such reason is, obviously, Germany's relative economic prosperity and political stability. But this is not the only factor that attracts Russian Jews to Germany. Some prefer to stay in Germany, even if they have the possibility to go to the United States, because of Germany's viable welfare state. Health insurance, unemployment aid, subsidized housing, and tuition-free schools make a new start easier even if high unemployment rates make it harder to find work. Others make their decision based on Germany's relative geographical and cultural proximity, especially if they leave behind close relatives. After all, German citizenship today means unlimited access to all other states of the European Union.

Because of this specific situation, the Jewish communities feel obliged to "create" Jews out of the immigrants. While the refugees know they are in Germany because they are Jews, and still remember the *evrei* [Jew] inscribed in their Soviet passports, they usually do not know what it means to be Jewish. To transmit Jewish knowledge and to provide attractive religious services may well be the most difficult challenge for a community that does not even have the spiritual leadership to satisfy its own modest demands. There are hardly any young German-speaking Jews who are able and willing to become teachers and rabbis in the Jewish community. In this respect, the Heidelberg University for Jewish Studies has provided very few concrete results. However, it constitutes the framework for a future Jewish education in that it encourages the new teachers, cantors, and rabbis to emanate from the immigrants themselves. A few years ago, this university advertised scholarships for Russian students in Jewish Studies, and a remarkably high number of potential new students have applied so far.

While most of the children of the Eastern European Jewish DPs by now have integrated well into German society, the new arrivals from the former Soviet Union are just at the beginning of this process of integration. When the Russian-Jewish immigrants arrive in Germany, most of them are first housed in state-run camps, most notably in former army barracks vacated by the Allied troops. According to a complicated formula, each German state receives a certain number of immigrants who are then distributed to cities with Jewish communities. While the size of the city and its Jewish community plays a certain role, other factors include living space capacity and the number of Soviet Jews who came in the 1970s and 1980s. Thus, the distribution is not equal.

In many places it is impossible to speak of an integration of the newcomers. There is very little previous Jewish life into which the newcomers can integrate. In most smaller places the "Russians" constitute the vast majority of Jews. Still, in most of the cases, the Jewish communities try hard to accommodate the needs of the refugees with the help of local authorities. This means that many Jewish communities today resemble social welfare agencies. They—and in smaller places this often means the one or two active Jewish families and perhaps a hired secretary (who in many cases is already one of the "veteran" Russians who came in 1990 or 1991)—help them find apartments and also arrange language instruction.

What about the German-Jewish community itself? Statistics from the 1960s and 1970s document the readiness with which young Jews left Germany. Indeed, among Western states, Germany had for a long time certainly one of the highest rates not only of donations to Israel but also of *aliyah*. Without Russian immigration, Germany's "old" Jewish community would have dwindled further during the 1990s. The picture today is more complex, however. While it is still true that a relatively large part of students active in the community leave Germany after graduating from high school, their destinations are now more diverse. Few continue their studies in Israel. The United States and, in recent years, England have become more popular places to go. Thus, the overall picture has many different aspects: The majority of Jews remain in Germany, but the majority of the most engaged ones leave, although not necessarily for good. These developments make it extremely difficult to predict the future of a Jewish community that demonstrates, simultaneously, rapid numerical growth and a loss of its most active young members, a renewed interest in Jewish matters and a desperate lack of religious leadership, a strong sense of renewal in the shadow of the Shoah and a relatively high integration into non-Jewish society.

Jews and Judaism in German Society

Jews are a minuscule minority in today's Germany, constituting not more than 0.1 percent of the total population. Their voices, however, cannot be dismissed or silenced. Whenever there are major public debates on the German past, spokespersons of the Jewish community are given prominent space.

It is telling that all leading representatives of postwar German Jewry, from the volatile Bavarian State Commissioner Philipp Auerbach (who committed suicide in 1952 after a spectacular trial against him that failed to prove that he had embezzled restitution money) and the longtime secretary general of the Central Council, Hendrik van Dam, to the Central Council's most recent presidents (Werner Nachmann, Heinz Galinski, Ignatz Bubis, and Paul Spiegel) were all German-born Jews, while the majority of Germany's Jewish community were of Eastern European background. The 1992 election of Ignatz Bubis as president of the Central Council of Jews in Germany marked a significant change of image for the German-Jewish community. Bubis succeeded the stern Auschwitz survivor Heinz Galinski and Galinski's predecessor, Werner Nachmann, who had enriched himself with millions of German Marks of reparation money. Bubis, who had survived the Holocaust as a child, symbolized a new optimism among German Jews and was one of the best-known figures in the German public. He was even suggested as a candidate for the federal presidency in the 1990s. After Bubis's untimely death in 1999, the elections to determine his successor were, for the first time, a highly visible public issue in Germany. Perhaps for the last time, a Holocaust survivor, Düsseldorf community president Paul Spiegel, was elected president of the Central Council in January 2000.

In contrast to pre-Nazi Germany, there are today only a handful of prominent German Jews in the public sector. For many years not a single professing Jew has been a member of the Bundestag. Today a few well-known younger Jews, such as Michel Friedman for the Christian Democrats and Professor Micha Brumlik for the Greens, are active in political life. Together with the late Ignatz Bubis, who was a leading member of the Free Democrats, these Jewish politicians all came from Frankfurt am Main.

Since the 1960s and 1970s, German public discourse has been characterized by a culture of memory, which began with modest exhibits and local memorials and reached its peak in the 1990s with the construction of several Jewish museums and the enormous debate regarding the Berlin Holocaust Monument. In the 1980s and 1990s the German public began discussing matters of the unpleasant German past with a heretofore unknown openness—starting with the Historians' Debate and continuing to include discussions on the Goldhagen book, the Walser speech, the Wehrmacht exhibit, and Nazi slave-labor reparations.

Here again the larger German development was decisive. It was the generation of 1968 and the issues of 1968 that influenced the further outlook of both progressive and conservative Jewish intellectuals. The early identification of many young Jews with the student revolt, just as their later disappointment with the anti-Semitism hidden behind its anti-Zionism, shaped the critical Jewish voices that first emerged in opposition to the official leadership of the Jewish communities, but then—at least in the Fassbinder scandal—transcended traditional affiliations. As Jewish intellectuals like Micha Brumlik, Dan Diner, and Henryk Broder made clear, their growing disappointment with the German left caused them to reconsider their Jewish identity. On the other hand, minority conservative Jewish opinion (for example, as represented by the TV journalist Richard Loewenthal in the 1960s and 1970s or the historian Michael Wolffsohn in later decades), was also deeply influenced by the student revolt, albeit in opposition to it and to its perceived values.

More noticeable than any internal Jewish discourse is the immense German interest in Jewish matters, especially in the cultural and scholarly spheres. Jewish museums were built in Frankfurt am Main, Berlin, and many smaller places in the 1980s and 1990s; another is currently under construction in Munich.[9] There are numerous non-Jewish klezmer bands and even a non-Jewish synagogue choir. Jewish bookstores in Munich and Berlin prosper from the patronage of a primarily non-Jewish clientele. Without any significant Jewish student population, Germany is becoming a major center in the field of Jewish Studies. Within the last decade, an array of new chairs and research institutions have appeared in Duisburg, Potsdam, Halle, Leipzig, Munich, Düsseldorf, Aachen, and Frankfurt am Main.[10] On a more popular level, the new kosher cafés around the restored golden dome of Berlin's Oranienburger Strasse synagogue (which houses an archive and a museum, and is no longer a house of prayer) are popular meeting places for non-Jewish guests. TV films, series, and miniseries on Jewish life, such as the film adaptation of Viktor Klemperer's diary during the Nazi period, are marketed at the most prominent viewing times. Jewish cultural festivals have become regular events of local culture in Berlin, Munich, and many other places. It is fashionable to be Jewish in today's Germany. Even the number of conversions to Judaism testifies to a situation that many observers may find more than a bit odd.[11]

This boom of a "non-Jewish Jewish culture" is an ambiguous development. On the one hand, the Jewish community is simply overburdened with this enormous interest in Jewish culture; on the other hand, this interest in Jewish culture evokes interest among Jews as well, along the lines of, "If it's that fascinating for *them,* there must be something in it for *us* as well." In contrast to similar developments in countries such as Poland or Spain, there is still enough of a Jewish community to take active part in these endeavors—or sufficient attraction on the part of Germany to bring in foreign "experts." The Berlin Jewish Museum may prove this point. Its first director came from Israel and, later, both its director and deputy director were German-born American Jews, while its architect, Daniel Libeskind, is a Polish-born Jew who holds a professorship at the University of California, Los Angeles. On a different level, the Lauder Foundation, the American Jewish Committee, and of course the Lubavitch religious movement, have become active in Germany.

While the interest in Judaism among the non-Jewish population is remarkable, the efforts to uphold the basis of religious life among the Jewish community are often frustrating. In 1999, there were 24 rabbis listed in the directory of community rabbis, as well as 4 Chabad (Lubavitch) rabbis. In a few places, such as Brandenburg, the community rabbi comes from the Lubavitch movement. Chabad develops quite a few activities in the larger (and now also some smaller) communities, especially programs related to children. The only local Jewish summer camps in Germany are run by Chabad, which solves the language gap by recruiting young American women who speak to the children in Yiddish. These summer camps have been among Chabad's most successful activities in Germany. In recent years, Chabad has also initiated the annual Hanukkah lighting of the Menorah in German public places.

On the other side of the religious spectrum, the Reform and Conservative movements have made considerable inroads in recent years. Both developments have their roots in nineteenth-century Germany, but virtually disappeared with the destruction of German Jewry in the 1930s. Religious Jewish life in postwar Germany was dominated by Eastern European Jews and therefore led to the establishment of Orthodox synagogues. In only one Berlin synagogue (in *Pestalozzistrasse*) and in Saarbruecken was the prewar organ tradition revived. However, even there Reform services remained in the tradition of prewar Liberal German Judaism, with segregated seating and no active role of women in the service. In the 1980s the first egalitarian services were introduced in Berlin and Frankfurt am Main, a practice then followed in a few other cities. Many synagogue members originally came from the small American Jewish community in Germany. Although they were established outside the structure of the main Jewish community, the Liberal Berlin and Frankfurt congregations were granted space within the *Gemeinde* [community] in the later 1990s. Other liberal congregations, as in, for example, Munich and Cologne, remained outside the *Gemeinde* structure or founded a separate association of communities, such as in Lower Saxony. In 1995 the small and new congregation of Oldenburg in Northern Germany hired the first woman rabbi in Germany. She is presently the only Conservative rabbi in Germany.

Most Jews in Germany are what is often termed "non-practicing Orthodox." This means they do not attend synagogues on a regular basis, but visit Orthodox synagogues during the High Holidays or family celebrations. Developments in recent years show the first signs of a more modern approach to the phenomenon of empty synagogues. Besides the Liberal congregations, which are united in an organization together with their Swiss and Austrian equivalents, there are a few modern Orthodox rabbis who try to replace the more Eastern European-like services in their synagogues. They have initiated youth services, beginner's services, special Kabbalat Shabbat events, and regular German sermons. With the few exceptions of the largest communities, there is usually only one synagogue in town. This situation requires a certain amount of compromise in order to serve all community members. Berlin is the only German community that employs an Orthodox and a Liberal rabbi. In 2000, a Liberal Rabbinical seminary opened in Potsdam, and one year later the Heidelberg University for Jewish Studies established the basis for a rabbinical education. The fruits of those efforts still remain to be seen.

In conclusion we may say that, while much has changed and is still changing within the Jewish community, we should not exaggerate the transformations. Even though, ironically, Germany is the only European country with a rapidly increasing Jewish community, it will remain an almost invisible minority of 0.1 percent of Germany's 80 million inhabitants. With less than 100,000 Jews spread over more than 70 communities, most Germans will never encounter a Jew. The prospects for a Jewish revival should be seen realistically. Perhaps 20 or 30 percent of the immigrants will in some way remain active within the Jewish community once they have settled and started to work. Few of them will be able to contribute much to religious Jewish life in the near future. However, the structure of German-Jewish communities, with their centralized administrative system coupled with, in most states, obligatory Jewish religious education, enables the systematic education of the young generation. Already, many of the children resemble their German-Jewish counterparts in that they speak German, participate in Jewish communal youth activities, and demonstrate an orientation toward Israel. If this young generation, which today is mostly Russian, succeeds in creating its own religious and cultural leadership and in counterbalancing the path of forced assimilation taken by their ancestors, there may indeed be cause for cautious optimism regarding a future Jewish life in Germany.

Even more than in other European countries, the future of German Jewry is closely tied to the success of the experiment of European integration. For German Jews this vision is especially attractive. To identify as European rather than as German Jews would enable them to identify with a promising future rather than with a bleak past.

Notes

1. Unless otherwise noted, the data for the German-Jewish communities are taken from *Mitgliederstatistik der einzelnen jüdischen Gemeinden und Landesverbände in Deutschland per 1. Januar 1999,* edited by the Zentralwohlfahrtsstelle der Juden in Deutschland (Frankfurt am Main, 1999). In contrast to most other western countries, and especially to the Unites States, the term "Jewish community" has a clear legal meaning in Germany. There is one Jewish *Gemeinde* in a town (with the exception of the one Orthodox congregation in Berlin), and it usually includes most religious, cultural, and

social activities. In addition, it is officially recognized by the state and supported by tax money from its members.

2. For more details see my book, *After the Holocaust: Rebuilding Jewish Lives in Postwar Germany* (Princeton: Princeton University Press, 1997), 11–18.

3. Wolfgang Jacobmeyer, "Jüdische Überlebende als Displaced Persons," *Geschichte und Gesellschaft* 9 (1983): 436.

4. Cf. Günter Bernd Ginzel, "Phasen der Etablierung einer Jüdischen Gemeinde in der Kölner Trümmerlandschaft 1945–1949," in *Köln und das rheinische Judentum. Festschrift Germania Judaica, 1959–1984,* ed. Jutta Bohnke-Kollwitz (Cologne: Bachem, 1984): 446–47.

5. There is by now a long list of publications on Jews in the GDR. In English, see Robin Ostow, *Jews in Contemporary East Germany: The Children of Moses in the Land of Marx.* (New York: St. Martin's Press, 1989).

6. On German-Jewish reactions to the Weizmann visit, see *Der Spiegel,* January 22, 1996, 33–35.

7. Madeleine Tress, "Soviet Jews in the Federal Republic of Germany: The Rebuilding of a Community," *Jewish Journal of Sociology* 37 (1995): 39–43.

8. Some individual opinions have been collected in Irene Runge, ed., *"Ich bin kein Russe": Jüdische Zuwanderer zwischen 1989 und 1994* (Berlin: Dietz, 1995).

9. See two recent publications on the topic: Sabine Offe, *Ausstellungen, Einstellungen, Entstellungen: Jüdische Museen in Deutschland und Österreich* (Berlin: Philo, 2000); and Thomas Lackmann, *Jewrassic Park: Wie baut man (k)ein Jüdisches Museum in Berlin* (Berlin: Philo, 2000).

10. See Michael Brenner and Stefan Rohrbacher, eds., *Wissenschaft vom Judentum: Annäherungen nach dem Holocaust* (Göttingen: Vandenhoeck & Ruprecht, 2000).

11. This phenomenon is well described by Ruth Ellen Gruber, "Filling the Jewish Space in Europe," *International Perspectives* 35, ed. The American Jewish Committee (September 1996): 23–35.

CHAPTER FOUR

HOME AND DISPLACEMENT
IN A CITY OF BORDERCROSSERS
Jews in Berlin 1945–1948

ATINA GROSSMANN [*]

Conquered by the Soviets in the chaotic weeks between April 24 and May 14, 1945, Berlin became a multinational polyglot city of bordercrossers (*Grenz-gänger* in popular parlance) when the Americans officially moved into the city on July 4 and it was divided into four sectors. The "greatest pile of rubble in the world" [*grösste[r] Trümmerhaufen der Welt*], as both its residents and occupiers both sarcastically dubbed it,[1] the vanquished Nazi capital was a city of women, refugees, and foreigners. It was crowded with returning soldiers and prisoners of war; liberated slave laborers from many different countries; ethnic German expellees and refugees from the East; repatriated political exiles (especially Communists returning to work with the Soviet Military Administration, SMAD); Jews emerging from hiding, forced labor, or concentration camps, or fleeing renewed persecution in Eastern Europe; and Allied troops (including a highly visible collection of former German Jews).[2] Moreover, huge numbers (by some estimates as many as a half-million) of displaced persons of multiple nationalities were streaming into some 50 transit camps in Berlin. Thousands of refugees from Soviet and Polish occupied territories in the East, mostly ethnic German (but also surviving Jews), poured into the city daily, at the same time as Allied officials struggled to repatriate freed foreign laborers, prisoners of war, and concentration camp inmates.[3] The U.S. diplomat Robert Murphy recorded his first impressions of the occupied city:

Two months after their surrender, Berliners still were moving about in a dazed condition. They had endured not only thousand-plane raids for years, but also weeks of Russian close-range artillery fire. In addition to three million Germans in Berlin, thousands of displaced persons were roaming around the shattered city."[4]

Rubble

In carved-up and bombed-out Berlin, still carrying traces of its pre-Nazi Weimar cachet, defeated Germans, together with hundreds of thousands of their former enemies and victims, became literal bordercrossers on the surreal stage of a broken city. Ruth Andreas-Friedrich titled her diary of war's end *Schauplatz Berlin,* and Curt Riess, a Berlin Jew who had returned as an American journalist, depicted his former hometown, with all its cinematic and operatic qualities, as "hardly like a city anymore, more like a stage on which the backdrops are just standing around."[5] Hans Habe, another returning Jewish refugee in American uniform, wrote—surely reflecting also on his own bizarre position—"Life in general has a strange, unreal, make-believe quality."[6] This initial sense of unreality was exacerbated by the Soviet military administration's decision in June to place Berlin on Moscow time, leaving the already disoriented city brightly lit at midnight and dark at 7 A.M.[7]

Shocked and fascinated descriptions of Berlin's rubble abound in both literature and cinema. One chronicler tried to render his impressions for his hometown audience by asking them to imagine the scene if one were to:

knock down every building between 34th and 59th Streets and between Eighth and Park Avenues. Then reduce to a burned out shell seven of every ten homes and apartments between 60th and 86th Streets on the West Side, and in the same way that you might sprinkle salt on an egg sprinkle destruction on the remaining sections of just Manhattan.[8]

"The city was like a vast archeological excavation where only foundations could be traced, with an occasional bit of wall," the American Jewish writer Meyer Levin noted with some satisfaction,[9] while John Dos Passos recorded that, "The ruin of the city was so immense it took on the grandeur of a natural phenomenon like the Garden of the Gods or the Painted Desert"[10] Or, as one American Jewish GI wrote home sarcastically (and a bit jubilantly) on stationary he claimed to have confiscated from Hitler's destroyed Chancellery, Berlin certainly was "all it was cracked up to be."[11] For every Berliner, authorities estimated, there were 26 cubic meters of ruins.[12]

The material damage, however, was less severe than it appeared on camera and in the countless dramatic reports by both awed and triumphant occupiers and shell-shocked Berliners; the infrastructure was remarkably intact and ready for rather rapid reconstruction. Many complained that the restoration of order meant that "looting became systematic" in the guise of *demontage* of German materiel and equipment for use in the shattered Soviet economy and that these "reparations succeeded rape" as the most feared and resented aspects of Russian retribution. Yet the Western Allies found, somewhat to their displeasure, that everything crucial to the running of the city had already been organized by the Soviet Military Administration.[13] Even before the battle of Berlin was over, the Soviets ordered restaurants and cabarets to open, radio Berlin returned to the air on May 4, and by May 14, the Berlin subway was sputtering back into service. The first Soviet film was screened on May 22. On May 27, 1945, the Renaissance Theater reopened and Marshall Besarin, the relatively popular Soviet *Stadtcommandant* (soon to be killed in a motorcycle accident) and the Soviet-dominated city magistrate declared "Long live Berlin!"

Maneuvering their way through a multioccupied city, relying on their wits, connections, and the black market for sustenance, inhabitants of Berlin moved between sectors and differing models of denazification, democratization, and reconstruction provided by four victorious occupiers. They crossed in and out of identities as victims or perpetrators, liberated or conquered people. They appeared in diaries, memoirs, and press accounts as hapless victims of Nazi betrayal, Anglo-American bombings, and Soviet plunder and rape; as rightfully subjugated former citizens of a criminal regime; or as "against all odds" survivors of Hitler and the Final Solution, struggling with dilemmas about whether to stay and participate in reconstruction or to depart "cursed German soil" as quickly as possible.

In this article, I focus particularly on Jews in Berlin, a surprisingly visible and significant group in the immediate postwar period. Indeed, the scope and variety of the Jewish presence in the vanquished former capital of a regime that had succeeded in exterminating most of European Jewry was quite extraordinary. Shortly after war's end, some 6,000 to 7,000 Jews were counted as Berlin residents. It is crucial to note here that these figures are imprecise and confusing and depend heavily on when exactly the count was taken and how "Jew" was defined. Two-thirds of those identified as Jewish survivors in Berlin shortly after the war were intermarried or the children of mixed marriages. Of the 5,000 to 7,000 Jews who had actually gone underground, at most 1,400 made it to liberation. Jewish survivors in Berlin, then, represented a high proportion of the 15,000 Jews who survived within the entire *Reich,* but only a fraction of the 160,000 who had been registered as members of Germany's largest and most vibrant Jewish community in 1932.[14] Still, despite the Nazi pledge to make Berlin free of Jews (*judenrein*), Jewish life in the capital of the Third Reich had never completely stopped.

It survived in precarious niches; underground among the Jewish *Uboote* [il-legals] hidden in factory lofts, apartments, and the shacks of Berlins' many garden plots (*Schrebergärten*), on the grounds of the Weissensee Jewish cemetery, and both officially and secretly in the strange ambiguous world of the Jewish Hospital under the eyes of the Gestapo.[15]

Surfacing

No sooner were areas of the city liberated by the Soviets than it seemed that the Jews were back in the open. German memoirs speak of Jews disappearing but then suddenly, surprisingly, reappearing in the spring of 1945. In Jewish memoirs, the same stories are told over and over again: the anxious wait as the Soviet tanks pounded closer, the struggle to convince disbelieving Red Army soldiers that the yellow stars were genuine and not the SS disguise they'd been warned about, that not all *Ivrey* were *kaputt* (and in the case of women, the desperate effort to avoid rape), and then the miraculous *deus ex machina* appearance of a Yiddish-speaking Red Army officer who announced, "Brider, ihr sayt frei," [Brothers, you are free] but sometimes not until after the *Sh'ma* had been recited as proof. Even as the fighting still continued in the center of Berlin, the young Hans Rosenthal emerged from his hiding place in a Berlin garden colony [*Schrebergarten*] and reported to the neighborhood *Anti-fa* committee, reclaiming his name and acquiring a new identity card certifying his Jewishness.[16]

Already on May 9, 1945, one day after the unconditional surrender, the apparent presence of so many Jews, the formerly hidden and the newly arrived, so soon after the end of a regime committed to the extermination of Europe's Jews, sufficiently unnerved the German journalist Margaret Boveri that she commented in a surprised and somewhat irritated tone on her encounter with a young "Rabbi" on a bicycle. Having successfully hidden himself under a false name and armed with two prized possessions, he was now biking through the ruins of Berlin carrying a radio:

> So it is no wonder that important positions are crawling with Jews, they have simply crept out of obscurity. Reinforcements are also supposedly coming from East Europe, especially from Poland—those who are smuggling themselves in with the refugee treks.[17]

New Yorker writer Joel Sayre in his "Letter from Berlin," dated July 28, 1945, also described an encounter in the midst of the rubble:

> Next we got to talking with a pale youth who was carrying a portfolio. He told us he was a Jew and showed us his card to prove it. Jews and half-Jews in

Berlin have identification cards issued by the Russians. Each card has the bearer's photograph, declares that he is a victim of National Socialism, and asks that he be given special consideration.[18]

By June 6, police registration was reinstated by the occupiers. Jews had received ID cards from the reconstituted *Gemeinde* and their "Victims of Fascism" (*Opfer des Faschismus,* OdF) insignia even earlier. Registrations that only days, certainly weeks, before would have meant deportation and death now had concrete benefits in terms of housing and increased rations. On June 14, the first postal delivery—crucial for tracking down the lost—arrived in civilian homes and the first mostly elderly returnees from Theresienstadt concentration camp were asked to register with the *Gemeinde.* After the arrival of the Americans and British, Jewish soldiers subverted antifraternization regulations to contact survivors—both those they knew about and those whom they simply encountered on the street—and quickly provided them with food and sometimes jobs.[19] The battle over the definition of, and access to, status as an OdF was immediately launched and on the most material level of food, clothing rations, and positions with the occupiers.

My own grandfather's papers, recently discovered in a closet when I was clearing out my mother's Upper West Side Manhattan apartment after she had moved to a nursing home, tell one story of these drastic shifts of identity. A March 1945 receipt under a false name from a lodging house in the Berlin suburb Lehnitz still marked him as a hunted illegal. The next form dating from August 13 was a modest typed certificate from the reconstituted *Jüdische Gemeinde,* Berlin, Iranische Strasse, certifying that Heinrich Busse was a full Jew and had lived hidden. A year later, on July 15, 1946, a more official *Ausweis Nr. 2584* (identity card) from the *Gemeinde* confirmed that he was of the mosaic faith, had worn a star, and had lived as an "illegal"; it came with ration stamps for a pullover, socks, shirt, and food. On August 30, Heinrich was a Berliner again; he had a full *Ausweis* with photograph issued by the *Magistrat der Stadt Berlin, Hauptausschuss* OdF, certifying him, in German and Russian, as a full-fledged OdF. He was now stamped both as a Jew and a victim of fascism.

The designation Jewish, however, was elastic and subject to much contestation. It encompassed Jewish *Uboote* or "illegals," as they called themselves, emerging from underground, Jews who had survived more or less above ground in mixed marriages, as well as in concentration camps, and liberated slave laborers. The latter were often *Mischlinge* (partial Jews) or partners in mixed marriages. Emigrated former German Jews returned to their home city in Allied uniform. Many—their collective story remains, remarkably, untold—came as new Americans. Konrad Wolf, the future GDR filmmaker, arrived with the Red Army; Hans Rosenthal's cousin

Heinz Renner reappeared in British uniform as Harold Ramsey.[20] Eastern European Jewish soldiers in all four allied armies often spoke Yiddish and hailed from the same towns and villages in Russia and Poland. Within a short time, other former Berliners slipped back to try and reclaim property, find friends and relatives, or to participate in a hoped for reconstruction of a new democratic Germany; the latter group included some 3,500 to 4,000 Communist exiles, in some way identified as Jewish, who returned from Moscow, London, Mexico, and elsewhere.[21] Jews trickled back from the death camps (especially Auschwitz). Others were repatriated from Theresienstadt, and then in 1947 en masse from Shanghai.

Finally, there were the displaced persons: the troublesome Polish-Jewish "infiltrees," survivors of the camps, ghettoes, hiding, and partisan movements, as well as returnees from the Soviet Union where at least 150,000 Jews, mostly Polish, had found a difficult but relatively safe refuge. Fleeing renewed persecution in Poland where they had hoped to find traces of lost family and property, they were funneled into the city in increasing numbers by the "open secret" of the underground Zionist *Bricha* network that planned to use the DP camps in the American zone as a waystation to Palestine.[22] Starting in November 1945, the flight of Eastern European Jewish survivors reached a high point after the pogrom in Kielce, Poland, on July 4, 1946, in which a charge of ritual murder led to the massacre of at least 40 Jews who had tried to return to their hometown.[23] During the brief liminal period from 1945 to 1948 when the occupied and officially divided city was still open to bordercrossers, all these quite different groups of Jews staked out a public presence that not only would have been unimaginable before May 1945 but has been largely forgotten today.

The tentative but remarkably rapid restoration of peaceful civil society, first by the Soviet Military Administration (SMAD), and then by the other three victor powers and their German (not infrequently Jewish or partially Jewish) collaborators, was marked in contemporary accounts by events with a specifically Jewish component. Surviving Jews were often deployed as instant bureaucrats or public safety officials. Hans Rosenthal, freed from his *Schrebergarten* hiding place, was immediately recruited for the local *anti-fa* committee. Gad Beck, a member of the Zionist youth resistance group *Chug Chaluzi,* had barely escaped from his bunker in the Jewish Hospital when he was briefly installed by the Soviets as a "representative for Jewish questions."[24]

Already on May 8, the first marriage in liberated Berlin was celebrated in Charlottenburg between two people who had not been allowed to marry under the Nuremberg Laws. On May 12, the first Jewish religious service was reported in the reopened synagogue on the Lotringer Strasse. And on May 11 (or perhaps May 12, the sources differ) another Jewish religious ceremony, also claimed as the first, was presided over by a Soviet Red Army chaplain, in the *Jüdisches Krankenhaus* [Jewish hospital] in the Iranische Strasse, where numbers of Jews had survived.[25] The SMA offered 400 Marks and privileged rations to returnees from the concentration camps. Rabbi Martin Riesenburger, who had served throughout the war at the Jewish Old Age Home (and deportation center) in the Grosse Hamburger Strasse and then at the Weissensee cemetery, advertised on the radio and on the remaining building walls for Jewish children to "contact him so that he could organize the first classes in Jewish religion in the city after liberation."[26] Committee for American Relief (CARE) packets from the American Joint Distribution Committee (JOINT) began arriving with "Butter, corned beef, chocolate, powdered milk, and sugar," plus the most valuable currency of all, cigarettes to be traded on the flourishing black market. In July, some 200 people gathered for a memorial service in the "eerie setting" of the cleaned-up stone ruins of a synagogue in Charlottenburg in the British sector. The young Zionist Lithuanian–American Jewish GI Kieve Skiddel, who worked as an Army interpreter in Berlin, described to his wife an "impressive in the extreme" service where everyone "wept" and "one of the men switched on the Eternal Light which had been out since I don't know when." The ceremony, a conscious reassertion of German-Jewish liberal religious identity, began, heartbreakingly, with a familiar recitation of the *Shehechiyanu*, the Hebrew prayer thanking God for having allowed one to survive until the present moment. It proceeded however to a sermon appealing to the values of the Enlightenment and was accompanied by Lewandowski's ritual organ music, which incorporated in its melody, to the GI's dismay, what he heard as "Arioso" by Handel. Both moved and nonplused, Skiddel, raised in an Eastern European tradition, commented that it "had the character of a reform service," but "there wasn't a trace of that chill."[27]

A year later, the Berlin Jewish Club, supervised by U. S. Army chaplain Herbert Friedman, was serving about 450 Jewish Allied soldiers and civilians. The club was an important site for the encounter among the various occupiers, especially for the squabbling Soviets and Americans, who could recognize each other as fellow Jews and even *Landsleute* [countrymen]. German served as a common language because the Russian officers could often speak German, and "if one of the Americans happened to be a Jewish boy who spoke German-Yiddish, the Russian and the American found some common ground there where they could understand each other's words."[28] Kieve Skiddel commented in July 1945 that, "It strikes me that the proportion of Jews among the higher ranking Russian officers is uncommonly high. I haven't enough to go by naturally, but I did actually talk with as many as three majors, one captain and two senior lieutenants."[29] In April 1946, an enormous public seder for over 2000 soldiers from the four armies as well as surviving local Jews was held in the *Schöneberger* [city hall], which would later become famous as the site of John F. Kennedy's "I am a jelly-doughnut" speech honoring the citizens of West Berlin. Heinrich Busse, the still malnourished Jewish *Uboote* offered his daughters in London a rather pragmatic rendition of the celebrated event in typical Berlin sardonic wit: "There was a very good meal for free, but in exchange one had to put up with hours of an English-Hebrew service as part of the bargain, and not a single soul understood a word."[30]

Berlin Is Back

Virtually overnight, vibrant urban life, with its flourishing theater, cinema, press, cabaret (and black market), materialized and Berliners reasserted their cherished self-image as plucky good-humored survivors. This recovery from a life "of bowed heads—looking for cigarette butts . . ." (as the American military paper *Stars and Stripes* unkindly put it)[31] depended in important ways on the return to public view—and indeed the showcasing—of Jewish journalists, actors, and theater directors with their links to Weimar (and exile Soviet or American) culture. "*Berlin Is Revived!*" the *Berliner Zeitung* already proclaimed on May 21, 1945, and other headlines announced, "*Berlin Is Back,*" suggesting naively that reconstructing Berlin could be a bit, in Wolfgang Schivelbusch's words, "like opening a time capsule" untouched since 1932.[32]

The resurrected memory of Weimar, a fascination with Nazi-banned modernism, obeisance to Soviet cultural policy calling for peace and progress, and general dependence on Allied (first Soviet and then four-power) licenses, produced a manic plethora of cultural events. Programs were printed in a babel of languages and included long explanations for the culturally starved audiences; the intensity of the theater experience was only heightened by the surreal theatricality of the surroundings. Forty-six plays were presented in Berlin in the first postwar year of 1945 to 1946 to ecstatic audiences in ice-cold halls, with programs ranging from "Shakespeare to Wilder, from Hebbel to Brecht, from Gorki to Weisenborn, from Offenbach to Weill."[33] Banned stars such as Käthe Dorsch returned to the stage. Elisabeth Bergner's return to Berlin was treated as front-page news. Jewish actors Ida Ehre, Lilli Palmer, Elisabeth Bergner, Curt Bois, and Ernst Deutsch returned to stage and screen, and "Almost all directors at Berlin theaters were of Jewish origin, about ten Jewish actresses returned to East Germany."[34]

Hans Rosenthal garnered a job with Allied licensed radio and almost immediately became the host of a popular radio broadcast, *Pulsschlag Berlins,* foreshadowing his later career as West Germany's most prominent television talk-show host. Despite the murder of his parents and his younger brother, and his rapid disillusionment with the Communists he had initially served so eagerly, Rosenthal delighted in an irrepressible zest for life. Like many survivors in ruined postwar Berlin, he experienced the exhilaration of survival and a passionate desire to catch up on his lost youth. He wanted to start anew, to fall in love. On August 30, 1947, at the age of 20, he married a German.[35] Henry C. Alter, a Viennese Jew, was the American officer in charge of film licensing for Berlin. One of his colleagues was Billy Wilder, who returned in 1945 from Hollywood to the city where he had spent his formative years. Many of the Soviet cultural officers were also Jews.[36] At the Soviet club *Die Möwe* [Club Seagull] in the Neue Wilhelmstrasse, Soviet and American cultural officers and German intelligentsia, many of whom had returned from exile, socialized and feasted on cheap borscht, sausage, beer, and of course vodka.[37] As Frank Stern has pointed out, many of the very early licensed films (*Professor Mamlock, Morituri,* and *Die Mörder Sind Unter Uns* are the best known) have Jewish (or coded Jewish) themes that were also assumed to be amenable to the censors.[38] The relatively large representation of Jews among U.S. occupation officers continued until the heating up of the Cold War in 1947, when the military government moved to dismiss anyone who had not been a citizen of the United States for at least ten years. This decision was clearly also aimed at Jewish émigrés, many of whom had become suspect because of their anti-German and pro-leftist sympathies.[39]

On September 7, 1945—ironically it was Rosh Hashanah—the first major theater production premiered in Berlin. Lessing's classic play *Nathan the Wise,* with Paul Wegner in the title role and Fritz Wisten directing, had been rescued, as a Berlin critic put it, from "the stage silence to which racial fanaticism had damned it."[40] In his recently published autobiography, the German-Jewish literary critic Marcel Reich-Ranicki, who returned to Berlin in Polish uniform and in the service of the Polish Communist secret police after having survived (and escaped) the Warsaw Ghetto, describes the event. He went to the theater expectantly, eager to observe how a German audience would now react to the long banned play about a Jew "whose wife and seven sons had been burned." But Reich-Ranicki was disappointed, for the audience was not German at all. The theater was filled rather with the officers of the four occupying powers, most of them, he noted, "Jews who spoke amazingly good German." Not surprisingly of course, because many of them were—or at least had been—German; "they were the exiles and refugees who now gathered together in a Berlin theater, not far from the ruins of the Reichstag and the Reichs Chancellery, under the sign of Lessing."[41]

So there was German-Jewish culture in Berlin right after the war, even as the city was becoming an important entry point for Polish Jews fleeing westward to the American zone. Indeed, it was visible in a manner quite disproportionate to the number of surviving German Jews who had remained or returned. The German-Jewish return was relatively tiny, and in many cases, temporary. But especially in those early postwar years, it was highly visible and much commented upon. It was even more noticeable because the returnees appeared so often in occupier uniform. One of Marcel Reich-Ranicki's first excursions in the Berlin he had adored as a child took him to the apartment of Reinhold Klink, a beloved teacher from his liberal (mostly Jewish) Werner Siemens *Realgymnasium:* "Quite by the way, he remarked that he received visitors often now. The guests usually wore American or English uniforms. They were his former Jewish pupils."[42]

Some Berlin Jews working for the Americans had never even left Europe. When Lothar Orbach returned from eight months in Auschwitz after he had been denounced while living underground, he went straight home, rang a doorbell with his name on it, and found that his mother was still alive, busy, and already at an *anti-fa* meeting. His three older brothers who had managed to emigrate were back as well, all in U.S. uniform and working for army intelligence. Lothar too quickly became an army investigator and interrogator.[43] When Kieve Skiddel, who had entered Berlin with the first wave of Americans in July, spied his first Jew on the streets of Berlin he immediately recruited him to work for the military government. The young man had been hidden with his parents by a "a simple man, a building worker in the Berlin subway system."[44]

Transit Station Berlin:
Displaced Persons, Allies, and German Jews

As the city came to life again, so did many of its most desperate aspects. Invoking memories of the upside-down inflation world of the early 1920s, Berlin was a center of crime, prostitution, and the inevitable black market. A boom in fortune telling and the occult serviced those who could no longer discern what was real and what was surreal, nor what had happened to their world and their loved ones. In the early years, Jews, with their designations as victims of fascism (*OdF*) and links to the military government and relief agencies, did have privileged access to the black market bonanza enjoyed by American GIs and officers stationed in Berlin. Especially, "[D]ruing the first months of the four-power occupation," U.S. troops "sent home more money than they were paid" and a grand booty of Leica cameras, Meissen china, Zeiss binoculars, and antique jewelry. They collected large sums of dollars, exchanging, for example, the occupation marks for a watch with the proverbial Russian peasant soldier who had never owned a timepiece and dreamed of sending it home so "his wife could barter it for a cow."[45] "A Mickey Mouse watch was worth more than a jewel-studded trinket from Cartier" the American commander in Berlin, Frank Howley, recorded.[46] As John Dos Passos recalled, "At the further end of the Tiergarten were crowds of furtive people with bundles under their arms scattered in groups over a wide area that looked like an American city dump. That was the black market."[47] Despite frequent protestations by Jewish military government and relief officials, pointing out that the black market was quite simply the only viable economy available in the immediate postwar period and that everyone was forced to participate, occupiers and Germans alike were of the opinion that it was the uprooted, traumatized Polish-Jewish "dee pees"—as the GIs called them—illegally jumping borders to enter Berlin who committed many of the crimes and black market offenses.

The story of surviving Jews in Berlin cannot be separated from the larger story of millions of non-Jewish (ethnic German and East European) refugees pouring westward, but it especially should not be disconnected from the experience of the mostly Polish-Jewish displaced persons who poured into "transit station" Berlin from Poland via Stettin, hoping to move westward to the American zone and eventually out of Europe. Berlin was unusual in occupied Germany because of the significant number of Jews who had survived in the capital and also because of the highly visible presence of Jews, in and out of Allied uniform, returning from the camps, slave labor, or exile. But it was the daily arrival of at least several hundred non-Berliner Jewish survivors in the officially closed city that caused what one U.S. officer termed a "red-hot" crisis for local and Allied authorities. Squabbles about the "Polish Jewish problem held center stage" at a surprising number of Allied *Kommandatura* sessions.[48]

The flow of Jews fleeing Poland and hoping for passage into the American zone and eventually to Palestine or other new homes seemed unstoppable. Colonel Howley, who had been the commander of Berlin's U.S. sector, recorded in 1951:

> Something drastic had to be done. At one time, we considered throwing a barricade around the city, but that would only have caused camps to spring up on our doorstep . . . The only thing we really could do was to maintain control over the refugees passing through, giving them one meal at night and shipping them out the next morning.[49]

Despite the best efforts of American occupation officials to stem the flow or at least to move new arrivals out quickly to larger camps in western Germany, the numbers of Jewish DPs continued to grow. U.S. military government had initially resisted forming DP camps in Berlin, especially since, "the Jewish population resident in Berlin in the main did not desire to have a camp created for them, stating that they had seen enough of camps."[50] Much to their annoyance, however, the U. S. military government authorities could not as easily, guiltlessly, and unilaterally ban all Jewish DPs from their zone in Berlin as the British, French, and certainly the Soviets did. The

British, preoccupied with the crisis in Palestine, flatly said no; the French pleaded poverty and lack of resources, and the Soviet general with "a puckish smile on his face," rather gleefully noted that the refugees all snuck out of his sector into the West anyway. The U.S. military government officer responsible recalled, "Everyone was irked by the way we were being browbeaten into assuming responsibility for all of the Polish Jews, regardless of what sector of Berlin they were in."[51]

The Americans constantly struggled with the persistent infiltrees and the tensions they produced with the Germans and among the Allies. All decisions regarding Berlin had to be cleared by four contentious occupying powers. Relief work had to be coordinated with various independent agencies like the United Nations Relief and Rehabilitation Administration (UNRRA), which was officially in charge of displaced persons, and the major Jewish organizations, American Jewish Distribution Committee (AJDC or JOINT) and the British Jewish Relief Unit, which also continually argued amongst themselves and with the Allies. The major challenges were acquiring enough "food, coal, motor fuel, and transport,"[52] but even seemingly minor problems were always on the verge of becoming international incidents; one example was the U.S. effort, vigorously opposed by the British and Soviets, to sanction Yiddish as an approved language for postal service in and out of Berlin. American occupiers were clearly frustrated by the circles being run around them—with help from many sympathetic officers—by U. S. Army rabbis, American Jewish relief agencies, and Palestinian *Bricha* agents determined to smuggle Jews from Eastern Europe into the American sector and eventually the U.S. zone in the West.[53]

By 1947, over 1,000 Jewish infants and children were housed in camps in the American sector, and 6,000–7,000 Polish Jews were settled into DP camps under UNRRA management in the U.S. controlled suburb of Zehlendorf (Schlachtensee Düppel, which had been a camp for Soviet POWs, and Mariendorf were the best known). About 200 people a day "arrived and left, all put through delousing, medical checks, and cleaned up; none were allowed to leave unless they were free of disease and [had] proper clothing." As if surprised, an American officer noted, "We had a large number of stateless persons. The Germans certainly had mixed up a lot of people in Europe."[54] The camps were quickly pulled into "shape, spic and span, spacious and well-organized," and the Americans boasted that they had become a "showplace for visitors interested in seeing how comfortable DPs could be made and how sensibly they could be cared for." In the fall of 1946, in one of the many brilliant public relations moves that developed between the Americans and the DPs, General Lucius Clay participated, with tears in his eyes, at a *Yizkor* memorial service in the synagogue at Düppel DP center.[55]

The DP camps in Berlin, while certainly not entirely isolated from the official *Gemeinde* [community] comprised mostly of German Jews, developed a lively existence of their own. Three schools and two summer camps opened; some 70 Jewish DP students registered at Berlin universities. In fall 1946, the Herzl Public Hebrew School had 400 students; altogether almost 1,000 children attended school. Zionist youth organizations of all stripes, from the right-wing *Betar* to socialist *Hashomer Hatzair,* flourished, providing support and a vision for the future to the many young single survivors of exterminated families. An AJDC mobile film unit toured the camps, showing Yiddish and Hollywood films ("When Irish Eyes Were Smiling" seems to have been particularly memorable). Legal aid teams worked to straighten out the status of the many "infiltrees." Yehudi Menuhin came to play, and was greeted with an icy boycott for having had, in the name of peace and reconciliation, agreed to a joint appearance with the German conductor Wilhelm Fürtwangler.[56]

By autumn 1946, the Soviets forced the *Bricha* underground network to curtail its "flight and rescue" missions, but still, tens of thousands of mostly Polish Jews would pass through Berlin from November 1945 through January 1947. Several thousand of the estimated 90,000 people who had taken that route remained, at least temporarily, in Berlin.[57] The one point on which everyone—the local *Gemeinde,* the Americans, the other occupiers, the Germans, and the DPs themselves—could agree was that there would be no future for Eastern European Jewish DPs in Berlin, in fact nowhere in Germany (or probably in Europe). Indeed, it was directly in response to the mass influx of Jewish DPs that in December 1945 the liberal U. S.-licensed *Tagesspiegel* editorialized:

> So one may hope that the millions of sacrifices [*Opfer*] by the Jews have not been brought in vain, but that rather after hundreds of years of effort it will finally be possible today to solve the Jewish problem in its totality [*das jüdische Problem in seiner Gesamtheit zu lösen* (*sic*)]; namely, on the one hand, through emigration of the homeless Jews and, on the other hand, through the complete assimilation of those Jews who wish to remain in Europe.[58]

Of course, most of the DPs themselves wanted nothing more than to escape the "cursed soil" of Germany. Much more divided in their sentiments about remaining in Germany, the German Jews living in Berlin shared German and Allied anxieties about the Eastern European survivors in their midst, but by no means as crassly or censoriously as is often assumed. The *Gemeinde* paper *Der Weg* [*Zeitschrift für Fragen des Judentums*], which commenced publication on March 1, 1946 as the voice of the Berlin German-Jewish community, judged the DPs, "aliens in Germany who also want to remain that way."[59] Hans Habe complained that "These survivors of mass murder were not necessarily the best elements among the Jews," while simultaneously expressing his outrage that "Not a single attempt has been made to call the German Jews back; the ones who returned were in for bitter disappointments."[60] Nonetheless, *Der Weg* tirelessly pointed out the logical error characterizing all the uproar about DPs and their black-market activities; it was after all not the DPs who were responsible for anti-Semitism but anti-Semitism that was responsible for the plight of the DPs.

German Jews were not willing to join—at least officially—in the general condemnation of DP petty crime. They insisted on how minute the DPs' vices were in comparison with those perpetrated on all Jews by the Germans. Calling for sympathy, *Der Weg* published photographs depicting DP children playing behind barbed wire, without sufficient space, clothes, and care. The paper sought to humanize and explain the motivations of the "infiltrees," presenting, for example, the story of a young man who had fled to Russia with his young wife and child. His family did not survive their flight; when he returned to Poland grieving and alone, none of his possessions remained, but "every corner in his birthplace reminded him of his wife and child—the attitude of the population was anything but friendly." So he fled west and landed in a DP camp in Berlin.[61] *Der Weg* was also careful to report common activities. In November 1946 some 1,000 children from the DP camps and the *Gemeinde* enjoyed a joint excursion to a performance of *Robinson Crusoe* at the Neue Scala. On OdF Day they marched together in the commemorative parades.[62]

Return and Tentative Rebuilding

However, at the same time as Germans complained, German Jews worried, and the Allies tried (unsuccessfully and rather halfheartedly) to halt the flow of Eastern European Jews, the return of Berlin Jews was celebrated with some fanfare. The repatriation in 1947 of 295 Berlin Jews from Shanghai was a huge media event and was treated as a relatively unproblematic case of the lost natives coming home after 22 days on an American troopship and a 5 day train ride from Naples. Berlin papers described in great detail how 71-year-old Martin Hamburg, the former London correspondent of the *Berliner Tageblatt*, returned with the same faithful dog that had accompanied him to Shanghai in 1939. The actor Martin Rosen, liberated from Auschwitz, was photographed at the Görlitzer train station as he embraced his eight and one-half-year-old daughter Eva whom he had sent to safety in China when she was only five months old (her mother was not mentioned).[63] The returnees were first taken to the Reinickendorf DP camp where, in sharp contrast to the reception of Eastern European survivors, they were "entertained lavishly."[64]

The miraculous survival and return to Berlin of one seven-year-old child was celebrated with great publicity. As reported on February 7, 1946, Peter Dattel, the youngest child survivor of Auschwitz, was also the only 1 of 8,000 deported Berlin children to have survived; of the adults, barely 100 had returned. Thanks to the heroic efforts of other inmates, determined to rescue at least one child, mother and child somehow managed to stay together in the medical experimentation block. But liberation found the mother in another camp, searching frantically for her son. The child, who barely remembered his pre-Auschwitz life, was taken in by foster parents in Czechoslovakia; Jewish and Czech authorities had then cooperated to assure a reunion with his mother, who had finally returned to Berlin. Peter Dattel's singular homecoming was marked by a festive event at the *Gemeinde,* attended by members of the occupying powers, the local *anti-fa* committees, the Berlin magistrate, and the Czech military attachés. Fellow Auschwitz survivor Julius Meyer, representing the OdF, used the occasion for public antifascist ritual, articulating the survivors' pledge to look forward with hope rather than backward with agony:

> We survivors of this murderous system want to deploy all our efforts to assure that Peter Dattel will become a happy child [*Menschenkind*] whose life will not be destroyed by enmity and persecution.

While the dramatic narrative served as an antidote to the tragic search and death notices usually published in *Der Weg,* it was clear that the story, like that of most rescued children reunited with parents from whom they had been traumatically separated, was not unproblematic. Mother and son, it was noted, no longer spoke the same language, and the implication was clear that this was meant in more than the linguistic sense. Indeed, the child was so terrified of leaving his foster family in Czechoslovakia that he had to be forced into the car taking him home to Berlin. Peter's mother's name or presence at the ceremony was not mentioned. As the first anniversary of liberation approached, *Der Weg* spoke for its readers, "Rescue has come, but we still await salvation."[65]

The advertisement and announcement pages of *Der Weg* tell these ambivalent stories most eloquently; they are filled with notices pleading for any word of lost loved ones alongside a beginning trickle of wedding, birth, and Bar Mitzvah announcements. Brave new bulletins bordered the unspeakably tragic. The first Bar Mitzvah and engagement notices were printed on August 23, 1946.[66] In October the Jewish community leader Julius Meyer and his wife announced the birth of their daughter Renate. On the same page, "A desperate wife and mother" was "searching for her husband and five children" (including twins born in 1927).[67] In post-catastrophe Europe where so much survivor energy was bound up in trying to locate, or at least to find traces of, the dead and missing, people pleaded that they would be grateful for "any, even the tiniest information." People were loath to accept the news that Heinrich Busse relayed to still hopeful relatives abroad in December 1945:

> I am very much afraid that we will all have to accept the awful fact that there is no more hope. Whoever hasn't returned by now, will, as the *Gemeinde* tells me, hardly have the possibility of reporting or suddenly surfacing with the countless refugees who are crisscrossing the country. All the search actions are only a tranquilizer, because how are we to find anyone in the midst of these millions upon millions, especially given the lack of lists and documentation.[68]

Obituaries referred both to the present, painfully soon after liberation, and to deaths that had been unmarked during the war. Scattered family members placed death notices for relatives without graves: "In anguished memory of our beloved mother, mother in-law and grandmother, born 22.17.76, perished in Birkenau," signed by her children in South Africa, Palestine, Shanghai, and Berlin.[69] Another family simultaneously announced its emergence from illegality, the reunion with their mother returned from Theresienstadt, and the death of the father in Theresienstadt.[70] The advertising section of *Der Weg* also documented the current daily life of a small, traumatized, but undeniably lively community in the making. It featured the ubiquitous ads for magicians and seers, feeding on hopes that perhaps the occult could make the lost visible again. While many items declared departures for new homelands, others offered the services of re- or newly established Jewish doctors, dentists, lawyers, hoteliers, storekeepers, and antique dealers. The first kosher butcher opened in Schöneberg on July 1, 1946.

In March 1946, when *Der Weg* distributed its first issue, the community counted 7,768 members, living in 5,640 households (not including the large numbers who passed through Berlin DP camps). Most of those counted were single survivors and lived, as the paper perceived, "in a loneliness without end."[71] A year after the war ended, *Der Weg* took grim statistical inventory. In 1925 during the Weimar Republic's "Golden Twenties," Berlin counted 172,672 registered Jews, 4.3 percent of the general population. In 1933 there were 160,564. In June 1941, 67,000 Jewish-identified Jews (*Glaubensjuden*) remained in Berlin; in October when the deportations began, still 66,000. Then the decimation proceeded more rapidly: 55,000 in January 1942; 25,000 in March 1943 after the *Fabrikaktion* had deported many slave laborers; 17,000 in April; and then by December 1, 1944, 5,500, including about 1,000 who had been transported in from other parts of the country. On April 1, 1945 as the Russian tanks approached, an estimated 5,100 Jews resided in Berlin, above and below ground, most of them in mixed marriages. In February 1946, a census of *Glaubensjuden* in Berlin counted 3,004 men and 3,299 women. Of the 6,303 only 70 were under 6 and 1,340 were between 40 and 50 but 1,684 were over 60.[72] The relatively large number of elderly was completely atypical for survivors and reflected the fact that most members of Berlin's early postwar community had not been deported to labor or death camps, but had survived in hiding, in mixed marriages, or in exile (and in some cases in Theresienstadt concentration camp).

Debates over Past and Future

Because of these numbers and because of the city's emblematic status in both German and Jewish history, Berlin remained a unique center for a continuing German-Jewish community. Inevitably, it also became a center of anguished debate and sometimes bitter controversy about what that might or should mean. *Der Weg* chronicled all of this ferment: the divisions among those who had survived underground, those who had returned from the camps, and the émigrés who had returned from exile; the endless cogitations about whether it was better to stay or to leave, whether the task at hand was simply to administer a fading remnant community [*Liquidationsgemeinde*], or attempt to build a new German-Jewish life. The paper documented the increasing (rather than diminishing) anger and anxiety about continued anti-Semitism and lack of remorse among Germans. It debated whether to join with other victims of fascism in the VVN (Association of Persecutees of National Socialism), established on November 23, 1946, with 181 delegates representing 20,000 persecuted survivors, or to remain separate in exclusively Jewish associations.

All aspects of past and future were subject to intense argument. There were disputes between those who were fully Jewish and those who were not, between those with non-Jewish partners to whom they owed their survival and those who did not want to include non-Jews in the community (and the compensation that, it was immediately claimed, was due that community). Among those who wanted to leave, there were disagreements between those hoping to head to Palestine and those seeking other destinations. After all, the U. S. consulate in Berlin opened for business on April 1, 1946, and as one American reporter astutely observed of both German and DP Jews, "Palestine is a kind of magic word among them which means not so much Palestine as some never-never Utopia of which they dream. It might be anywhere they could live freely."[73] Arguments abounded about whether the Jewish remnants in Berlin should define themselves as German Jews or Jews in Germany, and over who counted as Jewish at all. The latter was an especially crucial question because of the prominence in the community of those who were partially Jewish or who had non-Jewish spouses to whom they were often especially indebted and devoted.[74]

Such questions assumed even more urgency because of the very real material benefits in terms of privileges and compensation now attached to a Jewish identity. Right after liberation, outside observers like the American soldier Kieve Skiddel were convinced that as far as Berlin's Jews were concerned, "What they want is 1) food and 2) a chance to get out of Germany."[75] But a year later, those who wanted to reclaim German citizenship defended themselves, insisting that they were not "bad Jews . . . because we want to stay and work there where we, thanks to our birth and language, our worldly culture and lifestyle, belong."[76] At the same time, German Jews struggled with their ambivalent feelings about contributing to the recovery of the German nation and economy. This tension was felt less keenly by the Eastern European DPs who carried no obligation whatsoever to German reconstruction (to put it mildly). On the other hand, several thousand Jewish Communists who had returned from exile (mostly in the West, in London and Mexico) were explicitly committed to building a new democratic Germany in the Soviet zone.[77]

In its very first issue on March 1, 1946, *Der Weg* posed key questions about the future: defining themselves as *Judische Mitbürger* [Jewish fellow citizens]—the term that remains current in today's Germany—the editors adopted a wait-and-see attitude towards their participation in the reconstruction of Europe and Germany. Germans, they seemed to be insisting, needed to prove themselves worthy of the Jews staying or returning; equally obvious was their intense hope—soon dashed—that the reconstructed postwar Germany would be welcoming. As the lead first article stated, in a rather astonishing expression of undaunted German-Jewish enlightenment tenets, the journal wished to "contribute to totally eliminating the rift between Jews and non-Jews that has been ripped open by a twelve-year uninhibited hate campaign against Jewish people." They proceeded to note gravely, as if any readers in 1946 were in need of reminding, that, "despite all efforts the anti-Semitic poison that Hitler infused into the German *Volk,* and not only since his coup d'état, has not yet been everywhere totally absorbed/eliminated."[78]

Views on the proper future for Jews in Germany inevitably reflected experiences in the immediate past. Those who had survived underground as "illegals" tended to have both the most positive and the most narrow perspective on their former fellow citizens. Often they were the most hopeful about the possibilities of reconciliation and cooperation for building a new democratic Germany. Their voices were particularly powerful in Berlin where the largest number of Jews had been hidden. During the worst of the Nazi years, often isolated in their hiding places, they had encountered primarily the best of the Germans. They generally owed their survival not just to one individual but to entire networks of people, albeit mostly unorganized, willing to help or at least to tolerate others who did. Hans Rosenthal, who became a leader of the "reconciliationist" faction in the community even as he developed his radio (and later, television) career as one of Germany's best-known *conferenciers*, put this into perhaps extreme form in his memoirs. It was, he insisted, the memory of three elderly women who protected and mothered him in a working-class Berlin garden colony [*Laubenpieper Kolonie Dreieinigkeit*] that sustained him in his identification with the new Germany. They had made it possible, "after this terrible time for Jews for us to live freely (without reservation) in Germany, for me to feel as a German, to be without hatred, a citizen of this country."[79] At the same time, accounts in *Der Weg* made clear that the "illegals" found themselves on the defensive, prodded into protesting that they too had suffered, albeit in different ways than those who had actually been in the camps.

Those who had survived with the aid of non-Jewish partners struggled to convince fellow Jews and the occupiers that they too deserved aid and sympathy. One woman wrote in broken English to the U.S. occupation authorities:

> Being a Jewess I was apprehended in the year 1944 by Gestapo upon denunciation and abducted to Theresienstadt. My husband who was not a Jew, died with grief. In consequence of this, my dwelling was unattended for a longer space of time . . . I cannot believe that after all my ghastly experiences during the time of Nazi rule people may leave me in the cold flat, and I beg to ask for checking whether I cannot be helped. I am adding that I am 69½ years of age.[80]

Non-Jewish partners whose families had often lost German relatives in the war also sought recognition and equal benefits from the associations of persecutees and victims, the *Gemeinde,* and the Allies.

Compensation and Commemoration: Early Debates

The intensity of these early debates about identity, memories of the very recent past, and relative guilt and victimization was fueled by concrete questions of livelihood, money, and property. They revolved around the most banal issues of everyday life: from the most urgent needs for food, clothing, and housing to the reparation of bank accounts and property. The special office for the restitution of Jewish property in the Schlüter Strasse, corner *Kudamm,* was undoubtedly one of the most important addresses for Berlin Jews shortly after the war. *Wiedergutmachung* [reparation] was immediately on the agenda and the determination to extract monetary compensation was inextricably linked to the memorialization of the dead. Indeed, all the thorny topics still agitating current discourse about the Holocaust, such as the architecture of memorials, how best to provide reparations to the victims and punishment for the perpetrators, or the place of Jews in postwar Germany, were aired in *Der Weg*.

Debates about the proper forms and mode of memorialization commenced almost immediately; there was not, it seems, a moment when survivors did not conceive of themselves consciously as witnesses with an obligation to tell their stories, on behalf of themselves and those who had perished. *Der Weg* published numerous memoirs and diaries of persecution and survival. Shortly before Rosh Hashonah in 1946, 2,000 Berlin Jews, including children from the community's orphanage and DPs from the various camps marched in the first Day of Remembrance, an OdF gathering on September 22, 1946. At a time when people still moved relatively easily across the open borders between the Soviet and Western zones, the Jewish and antifascist experiences were, as Michal Bodemann has argued, still closely linked, despite deep disagreements about the relative status of antifascist "resisters" and "victims" of fascism.[81] On the eve of Yom Kippur in 1946 at Kol Nidre services in Weissensee cemetery, the cornerstone of a future memorial was laid, but its precise shape and form was left open to further discussion. In April 1947 the blueprint, designed by the sculptor Cramer, was published. Despite what appears to have been considerable discussion, no resolution was found.[82]

Revenge and Reconciliation

With its personal announcements, ads for goods and services, notices of public events, personal testimonies, and heartfelt polemics, *Der Weg* served both as a community newsletter and a forum for arguing about and making sense of a disrupted past, difficult present, and endlessly contested future. Probably reflecting the shell-shocked mood of its small community of German-Jewish readers, the paper often seemed to carry a split personality. At points it read, in surreal time capsule form, like a revived smaller version of a *Central Verein* [Association of Germans of Jewish Faith] journal, in its honoring of the Jewish contribution to German *Kultur*. Articles appeared about the Jewish salons of Henriette Herz and Dorothea Schlegel and other German-Jewish luminaries, celebrating the memory of the destroyed German-Jewish symbiosis, as if insisting on that history could somehow lead to its resurrection.

But *Der Weg* was quick to report acts of revenge as well as struggles around reconciliation. Clearly, Jewish survivors played important roles in the sighting, identification, and (at least initial) bringing to justice of Nazi criminals. The May 17, 1946 issue tells the story of the Eisenmann family's excursion to a boxing match at which they encountered the Gestapo man Müller. Soviet authorities were called and he was immediately taken away. A week later, a Jewish theatergoer recognized an SS guard from Auschwitz at the Metropol Theater; she too was handed over. Such confrontations—and they seem to have been frequent—provide another lens on the vexed questions about Jewish revenge (or the lack thereof), and suggest also at least one powerful reason to stay in the land of the murderers after liberation: the drive to expose and punish the guilty. At least in the beginning, it seems, Jewish survivors felt that they could count on Allied support and gratitude, especially from the Soviets and Americans, for these acts of vigilante justice. Much energy was also expended in the early postliberation days on settling accounts with Jewish collaborators, particularly the dreaded "Jew catchers," who had, toward the war's end, become one of the greatest dangers for Jewish illegals in Berlin. The capture of the notorious (and beautiful) "catcher" Stella Kübler was noted with satisfaction; she would "no longer be able to do any harm."[83]

There were other forms of revenge as well. Lothar (later Larry) Orbach had spent most of the war hidden in Berlin and, not unlike the young half-Jewish Zionist Gad Beck who recorded with glee his homosexual as well as political adventures underground, he had lived a nerve-wracking life not without its pleasures. In his memoir, which reads like a heterosexual version of Beck's account, Orbach recalls the thrill of wartime Berlin, his love affairs, his contacts with Communist resisters, his hideouts in seedy pool halls and brothels. With a certain degree of embarrassment and disbelief, he confesses:

> my years of hiding from the Nazis in war-torn Berlin included quite a few "nice days." It may seem blasphemous to recall that time of darkness and to remember also the flashes of light and warmth—to speak of romance, friendship, delight, and adventure in the midst of murderous oppression. But that is the way it was.

But Orbach also spent "eight months in the hell of Auschwitz and Buchenwald," after nearly two years underground in Nazi Berlin. When he returned to Berlin in 1945, his mourning for all that was lost and his relief at finding his mother still alive mingled with intense feelings of triumph and revenge: "I wore the dark blue Eisenhower jacket the Americans had given me so that any Nazis I might meet could appreciate the dramatic reversal in our relationship." Like virtually all diarists of postwar Berlin, he described rapes committed by Red Army soldiers. In the train taking him home, he heard Russian soldiers raping a German girl:

> No one raised a hand to help her; there was no sound but her screams. So much for the Master Race who, in Auschwitz, I had watched slam the head of a Jewish baby into the wall of a shower room. The baby had died instantly,

his brain protruding and his blood spurting; they had laughed, full of triumph and swagger. Now they were too meek even to protect one of their own children. Nor did I intervene; these were people who had set me apart, told me I could not be one of them.

Sitting in the train eating his American rations, he refused pleas for help, except to stuff some Spam into the mouth of a crying baby. Hired by the U.S. Army as an interrogator, Orbach felt, "I was grateful for the chance to be involved in a small way in the process of retribution." His acts of retribution also extended beyond those sanctioned by his American employers. Immediately after his return to Berlin, he went straight to the apartment of a Jew catcher, thoroughly beat him up, dragged him out, and turned him over to a Russian officer. It "was only a token gesture," Orbach conceded; the man was released shortly thereafter. "But the fact that it was a score settled, no matter how trivial in the larger scheme of things, relieved me of a burden, and helped me close the book on a long nightmare."[84]

In gratitude to the Soviets who liberated him, Marcel Reich-Ranicki returned to Berlin in the service of the Polish Communist police; "In order to see Berlin again, " he reflected, "who knows, maybe I would have even made a pact with the devil." Yet, the temptation had as much to do with the revenge as it did with nostalgia: "The defeated Germany, forced to its knees, fascinated me more than any other land on earth."[85]

The urge for revenge or at least some kind of compensation also, of course, expressed itself in the drive for material advantages, whether this took the form of better rations, restoration of property, or access to positions and black-market goods. At the same time, gratitude for survival led some to accept German pleas of innocence uncritically. The *Gemeinde* criticized Jewish jurists for cynically (or sentimentally) defending Germans in their denazification proceedings. Even if Germans had been personally helpful, it warned, such a "subjective" judgement did not take into account that the same people might very well have sent others to their death.[86] In a particularly ironic and perverse manifestation of the corruption produced by defeat, occupation, and apparently arbitrary punishment, former Nazis ("*Pgs*," party comrades) turned to the "black market in grandmothers," approaching Jewish survivors and offering money or food for a certificate (the famous *Persilschein* named for a detergent that did a particularly good job of whitewashing) that certified a Jewish relative as well as good behavior toward Jews during the Nazi years. Americans disgusted by this traffic in expiation reported that Jews were seen as so privileged that "some Germans after the war actually gave themselves a KZ tattoo."[87] With the more obvious anti-Semitism of the occupation years, also came a bizarre philo-Semitism. By June 1946, the Jewish *Gemeinde* in Berlin had registered some 2,500 petitions for entry and had to "create a special commission to cope with this phenomenon."[88] Some of these requests came from Jews who had left the *Gemeinde* and now found membership morally or materially beneficial; but many came from non-Jews. Some had married into the religion, but had tried to reverse their conversion to Judaism during the Nazi years and now wanted to reclaim it; others were new converts, seeking repentance or rehabilitation by identifying with Jewish victims.[89]

Borders Closing

By 1947, as the intensification of the Cold War obscured attention to Nazi crimes and the links between East and West Berlin became more fraught, the Jewish community's tone, as reflected in *Der Weg,* seemed to change. The sometimes manic exhilaration of the immediate postwar period faded. German Jews expressed more pessimism about German penitence and willingness to engage the past. Fewer search notices and more statements confirming deaths appeared. More and more ads said farewell "before our departure for the USA."[90] In the bitter winter of 1946 to 1947, community leader Hans Erich Fabian confessed that Germany had now become *unheimlich* to him; anti-Semitism more, not less obvious. Hopes for reconstructing a truncated but viable German-Jewish community seemed rather thoroughly dashed; by February 1947, disappointment was the motto:

> When we see that anti-Semitism in Germany today is becoming stronger by the day, that wide circles of people have learned nothing on this score and [worst of all] don't want to learn anything.[91]

In March 1947, one anonymous Jewish *Heimkehrer* [returnee] was diagnosed as having "unprecedented depression."[92] Jews living in occupied Germany were acutely aware that it was not the dead six million (and that was the figure cited) whom resentful Germans noticed, but the handful who were present. Visible, in Allied uniform, with some power in antifascist councils, as cultural officers and arbiters, Jews were perceived once again as much more numerous and powerful than they actually were.[93] Familiar anti-Semitic stereotypes and ressentiments were loudly voiced: there were complaints about the disproportionate number of Jewish lawyers and "the unfair advantage" they enjoyed over "Aryan" colleagues tainted by their Nazi past. The Jews hanging on in Berlin yearned for more understanding of their choice to remain (at least for the moment) but they were entirely sympathetic to the many who refused to return. They were outraged at the temerity of those who, like the Social Democratic politician (and KZ veteran) Kurt Schumacher, chastised Jews for their manifest disinterest in returning to rebuild their ruined land.[94] They were painfully cognizant of their isolation; Fabian noted that, "the best of us have fallen victim to the persecutions," and those who remained had only very limited psychic and physical energy.[95] Fabian himself would soon emigrate. The Berlin Jewish world was narrowing.

Crossing Borders, Shifting Identities

On July 4, 1946, a year after the Americans entered Berlin, Heinrich Busse, my grandfather, reacquired his German civil identity. He was issued real Berliner identification, signed not by occupation or *Gemeinde* authorities, but by the Berlin police chief, listing his citizenship as "German" and omitting any mention of religion. By June 27, 1947, however, he also possessed a much more valuable document. Printed in French and English, a *Titre de Voyage* or "Travel Document in lieu of a national passport," allowed him to enter Folkesstone, England, on October 20, 1947 and rejoin two daughters who had fled to England as domestics in early 1939. Heinrich Busse was a very German Jew, who at times briskly described his life in the underground as just another challenge to a hardened German gymnast for whom "there was no such thing as bad weather, just inappropriate clothing."[96] For him, the real recognition of the irrevocable loss of his *Heimat* and the need to find another or a substitute one came only after the war had ended and his many losses were confirmed. He realized that despite the hopeful excitement of liberation, which had made him feel as if "newborn," there would always be—as he put it in a birthday letter to his 36-year-old married daughter in London on June 18, 1946—"a sediment of mourning in the cup of your and all of our joy in life and ability to experience pleasure."

Only in 1947, over two years after his liberation, when Busse had left Berlin behind forever, did he begin to articulate the enormity of the German-Jewish catastrophe and the persistence of anti-Semitism. He acknowledged to a former rescuer, " . . . always, as you may know, I considered myself more as a German than as a Jew, and rejected the stupid and artificially constructed division between people who have lived in one land for many hundreds of years." Safely arrived in London, his perspective shifted. "Due to the very sharp and general condemnation of Germany—not only here [in England] but everywhere abroad, I have myself become more self-critical and perhaps more clear-sighted."

Ironically (and tellingly) Busse was most bitter, not about the mass of Germans whom he had long since written off, but about the minority of good Germans. They had helped him survive and he had maintained faith in them throughout the darkest days, even after his wife was deported to her death, even after the rest of his family had either emigrated or been murdered.

During the war, the "illegals" and those living in mixed marriages [or as *Mischlinge*], had relied on the help and cooperation of Germans. Even at their most desperate times, those in hiding or in touch with resistance news felt somehow vindicated in thinking that they were dealing with a "real" if minority Germany, with whom they might join in reconstructing their homeland after the Nazis were defeated. After liberation, Jews were shocked and aggrieved by the sentiments revealed among even the "decent" minority. Their rescuers complained about ungrateful Jews who received special favors from the occupiers, or who were quick to emigrate, leaving their helpers behind hungry, cold, and self-pitying in a devastated city, or who (in Allied uniform) treated them insensitively in denazification procedures. Confronted with Germans preoccupied with their own misery and indifferent to, or in denial about, what had happened to their Jewish compatriots—what observers termed "the enigma of German irresponsibility"[97]—surviving German Jews felt the force of anti-Semitism even more painfully than when hiding in a friendly *Schrebergarten*.[98]

Busse was shocked and horrified by a hectoring letter from an old business acquaintance, the furniture maker Hermann Paul, who had sheltered him during the war's chaotic final months (at great personal risk, but not without hope of advantage after Germany's inevitable defeat). Smarting from the miserably cold winter of 1947, Paul complained that Busse, now safe in England, was ungrateful, insufficiently generous with his CARE packages, and moreover, had taken off with a radio that could have brought a small fortune on the black market. Suddenly, it seemed to Busse, he was no longer the fellow Berliner who had needed help, but just another Jewish war profiteer. He responded fiercely:

> I was speechless. . . . Even you seem to be accepting this silly as well as pernicious "Antisemitism." . . . I am not indifferent to what you think of me. Not in the least do I want to minimize or deny that I owe you much thanks. You behaved decently and with courage, quite unlike the overwhelming majority of Germans, toward a criminal, treacherous, and in every way deeply contemptible regime. I have expressed this to you repeatedly. But I must tell you one thing in regard to your current attitude and your outrageous version of events. As much as I value your help and your previous rejection of National Socialism—your brother Erwin had himself at the time not been shy about declaring that under the existing circumstances [late in the war] the dangers of taking me were not so great, the benefits of helping someone persecuted possibly greater. I completely understood that, and would never have thought about even mentioning this. Now however, it is necessary. Because it might at least make you—I have no such hopes anymore about your brother Erwin—more thoughtful.[99]

In another letter from London, Busse responded passionately to the laments of a young woman who had supported him during his years as an *Uboote*. She was, he insisted, so immersed in her own experience as a victim of war, defeat, and victors' justice that she had lost all sense of moral and historical proportion:

> You have no idea how provocative it feels to those whom it affects when you now ask when will the liberators finally have satisfied their bloodthirstiness against us. When you as a German accuse them of horrendous tortures, after the entire world is still stunned with horror over the exposed and still not really admitted, somehow excused or trivialized, atrocities of the Germans, of which no one wants to be guilty or even involved. When you, despite all that has happened, literally write, "and after all, our hearts and hands are pure and with them the blood is flowing out of their collars," and other stuff like that, you refer personally to yourself and yours, but you can't possibly assume that the same would hold for the Germans as a whole and that one can expect the world simply to forget the horrors of Hitler, with which after all the broad masses generally identified.[100]

He did not want to live in a city where he had to explain even to his friends, "the not in the remotest way comparable difference between the conditions in Berlin or Germany now with those in Auschwitz, Belsen, etc."[101] On December 21, 1948, Heinrich Busse crossed his last border; the United States Immigration and Naturalization Service admitted the 74-year-old to New York City where he became an enthusiastic resident of Morningside Heights.

Staying Home, Traveling Letters

But there were also other resolutions, other ways to situate the conflict of being a German Jew post–May 1945. The debates about whether to stay or go, to stay away or return, were played out in countless conversations and letters that moved back and forth between Germany and the multiple emigration destinations. Some of them are mirrored in the papers of Sigmund Weltlinger,[102] a Berlin Jew who stayed home and felt at home; an exception to the general rule observed by an American Jewish military government official: "The fact that the German people feel no compulsion to make amends for the crimes of Nazism is the most important reason why a substantial part of the few remaining German Jews have decided to emigrate."[103]

Weltlinger was appointed the first Commissioner for Jewish Questions with the postwar Berlin *magistrat* and later served as a conservative Christian Democratic (CDU) deputy in the Berlin Assembly. From February 1943, after their children had been sent to England, he and his wife had lived concealed in Berlin with friends. Like many *Uboote*, they rarely left their hiding place, made it through several terrifying house searches, and had relatively little sense of what was going on around them.

Like Busse, Weltlinger wrote letters in a strongly defensive mode. He, however, was defending himself not against aggrieved Germans but against uncomprehending Jews who questioned his decision to stay in Berlin. On July 8, 1946, his niece Resilotte Lisser, now living at 750 Riverside Drive in New York, a classic Washington Heights (Fourth Reich, as the refugees dubbed it) refugee address, wrote to her uncle and aunt in Berlin. She tried to persuade her only remaining close relatives to come to New York: "What a life we have here in freedom—it is good to live here." She assured them that everyone could find work and that they would not be a burden. On March 3, 1947, she tried again, reflecting the thoughts of the vast majority of her fellow German Jews living in that *Viertes Reich* on the problematics of what it meant to be home. "No, for us there can be no going back, even if in my thoughts I am often back "at home." But it was all only a dream, my youth, and everything to do with it. I am at home *here* and happy!" She had a four-year-old American daughter with blond braids.[104]

Weltlinger however did not want to leave Berlin. He had only just emerged into its daylight again, and he found the city open and fascinating in all the ways suggested at the beginning of this article. In the hard years of 1946 to 1947, he and his wife, like so many Berliners, went to the theater, heard Fürtwangler conduct Menuhin, and admired Gründgens, Dorsch, and many other great actors and actresses on the reopened, if unheated, stages. He was a minor big shot, privileged now as a Jew with good contacts to the Allies, enjoying the many receptions and parties with German and occupation officials.

Inevitably, there are silences and ruptures and inconsistencies in his stories. He reported how well they were living, better than most Berliners; his wife was greeted at receptions as *Frau Stadtrat*. But he also pleaded for shipments of food and clothing to be sent from New York; not to the JOINT please, where everything supposedly got lost (presumably to the DPs) but to the U. S. Chaplains Office, Jewish Relief Unit. On September 9, 1946, he carefully chronicled the lost and murdered; listing the names of those "unfortunately gassed," " . . . actually most of our old friends—one mustn't think about it." Yet he and his wife stayed on even as their children made new lives abroad. "We have found a new and stimulating circle which makes a lot of music. We hear good operas and concerts. Berlin is right up to par," he contended in 1951.[105] Weltlinger was not convinced by all the letters begging him to join the emigration, reporting on new lives. He continued to campaign for the Berlin Jews to return to a place he still considered home and mistrusted their insistence that they had created new homes.

But Weltlinger was unusual. Hans-Erich Fabian, the community leader, had expressed the dominant sense of unease in his lead article in *Der Weg* on January 31, 1947, when he acknowledged that postwar Germany had become irrevocably alien [*unheimlich*]. He struggled with the notion of a *Liquidationsgemeinde* and finally resorted, as did others, to the minimalist argument that some Jews must remain in Berlin, at least to help and guide the many refugees from the East who would continue to pour through. Sigmund Weltlinger even made the prescient (by about 40 years!) comment that an ongoing Jewish community was necessary if only because Berlin was the logical destination for a future but inevitable exodus of Jews from the Soviet Union.[106] Fabian, for his part, understood clearly all the reasons why Jewish life in Berlin should end, but still he lingered; it would after all mean the final loss of a long and cherished tradition. Eastern European Jewry had provided the basis for Jewish religion and ritual, but, he insisted, German Jewry had offered an important road out of the Ghetto into the civilization offered by the West. To finally close the door on that legacy would be hard to endure, Fabian lamented.[107] Yet, he too, departed (much more unhappily than most) for New York.

By 1948 to 1949, the situation in Berlin changed dramatically: currency reform, blockade, and airlift sealed the division of the city and transformed its status (for both sides) from vanquished Nazi capital to plucky Cold War ally. The final separation of Berlin into East and West also basically eliminated the Jewish DP problem for Berlin. Almost all of the stubbornly remaining (ca. 6,500) DPs in Berlin were flown out into the Western U.S. zone in empty Airlift planes returning to their base at Rhine-Main, another step toward the normalization of divided Berlin. The borders in Berlin were closing. The bordercrossers, even the most determined, were leaving or thinking about leaving (some of them, of course, were still thinking about it 55 years later). Jewish aid organizations curtailed their programs in Berlin; if Jews decided to stay, then that would be their own personal responsibility.[108] The burden was placed on the small numbers of Jews, both native German or Eastern European, who remained in the land of the murderers; a situation that would not fundamentally change until the fall of the Wall set the stage for a new phase of revived and multifaceted if still problematic and evolving Jewish life in Berlin.

Notes

* I am, as always, grateful to members of the German Women's History Study Group in New York City for their incisive criticisms and suggestions. I am also grateful to the Sawyer Seminar on "Archives, Documentations, and the Institutions of Social Memory" as well as the Program in the Comparative

Study of Social Transformations at the University of Michigan Ann Arbor for inviting me to present portions of this work in progress in November 2000 and March 2001.

1. West Berlin Senat, *Berlin: Kampf um Freiheit und Selbstverwaltung 1945–1946* (Heinz Spitzing Verlag, 1961), 10. Col. Frank Howley uses the same terms in his *Berlin Command* (New York: Putnam, 1950), 8. Indeed, the historian is generally struck by the ubiquitousness and repetitiveness of certain phrases and expressions.

2. See for example Hans Speier, *From the Ashes of Disgrace: A Journal from Germany 1945–1955* (Amherst, MA: University of Massachusetts Press, 1981).

3. Estimates of refugee numbers in the summer and fall of 1945 vary greatly, depending on who is counting whom, how, and when. John J. Maginnis, *Military Government Journal, Normandy to Berlin* (Amherst: University of Massachusetts Press, 1971), 278–79, refers to 15,000 daily. Eugene Davidson in *The Death and Life of Germany: An Account of the American Occupation* (New York: Alfred A. Knopf, 1959), 77, counted 25,000 to 30,000 refugees daily. See also Landesarchiv Berlin (LAB) OMGUS 4/24–1/4 for discussions on efforts to keep refugees out of the beleaguered city.

4. Robert Murphy, *Diplomat Among Warriors* (New York: Collins, 1964), 264. Former ambassador Murphy became the political advisor to U.S. military government in Germany.

5. Ruth Andreas-Friedrich, *Schauplatz Berlin. Tagebuchaufzeichnungen 1945 bis 1948* (Frankfurt am Main: Suhrkamp, 1984); Curt Riess, *Berlin! Berlin! 1945–1953* (Berlin: Non Stop Bücherei, 1953), 174. The notion of Berlin in ruins as a kind of surreal theatrical or operatic stage set was invoked by many observers—and filmmakers—at war's end. See the large number of films made in the ruins; exemplary perhaps are Roberto Rossellini's *Germania Anno Zero* and Billy Wilder's *A Foreign Affair.*

6. Hans Habe, *Aftermath* (New York: Viking, 1947), 185.

7. See for example, Davidson, *The Death and Life of Germany,* 75.

8. Julian Bach Jr., *American's Germany: An Account of the Occupation* (New York: Random House, 1946), 22.

9. Meyer Levin, *In Search: An Autobiography* (New York: Horizon Press, 1950), 384.

10. John Dos Passos, *Tour of Duty* (Boston: Houghton Mifflin, 1946), 319.

11. Kieve Skiddel, unpublished letter home to his wife in New York, July 3, 1945. I am grateful to Professor Arthur Goren, Columbia University, for giving me copies of these extraordinary letters.

12. Film Nr. 5. Landesarchiv Berlin (LAZ) Nr. 2722. "Bericht über die Zeit seit dem Einzug der russischen Armee" [report on the time after the entry of the Russian army].

13. Davidson, *The Death and Life of Germany,* 75; Jean Edward Smith, *The Defense of Berlin* (Baltimore, MD: Johns Hopkins Press, 1963), 67.

14. To the total of ca. 15,000 Jews (of a pre-1933 Jewish population of about a half-million) who survived within the Reich must be added perhaps 50,000

Jewish forced laborers who were liberated on German territory at the end of the war. See Frank Stern, "Antagonistic Memories: The Post-War Survival and Alienation of Jews and Germans," in *Memory and Totalitarianism, Volume I, International Yearbook of Oral History and Life Stories,* ed. Luisa Passerini (New York: Oxford University Press, 1992), 23. The survival statistics for Berlin, as well as for Germany as a whole, are inconsistent and varied according to who is counting whom when, and depending on how "Jewish" and "end of war" are demarcated. Andreas Nachama, "Nach der Befreiung: Jüdisches Leben in Berlin 1945–1953," in *Jüdische Geschichte in Berlin. Essays und Studien,* ed. Reinhard Rürup (Berlin: Edition Hentrich, 1995), 268–69, quotes reports similar to those used by Frank Stern, estimating that there were about 7,000 Jews in Berlin right after the war. 1,500 had survived the camps, 1,250 had been *Uboote* in hiding, and ca. 4,250 had been spared deportation because they lived in mixed marriages; of these, 2,250 were so-called star wearers, while the rest were privileged due to their Christian-identified children. Stern's corresponding figures are 1,155 camp survivors, 1,050 "illegals," and 2,000 mixed marriage partners, and another 1,600 exempted from wearing the star. Nachama also counts the pre-Nazi Jewish population of Berlin as about 200,000, which presumably includes those not officially registered as Jews. Michael Brenner notes that "more than ⅔ of the seven thousand members of the Berlin Jewish community of 1946 were intermarried or children of mixed marriages." See Brenner, "East European and German Jews in Postwar Germany, 1945–50," in *Jews, Germans, Memory: Reconstructions of Jewish Life in Germany,* ed. Y. Michal Bodemann (Ann Arbor: University of Michigan Press, 1996), 52. Marion Kaplan, on the other hand, in her book, *Between Dignity and Despair: Jewish Life in Nazi Germany* (New York: Oxford University Press, 1998), while also noting the general survival figure of "approximately 15,000" surviving German Jews "within the pre-1938 borders," cites Konrad Kwiet and Helmut Eschwege in their *Selbstbehauptung und Widerstand: Deutsche Juden im Kampf um Existenz und Menschenwürde, 1933–1945* (Hamburg: Christians, 1984) to state, p. 228, that "between 3,000 and 5,000 Jews came out of hiding in Germany. In Berlin, a city that once encompassed 160,000 Jewish Berliners, about 5,000 to 7,000 Jews hid, of whom only 1,400 survived." Here, on the one hand, she counts only those Jews who were hidden, and not those (included for example by Nachama, Stern, and Brenner) who had survived more or less above ground in mixed marriages (or had themselves been "mixed"); on the other hand, she cites a somewhat higher number of surviving *Uboote.* The interesting story here may not be the precise numbers but the variations of classification, and how they differ according to when and by whom the counting is done.

15. There is a relatively large body of literature—historical, memoir, diary, and fictional (and semifictional)—on Jews who survived in Berlin. See, for example, besides the memoirs cited in note 16, Leon Brandt, *Menschen ohne Schatten: Juden zwischen Untergang und Untergrund 1938 bis 1945* (Berlin:

Oberbaum Verlag, 1984); Leonard Gross, *The Last Jews in Berlin* (New York: Simon and Schuster, 1982); Erika Fischer, *Aimée und Jaguar: Eine Liebesgeschichte, Berlin 1943* (Cologne: Kiepenheuer and Witsch, 1994); and David Wyden's *Stella: One Woman's True Tale of Evil, Betrayal, and Survival in the Holocaust* (New York: Simon and Schuster, 1992), the story of a notorious Jewish Jew catcher.

16. Hans Rosenthal, *Zwei Leben in Deutschland* (Bergisch Gladbach: Gustav Lübbe Verlag, 1980). See also Gad Beck, *Und gad ging zu david: die erinnerungen des gad beck 1923 bis 1945,* ed. Frank Heibert (Berlin: edition diá, zebra literaturverlag, 1995), 187, in English, *An Underground Life: The Memoirs of a Gay Jew in Nazi Germany* (Madison: University of Wisconsin Press, 1999). Inge Deutschkron in *Ich trug den gelben Stern* (Munich: Deutscher Taschenbuch Verlag, 1987), 179–81, describes painfully how fear of the Gestapo turned into fear of rape by Red Army liberators.

17. Margaret Boveri, *Tage des Überlebens. Berlin 1945* (Munich: Piper, [1968]1985) 127–28.

18. Joel Sayre, "Letter from Berlin," *The New Yorker,* July 28, 1945 (July 14 dispatch). One wonders of course whether Sayre fully meant the irony of his translation of "Sonderbehandlung."

19. In a letter dated July 8, 1945, the American Jewish soldier Kieve Skiddel describes meeting a Jewish father and son on the street in Berlin, amazed to discover that there had been Germans who hid Jews: For two-and-a-half years a building worker in the Berlin subway system had hidden the father and son. His own children "have gone to war and he knows nothing about them. He took in this family of three, though it would have meant his neck if he had been discovered."

20. See Konrad Wolf's 1968 semi-autobiographical DEFA film *Ich War Neunzehn,* which chronicles the return to Berlin in 1945 of a German refugee soldier in the Soviet Army.

21. Figures from Frank Stern, "The Culture of Dissent: Jewish Writers and Filmmakers and the Re-Casting of Germany," paper presented at German Studies Association, Atlanta, October 1999.

22. See Nachama, "Nach der Befreiung," 272; Angelika Königseder, "Durchgangsstation Berlin: Jüdische DPs 1945–1948," in *Überlebt und unterwegs: Jüdische Displaced Persons in Nachkriegsdeutschland* (Fritz Bauer Institut Jahrbuch, Frankfurt am Main: Campus, 1997), 189–206; and Königseder, *Flucht nach Berlin: Jüdische Displaced Persons 1945–1948* (Berlin: Metropol, 1998). See also Maginnis, *Military Government Journal* 323–329, for a detailed (and candid) discussion of the Polish-Jewish refugee crisis and the considerable problems it posed for the Allied Kommandatura and especially the American occupiers. On Kielce, see Abraham J. Peck, "Jewish Survivors of the Holocaust in Germany: Revolutionary Vanguard or Remnants of a Destroyed People?" *Tel Aviver Jahrbuch für deutsche Geschichte* 19 (1990): 35. On the *Bricha* network that transported Jews into the American zone of Germany and Italy for eventual *Aliyah* to Palestine, see especially Yehudah

Bauer, *Flight and Rescue: Bricha* (New York: Random House, 1970) and Idith Zertal, *From Catastrophe to Power: Holocaust Survivors and the Emergence of Israel* (Berkeley: University of California Press, 1998).

23. See Abraham J. Peck. "Jewish Survivors of the Holocaust in Germany," 35. Most sources now agree that 42 Jews were killed in the Kielce pogrom. An estimated 62,000 Jews left Poland from early July until late September 1946.

24. On the remarkable Zionist youth resistance group *Chug Chaluzi*, see in addition to Gad Beck's memoir, Brandt, *Menschen ohne Schatten.*

25. *Berlin: Kampf um Freiheit und Selbstverwaltung,* 54.

26. Martin Riesenburger, *Das Licht verlöschte nicht. Ein Zeugnis aus der Nacht des Faschismus* (Berlin: Union Verlag, 1958, 1960, 1984), 54–59. See also Frank Stern, "Antagonistic Memories," 22.

27. Kieve Skiddel, unpublished letter, July 15, 1945.

28. Oram C. Hutton and Andrew Rooney, *Conquerors Peace: Report to the American Stockholders* (New York: Doubleday, 1947), 67.

29. Kieve Skiddel, letter, July 17, 1945.

30. Heinrich Busse, letter, April 20, 1946.

31. Douglas Botting, *In the Ruins of the Reich: Germany 1945–1949* (London: Allen and Unwin, 1985), 85. Joel Sayre wrote in his "Letter from Berlin," *New Yorker,* July 28, 1945 (July 14 dispatch), "The butt collecting in Berlin, I do not hesitate to say, is the most intensive on earth, and I am not forgetting the *Kippensammlung* on the Bowery and in the Middle East."

32. Wolfgang Schivelbusch, *In a Cold Crater: Cultural and Intellectual Life in Berlin 1945–1948* (Berkeley: University of California Press, 1998), 28.

33. Walter Karsch, "Bekenntnis zum Theater. Rückblick auf die Berliner Spielzeit 1945/46," *Berliner Almanach* (Berlin: Lothar Blahnvalet, 1946), 70.

34. Stern, "The Culture of Dissent."

35. Rosenthal, *Zwei Leben,* 126.

36. Schivelbusch, *In a Cold Crater* describes wonderfully this cacophonous cultural scene.

37. See for example the lively descriptions in Carl Zuckmayer (himself just returned from exile on a farm in Vermont), *Als wär's ein Stück von mir. Horen der Freundschaft* (Vienna: S. Fischer Verlag, 1966), 551–52.

38. See Frank Stern, "Facing the Past: Representations of the Holocaust in German Cinema since 1945," Joseph and Rebecca Meyerhoff Annual Lecture, June 14, 2000, United States Holocaust Memorial Museum.

39. See among many sources, Eugene Davidson, *The Death and Life of Germany,* 165. See also Hans Georg Troller's poignant autobiographical Austrian film, *Welcome to Vienna,* which depicts the young Jewish native's return to Vienna as an American cultural officer.

40. Karsch, "Bekenntnis zum Theater," 76. Karsch was not kind to Wisten.

41. Marcel Reich-Ranicki, *Mein Leben* (Stuttgart: Deutsche Verlags-Anstalt, 1999), 319.

42. Reich-Ranicki, *Mein Leben,* 53.

43. Larry Orbach and Vivien Orbach-Smith, *Soaring Underground: A Young Fugitive's Life in Nazi Berlin* (Washington, DC: Compass Press, 1996), 334.

44. Skiddel, letter from Berlin-Lichterfelde, July 8, 1945. Coincidentally, Marion Kaplan tells a later version of this family's story in her *Between Dignity and Despair*, 217–20. In her account, based on memoirs of the mother Irma Simon, the rescuer was a blacksmith with communist sympathies.

45. Davidson, *The Death and Life of Germany*, 84.

46. Frank L. Howley, *Berlin Command* (New York: Putnam, 1983), 91.

47. Dos Passos, *Tour of Duty*, 319.

48. Maginnis, *Military Government Journal*, 326.

49. Howley, *Berlin Command*, 88.

50. Lt. Col. Harold Mercer, chief of Displaced Persons and Welfare Section (OMG), 5 February 1946, LAB OMGUS 4/20–1/10.

51. Maginnis, *Military Government Journal*, 326–27.

52. Maginnis, *Military Government Journal*, 278.

53. On the relationship of Jewish displaced persons, the *Bricha*, and Jewish relief agencies to the American occupiers in Berlin and throughout Germany, see, among many sources, Maginnis, *Military Government Journal*; Abraham S. Hyman, *The Undefeated* (Jerusalem: Gefen, 1993); and *In Defense of the Survivors: The Letters and Documents of Oscar A. Mintzer, AJDC Legal Advisor, Germany 1945–46* (Berkeley: Judah Magnes Museum, 1999).

54. Maginnis, *Military Government Journal*, 299.

55. Abraham S. Hyman, *The Undefeated* (Jerusalem: Gefen, 1993), 281.

56. See for example, Hyman, *The Undefeated*, 340.

57. Nachama, "Nach der Brefreiung," 272. See also Angelika Königseder, "Durchgangsstation Berlin: Jüdische DPs 1945–1948," 189–206. All these numbers are inexact. The Berlin Sector/Public Welfare Branch of the Office of Military Government estimated on June 20, 1947, that there were 8,000 German Jews in Berlin receiving aid from the American Joint Distribution Committee, plus 6,300 Polish Jews in two DP camps. Another memorandum on June 20, 1947, for the Jewish Agency for Palestine counted 8,000 persons in Düppel and 4,000 in Wittenau camps.

58. K. E., "Juden in Deutschland," *Der Tagesspiegel* 39 (December 5, 1945): 3

59. Hans-Erich Fabian, "D. P.," *Der Weg* 2 (February 14, 1947): 2.

60. Habe, *Aftermath*, 124, 132. On the lack of interest in the return of Jewish academics or professionals, see Frank Stern, "Academia without Jews: The Universities in the Wake of *Entjudung*," in *The Whitewashing of the Yellow Badge: Antisemitism and Philosemitism in Postwar Germany* (Oxford: Pergamon, 1992), 158–212. On the bitter disappointment of returnees, see also Anthony Heilbut, *Exiled in Paradise: German Refugee Artists and Intellectuals in America From the 1930s to the Present* (New York: Viking Press, 1983), 325–49.

61. Ernst-Günter Fontheim, "Befreite Juden," *Der Weg* 1 (September 6, 1946): 5–6.

62. *Der Weg* 1 (November 22, 1946): 2. See also, commentary on "Lagerleben," *Der Weg,* 1 (August 30, 1946): 1–2.
63. *Der Weg* 2 (August 29, 1947): 3–4. The story was also covered by the general Berlin press.
64. Landesarchiv Berlin (LAB), Film Nr. 5, LAZ Nr. 2722, from OMGUS files 4/20–1/10. Translation of the article is in *Der Telegraf* from August 22, 1947, "Odyssey of a Berlin Emigrant through Asia—Return of 295." The report notes that 10,000 German Jews remained in Shanghai.
65. *Der Weg* 2 (February 7, 1947): 2–3.
66. *Der Weg* 1 (March 23, 1946): unpaginated.
67. *Der Weg* 1 (October 10, 1946): unpaginated.
68. Heinrich Busse, letter, December 1945. Original text: "Ich fürchte sehr, wir werden uns alle mit der furchtbaren Tatsache abfinden müssen, das jetzt keine Hoffnung mehr auf Erfolg besteht. Wer bis jetzt nicht wieder hier ist, wie mir auf der Gemeinde gesagt, wird schwerlich noch eine Möglichkeit haben, sich zumelden oder mit den zahllosen das Land durchziehenden Fluechtingen aufzutauchen. Die Suchaktionen selbst sind nur ein Berühigungsmittel, denn wie soll man praktisch jemand aus den Millionen und Abermillionen herausfinden, noch dazu mangels aller Listen und Aufzeichnungen."
69. *Der Weg* 2 (December 20, 1947): unpaginated.
70. *Der Weg* 1 (March 1, 1946): unpaginated.
71. *Der Weg* 1 (March 8, 1946): 1.
72. *Der Weg* 1 (March 29, 1946): 3. See also see Elisabeth Freund's remarkable diary for a record of the year of 1941 in Berlin, as experienced by a female Jewish slave laborer; Carola Sachse, ed., *Als Zwangsarbeiterin 1941 in Berlin: Die Aufzeichnungen der Volkswirtin Elisabeth Freund* (Berlin: Akademie Verlag, 1996).
73. Rooney and Hutton, *Conquerors Peace,* 86.
74. In addition to those Jews who had already been intermarried during Third Reich, memoirs point to liaisons and even marriages with rescuers. See for example, Beck, *und gad ging zu david,* pp. 180–181 and Kaplan, *Between Dignity and Despair,* 217–220.
75. Kieve Skiddel, letter, July 24, 1945.
76. *Der Weg* 1 (April 5, 1946): 3.
77. In one debate on whether to aid with German recovery, a headline in *Der Weg* (April 19, 1946): 1 asked "Hassen Wir?" The article concluded that "love thy neighbor as thyself" is a key Jewish tenet, and that even if Jews cannot love, they will not hate. There is a relatively large amount of literature on the relatively small group of Jewish Communists who returned to work in the Soviet zone. Many estimate 2,000; Frank Stern estimates 3,500 to 4,000 but he includes many who had claimed not the slightest identification with Judaism. See for example, Jeff Peck and John Borneman, *Sojourners: The Return of German Jews and the Question of Identity (Texts and Contexts)* (Lincoln: University of Nebraska Press, 1995); Bodemann, ed., *Jews, Germans, Memory.*

78. *Der Weg* 1(March 1, 1946): 1. For a discussion of such debates among Jews of German origin, see the recent dissertation by Jael Geis, *Übrig sein-Leben "danach": Juden deutschen Herkunft in der britischen und amerikanischen Zone Deutschlands 1945–1949* (Berlin: Philo, 2000).

79. Rosenthal, *Zwei Leben in Deutschland*, 80.

80. LAB Berlin. OMGUS 4/20.

81. See Y. Michal Bodemann, "Reconstructions of History: From Jewish Memory to Nationalized Commemoration of Kristallnacht in Germany," in *Jews, Germans, Memory*, ed. Bodemann, 190–95. See also Jeffrey Herf, *Divided Memory: The Nazi Past in the Two Germanys* (Cambridge MA: Harvard University Press, 1997), 69–105.

82. See *Der Weg* 2 (April 10, 1947): unpaginated.

83. *Der Weg* 1 (March 15, 1946): 3. See also Peter Wyden, *Stella* (New York: Simon and Schuster, 1992). For an interesting analysis of discussions about revenge among German-Jewish survivors, se Geis, *Übrig sein-Leben "danach,"* 207–38.

84. Larry Orbach and Vivien Orbach-Smith, *Soaring Underground*, 330–34. It is worth noting that those precious pieces of U. S. military clothing or other goods spontaneously offered by GIs to survivors were likely to eventually get Jews (especially DPs) into trouble for possessing "stolen" or otherwise illegally acquired military property. On underground adventures see also Gad Beck, *und gad ging zu david. Die erinnerungen des gad beck 1923 bis 1945,* now also available in English from University of Wisconsin Press.

85. Reich-Ranicki, *Mein Leben,* 316.

86. *Der Weg* 1 (March 15, 1946): 1.

87. See Hutton and Rooney, *Conqueror's Peace,* 82. The "black market in grandmothers" is an obvious cynical reference to Nazi racial policy defining who counted as a Jew. See also *Der Weg* 1 (March 22, 1946): 2. Brenner also notes this phenomenon, "East European and German Jews," 58.

88. *Der Weg* 1 (June 28, 1946): 1. Brenner, "East European and German Jews," 58. See also Frank Stern, *The Whitewashing of the Yellow Badge.*

89. For one version of this quest for identification with the victims, see the postwar Berlin life of Lily Wust after her Jewish lover Felice Schragenheim was deported and killed, as described by Erika Fischer in *Aimee and Jaguar,* 257–92.

90. *Der Weg* 2 (January 3, 1947): 3.

91. "Wenn wir sehen, dass der Antisemitismus in Deutschland heute tagtäglich stärker wird, dass weite Kreise auch auf diesem Gebiete nichts gelernt haben und nichts lernen wollen." *Der Weg* 2 (Feb. 28, 1947): 2. See also Hans-Erich Fabian, "Unheimliches Deutschland," *Der Weg* 2 (January 31, 1947): 1.

92. *Der Weg* 2 (March 14, 1947): 4.

93. See the interesting discussion of "*Jüdische Rache*" [Jewish revenge] perceived by Germans, especially among emigrated German Jews serving with the occupation forces, in Theodor W. Adorno, *Soziologische Schriften II, Gesammelte Schriften,* vol. 9.2 (Frankfurt am Main: Suhrkamp, 1975): 258–61.

94. *Der Weg* 1 (December 6, 1946): 1–2.
95. *Der Weg* 2 (January 31, 1947): 1.
96. Heinrich Busse, letter, December 12, 1945.
97. Moses Moskowitz, "The Germans and the Jews: The Postwar Report. The Enigma of German Irresponsibility," *Commentary* 2 (1946): 7–14.
98. Frank Stern in *The Whitewashing of the Yellow Badge* posits that anti-Semitism was in many ways more visible in Germany after the war than before. For one German-Jewish perspective on postwar Germans, see Hannah Arendt's much quoted lament about Germans' "deep-rooted, stubborn, and at times vicious refusal to face and come to terms with what really happened." "The Aftermath of Nazi Rule: Report from Germany," *Commentary* 10 (1950): 342–43.
99. Heinrich Busse, letter to Hermann Paul (n.d. 1947). Original: "Mir ist nicht gleichgültig wie Sie über mich denken. Nicht im geringsten will ich verkleinern oder bestreiten, dass ich Ihnen viel Dank schuldig bin. Sie haben sich anständig und mutig behommen, anders als die völlig überweigende Anzahl der Deutschen gegenüber einem verbrecherischen, verlogenen und in jeder Hinsicht tief verächtlichen Regime. Ich habe Ihenn dies wiederholt zum Ausdruck gebracht. Eins aber muss ich Ihnen angesichts Ihrer jetzigen Haltung und mich aüsserst empörenden Darstelling jetzt doch erwidern. So sehr ich Ihre Hilfsbereitschaft und Ihre frühere Ablehnung des Nationalsozialismus anerkenne—ihr Bruder Erwin selbst hat sich garnicht gescheut zu erklären, die Gefahr meiner Aufnahme halte er unter bereits vorliegenden Umständen für nicht sehr erheblich, der Nützen aus solcher Unterstützung eines Verfolgten könne sogar grösser sein. Ich habe ihm das nicht im geringsten verdacht und es hätte mir fern gelegen, diesen Umstand Ihnen gegenüber jemals zu erwähnen. Jetzt aber ist es nötig. Weil es vielleicht wenigstens Sie (bei ihrem Bruder Erwin habe ich diese Hoffnung nicht) zu einer Nachdenklichkeit bringt."
100. Heinrich Busse, letter to Hohenwalds in Berlin, April 11, 1947. Original: "Du machts Dir keine Vorstellung davon, wie aufreizend es auf die unmittelbar Betroffenen wirken muss, wenn Du jetzt fragst: wann werden die Befreier endlich ihren Blutdurst an uns gestillt haben? Wenn Du als Deutsche ihnen grausame Folterungen vorwirfst, nachdem die ganze Welt noch immer starr vor Entsetzen ist über die aufgedeckten und jetzt von den Deutschen noch immer nicht recht zugegeben, irgendwie entschuldigten oder verkleinerten Greultaten, an denen jetzt niemand schuldig order beteiligt gewesen sein will. Wenn Du trotz alledem wörtlich schreibst, "dabei sind unsere Herzen und Hände rein und ihnen läuft das Blut schon aus dem Stehkragen" und dergl. mehr, so meinst Du zwar Dich und Die Deinen persönlich, kannst doch aber unmöglich annehmen, das Gleiches für die Deutschen schlechthin gelten kann und dass von der Welt verlangt werden kann, die Untaten Hitlers, mit denen sich die breiten Massen doch weitgehend identifiziert hat, einfach zu vergessen."
101. Heinrich Busse, letter, April 11, 1947.

102. *Nachlass* Siegmund Weltlinger, LAB, Rep. 200, Acc. 2334. Others would come back later, when the situation in Berlin had stabilized, after the division of the city and the formation of the Federal Republic. For example, Hans E. Hirschfeld, whose *Nachlass* also lies in the Landesarchiv Berlin, a veteran of World War I and member of the Hamburg Workers and Soldiers Council, he had fled to the United States from France in 1940 via the Pyrennees and Lisbon, but after eight unsatisfying years in the United States, working for the Office of Strategic Services (OSS), and continuing to feel himself as exile rather than emigrant, he returned to Germany to work for Ernst Reuter's Senat. These men were the minority—absolutely—but in Berlin they loomed large. See LAB, Rep. 200, Acc. 2014.

103. Moskowitz, "The Germans and the Jews," 13.

104. *Nachlass* Weltlinger, letter from Resilotte Lisser, July 8, 1946. Original: "Nein, für uns gibt es kein Zurück, wenngleich ich in Gedanken oft 'zu Hause' bin. Es war ja alles nur ein [illegible] Traum gewesen, meine Jugend und alles Dazugehörige. Ich bin jetzt hier zu Hause und glücklich!"

105. *Nachlass* Weltlinger, letter to Mrs. Mally Corey, December 1, 1951.

106. *Nachlass* Weltlinger, for example, letter to Max, December 15, 1949.

107. Hans-Erich Fabian, "Liquidationsgemeinden?," *Der Weg* 2 (May 2, 1947): 1–2.

108. The Jewish Agency (for Palestine) closed its doors in Germany on September 30, 1950. The World Jewish Congress, under Nahum Goldmann, was (and not without enormous controversy) the only Jewish international political organization that maintained a presence in Germany. Most Jews argued that "if Jews in small or larger groups choose to continue to live among the people who are responsible for the slaughter of six million of their brothers, that is their affair." See *Archives of the Holocaust. Volume 9, The Papers of the World Jewish Congress 1945–1950: Liberation and the Saving Remnant,* ed. Abraham J. Peck (New York: Garland, 1990), 398ff.

CHAPTER FIVE

JEWISH EXISTENCE IN GERMANY FROM THE PERSPECTIVE OF THE NON-JEWISH MAJORITY

Daily Life between Anti-Semitism and Philo-Semitism

WOLFGANG BENZ

One-third of the 82 million citizens of the Federal Republic of Germany do not know how many Jews live in Germany; another third guesses the figure to be in the millions; a mere 3 percent guess between 50,000 and 100,000, which is closer to the truth (between 70,000 and 80,000 Jews live in Germany today). Given the degree of attention paid to Jews in public life, this ignorance is rather astounding. The minority—one-one thousandth of the population of Germany professes Judaism as its religious faith—lives caught between anti-Semitism and philo-Semitism, in a tension caused both by hostility toward and excessive attention paid to Jews. This becomes evident from state actions and public ceremonies, such as the annual November 9 commemoration of the November Pogrom of 1938, or the ceremony on January 27, the day that Auschwitz was liberated. It is also clear from the way that prominent Jewish figures are called upon to comment on events and incidents in daily political life and in commemorative culture. There are three men of different backgrounds and generations who present themselves as Jews in the public intellectual life of the Republic: the recently deceased sociologist Adolph Silbermann, the literary critic Marcel Reich-Ranicki, and the politician Michel Friedmann. Their intellectual brilliance, understood as a "Jewish" characteristic, meets the expectation of their audience.

What the non-Jewish majority perceives as Jewish is of course not the same as how a Jewish individual perceives his own identity, nor does it depend on whether the Jewish community recognizes that individual as Jewish. This can be illustrated by the following example. Ladislaus Szücs, born in Transylvania in 1909, was deported to Auschwitz as a Hungarian Jew. He died in January 2000 in Cologne. Because he was not a member of the Jewish community, he was denied a Jewish burial. At the request of the family, a Catholic priest offered his services at the funeral and went to great efforts to provide a general humanistic funeral service devoid of Christian content. When, out of habit, he mentioned Jesus Christ in his address, he interrupted himself and glancing toward the mourners cried out, "Oh God, that is not what I had wanted here."[1]

⚭ ⚭ ⚭ ⚭ ⚭

The Jewish minority is flourishing as a theme in literature and in other areas of public culture. Klezmer music and Yiddish songs have been elevated to trademarks of Jewishness, resulting in an inflated folklore consumption among the non-Jewish majority. Jewish cookbooks are just as much a part of this trend as is the rediscovery of decaying Jewish life in Odessa, Czernowitz, Prague, and Cracow popularized through cultural tourism. Reconstructing destroyed synagogues has become a matter of personal interest for many communities. The Jewish Museum in Berlin, an institution that has been in the process of being built for many years now, enjoys public attention and interest to a degree not comparable to any other project. One example of how Jewish history is appropriated is offered by an exhibition on the daily life of persecution under National Socialism, which was created in Berlin by a history workshop project and installed in a stationary above-ground subway car. The exhibition, having been destroyed by arson, was recreated and presented on Holocaust Memorial Day, January 27, in a special subway car that traveled back and forth through the city the entire day.[2]

Attention is paid to Judaism by the approximately 70 associations that work toward Christian-Jewish reconciliation. The associations, which are overseen by the German Coordination Council, organize the "Week of Brotherhood" each year, which opens with a philo-Semitic rally in which politicians from all parties are notably present. These Christian-Jewish societies, which were formed on the insistence of the Americans during the period of occupation from 1945 to 1949, engage in dialogues over biblical exegesis and the theological meanings of genocide, and they propagate religious tolerance between Christians and Jews.[3] Functioning quite differently are the Protestant zealots in southern Germany, who run the "Mission Union for the Spreading of the Gospel—Light in the East" and who mostly pursue

Jewish immigrants from the former Soviet Union. The German Protestant Church, aware of these missionary activities, has distanced itself from this organization.[4] There is also the German-Israeli Society, founded in 1966 and with over 40 regional branches throughout the country. The Society maintains contact with Israel as a sign of political solidarity with Judaism.

The identity problems of the Jewish minority arouse intellectual curiosity among the non-Jewish majority. This has become a common theme in literary studies and among cultural sociologists. As the component of its own literary genre—the self-reflection of the "second generation"—it has increasing appeal in the media and with the public. It finds expression in collected essays, magazine articles, newspaper cultural pages, and scholarly lectures and encompasses both the scholarly intellectual brilliance of Jewish professors as well as such diverse literary forms as the magnificent and on-the-mark diagnoses of Henryk Broder, the memoirs of Reich-Ranicki,[5] the emotionalism of the moralist Ralph Giordano,[6] and even lower polemic forms by frustrated second-rate writers who also want a part of the action.

Esther Dischereit, a German-Jewish author, describes in her book *Übungen jüdisch zu sein* (Exercises to be Jewish) the patronizing view of the well-intentioned majority that regards the Jewish contribution to German culture foremost as its own loss. The Jewish emigration from Germany and the Holocaust are seen from this perspective as having diminished the German cultural legacy, because Einstein died as an American and because Felix Nußbaum, who was murdered as an outcast, is regarded foremost as a victim of the Holocaust and not as a German painter. Esther Dischereit notes how the regret over the loss of Jewish culture becomes self-pity, expressed in comments such as "Jewish culture joined German culture, making it more prolific. Germans then have deprived themselves of an invaluable intellectual bounty. This is a telling sentence spoken by the good guys, the well-intentioned of the Republic."[7] The *Allgemeine Jüdische Wochenzeitung,* a weekly Jewish newspaper, published a satirical piece with rules on how the majority should deal with the Jewish minority, compiled from a list of the most commonplace stereotypes: Not all Jews are Israelis, or rich, or geniuses, or religious, nor are the Jews the conscience of humanity, as is often inferred from the 2,000 years of persecution and then linked to a request for help in solving any and all problems of non-Jews ("Of all people, you as a Jew must understand . . ."). In addition to recommending that non-Jews not try to entertain Jews with Jewish jokes, the article concludes with a piece of advice: Learn to deal with the guilt feelings harbored as descendants of the perpetrator society without involving the Jews.[8]

The other extreme of the conflict, daily anti-Semitism and hostility toward Jews, is an easier attitude to describe than philo-Semitism, which is openly expressed in the eager attention paid to Jews and in the appropriation of their concerns. Public opinion researchers predict a long-term decrease in anti-Semitic injuries in Germany. Those who have been the targets of anti-Semitic injury, however, complain of the disparity between the increasing directness of the anti-Jewish sentiment directed at them, the crudeness of the incorrigible offenders, and the composed public response to the regularly reported anonymous attacks on Jewish cemeteries, religious institutions, memorial sites, and gravestones.

In Germany, showing open anti-Semitism is regarded with disdain, as is denial of the genocide. This forces anti-Semites to be more restrained and encourages the deniers to act from the safety of concealment. The Office for the Protection of the Constitution registers the increase in propaganda crimes alongside the violent acts against foreigners, but it cannot identify the significance of anti-Jewish attitudes as a motivating factor in the crimes. More so than the number of individual acts of propaganda or the ideology of rightwing extremists, it is latent hostility toward Jews that determines the political climate of the country.

The everyday anti-Semitism of quiet agreement toward "the Jews"—an agreement that rests on the age-old belief that Jews are different—is most effectively maintained by the tirades of right-wing extremist inflammatory publications. Legends and myths are revived and newly constructed in these works to offer simple explanations of the world based on old stereotypes such as the "Jewish world conspiracy," the supposed disproportion of Jewish influence in the cultural and financial world, and so on.

With headlines and insinuations the legends and myths appeal to the latent feelings that Germans have of being threatened, of having suffered an injustice, of having to defend themselves against further ignominy. Simple explanations founded on clear recriminations are offered in place of the complex facts: "the Jews" as a mysterious and unpleasant minority; "the onslaught of foreign criminals" to Germany; the supposedly falsified German history. These are the hackneyed ideas behind the repetitious claim that the German people have been deprived of self-determination; that they suffer under the dictatorial Allies of World War II; and that they must engage in a kind of war of liberation.

Ignatz Bubis, chairman of the Central Council of Jews in Germany, was one of the most popular politicians of this decade. He overcame his distorted image as "the Jewish speculator," as he was known from Rainer Werner Fassbinder's anti-Semitic play *Der Müll, Die Stadt und der Tod* [Garbage, the City and Death],[9] and replaced it with the image of the omnipresent advisor to the majority population and educator of German youth. The figure of Bubis reflects both the ambivalence of Jewish life in Germany and the impression, which is closely related to this ambivalence, that the majority of society has of Jews in Germany. The response to the suggestion by one weekly newspaper that Bubis should campaign for the position of federal president is an indication of the problems that the majority has with the minority. Readers responded with complete earnestness and considerable anger. Some tried to use irony: "It is always at great expense and high costs when leading politicians from Bonn must travel to Jerusalem to receive their directives." Others vented their feelings using invectives: "A people, who according to orders, almost annihilated the Jews is now supposed to get lucky with a fat rich Jew."

One typical reply included the comment: "He will always be a stranger among us, even if you go on telling such wonderful things about him until we are moved to tears." Such exclusionary judgments reveal a basic attitude that is reminiscent of the propaganda of National Socialism. The discrimination and retraction of the rights of Jews began, of course, with defining German Jews as "strangers," which meant that they were obliged to put up with a lower legal status. Ever since the establishment of Israel, however, those who express such ideas feel a sense of justification, pointing out that all Jews have a right to live in that country. Even Ignatz Bubis, recognized as someone who won sympathy and was well liked, experienced that reaction repeatedly.

It is illegal to openly articulate anti-Semitism in the Federal Republic. That has been a part of the law of the political culture in Germany since Auschwitz. Anyone who breaks this taboo risks losing his or her position and reputation, at least initially following the incident. When anti-Semitic or xenophobic judgments are expressed in less spectacular situations, in front of a smaller public or within an association, as a regular customer at a bar or in daily social contact, it is usually not punished.

In the fall of 1992, Father Basilius Streithofen, a Dominican who was well known as a powerfully eloquent and pugnacious speaker and who was close to the former Federal Chancellor Helmut Kohl, once gave a lecture in which he said that Jews and Poles were the biggest exploiters of the German taxpayers. Certainly over the past decades a considerable number of Germans had heard similar comments about the restitution and compensation payments of the Federal Republic. But because he made his comments in public, the religious leader was charged with inciting the public. He justified himself with the often heard demand "that an end must finally come to this confrontation with the past" and that we must ensure that "great-grandchildren are no longer held responsible for the guilt of the Nazi era." Not wanting to accuse the priest of being a nationalistic demagogue (one who propagates the old anti-Semitic clichés of the Jew who doesn't work, exploits others, and leads the life of a parasite), we must then find another explanation for his language; for example, apparently in using the stigma of "exploiter" he intended in some way to diminish the guilt and strain that he felt vis-à-vis Jews and Poles.

In May of 1993, the state prosecutor closed the case against Streithofen. He had come to the conclusion that the comments of the priest did not warrant the charge of inciting the public [*Volksverhetzung*] because the offense only applied to the "native part of the population." After protests from the regional association of the Jewish community in Lower Saxony, the legal proceedings were resumed, and Father Basilius ended up paying a fine to a charitable cause. An anti-Semitic scandal had come to an end. That it was caused by a Catholic priest was a coincidence. The Streithofen case had nothing to do with the old tradition of Christian anti-Judaism. The small relic of hostility toward Jews stemming from Christian roots—based either on theological grounds or the practice of popular religious traditions—that one occasionally hears about in connection with sect pilgrimages, pejorative religious pictures, or anti-Semitic passional texts, does not play a role in the current public discourse in Germany.

The mobilization of traditional hostile images and prejudices keeps daily anti-Semitism alive. The tendency to make these public has increased in recent years. At the same time, however, anti-Semitism as a personal attitude, as a political, cultural, or social model in Germany, is on the decline according to the results of empirical social research. In Nuremberg in the spring of 1994, cleverly designed "notices of deportation" were mailed to Jewish citizens and foreigners. With a stamp, file number, and the federal eagle on phony letterhead of the "Federal Office for the Recognition of Foreign Refugees" the memory of the Gestapo deportation lists were used in an expression of anti-Semitism.

Another equally concrete example shows how old stereotypes, crystallized by a current discussion, can appear in a new form: On Deutschlandfunk, a nationwide public radio station, a commentary was broadcast in early September 1992, that, under the heading "Shalom—Jewish Life Today," attempted a kind of reckoning with the "Jewish confrontation with past." On the part of the Jews, we are told, when regarding and assessing the Holocaust one hears "much, much too often the flagrant distortion of views, premature judgements in ordering the facts, blindness for connections." Non-Jews also suffered under Hitler, the report continued, they too were tortured and murdered, but that doesn't concern the Jewish commentators; they are much too fixated on their own past. The author, completely candid and without any fear of exposing himself, let the Jews know what they should really be concerned about:

> What about a Jewish confrontation with Marxism and with the devastating consequences of the Marxist-Leninist dictatorships? At the very latest now while they are collapsing, it is time to critically address their brutality and contempt for humanity, even self-critically: A large number of Jews were coper-

petrators. It is worth analyzing the charitable work of the Jewish community in the unlawful GDR. The mild verdicts on Jewish authors Stefan Heym and Anna Seghers are characteristic, just to name two striking examples. Both are, or rather, were loyal sympathizers of the GDR dictatorship. Their own fame was more important to them than humanity.

One has to regard these sentences as a new variety of the repression, defensiveness, and reckoning that we have long been familiar with and as a manifestation of latent anti-Semitism.

In addition to the old familiar tradition of anti-Semitism, there is now a new one. Anti-Zionism as a new form of anti-Jewish sentiment was a component of the GDR state doctrine, spread through anti-Israeli pamphlets and repeatedly evoked in expressions of solidarity for the Palestinians and Arab nations. Not only were political positions toward the Federal Republic instrumentalized, but hostile anti-Jewish images were also transmitted. Clearly, the official hostile images of Israel and of international Jewish organizations propagated over time had a long-term impact. That these hostile images of "international Jewry" are suspiciously similar to the older stereotypes of a Jewish conspiracy and to the idea promoted by the National Socialists only adds to their effectiveness.[10]

The Jews in the GDR were not only marginal in number. Their role as victims barely figured into the state ideology, which claimed legitimization through the communist resistance struggle against Hitler Germany. In contrast to the Federal Republic, no efforts were made toward paying restitution or reparations. The last parliament of the GDR did, however, express to the Jews its desire to be forgiven for the National Socialist persecution, and it opened the borders to Jewish emigrants from the Soviet Union. This explains how the new communities in Potsdam, Rostock, Dessau, and Schwerin came to be established. They were comprised solely of these immigrants—and they tackled the same problems of integration and all the social and cultural difficulties symptomatic of the structural changes encountered by Jewish communities throughout all of Germany at that time.[11]

According to research based on opinion polls, anti-Semitism in Germany is not a major problem: Anti-Jewish tendencies are generally declining, even when 16 percent of the population in West Germany, and four percent in East Germany (Emnid-opinion poll 1992) are identified as anti-Semitic. Results of a more recent study (Forsa-opinion poll 1998) suggest that every fifth German is latently anti-Semitic.[12] Manifest anti-Jewish hostility is less commonly ascertained.

In contrast to crude, straightforward, or indiscriminate anti-Semitism as it was articulated before 1945, hostility toward Jews is difficult to recognize today. The problem of anti-Semitism in present-day Germany is more complex and must be viewed with more differentiation.[13] If someone who is not Jewish claims to have many Jewish friends, then caution is due because usually an anti-Semitic remark will directly follow. In general, depending on the speaker's degree of education, the remark comes concealed as a question or expressed as a doubt, a "justified" doubt "in the name of truth" (such as whether so many Jews were really murdered in Auschwitz as is claimed; whether Cyclon B worked the way witnesses, perpetrators, and historians attested; whether the Jews were perhaps themselves responsible for the Holocaust; and so on). Such questions, however, always deal with stereotypes.

Traditional prejudice against Jews has always suspected them of having a particularly strong business sense (stereotypes of the profiteer or haggler), or the supposed thirst for revenge conveyed in the Old Testament ("An eye for an eye, a tooth for a tooth"), or the belief that Jews have a constitutional aversion to the toil of hard work (stereotypes of the "parasite" or "sponger"). They are accused of harboring ambitions to take over the world, symbolized by the "international Jews of finance" or by suggestions of a "Jewish world conspiracy." The absurdity of such constructs is shown by two completely opposing clichés: on the one hand, the Jew as bolshevist, as creator and instigator of the communist world revolution ideology, and on the other, the Jew as the incarnation of capitalism, represented by the figures of the stock-market bull, banker, or finance magnate. Both images, that of the plutocrat and that of the bolshevist, were cultivated by Goebbels and had a lasting impact. They are founded on older anti-Semitic notions.

The most spectacular example of often thoughtless everyday anti-Semitism was precipitated by a rather dim-witted counter-bassist of the Berlin German Opera who thought it would be funny to sign his hotel bar bill with the name "Adolf Hitler" while in Israel in June 1997 for a guest concert. In an attempt to limit the damage, the orchestra and conductor quickly, clearly, and effectively distanced themselves from the musician (who was dismissed and forced to return to Germany without delay). But the general impression remained that Germans, when intoxicated, often express what they would otherwise only dare think when they are sober. In this case, it was typical that the offender was not considered an anti-Semite. Indeed, he had not previously drawn attention to himself, but apparently had acted from his subconsciousness[14] while under the influence of alcohol.

Another equally instructive case of collective aggression occurred in Adelsdorf in Franken, not far from Erlangen. Holocaust survivors, former citizens of the community, noticed during a visit there in 1996 that a street was named after the former NSDAP (National Sozialistische Deutsche Arbeiterpartei) regional group leader [Ortsgruppenleiter]. Apparently no one had noticed this before, but now a major discussion ensued. Citizens organized an event, a candlelight procession, to apply pressure to the demand that the street be renamed. Five retired Germans formed a counterdemon-stration, yelling "Jews out!" [*Juden raus*]. In the summer of 1998 they were fined as a result.[15]

Anti-Jewish hostility—which finds expression in the relativization of the Holocaust, in the defamation of Jewish figures, in an articulated hostility to-ward Israel, in appeals to vague feelings of unease—carries an impact that goes well beyond the ideas of the right-wing conservative and right-wing ex-tremist clientele. In other words, in right-wing extremist tabloids such as the *Deutsche Nationalzeitung,* one can read in concrete terms what others throughout country think and say only after a few beers. This includes, of course, the desire of many to be freed from the memory of the National So-cialist genocide, to have the dimensions of the Holocaust reduced at the very least, and to see the Holocaust compared to the atrocities of other nations. Above all, this includes a false understanding of Judaism that defies any cor-rection. "The Jew" continues to be seen as rich, successful in business, money-grubbing, and greedy for profits. He is still defined as embodying racially determined characteristics and is discriminated against as an out-sider. In combination with the stigma of being foreign (expressed, for in-stance, by the question posed to German Jews of whether their true home isn't really Israel, or in the compliment on how well they have mastered the German language) comes the accusation of a world conspiracy "proven" by the notorious stereotypes that Wall Street is controlled by Jews and that the Communist revolutionary regime in Russia in 1917 was dominated by Jews.

Anti-Semitism serves in everyday life to explain the world, an under-standing at the expense of others. Anti-Semitism requires an aura of uncer-tainty and thrives on whispers and in a thicket of insinuations and suspicions; anti-Semitism is an undefined agreement to exclude others. Latent anti-Semi-tism manifests itself in a nonpublic discourse about a minority as a symbol for the consensus of the majority. Everything disagreeable is delegated to "the Jews," even though it actually has nothing to do with their existence (or at least only indirectly). Jews are viewed as a tangible reminder of the burden of German history, a reminder that generates feelings of shame and insecurity, which in turn leads to German insolence and recriminations: How long will the restitution payments continue? Will forgiveness never be granted? Must we forever feel guilty? The aggression is disguised in the form of a question.

That Jews have not given cause for these questions is unimportant, for within this agreement the old function of scapegoat is given a new form. Anti-Semitism is not a phenomenon caused by Jews. Nor is it a response to Jewish qualities or behavior. Rather, anti-Semitism is a defect in the ma-jority population, a defect triggered by frustrations and fears, stimulated by propaganda and suggestiveness, and nourished by traditions and con-ventions. Desecrated Jewish cemeteries, defaced monuments, swastikas on synagogues, anonymous letters to prominent Jews, hostile articles in the right-wing extremist press—these are all demonstrations of the exclusion and rejection committed by a few individuals who can be certain of receiving a much greater amount of approval for their actions than is made public. That is the problem with everyday anti-Semitism, and the problem exists not just in Germany.

"The epoch of the Jew in Germany has ended once and for all." This often cited quote from Leo Baeck was considered the farewell to the hope of Germans and Jews ever living side by side. The dream of intellectual symbiosis and social assimilation vanished in Auschwitz, Treblinka, and in the other places of genocide, in the ghettos such as Theresienstadt and Riga, and also in the stations of emigration and flight from Hitler Germany. Baeck, once a rabbi in Berlin and president of the *Reichsvertretung der deutschen Juden* [Representation of Jews in Germany], spoke these words following the extermination of German Jewry by the Nazi state and following his own liberation from Theresienstadt.

Baeck, a figure who stood for intellectual Germany Jewry, was not the only one to regard Jewish life in Germany after Auschwitz as unthinkable. His prophecy, articulated in December 1945 in New York, was by no means visionary. Given the situation, it was quite realistic: Before the National Socialist persecution of Jews began, just over one-half million Jews lived in Germany. Between 1933 and 1945 approximately 270,000 were able to emigrate. More than 200,000 were deported to ghettos and extermination camps, where some 165,000 were murdered. About 15,000 Jews survived outside the concentration camps, most of them as partners in mixed marriages with non-Jews. A few had been able to hide in the underground.

The Jews who were liberated from the concentration and extermination camps and who remained after 1945 for a time in Germany as DPs (displaced persons) under the care of the Allied authority were just waiting until they had regained their strength and were able to emigrate; waiting until the formalities of their emigration to a country willing to offer them a home— the United States? Palestine? some other country?—were arranged. This process, of course, took years. Most of the Jewish survivors came from Hungary, Czechoslovakia, Poland, and other Eastern European countries. In the early postwar years a new wave of anti-Semitism broke out in Poland (and elsewhere) and escalated into pogroms. Even these emigrants regarded Germany merely as a way station.[16]

These Jews unintentionally influenced the recommencement of Jewish life in Germany. They gathered in the American zone of occupation, where the U.S. Army, the United Nations Relief and Rehabilitation Administration (UNRRA), and the UNRRA's successor as of July 1947, the International Refugee Organization (IRO), erected camps, mostly in Bavaria, in

Deggendorf, Landsberg, Munich-Freimann, Feldafing, and the longest existing camp, named "Föhrenwald," located in the district of Wolfratshausen. A total of 200,000 Jewish DPs lived in Germany between 1945 and 1950. The camps in the American and British zones of occupation became centers of Jewish culture and Jewish religion in Germany. But the synagogues and schools, newspapers and theater groups only continued the life of the ghettos. The majority of eastern Jewish ghetto inhabitants had no interest in their German environment; they strictly refused contact with non-Jews.[17]

Some managed to emigrate to Palestine illegally or to enter the United States legally under the regulated quota system. For most of them, however, it was with the founding of the State of Israel that their dream was fulfilled. By 1950, the camps had emptied. Only a remnant of Jewish people remained, many of whom had been too old or sick to emigrate, or whose visa problems remained unsolvable, or who were no longer capable of adjusting to a new place after having experienced so much suffering. Munich was the transit and exit station for about 120,000 Jews until 1952, when the IRO terminated their care of the Jewish DPs. It became evident that approximately 12,000 Jews wanted to remain in Germany and not only because they were ill or exhausted, but also because they had established new lives or had married.

The Jewish survivors in the DP camps encountered resentment and hostility from the Germans, who perceived the survivors as a reminder of their repressed guilt. This hostility continually found expression in anti-Semitic incidents, as in the raid on the Föhrenwald camp on May 28, 1952. Hundreds of customs officers and members of the criminal and state police surrounded and stormed the camp; they were armed and accompanied by bloodhounds. All of this was done just to check shops and kiosks, in which undeclared goods were believed to be housed. The 2,000 Jews in the camp were reminded of the murder operations of the Nazis in the ghettos and concentration camps. The keepers of the peace beat Jews, uttered anti-Semitic and Nazi-like threats, declared that "the crematoria and gas chambers still existed" and that this was "just the beginning." The representatives of the Jewish relief organization American Joint Distribution Committee informed the secretary of state in charge of refugees in the Bavarian ministry of interior, who intervened in order to put an end to the illegal operation.

According to official statistics, between 70,000 and 80,000 Jews live in the Federal Republic today. This sum represents the number of registered members of the Jewish community. Only a few of them are survivors from pre-Hitler German Jewry, in other words, Jews who returned from the camps, came out of hiding, or were in some other way rescued. Most of them, and in fact the largest group until 1990, were Jews from the DP camps and their offspring. They had migrated from Poland, Lithuania,

Hungary, and Czechoslovakia after the Holocaust and then remained in Germany. The number of Jews living in Germany has more than doubled in the last decade. Joining the 30,000 people who in 1990 to 1991 were registered as Jews living in Germany (this number includes the 400 who lived in East Germany), immigrants from the successor states of the Soviet Union came and continue to come to Germany looking for a new home.

When Jewish victims were liberated at the end of Nazi rule and lived in DP camps in Germany, it was not intended that a Jewish presence in post-Hitler Germany would be permanent. The position of official Jewry was that it was by no means desirable. As a result of the Holocaust, it was considered a matter of certainty by Jews throughout the world that Germany would be off-limits to Jews, similar to the situation in Spain after the expulsion of Jews there in 1492. Zionist politicians and Jewish officials of international organizations had agreed that the remaining Jews in Germany and the temporary living arrangements created by the DP camps would have to disappear as soon as possible. As early as 1948, the year that Israel was founded, the Jewish World Congress declared that soon no Jews would ever set foot on German soil again. Germany's function as a way station within the country of the murderers was to end in the 1950s, as soon as the last camp inhabitant had departed. This opinion was also embraced by Zionist politics, which needed every Jew it could get to help in building up Israel. At the beginning of 1950, the Jewish World Congress in Frankfurt am Main passed a resolution declaring that the Jewish organizations in Germany were only to have a provisional character: As soon as they had helped the last Jew to emigrate from Germany, they would be dissolved.

But ten days later, on July 19, 1950, the Central Council Committee of Jews in Germany was established, giving the signal that there were indeed Jews who lived in Germany and who wanted to remain there. This was difficult for many reasons, in particular because the mass immigration to Israel between 1948 and 1953 had drained the camps of the cultural and intellectual substance that had once developed there.

The rich religious life and cultural diversity in the DP camps could not therefore be turned over to the newly founded Jewish community. In Munich, for example, the leadership positions in the community were defended by the few surviving German Jews against the numerically much stronger Eastern European Jewish immigrants. In southern Germany, Eastern European Jews made up the lion's share of the community. In Munich, for example, they comprised more than 79 percent during the 1950s. Relations between the two groups were tense: The highly assimilated German Jews had difficulties with the Eastern European Jews, who spoke Yiddish, lived more strictly according to the Jewish religious laws, and whose appearance made them recognizable as Jews.

German Jews, in turn, felt accused of being lax in their faith, not conveying much Jewish spirituality, and being much too closely connected to non-Jews, which was apparent from their high number of mixed marriages. German-Jewish identity, often misunderstood as a German-Jewish symbiosis and still considered vital by interested non-Jews even after the Holocaust, was regarded by Eastern European Jews with skepticism, a lack of understanding, and disapproval.

These early problems are an integral part of the history of the establishment of the Jewish community in Germany, and they continue to exist up through the present. The new beginning of Jewish life in Germany after 1945 was characterized by the tension created from the social, cultural, and psychological problems involved in having survived. In the 1950s a religious justification for Jews remaining in Germany was expressed by a prominent rabbi: Jews are a monument for the German people; Jewish existence keeps the memory alive, causing people to reflect and to take stock of themselves. More than a few Germans seek out reconciliation: "And from within this situation, the small remnant of Israel present in Germany acquires a totally different perspective and significance. . . . I have never seen such an openness for Jewish thought, almost a longing for Jewish values, in groups of other peoples, as I see it today and here. Amidst this development and faced again with an increase in antisemitism, Jews in Germany carry a major responsibility and with it the possibility for a future and justification of their existence."[18]

The cultural and social life of the Jewish community in Germany as well as the politics of the Central Council of Jews in Germany remains dominated by this mission even today. In the Jewish adult education centers and in the Jewish cultural community centers, the awareness of the Holocaust, the memory of the persecution and extermination, and the reflection on this memory play an important role. It is impossible to overestimate the psychological difficulty of living as a Jew in Germany. Many Jews suffer from the pressure of having to justify themselves to relatives and friends who don't live in Germany or from feelings of guilt toward the murdered family members. Micha Brumlik, one of the most witty and critical spokesmen of the second generation, described this feeling of being a stranger among Jews, when he attended an international Jewish student seminar in Antwerp, as "the alienating realization that a Jew in Germany is considered to be a kind of monster, not only by the Germans but also by other Jews. We were treated by most of the U.S. and Latin American students with such care and understanding as if we—in 1972—had just escaped the hell of the concentration camps while the Belgians, British, and Israelis viewed us either with suspicion or as traitors."[19]

One aspect of the Jewish experience in Germany is the particular pain Jews suffer as a result of intentional or unintentional exclusion and tactlessness and their suspicion of new manifestations of anti-Semitism and xenophobia. The ubiquitous fear of right-wing extremists can quickly escalate into paranoia. Non-Jews tend to be more fearful than they are sensitive when dealing with Jews. They sway between philo-Semitism, which presents itself as a "willingness toward reconciliation" amidst stereotypical assertions that one has many Jewish friends and is personally engaged and affected, and, on the other hand, the everyday taboo of the past. These attitudes reveal themselves, for example, in the attempt to avoid certain words and labels such as "Jew," which is replaced with "background" or "descent." At the same time, however, the vocabulary of Nazi jargon such as "Aryan," "exterminate," "final solution," and "special treatment" still continues to be used without reflection. This paves the way for misunderstandings.

When Jews are mistrustful and in certain cases suspect anti-Semitism, the non-Jew in Germany often lacks the understanding and willingness to put himself in the place of the German Jew or Jewish German. He is not willing, for example, to imagine that they, as members of the second and third generation after the Holocaust, live in a "ghetto of fear and isolation,"[20] that Jews in Germany are traumatized by the feeling of having escaped the inferno and of living among their murderers. What psychoanalysts refer to as "survivor syndrome" is for many a very present reality. In addition to the individual trauma, there is not only the obligation to justify to oneself one's very existence in Germany, but also to legitimize oneself politically, culturally, and socially to the entire world. Rafael Seligmann, a publicist and novelist who explicitly regards himself as a "German Jew" and propagates integration with a sense of mission, is aware of the difficulties involved in such an existence: "We represent the model Jew. We are the alibi for a purified German society after Hitler. We supposedly yearn for normality. In truth, however, we are addicted to the neurotic life of living as a Jew in Germany. The German, however, values us as exotic reminders of the horror."[21]

In 1949, following the establishment of the Federal Republic of Germany, John McCloy, the American high commissioner and thus one of the Allied guardians of the new state, said that the test of this young German democracy will be how it deals with the Jews. Following the major efforts made toward restitution and reparations for material wrongs in the 1950s, Jews were not an issue of public interest for the majority of the society in Germany, both in the GDR and in the Federal Republic. The American TV series "Holocaust," because its trivial portrayal of the Jewish genocide facilitated in the 1970s emotional identification, created the impetus for a confrontation that overcame the limitations of the intellectual and professional preoccupation with the topic.

Rainer Werner Fassbinder's anti-Semitic play *Der Müll, Die Stadt und der Tod* [Garbage, the City and Death], in which the role of the Jew as speculator figured prominently, created a commotion for a period in the mid-

1980s. Jews, including Ignatz Bubis, the later chairman of the Central Council of Jews in Germany who was caricatured in the play, prevented the play's performance in Frankfurt am Main. The discourse was ignited once again at the end of the 1990s when, in the name of artistic freedom, a Berlin theater announced its plans to present the play, claiming that the public had a right to see it (although the text is both published and available in a film version). Because the project was unable to win the support of organized Jewry from the start, the theater threatened to invite an Israeli company from Tel Aviv to come and stage the play, in Hebrew, as a guest performance.

In the 1980s the West German media was occupied with the discussions about guilt and responsibility for the Holocaust that were generated by the Historians' Debate. These discussions were then continued at the end of the 1990s as a result of the debates that ensued over Daniel J. Goldhagen's book and its charges of German eliminatory anti-Semitism. The public vehemently took the side of the Jewish-American interpreter of the German character against that of the historians, who appealed to serious research and pointed out that staged publicity should not serve to replace serious argumentation. Moreover, the Goldhagen Debate, like the admiration that Hollywood director Steven Spielberg enjoyed for his film *Schindler's List* and for his later activities, suggests that there are many Germans, particularly among the younger generation, who are emotionally, morally, and intellectually engaged on behalf of Jews. This is illustrated as well by the decade-long discussion over a central memorial for the murdered Jews that is to be erected in Berlin and even by the debate that the author Martin Walser triggered when, amidst applause from German dignitaries, he demanded a seemingly liberating end to the discussion of the German past.

The increased distance in time from the Holocaust does not play a role for the Jews as victims. For non-Jews, however, it provides the main argument and is appealed to in their call for "normality": "Can you all never forget? That was all so long ago." When Jews answer this typical comment with "no," a bitterness resurfaces. Their position is dismissed or judged to be "unforgiving," confirming subliminal feelings of prejudice and latent anti-Semitism. Salomon Korn, chairman of the Jewish community in Frankfurt and one of the important voices in the discourse over Jewish life in Germany, clearly articulated the Jewish position: "After all that has happened, it is perfectly normal that we still cannot deal normally with one another today."[22]

Notes

1. Ladislaus Szücs, *Zählappell. Als Arzt im Konzentrationslager* (Frankfurt am Main: Fischer Taschenbuch, 1995); Helen Quandt, ed., *Salz der Tränen. Zeichnungen von Ladislaus Szücs* (Düsseldorf: Mahn- und Gedenkstätte, 1999).

2. "'Jüdisches Leben' in fahrender S-Bahn," *Der Tagesspiegel* (January 26, 2000).

3. Joseph Foschepoth, *Im Schatten der Vergangenheit. Die Anfänge der Gesellschaft für Christlich-Jüdische Zusammenarbeit* (Göttingen: Vandenhoeck & Ruprecht, 1993).

4. Henryk M. Broder, "Die Juden zuerst," *Der Spiegel* (July 13, 1998): 29.

5. Marcel Reich-Ranicki, *Mein Leben* (Stuttgart: Deutsche Verlags-Anstalt, 1999).

6. Ralph Giordano, *Die zweite Schuld oder Von der Last, Deutscher zu sein* (Hamburg: Rasch und Röhring, 1987); *Wenn Hitler den Krieg gewonnen hätte* (Hamburg: Rasch und Röhring, 1989); *Wird Deutschland wieder gefährlich? Mein Brief an Kanzler Kohl—Ursachen und Folgen* (Cologne: Kiepenheuer und Witsch, 1993).

7. Esther Dischereit, *Übungen jüdisch zu sein* (Frankfurt am Main: Suhrkamp, 1998), 20ff.

8. "Der Koschere Knigge. Über den Umgang mit 'jüdischen Mitbürgern,'" *Allgemeine Jüdische Wochenzeitung* (May 15, 1996).

9. See *Fassbinder ohne Ende. Eine Dokumentation anläßlich der Uraufführung von Rainer Werner Fassbinders Theaterstück "Der Müll, die Stadt und der Tod" im Kammerspiel von Schauspiel Frankfurt am 31. Oktober 1985* (Frankfurt am Main, 1985); Heiner Lichtenstein, ed., *Die Fassbinder-Kontroverse oder Das Ende der Schonzeit* (Königstein: Äthenaum, 1986).

10. See Wolfgang Benz, ed., *Antisemitismus in Deutschland. Zur Aktualität eines Vorurteils* (Munich: DTV, 1995).

11. Julius H. Schoeps, Willi Jasper, and Bernhard Vogt, eds., *Ein neues Judentum in Deutschland? Fremd- und Eigenbilder der russisch-jüdischen Einwanderer* (Potsdam: Verlag für Berlin-Brandenburg, 1999).

12. *Die Woche* (January 1999).

13. Werner Bergmann and Rainer Erb, "Wie antisemitisch sind die Deutschen?" in Benz, ed., *Antisemitismus in Deutschland,* 47–63; see also Werner Bergmann and Rainer Erb, *Antisemitismus in der Bundesrepublik Deutschland. Ergebnisse der empirischen Forschung von 1946 bis 1989* (Opladen: Leske und Budrich, 1991).

14. In an official notice the orchestra executive board expressed its "deep regret over the anti-Semitic incident which occurred during the Israeli guest concert and completely distanced itself from the orchestra member," *Tagesspiegel* (June 4, 1997); see "Der einsame Josef," *Frankfurter Allgemeine Zeitung* (June 11, 1997).

15. "'Juden raus'—Ruf geahndet," *Süddeutsche Zeitung* (July 17, 1998).

16. Angelika Königseder, *Flucht nach Berlin. Jüdische Displaced Persons 1945–1948* (Berlin: Metropol, 1998).

17. Angelika Königseder and Juliane Wetzel, *Lebensmut im Wartesaal. Die jüdischen DPs (Displaced Persons) im Nachkriegsdeutschland* (Frankfurt am Main, Fischer Taschenbuch, 1994).

18. Zwi Harry Levy, "Der 'Überrest Israels' in Deutschland," in *The Jewish Travel Guide* (Frankfurt am Main: 1953), 20; cited in Harry Maór, Über den Wiederaufbau der jüdischen Gemeinden in Deutschland seit 1945, (Ph.D. Dissertation, University of Mainz, 1961).

19. Micha Brumlik, *Kein Weg als Deutscher und Jude. Eine bundesrepublikanische Erfahrung* (Munich: Luchterhand, 1996), 105.

20. Rafael Seligmann, *Mit beschränkter Hoffnung: Juden, Deutsche, Israelis* (Hamburg: Hoffmann und Campe, 1991), 81.

21. Rafael Seligmann, "Nicht in jüdischer Macht. Von der Mehrheit allein gelassen, der Selbstisolation besichtigt—Erfahrungen im veränderten Deutschland," *Die Zeit* (November 25, 1999).

22. *Tagesspiegel Berlin* (November 11, 1999); see Salomon Korn, *Geteilte Erinnerung. Beiträge zur deutsch-jüdischen Gegenwart* (Berlin: Philo, 1999).

CHAPTER SIX

AUSTRIAN EXCEPTIONALISM
Haider, the European Union, the Austrian Past
and Present: An Inimical World for the Jews

ANDREI S. MARKOVITS

Introduction

This paper focuses on the developments pertaining to the controversy surrounding the coming to power of a "black/blue" coalition government in
Austria during the early part of 2000. It analyzes the antecedents to this event
and places it in the context of Austria's postwar political arrangements. While
the paper does not deal with the situation of Austrian Jews in particular and
also does not feature an analysis of Austrian anti-Semitism, it presumes the
latter ill to be a featured constant in the societal framework and cultural
arrangement that permitted the rise of Joerg Haider and Haiderism to the
pinnacle of the European Right at the beginning of the twenty-first century.

The paper has three parts.

The first part offers an argument as to why I think the European Union's
actions of boycotting the Austrian government was not only morally appropriate but also immensely effective despite virtual unanimity regarding its alleged failure.

The second part delineates in some detail the structural and cultural antecedents to the current situation. In particular, it analyzes the precursors in
Austrian politics that led to the rise of Joerg Haider and his particular brand
of politics. I will briefly describe a situation that will make clear the reasons
why the Europeans reacted to much more than Joerg Haider and the current
Freedom Party (FPOe). Indeed, they reacted to a particularly inadequate and
unwilling confrontation on the part of key Austrian institutions regarding

Austria's involvement with its Nazi past. It is in this context that I will look at some of the features of this missed opportunity, in particular the three main actors of Austria's postwar politics: the Social Democratic Party (SPOe), the People's Party (OeVP), and Mr. Haider's own party, the Freedom Party (FPOe).

The third and final part of the paper will argue how, paradoxically, it has been the "de-Austrianization" of Austrian politics, to use Anton Pelinka's apt formulation, or the secularization of its particularly parochial culture, the so-called *Lager* or political camps, that has led to the "Westernization" or normalization of Austrian politics, at least in form if not necessarily in content. In the wake of this Westernization, this secularization that has encompassed every possible aspect of public and private life, I shall conclude this essay on a rather optimistic note.

Part One: The European Union's Response

First of all, the European Union as such—as the entity "European Union (EU)"—did not take a stand against Austria. Rather, it was a coordinated action in which 14 members of the EU, each acting completely as its own individual sovereign, decided to boycott Austria on regular bilateral relations—or, more precisely—to contain bilateral relations with Austria strictly to an administrative level. Thus, no Austrian representative on the cabinet level was welcomed on any bilateral missions in the capitals of these 14 European countries. No Austrian ambassador was allowed to meet with cabinet members of the 14 governments. Moreover, the European Parliament passed resolutions condemning the formation of a coalition government in Austria that included the FPOe. Last, the European Commission declared unambiguously that Austria would be closely watched—and if the country was found to be in violation of the EU's strict human rights principles, the Commission reserved the right to start procedures to cancel Austria's membership in the European Council. Pursuant to the Amsterdam Treaty, this would be the first step toward Austria's expulsion from the EU. The driving forces behind these uniquely drastic steps were the German government, in particular Social Democratic Chancellor Gerhard Schroeder and Greens Foreign Minister Joschka Fischer; the French government, led by Conservative (RPR) President Jacques Chirac and Socialist (PS) Prime Minister Lionel Jospin; the Spanish government, led by Conservative Prime Minister Jose Maria Asnar; and the Belgians. It is important to point out that—contrary to the repeated claims by the Austrian government that the EU members' action was a spiteful social democratic cabal orchestrated by the Austrian Social Democrats who proved to be sore losers—the European reaction reached across party lines and spanned the gamut of the acceptable middle that has governed Europe so successfully throughout the postwar period: from center-left social democrats to center-right conservatives.

Second, it is important to point out that the Europeans' reaction in no way interfered with the Austrians' political articulations, nor did it intervene in any way with Austria's political sovereignty. It was not a preemptive strike or a fait accompli; instead it was merely an unambiguously clear reaction. The Europeans never told the Austrians for whom to vote, what government to have, or how to run their internal affairs. What they did say—and they did so loud and clear—was that Austrians were free to choose whomever they wanted, but that Europe was equally free not to like the Austrians' choice. (Or to use Daniel Cohn-Bendit's inimitable language: "You are free to have bad breath, but we are free not to like you for it.") Politics is clearly a contact sport and any action activates a reaction. That is the name of the game, and the Europeans reacted to something that they clearly found uniquely objectionable. And what they found so objectionable was the unique character and history of the FPOe coupled with Austria's meager attempts to come to terms with its Nazi past. These two factors were far more important than Joerg Haider's personality and particular leadership.

Third, Europe's reaction must also be seen in the context of its becoming a community of values, a community that—as the Germans like to point out—adheres with increasing intensity to something called a *Wertekanon,* a canon of values. It has also entered the political vernacular by the French terminology of *acquis communautaire,* which—especially in its German version of *europaeische Errungenschaften*—sounds haughty and arrogant but also helps establish an important baseline of values that any newly forming political entity needs for its internal as well as external legitimation. By the end of the 1990s, the EU no longer was merely a common market, a large bureaucracy regulating British beef, Swedish cigarettes, used cars, and French cheese, although it remains that, too. Rather, it has come to stand for basic values of human decency that, to be sure, are vaguely defined and rather broad, but that nevertheless have some important common denominators and a clear baseline that is accepted by all. One essential ingredient of this baseline has been that everything and anything associated with National Socialism and open racism is simply beyond the boundaries of the acceptable. This is a clear remnant of the Yalta world. And it is in fact different from the views and values concerning other forms of dictatorships and evil regimes, including Stalinism and all other forms of fascism. Does this make the latter legitimate? No, it certainly does not. Does it make it right that the Europeans took over six months to react in concert to Serbia's Slobodan Milosevic in the Kosovo disaster and well over one year to the massacres in Bosnia—not to mention that they could only act in concert under the leadership of the much-despised United States (which, of course, further added to the Europeans' dislike of Americans)? Or that some Europeans, like the French, cannot wait for the moment to conduct business as usual with a mass murderer like Saddam Hussein? No, once again, it certainly does not. Are the Europeans flawed? Yes, they most certainly are. Do they have a singularly applicable universal code of moral right? No, they do not. Do they treat all dictatorships equally? No, they do not. To be sure, it is easier to attack a small and weak thug like Serbia's Milosevic than a large and powerful one like Russia's Putin, whom all Europeans—as well as Americans—accommodated in his butchery of the Chechen people without even the threat of any ambassadorial pull-outs as signs of discomfort and protest, let alone the threat of any kind of boycott. But these severe and moral shortcomings do not mean that the Europeans then have to accept anything and everything, particularly developments in a country that had over the years clearly become part of the inside, part of the family, a status that Austria by all measures had clearly attained. But it is noteworthy that, unlike Austria, the FPOe had been ostracized from the European family as early as 1993, when it was excluded from the Liberal International by dint of its racist and anti-Semitic stands and thus became an ostracized party in the European Parliament that did not belong to any overarching and international factions, as did all other Austrian parties: the Social Democrats to the large Europe-wide social democratic faction; the Greens to the smaller but still important European Green faction; and the Austrian People's Party—the OeVP—to the parliamentary association of European conservative parties.

In the wake of the Europeans' unique reaction to the FPOe's entrance into the Austrian government, the question was frequently posed as to why the Europeans did not act remotely as emphatically and forcefully when—in 1994—Gianfranco Fini's *Allianza Nationale* entered the Italian center-right government under the leadership of Silvio Berlusconi's *Forza Italia*. The answer is twofold: First, the European Union was something entirely different in 1994 from what it had become by 2000. There is simply no doubt that, in the meantime, spurred by the Amsterdam Treaty, the EU has become actively engaged in a gradual state-building process: It has a clear capital; it has clear, though shifting, boundaries; it has a common currency; it has a central bank; it has a flag; in the wake of the Kosovo crisis, it now has a foreign and security (defense) minister rolled into one—Mr. Gasp, as the Germans call him—in Javier Solana, the former secretary general of NATO. It has two rapidly consolidating stock exchanges: in Frankfurt-London and in Paris-Madrid-Amsterdam-Brussels. Both may soon perhaps unite into one giant. All the EU lacks is an airline, which it almost has in the form of Airbus Industries, and a national anthem, which has been commissioned. Europe is in the process—however slow and cumbersome—of establishing a federation that, in certain key cases among which issues of political ethics and human values such as rejection of racism definitely take pride of place, supersedes the sovereignty of the individual states. These centripetal developments also exact clearer rules and a more specific concept of acceptable behavior and legitimate political discourse. In a sense, then, the federation has become like a club, which means that it has clear insiders and equally clear outsiders. For the insiders, however, certain rules apply that the club intends to enforce. This is also part of the state-building process. Thus, just like the federal government in the United States deemed it appropriate to impose its values on race relations on deeply reluctant southern states who tried to resist any reforms to their racist ways under the banner of state rights and state autonomy, so, too, does the EU as a budding federation reserve the right to impose certain sanctions on one of its members whom it has deems to have violated one of the club's major rules, one which construes the club's very identity and essence. The status of the EU was not this clublike, its construct as a federation not as far advanced in 1994 as it was in 2000.

Second, and far more important, the *Allianza Nationale* simply never evoked nearly the images and fears in Europeans as did the FPOe, which, in turn, has everything to do with the fact that Italian Fascism, though a heinously murderous and dictatorial political regime, was much closer to other fascisms in Europe than to National Socialism in Germany (and Austria), which was truly sui generis. Italian Fascism was not nearly as anti-Semitic as German National Socialism. Indeed, Jews from Vichy France fled to Fascist Italy because they felt safer under the latter. But most important, Italians helped defeat fascism themselves and hanged Mussolini in Milan. Nothing comparable ever happened in Germany or Austria, where the local population did not even make any credible attempts to challenge National Socialism (excepting the famous July 20 putsch against Adolf Hitler), let alone help defeat it. Adding insult to injury, it was the infamous SS Major Walter Reder whom a leading FPOe member, then serving as defense minister in the "red/blue" coalition government of the mid-1980s, welcomed with all military honors while he was wanted and condemned as a war criminal in Italy. Europeans knew this difference and have continued to feel it. Moreover, not having reacted to Haider would in no way render the Europeans' nonreaction to Fini's *Allianza Nationale*'s presence in the 1994 Italian government justifiable or acceptable. Just because one was negligent and remiss in certain instances does not mean that one therefore has the permission—indeed the obligation—to make being remiss and negligent a matter of policy, habit, and routine. Nazism is still not part of Europe's routine. This is one of the great legacies of the Yalta world. But with that world now fast becoming history, there is a new contest afoot to create a new order of things, which—indeed—includes a community and hierarchy of values.

The battle for a new hegemonic political and moral order has already begun. All one needs to do to see this is read the editorial pages of certain key European dailies, such as the *Frankfurter Allgemeine Zeitung,* with rigor and care. Nowhere is it a given that the values that had been associated with National Socialism will remain beyond the acceptable for good. In fact, I am convinced that National Socialism—unlike Stalinism—exerts a certain attraction on people, contains a certain seduction of evil, even eroticism, which makes it very powerful and attractive, be it to adult Europeans or to teenage killers in an upper-middle-class Colorado suburb. Hate sites on the Internet are almost exclusively associated with Nazism and are full of Nazi iconography. They invoke National Socialism, not Stalinism. While I am not an expert in pornography, I am quite certain that the prominence of Nazi pornographic imagery far outweighs that of any of its Stalinist counterparts. There are probably very few, if any, hate sites or pornographic web pages invoking the Cheka, the NKVD, or the KGB the way they habitually do the SS and other Nazi symbols. Alas, of the two major evils of the twentieth century, National Socialism appears to be much more popular as we begin the twenty-first century.

The European Union clearly put its foot down with this unique action against Austria. As Chancellor Schroeder aptly phrased it: "We have to make every effort to contain this to Austria. We may fail, but we have to make the effort." The EU clearly conceived of its action as the construction of a *cordon sanitaire* around Austria, or as the message to other European countries that parties such as the FPOe will not be tolerated and will remain beyond the politically acceptable in the European community. As such, it was a clear act of precedence setting. One needs only to read the Hungarian intellectual Miklos Haraszti's prescient analysis on the op-ed page of the *New York Times* to see how Haider and his legitimation by the conservatives in Austrian politics have become an attractive and acceptable political model to many Eastern Europeans.

What of the consequences of this action? Was it such an ignominious failure as many have claimed? Did the EU have to revoke the sanctions in September 2000 with egg on its face, having caused much ado about nothing? I beg to differ.

This boycott included many positive consequences from my normative vantage point, proving yet again that the only way one attains anything in politics is through pressure. There have never been any free lunches in politics, and there never will be. This case was not any different. None of the things to follow would have happened without the EU's action.

First, the EU's policy rendered Austrian President Klestil into a man of stature and importance to a degree that he clearly lacked before this event. The fact that he first objected to some candidates for ministerial positions in the proposed Schuessel government and exacted that they be replaced was already a very unusual, indeed unprecedented, step in Austria's postwar politics. Typically, heads of state in parliamentary democracies are merely titular and ceremonial figures who routinely approve cabinets whom the heads of government propose to them. President Klestil fully realized the gravity of the situation and reacted accordingly. More important still, he had the two coalition partners sign an unusual document that he had drawn up in which the two coalition partners committed themselves in the most explicit of terms to respect human rights in full, to remain cognizant and mindful of Austria's heinous Nazi past and its continued responsibilities on account of this past, and to maintain all the policies that have stood in Austria's good stead through the entire postwar period and rendered the country into one of the most stable and admired European democracies. This unique presidential act and document owe their existence solely to the pressure exerted by the 14 European governments on Austria.

Second, there is little doubt that Haider himself was completely surprised by the vehemence and seriousness of this reaction. A vain and publicity-conscious man, he suddenly found himself a complete persona non grata in the very world that was of paramount importance to him. While Haider's forced withdrawal from the national scene and his seeking refuge in his home base of Carinthia seemed merely a tactical move at the time—which it very well might have been—it nevertheless must have come at a great cost to his ego and also to his political efficacy. His withdrawal never would have happened without the EU's strong measure. To be sure, Haider continues to exert complete bolshevik-style control over the FPOe the way he did prior to the Europeans' act of ostracism. But the fact is that he had to cede the center of power; that he had been weakened in stature and immediate influence; that all politics, including Austria's, is potentially subject to the so-called Brutus effect in which absent leaders facilitate the emergence of vacua that then lend themselves to be filled by those that happen to be present or by other, less ostracized, rivals. The FPOe has not been immune to such a development. New space permits the rise of potentially new stars as has indeed happened in the FPOe's case, despite Haider's iron grip over the party. That Haider had to cede the limelight was solely attributable to the EU's boycott.

Last, and perhaps most important, the European response helped confirm a resistance to Haider and the new government in Austria that has been truly unprecedented. More than in the case of any other development in the Second Republic, there developed an oppositional force, a critical public that engulfed all of Austrian life and that created a democratic discourse and an atmosphere of contestation never before experienced in Austria, and quite rare anywhere in most advanced industrial democracies. Be it the twice-weekly demonstrations in the streets of Vienna or the regular public discussions among actors and audience that occurred after the conclusion of theater performances even in such staid loci of the established order like the venerable Burgtheater in Vienna, there developed a public space for debate and opposition that has surprised everybody, most of all the Austrians. There is no doubt that the vibrancy and viability of the Austrian opposition to the FPOe's governmental role and to Joerg Haider's politics in particular derived much strength and stamina from the knowledge that Austria's European neighbors remain far from indifferent to the fate of Austria and its continued liberal democracy. And if one reads the report of the "Three Wise Men" whom the EU empowered to assess the situation in Austria eight months after decreeing the boycott on January 31, 2000, one will find plenty of evidence that, far from being a whitewash of the Austrian government and the Austrian situation and a face-saving device for the EU, as many have alleged, this "white paper" contains matters of important substance. While complimenting the Austrian government (including its FPOe members) for having taken particular care to maintain democratic discourse and to safeguard human rights, and absolving it of any wrongdoing, the "Three Wise Men" used emphatic language in chastising the FPOe as a party; they characterized it as "right-wing populist with radical elements." In particular, the report blamed the FPOe for having repeatedly used xenophobia in its political campaigns, thus rendering such discourse completely acceptable (*salonfaehig* is the word used in the report) in contemporary Austria. The report concludes with perhaps the most important notion of all: that this unprecedented action by the EU lead to a routinized system of "preventive and monitoring measures," lest similar developments that violate "common European values" not become part of any member country's government.

Part Two: Structural and Cultural Antecedents

It is important to point out that one of the main reasons for the Europeans' unprecedented swift and vociferous reaction to the FPOe's entrance into the Austrian government has to be placed in the context of Austria's much less sincere, less vocal, and less serious attempts to come to terms with its Nazi past. This is particularly evident when compared to those of *West* Germany (in stark contrast to East Germany, a comparison that, though highly relevant to the larger discussion here, is beyond the scope of this paper).

Austria's exculpation began with the Moscow Declaration of 1943, which pronounced Austria as Nazi Germany's first victim. While certainly correct and appropriate in one sense, this categorization was far too flat and one-sided in terms of accounting for the other side of Austria's history, the one that welcomed the *Anschluss* [annexation] and thus the Nazis' political rule over what had now become the Ostmark province in the larger Third Reich.

After the war, Austrians could conveniently blame the *Piefkes* [Germans] as the evil occupiers and as the only ones responsible for National Socialist rule, and especially its resulting atrocities, since Austrians were occupied like everybody else in Europe. They, too, had become one of Hitler's victims, just like the Poles, Belgians, French, Norwegians, Czechs, and so on. "Anschluss—The Rape of Austria" (to use the title of a book by a respected British historian) became a well-worn metaphor in the international discourse on Austria, a discourse that helped decouple Austria from the Nazis and their crimes.

If one can—and needs to—criticize the West Germans for their inadequate confrontation with their Nazi past, one also needs to give credit where credit is due: No society in the world has ever tried to atone for a particularly heinous epoch of its history the way the West Germans have done for Germany's Nazi past. To be sure, this did not start until the 1960s, and the silent 1950s provided the appropriate cover-up and atmosphere to create a smooth continuity between the Third Reich and important structures of the Federal Republic. However, following the Auschwitz trial in 1963 in Frankfurt and the arrival of the '68ers on the scene of West German politics, the Nazi past became an integral part of the Federal Republic's public discourse in virtually every aspect of life. Here is merely a brief—and incomplete—list of key events in which this past assumed center stage in West Germany's public debate to a degree unknown in Austria until the Waldheim Affair in 1986. There simply exists no comparable list for Austrian politics:

1963: Auschwitz trial.

1969: First parliamentary debate about the expiration of the statute of limitation of murder committed by the Nazis.

1972: Willy Brandt's impromptu knee fall at the Warsaw Ghetto memorial.

1979: Second parliamentary debate about the expiration of the statute of limitation of murder committed by the Nazis.

1979: The airing of the television series "Holocaust," which created a watershed in the public debate about the Nazi genocide of the Jews among virtually all groups in West Germany.

1985: The Bitburg affair.

1985: President Richard von Weizsaecker's legendary speech of May 8, arguably perhaps the most important public address in the Federal Republic's history.

1985: Rainer Werner Fassbinder's play "Garbage, the City and Death."

1986: The Historians' Debate.

1988: Philip Jenninger's ill-fated speech in the Bundestag.

1989: The fall of the Berlin Wall on November 9 and the ensuing public discussion about the proper commemoration of this day in German history.

1996: The Goldhagen controversy.

1998: The Walser-Bubis confrontation.

1999: The Wehrmacht Exhibit.

1986 to 1999 and continuing: The controversy over the Holocaust Memorial in Berlin: its very existence; its proper shape; its size; its location.

2000: Compensation for slave labor under the Nazis.

2001: The Finkelstein controversy.

Whatever the causes, procedures, and eventual results of these issues might have been, they all led to major debates in virtually all venues of Germany's public. Thus, however flawed Germany's coming to terms with its Nazi past might be judged, the attempt to do so most certainly created a public culture of awareness that rendered silence and complacency impossible. One simply could no longer be a thinking German without having the legacy of the Holocaust in some way be part of one's identity. No matter how contradictory one might gauge the German effort, it has been, comparatively speaking, far and away the most thorough in the world. Coming to terms with the Holocaust has in some manner become part of contemporary German identity. It had not become that in the case of its Austrian counterpart until very recently, if at all. Haider would still be unthinkable in Germany. Then again, the regular violence and constant intimidation exercised by the new German right on a daily basis, mainly—though far from exclusively—in the country's eastern regions, are rather rare in Austria

To be sure, Austria's Nazi past has also been covered up both consciously as well as structurally by the particular Austrian political arrangement known as consociationalism, a system of top-level elite cooperation (critics would call it collusion) that derived its legitimation from a pre-Nazi Austrian trauma that was absent in Germany: the Austrian Civil War of 1934. This war was merely the logical consumption of a civil war–like relationship between the Socialist "reds" and the Catholic-conservative "blacks" that had plagued the entire First Republic ("the republic that no one wanted" as it has aptly been characterized) from its very beginnings after the collapse of the Habsburg Monarchy and the end of World War I until its demise at the hands of Austro-Fascism's "Fatherland Front" in 1934. In many ways, this trauma defined Austria's postwar arrangement and political life much more than the Nazi interlude. Lest 1934 reappear once again, the reds and the blacks set up a governmental system immediately following the conclusion of World War II in which both sides were guaranteed constant inclusion regardless of electoral outcomes as long as there was a rough numerical balance between the two. Thus emerged a long-lasting system of red-black cooperation and collusion that consolidated Austria's postwar political stability and economic comfort to the detriment of excluding those that did not quite fit the system. The FPOe and its followers were among those excluded. What is interesting—and unique in the Austrian case—is that a governmental arrangement that is usually designed to deal with exceptional situations demanding the coalescence of society's major institutions (Germany's Grand Coalition featuring the SPD and the CDU/CSU between 1966 and 1969; Israel's Likud-Marach Coalition in the late 1980s; and Britain's all-party coalition during World War II come to mind) became the government norm in Austria's Second Republic. After all, for 34 of the Second Republic's 55 years, Austria was governed by a Grand Coalition of some kind, with the OeVP furnishing the senior partnership in the coalition's first installment until 1966 and the SPOe assuming this role between 1986 and 2000 when the FPOe, under Haider's leadership, joined with the OeVP to form a new coalition. There have been two major reasons for this Austrian norm: to avoid the trauma of the 1930s—the battle between the reds and the blacks—and thus guarantee political stability and economic prosperity; and to exclude—rather than confront—anything related to National Socialism by keeping the FPOe at bay and out of the government. Thus, the governmental arrangements most common to the rest of Europe, so-called small coalitions, remained beyond the acceptability and feasibility of much of Austria's postwar history. This "Austrian exceptionalism" remained fully intact until the Social Democrats formed a small coalition with the FPOe in 1983. It is to the Social Democrats that I now turn my attention.

The Social Democrats/Socialists—the SPOe

Key leaders of Austrian Socialism were active supporters of Austria's *Anschluss* with Nazi Germany. (To be sure, many Austrian socialists wanted an *Anschluss* with Germany as early as 1920 but for a very different reason: The SPOe hoped that by Austria's jointure with Germany, the two jewels of the Second International—the SPD and the SPOe—might in fact create a social-democratic hegemony that neither one of them could attain in their respective countries on their own.) Thus, for example, Karl Renner, one of the SPOe's leading figures and later president of Austria in the postwar era, an intellectual with international contacts and experience, urged Austria to join up with Nazi Germany. Approval of the Nazis' arrival in Austria in March 1938 was not confined to the country's middle class but was also welcomed by many blue-collar workers who had hoped that the "socialist" dimensions of the Nazis' policies would create jobs for them in the newly constituted

Ostmark. Moreover, this wing of the party was always wary of what it perceived to be the inordinate presence of Jewish intellectuals in the SPOe's policy-making apparatus and among its leaders.

Banned under the Nazis, the Austrian SPOe reconstituted itself in 1945, thanks to the postwar circumstances. Adopting the November 1943 Moscow Declaration, the Socialists rebuilt the party on a very different foundation than the "Austro-Marxist" social democracy of the First Republic. Austria's 200,000 Jews—most of whom had voted for the Socialists because the Christian Social Party program contained a notorious Aryan paragraph and because the pan-German party was obviously not an option for them—were gone, either murdered or driven abroad. As Adolf Sturmthal, who had been an assistant to Friedrich Adler (head of the Labor and Socialist International) in the 1930s and who returned to Austria in 1945 as the chairman of "Friends of Austrian Labor" (which he had become while exiled in America), soon learned, the new SPOe was not warmly disposed toward returning émigrés. Though a few well-known figures like Oskar Pollak, the editor of the *Arbeiter-Zeitung,* did return to Vienna, the new party chair, Adolf Schaerf—later president of the Republic—made it clear that he regarded a flood of returning Jewish émigrés as a potential problem for the Socialists in a country with a long anti-Semitic tradition. Some key leaders of postwar social democracy, like lower Austria's Heinrich Schneidmadl, had reputations as anti-Semites, and Schneidmadl's wing of the party had always been wary of what it perceived to be the inordinate presence of Jewish intellectuals in the SPOe's top echelons. According to the British historian Robert Knight, when the subject of restitution of Jewish property was raised in postwar cabinet meetings, SPOe interior minister Oskar Helmer said, "I am for dragging out the matter."[1] It soon became clear that many of the exiles would not return to Austria. For example, Otto Leichter, who had been Otto Bauer's right-hand man before the war, and whose wife, Kaethe, had perished in Ravensbrueck, chose to remain in New York, where his son Franz became a state senator.

Immediately following the war, the reconstituted SPOe's emphasis on a pragmatism that was to fetishize neo-corporatist consociationalism as the only possible expression of political rule also meant a speedy accommodation with ex-Nazis whose past the party was willing to forget as long as they now proved to be its loyal supporters, followers, and functionaries. Particularly in Austria's southern province of Carinthia—Haider's home and his current bailiwick as this entity's governor—the SPOe openly wooed ex-Nazis to join its ranks and start a new life in a party whose pedigree, though far from innocent of complicity with the Nazis, was certainly the cleanest that this new republic could offer. Barring a complete integration of ex-Nazis into the postwar SPOe, the party pursued a parallel track that was designed to weaken its only serious political rival (and consociational partner) until the meteoric rise of Joerg Haider, the conservative OeVP's successor to the Austro-Fascists of the 1930s. Rather than have the bulk of Austria's 680,000 registered members of the NSDAP become supporters of the conservatives, the SPOe openly advocated the creation of a third force that was to become the political home of Joerg Haider and his friends. Euphemistically labeled *Verband der Unabhaengigen* [League of Independents] and still disenfranchised for the 1945 parliamentary elections by dint of its members' active cooperation with National Socialism, this group contested its first national poll under the new name of *Wahlpartei der Unabhaengigen* [Party of the Independents] in 1949, garnering 11.7 percent of the popular vote. It is precisely this origin of what was to become the FPOe in 1956 that has led Anton Pelinka, Austria's leading political scientist, to label the FPOe not a Nazi party but clearly "a party founded by former Nazis for former Nazis."[2] This distinction makes it unique among all European parties, even among its cousins of the far right like the *Vlams Blok* in Belgium, the *Front National* in France, the *Allianza Nationale* in Italy and the numerous small right-wing parties of the postwar period in Germany itself.

The SPOe's tacit tolerance and quiet courting of ex-Nazis turned open and vocal under the leadership of Bruno Kreisky beginning in 1970. Kreisky, an assimilated Viennese Jew of the educated middle class who spent the war years in Sweden, returned to Austria to a successful career in politics that—among other things—openly and knowingly used anti-Semitism as a tool to further his own personal interests as well as those of his beloved SPOe. Fascinated by the 30-year hegemony of Swedish social democracy, as were so many continental émigrés (Willy Brandt and Rudolf Meidner just to name two), Kreisky hoped that by weakening the conservative OeVP and strengthening the right-radical FPOe he, too, would be able to establish "Swedish" conditions in Austria where the bourgeois parties would be splintered, thus leaving powerful social democrats as the permanent rulers of the country. The active pursuit of this Swedish strategy coincided quite conveniently with Kreisky's personal dislike of Jews, which he expressed to anyone willing to listen, such as the German weekly *Der Spiegel*, to whom he called the Jews "an old but ugly [*ein altes aber mieses*] people" in a freewheeling interview. From ostentatiously kissing and embracing Yasser Arafat and Muammar al-Qaddafi during their repeated meetings in Vienna and elsewhere, to denouncing certain Israeli leaders, particularly Menahem Begin, in derogatory terms commonly used by German (and Austrian) Jews in their contemptuous references to Eastern European Jews (the so-called *Ostjuden*), Kreisky's personal aversions happened to be superb politics in the 1970s in a country where well over 70 percent of the population still harbored deeply felt resentment toward Jews. When

Kreisky and the SPOe first entered the government all by themselves in 1970, thereby breaking the traditional tandem of consociationalism in which they were the OeVP's junior partner, the socialists formed a minority government, which meant that they had to rely on tacit parliamentary approval of their governance on the part of Austria's third party—the FPOe. The party was led at the time by Friedrich Peter, the party's second leader who, just like its first, had been a high-ranking member of the SS; Kreisky and Peter became not only political allies but also personal friends. Kreisky defended Peter against Simon Wiesenthal's allegations that Peter's SS unit had been involved in mass killings of civilians in the Soviet Union: "The only thing that matters is the present, not the past," Kreisky said, to the delight of millions of Austrians who loved hearing Kreisky's repeated utterances that he, as a Jew, could speak with abandon whereas the same remained strictly taboo for "true Austrians." This sobriquet was used by Kreisky's rival Josef Klaus in the 1970 election campaign to differentiate himself from Kreisky who, by dint of his being Jewish, was presumably not a true Austrian. Studies by the Austrian linguist Ruth Wodak and by other Austrian social scientists demonstrate quite clearly that in the wake of Kreisky's thinly veiled anti-Semitic attacks on Wiesenthal, anti-Semitic discourse grew and became more legitimate in Austria's public domain. Four ministers of Kreisky's first cabinet and five of his second cabinet were card-carrying members of the National Socialist Party. Kreisky's agriculture minister, Hans Oellinger, had to resign after it was revealed that—unbeknownst to Kreisky—he had an "illegal" SS background. Unlike having been a member of the "illegal" SS, having belonged to the "legal" NSDAP bore no stigma in Austrian politics at all. Oellinger's successor was a man who had been a perfectly "legal" member of the NSDAP. In 1983, the Austrian socialists entered into an official coalition with the FPOe, thus forming for the first time in the Second Republic's history a so-called "small coalition." This type of coalition had become the governing norm in virtually all European democracies but remained impossible in Austria first and foremost by dint of the FPOe's unique connection to the Nazi past but also by virtue of the entrenched consociationalism of the two big parties who, if they could not rule alone, preferred each other as coalition partners. They thus guaranteed the smooth continuation of a well-oiled spoils system best known under the term "Proporz." In fairness to Kreisky and the SPOe, it should be mentioned that the FPOe's debut at the helm of Austria's government occurred under the chancellorship of Fred Sinowatz, Kreisky's immediate successor, and during a brief hiatus in the FPOe's postwar history when, in the course of the early 1980s, the party's liberal wing under Norbert Steger assumed a short-lived prominence only to be toppled by its current star, Joerg Haider, later in the decade. While the small SPOe-FPOe coalition lasted only until 1986, the taboo had been broken: The Social Democrats had granted the FPOe its first access to state power in Austria's postwar history.

The ugly collaboration between Austria's Social Democrats and ex-Nazis was aired for the first time in 2000 in what surely was going to be Austria's last trial involving the Nazi past. The 83-year-old psychiatrist Heinrich Gross was accused of having conducted under Nazi rule a euthanasia program in Vienna specializing in the multiple killing of children. Gross was a Nazi of the first hour: He was a member of the Hitler Youth as of 1932 and a member of the SA one year later; he experienced rapid career advancement as an active Nazi leader during a period when being a Nazi was illegal in Austria; he joined the NSDAP in 1938, two days after the *Anschluss* in March—in short, he was a Nazi by conviction, not by opportunism. After the war he engaged in a straight-up trade: He relinquished his NSDAP party book (membership number 6335279) and acquired a socialist one instead (SPOe membership number 011598). Under the full protection of the Socialist leadership, and as a special protégé of the old Trotzkyite Christian Broda, who served as Austria's minister of justice from 1960 until 1983 and who—together with Kreisky—was one of the Second Republic's most prominent and respected Social Democratic politicians, Gross was accorded every possible accolade, honor, and privilege that the Austrian Republic can bestow on an individual. Gross is merely an egregious example of a pattern that represents the still unwritten but all the more ugly side of postwar Austrian social democracy. Adding insult to injury, Gross's trial—barely begun—was halted indefinitely on account of his alleged physical and mental frailty. Yet another chance to come to terms with Austria's past was nipped in the bud.

The Austrian People's Party—OeVP: Conservatism in the Postwar Era

National Socialism helped in a way to make Austro-Fascism, the political regime of the OeVP's predecessor, appear much less harshly than would have been the case had National Socialism, first, not been a far more murderous regime than Austro-Fascism and, second, not been conveniently "foreign" which meant that the domestic evils of clerical fascism could conveniently be forgotten, and indeed—as was the case in certain instances—even extolled. Kurt Schuschnigg, for example, tried to resist Hitler's pressures as best he could only to succumb to a hopeless situation. These circumstances accorded Schuschnigg a position of prominence in the Second Republic as Austria's brave resister against Nazi might. His leadership of the "Fatherland Front," which, after all, was an openly fascist regime, was barely mentioned in public discourse of postwar Austria, and so if, then only in the world of the "red Lager." National Socialism's presence was strong enough to allow the OeVP much leeway in dealing with the OeVP's own fascist past. Yet, it was not strong enough to have the party resist incorporating Nazis among its ranks and flirt with anti-Semitism when it suited the party's purpose. After all, harnessing the force of anti-Semitism has never been to any party's detriment in Austrian politics. It has always been only a matter of how, never one of if.

Thus, the OeVP, just like the SPOe, had plenty of its own Nazi issues. Reinhard Kamitz, minister of finance in the 1950s, was a Nazi party member. The OeVP was, of course, not above using subtle anti-Semitism in its electoral campaigns and other political events when it saw the expression of such sentiments as beneficial to its cause. Thus, as already briefly mentioned, in his campaign against Bruno Kreisky, the OeVP's leader and chancellor's candidate Josef Klaus had the country covered with posters that featured his face and the simple statement "A True Austrian," clearly implying that Kreisky, a Jew, was not a true Austrian. In 1965 Taras Borodajkewycz, an Austrian Catholic with a traditional background in the elite of political Catholicism, the Cartel-Verband (CV), the nondueling student fraternity, made repeated and openly pro-Nazi and anti-Semitic remarks in his lectures at the School of Business [then *Hochschule für Welthandel,* now rechristened *Wirtschaftsuniversitaet*] in Vienna. As a consequence of his anti-Semitic remarks, Borodajkewycz's lectures were among the most popular at the school, where he became one of the students' heroes. Indeed, when his remarks became public on account of the meticulous note-taking of a young socialist student named Heinz Fischer, who subsequently became one of the SPOe's most prominent politicians during the Kreisky years and beyond, and when on the basis of this publicity the government proceeded to censor Borodajkewycz and initiate his early retirement, thousands of his student followers demonstrated on the professor's behalf and engaged in pitched battles with workers who, trucked into Vienna's center from the city's "red" suburbs, protested against anti-Semitism and neo-Nazism at Austrian universities. There were two huge demonstrations that turned seriously violent. In the course of one, Ernst Kirchweger, a survivor of Nazi persecution and a member of the Austrian resistance against Nazism, was beaten to death by members of the *Burschenschaften,* the right-wing student fraternities whose rituals continue to feature dueling. This, of course, was the milieu that spawned Joerg Haider and his associates. It was different and separate from the conservative student associations, but these two worlds formed close alliances on issues pertaining to anti-Semitism, Jews, foreigners, and "reds." As testimony to the tremendous changes that have occurred in the development of Austrian social and political life, we now experience a complete role reversal as to the FPOe's and the political right's supporters between the 1960s and now: Then, the bastions of the right (both radical and conservative) were the country's universities and its intelligentsia; today, it is the male, blue-collar working class that demonstrated against Borodajkewycz in 1965. Haider and his party have become anathema to Austrian universities and the country's intelligentsia. It would be unthinkable for Haider to deliver a lecture at an Austrian university. Wisely, he has never tried.

No discussion of the OeVP would be complete without at least the mention of the Waldheim affair. While even a superficial discussion of this controversy would be far beyond the scope of this paper, three things need brief mention here: First, Kurt Waldheim was not a member of the OeVP but most certainly of the very milieu that tied this party in an indirect but far from insignificant way to Austria's entanglement with National Socialism. The relationship on Waldheim's part—and that of the OeVP—to the Nazis was never as clear cut, never as obvious in its complicity with National Socialism as was the case with the FPOe. Still, a relationship existed. Second, most of the OeVP and its members, voters, and supporters, stood by Kurt Waldheim during the entire six years of his ill-fated presidency when—for the first time—an Austrian politician, indeed the country's head of state, was persona non grata in most European states. Thus, there existed a European precedent to the action that the EU initiated in the crisis surrounding the formation of the black/blue coalition in early 2000. Though far less coordinated than in the present situation, the fact then was that President Kurt Waldheim was unwelcome in most European capitals, which he used to visit on a regular basis as the former foreign minister of Austria, one of its most senior diplomats, and—most important—as two-term Secretary General of the United Nations. Third, it was the Waldheim controversy that spawned two dialectically related developments that were to influence Austrian politics: the first serious reckoning of the Austrian Nazi past on a major scale involving a public debate unprecedented in its intensity since the inception of the Second Republic, and the emergence of Joerg Haider as leader of a meteorically rising FPOe. It is to a discussion of this entity that we now move.

The Freedom Party—FPOe: Yet Another Austrian Exception?

There is no doubt that the last 15 years have witnessed a reemergence of the radical right in many European countries. The end of the Cold War, the break-up of old value structures, and above all the creation of multicultural and multiethnic societies in countries that have been largely monocultural and monoethnic, at least in terms of being virtually all white and all "Western" by their self-understanding, have led to the emergence of a bevy of right-wing activities in almost all European countries. From Sweden in the continent's north to Italy in its south, right-wing politics has emerged with a force (and violence) that was largely unknown in the first four decades of the postwar period. All of these movements—and one needs to consider them as such, not only as parties in which their significance has been much less pronounced and seemingly less important than their actual existence has been in the political space of all these countries—share a number of commonalties: In terms of their social composition, they are disproportionately male, disproportionately young (15 to 30 years old), disproportionately skewed toward the lesser educated segments of all their societies, and disproportionately dissatisfied with the trajectories of their societies and their futures in particular. (Interestingly, they have not hailed disproportionately from the unemployed, as has been commonly reported.) As to their beliefs, they feature a heavy dosage of xenophobia, nationalism bordering on the chauvinist variety, racism, anti-Semitism, antifeminism, anti-Europeanism, and also anti-Americanism. Similar to their fascist predecessors of the interwar period, with whom they share many ideological and social similarities but from whom they are also quite different, this new Right disdains all aspects of weakness and remains skeptical toward the liberal democratic order of their respective countries.

The FPOe fits this profile with a good measure of accuracy. Yet, it is also different in two key ways: First, as already stated, none of the other constructs of the new Right have been parties or movements for Nazis by Nazis; they all—without exception—include the crucial prefix "neo" in their self-identification and, more important, in their identification by scholars and experts. In this important manner, the FPOe in fact is not a party of the new Right. It very much hails from an old Right that not only experienced the world of state power but also exerted such a power in the most brutal ways throughout much of the European continent. But, second, the FPOe is indeed new in terms of its leadership's age, its iconography, and its habitus. Indeed, it is so new that its newness has also contributed to its immense success, making it the most significant new Right phenomenon anywhere in Europe. This "newness" consists of all the elements that have become associated with the term "Armani Fascism": young, dynamic, stylish—the antithesis to the fascists of yore, who, by dint of their age and image, have simply lost most of their relevance and appeal at the beginning of the twenty-first century. Hobnail boots, goose stepping, and one-arm saluting might still be attractive to a small fringe of right-radical young men who fancy themselves as the vanguard of a reborn fascist movement, but these symbols and the world that they represent remain unappealing to a large number of voters who are needed to bring a party like the FPOe to political power.

The FPO—as has been already mentioned—started out as the VdU in 1945. This entity was the direct successor to the *Grossdeutsche Volkspartei* of the First Republic and to the pan-German "third Lager" of the Habsburg Empire, arguably one of the most virulently anti-Semitic and German-nationalist movements anywhere in the German-speaking world at the end of the nineteenth and the beginning of the twentieth centuries. The VdU's associations were so identified with National Socialism that it did not even contest the postwar era's first parliamentary election in which the country's 680,000 Austrian members of the National Socialist party were disenfranchised of their voting rights. In the 1949 poll, the VdU, campaigning as WdU, attained 11.7 percent of the voters' support; in the 1953 poll it garnered 11.0 percent. This grouping was renamed FPOe in 1956 and has maintained this name ever since. The party hovered between an electoral high of 7.7 percent of the vote 1959 and a low of 5.0 percent in its brief liberal interlude in the early 1980s under Norbert Steger, Joerg Haider's immediate predecessor as party leader. That Steger's attempts at making the FPOe something akin to the German FDP nearly cost the party its parliamentary representation (Austria's cut-off threshold for legislative representation lies at 4 percent of the tally, as opposed to 5 percent in Germany) and was an ill-fated course is best demonstrated by the party's rapidly improving electoral fate under Haider, which can only be described as meteorically successful in each election: 9.7 percent, 16.6 percent, 22.5 percent, 21.9 percent, and, in the last election of October 1999, 27.3 percent, a tally that has catapulted the FPOe into becoming Austria's second largest party behind the rapidly slumping Social Democrats.

The FPOe was different from the other two Austrian parties of the postwar era in that it was never really a membership party. Even during this meteoric rise at the polls since Haider's incumbency as party leader, the party membership has more or less held steady at circa 40,000. In stark opposition to the continuity on the membership dimension, significant shifts in the social characteristics of the party's voters in the course of Joerg Haider's leadership have occurred: To be sure, the FPOe had always attracted more male voters than it did female, but the gender gap has become significantly more pronounced since Haider's presence at the party's helm. Moreover, here are perhaps the three most important changes that amount to major shifts in the electoral topography of Austrian politics well beyond the FPOe proper: First, under Haider the FPOe has become especially popular among Austria's young voters, in notable contrast to previous times when the party attracted older voters in disproportionate numbers. More telling still of the earthquake-like shifts in Austrian politics, today's FPOe attracts a majority of Austrian male, blue-collar workers, who—for one solid century—had been the immutable backbone of Austria's social democracy. Finally, a close corollary to the shift in class profile of the FPOe's electorate is the one in education: If throughout the first four decades of the Second Republic the FPOe's voters hailed disproportionately from those holding university degrees or equivalent professional credentials and belonged to such elite professions as doctors and lawyers, the exact opposite has been the case in the course of Haider's meteoric rise. The FPOe has become the party of choice for the least educated segments of Austrian society, while it has virtually disappeared among the country's intelligentsia and has attained a minoritarian position among its professional sectors. Sociologically speaking, the party under Haider has assumed the profile of a traditional party of the Old Left.

Ideologically speaking, until the 1970s the FPOe was basically a pro-German, indeed pan-German, right-wing party whose milieu overlapped considerably with Austria's dueling university fraternities as well as—at least in the early 1960s—with those groups that committed terrorist attacks and bombings in Italy's Alto Adige province, which—as the South Tyrol—these groups and the FPOe wanted to see as part of Austria because of the substantial majority of German speakers among its inhabitants. The first two leaders of the FPOe were members of the SS; the party's leading politicians often expressed openly anti-Semitic sentiments; and the party never drew a clear and decisive demarcation setting it unequivocally apart from the shadowy world of virulent neo-Nazism. It would not be an exceptional event in Austrian politics for various prominent FPOe politicians constantly to test the waters of the permissible in terms of accepted discourse in the country's public culture. Thus, some remark that was clearly anti-Semitic, pro-Nazi, derisive of Austrian nationhood, antiforeign, or in whatever way part of the FPOe's discourse, though only tenuously Austria's, would always be retracted half-heartedly by an apology of sorts that—to the to the careful listener—merely confirmed that the original statement clearly reflected the speaker's actual intent and views. But a retraction had been made in a pro forma manner, thus making it possible for the FPOe as a party and for the particular politician to have reestablished their credentials as legitimate players in what had become officially accepted language in postwar Austrian politics.

For fairness's sake, it is important to mention the small, but extant, liberal wing in the FPOe that embodied all the values and views of a classical liberal party in the European sense: little state, lots of market, freedom of the individual, secularism. Only in the course of the first half of the 1980s, under the leadership of Norbert Steger, did this wing become hegemonic inside the FPOe. Haider's successful putsch against Steger quickly eliminated this tradition from the party altogether, so much so that the victims of this purge departed from the FPOe and formed the "Liberales Forum," a liberal party with the talented Heide Schmidt at its helm. Her personal charisma carried this new party into the Austrian parliament for two legislative periods. However, with liberalism never having played a significant role in Austrian politics and the novelty factor having worn off, the Liberales Forum failed to pass the 4 percent threshold in October 1999, thus not making it into the current Austrian legislature.

Enter Joerg Haider, a brilliant mixture of new and old; of young, hip, post-modern and well-tanned androgyny espousing market liberalism in some areas and state protection in others, articulating Austro-chauvinism with a solid dosage of old-fashioned pan-Germanism, xenophobia, and racism, and launching relentless attacks on the red-black establishment that had run Austrian politics solidly since 1945. There can be absolutely no doubt that along with Bruno Kreisky, Joerg Haider has already become far and away the most important politician of Austria's Second Republic. Just like Kreisky, Haider, too, has come to dominate Austrian domestic politics like no other politician ever had, and has in the process—also like Kreisky—attained an international aura that has eluded all other public figures of the Second Republic.

Part Three: Conclusion

There can be no doubt that Austrian postwar politics was forever changed in the course of the last few months of 1999 and the first few of 2000. Haider's emergence as a political force has been part of a secularization process that has demystified and destroyed the old Lager. There will be no more automaticity in Austrian politics. In a country where politics was completely predictable for nearly 50 years, where the ratio of party members to voters was the highest in any modern country (fully one-third of the electorate belonged to one of the three dominant political parties), including those of the Soviet bloc, where the SPOe's membership in absolute numbers was nearly as big as the SPD's and the OeVP's and was in fact larger than the CDU's in a country that contained one-tenth of the population of the Federal Republic of Germany, party politics has been indelibly altered. Writers such as Robert Menasse have rejoiced in this secularization of Austrian politics and see the destruction of the old Lager as a welcome "Westernization" of a postwar Austria that these critics have always regarded as merely semidemocratic at best. This "de-Austrianization" of Austrian politics, to use Anton Pelinka's apt term once again, the end of "Austrian exceptionalism," means of course an opening of a hitherto blocked political space. This creates new possibilities and opportunities but it also unveils the ugly underbelly of Austrian life that had been safely tucked away under the firm cover of the old consociationalism of the Second Republic.

To be sure, this secularization of Austria, this pluralization of its political space, allows access to all kinds of political expressions that are not to my liking. Yet, there is also something very welcoming in this secularization: It renders the ugly sentiments that have contributed to Haider's inordinate success much less dangerous than would have been the case in the previous era of desecularized Austrian politics. Adherence to Haider and the FPOe, no matter how sincere and heartfelt, is not a passion. It has no religious overtones, no aspects of fanaticism. As such, this adherence is basically the expression of a politics that will not vanquish liberal democracy in Austria. That welcome arrangement has become far too ensconced in the country's political culture to be displaced once again.

Notes

1. Helmer's statement, "Ich bin dafür, die Sache in die Länge zu ziehen" [I am for dragging out the matter] is the main title of Robert Knight's book, *"Ich bin dafür, die Sache in die Länge zu ziehen": Die Wortprotokolle der österreichischen Bundesregierung über die Entschädigung der Juden* (Vienna: Amalthea, 1988).
2. Anton Pelinka, "Österreich und Europa: Zur Isolierung eines Landes," *Europäische Rundschau* 1 (2000): 3.

CHAPTER SEVEN

ANTI-SEMITISM
IN EAST GERMANY, 1952–1953
Denial to the End[1]

MARIO KESSLER

The attitude toward Jews and Jewish issues during the postwar years must be carefully examined, especially in the country from which the destruction of European Jewry emanated. Within that context, the initial attempt to come to terms with the past was emphasized more strongly in the Soviet zone of Germany than in the Allied zones. This explains why many Jew who had survived in Germany or in exile opted for the German Democratic Republic (GDR) as their future place of residence. The political orientation in the Soviet zone was shaped by the traditions of the German working-class movement before 1933 and was dominated by its communist wing. The SED [*Sozialistische Einheitspartei*], which had been in the process of Stalinization since 1948, also identified itself with the position taken by the Communist International [Comintern] for solving the "Jewish Question." They believed that in order to defeat anti-Semitism, Jews should give up their Jewish identity and participate fully in the communist movement. Within the parameters of this movement, Jews should struggle for a classless and just society. It was assumed that any form of anti-Semitism would fade away, given that the Comintern approach explained anti-Semitism via economic reductionism. In a truly socialist society, anti-Semitism would have no class basis. Zionism was rejected in all of its manifestations.[2]

During the years that followed, leading communist politicians frequently attributed much responsibility for the crimes of National Socialism to the German people—a topic which has gained importance due to the recent controversies surrounding Daniel Goldhagen's book, *Hitler's Willing Executioners*. One important example, albeit not the only one, is the declaration of the KPD [Communist Party of Germany] on June 11, 1945, which emphasized that "every German must have a feeling of guilt and a burning awareness that the German people bear a significant responsibility for the war and its consequences. It was not just Hitler who is responsible for these crimes against humanity! Partially responsible are also those ten million Germans who freely voted for Hitler in 1932, even though we Communists warned 'whoever votes for Hitler votes for war!'"[3]

While this declaration by the KPD did not exclude the genocide against Jews, it did not mention it in any particular way. This was in accordance with the Soviet way of viewing the Holocaust as only secondary to the Nazi regime. Yet, during the first postwar years—but only then—there were serious considerations about offering surviving Jews not only individual, but also collective compensation. This was criticized within the KPD. Already during its first meeting, the Berlin governing council of the organization Victims of Fascism [*Opfer des Faschismus;* OdF] announced its interest in limiting the range of people who would be entitled to compensation. "Victims of fascism," the *Deutsche Volkszeitung* argued, "are those Jews who were persecuted and killed based on Nazi racial delusions, are those Jehovah's Witnesses, as well as the so-called 'Arbeitsvertragssünder.'[4] But we cannot extend the range of 'victims of fascism' so far. They all suffered much, but they did not fight [the Nazis actively]."[5] After some debate within the KPD and the Victims of Fascism, it was decided to include the "racially persecuted in the 'category' of . . . victims of fascism."[6]

Nonetheless, the East German administration provided essential moral support to the Jewish victims of Nazism. This had several practical results already by the late 1940s. First of all, an "Association of Victims of Nazism" had been created, aimed at supporting those who had suffered.[7] Second, in public meetings officials exposed and vigorously condemned Nazi crimes. Third, the administration turned death camps and other sites of atrocities into hallowed grounds that East Germans, particularly schoolchildren, were expected to visit.[8] Fourth, officials distributed large numbers of books, brochures, radio programs, movies, and art works about Nazi policies and the concentration camps.[9]

After his return from Mexican exile in July 1946, Paul Merker, member of the SED *Central Secretariat*,[10] supported Jewish survivors of the Holocaust and their cause. He frequently reminded Walter Ulbricht, the party's deputy chairman (and de facto leader), that the SED had not produced any specific guidelines for the compensation of the Jewish victims of fascism. Merker also noted that—as in 1947 in Thuringia—the Liberal Democratic Party had taken the initiative for such actions.[11] As late as August 1947 the

Central Committee of the SED rejected Merker's arguments. This rejection was based on the assumption that any collective compensation for Jews would only promote anti-Semitism.[12] After considerable debate within the SED, a new policy was put into practice on October 5, 1949, two days before the founding of the GDR. This policy focused on the individual situation of recognized victims of the Nazi regime and offered the survivors significant social programs. There was, however, no official position on the question of restitution and compensation.[13] As it was, the Soviet military administration had issued orders number 124 and 126, which declared that all formerly Jewish companies of particular interest to the Nazi state should be confiscated as Nazi property. Thus, these companies were excluded from any restitution. Almost all cases were endlessly prolonged or finally dismissed in April 1950.[14]

First contacts between Israeli and German officials were established during the Israeli-Arab war of 1948 when weapons were being airlifted from Czechoslovakia to support the Israeli military forces, the Haganah. Following the request of Chaim Yachiel, the Israeli representative in Munich, Julius Meyer, president of the Jewish communities in the Soviet zone of Germany, arranged a meeting between Yachiel and Otto Grotewohl, co-chairman of the SED. On this occasion, Grotewohl is said to have expressed the solidarity of the SED with the struggle of the Jewish state for its independence. He promised his help in taking the Jews from the displaced persons camps in Germany to Israel, although this kind of camp did not officially exist in the Soviet zone. No concrete action followed, since Grotewohl was not given the necessary Soviet support.[15]

One month after the founding of the GDR, Hermann Matern, chair of the internal SED Central Party Control Commission (ZPKK), sent a letter to the SED Party Control Commissions on the local level. That letter specified the objectives and tasks necessary to examine the background of leading figures in the state, the party, and the economy. Nora Goldenbogen, the East German historian, has shown in the case of Saxony that the guidelines specifically mentioned the Jews as a group of particular interest. The reasons for that were their assumed connections with Zionism, with the U.S. Secret Service, as well as with a so-called Trotzkyist-Jewish movement. The large portion of the Jews within all listed émigré organizations was noted.[16] Matern's letter marked the beginning of a whole range of investigations, the results of which were forwarded to the ZPKK as well as to specially created commissions for the sake of comparison and analysis.

Jewish Communists were among the first victims of the early waves of inner party purges in 1950 and 1951, which propelled the Stalinization of the SED. The well-known journalist Rudolf Feistmann was pushed into suicide; his colleague Lex Ende did not survive the ostracism that was part of the expulsion from the SED.[17] Among the imprisoned and otherwise restricted were more party members of Jewish background. Yet, at this point a Jewish background was not really an important factor in background checks. What mattered was whether or not one came from Western exile, as well as what one did, or supposedly did, while escaping the Nazis. One exception to this was the questioning of Alexander Abusch by the ZPKK.[18]

There was an attempt to show some sort of connection between Abusch and Noel Field, the unwitting pawn in these political maneuvers, in order to present Abusch as a "conspirator." Abusch seemingly fit all of the criteria. He had spent his exile in the West and he was, as a Jew, an outsider who attempted to compensate for that through particular conformity. In addition, he admitted that he had contact with Erica Wallach, Field's foster child.

The contacts between Abusch and Wallach turned out to be purely coincidental. Abusch delivered a letter written by Wallach in Prague to her former friend Leo Bauer, who resided in Berlin. Shortly afterward, on August 24, 1950, Bauer was taken into custody as an "enemy of the party." He was later transferred to the Soviet Union and condemned to death. Pardoned to life imprisonment and finally released in 1956, he subsequently left for the West.[19]

Abusch's Jewish background was not a significant issue during his first questioning, which took place on July 10, 1950.[20] The second questioning, on November 10 of the same year, was much different. Max Sens and Hertha Geffke of the ZPKK put Abusch through an interrogation, in which they looked into the money he collected "from Jewish economic emigrants" and from selling passports during his exile in Mexico, his membership in the German-Jewish cultural organization Menorah, as well as the fact that he was not a member of the Jewish community. Of interest was also Abusch's relationship to Leo Zuckermann, at this time head of Wilhelm Pieck's office,[21] and, most of all, to Paul Merker.[22] In a subsequent letter, Abusch emphasized once more what he already insisted on during his interrogation: Not since his eighteenth birthday had he "been interested in Jewish questions," he had never "written about it, had no experiences for political work within this realm, and [he was]even married to a non-Jew."[23]

These facts are not as important as the way Abusch chose to deal with them. He wrote with the spirit of constant apology that he, as a youth, "had to liberate myself within bitter domestic feuds from the influence of Judaism" in order to join the working-class movement—as if it would disgrace a Communist to still be interested in Jewish affairs after Auschwitz. This, more than anything else, indicates how profoundly the climate had changed within the SED apparatus.[24]

Abusch's meeting with Erika Wallach, who meanwhile had been imprisoned and taken to the Soviet Union, was deemed too brief to be important.[25] Abusch managed to avoid being thrown deeper into the whirlpool of the purges. He was expelled from the SED Politburo but never imprisoned. Later Abusch experienced some degree of rehabilitation, insomuch as he became minister for cultural affairs and deputy president of the Council of Ministers. Yet, Abusch never returned to the inner circle of power—the Politburo.

Paul Merker turned out to be a more suitable sacrificial lamb: Unlike Abusch, he was not Jewish. Thus, one could more easily reject any charges of anti-Semitism. Already in Mexican exile, Merker supported compensation and restitution of Jewish victims of National Socialism. He urged punishment of those guilty of crimes, and he sought to assure "our Jewish friends and comrades in struggle" that a new democratic order in Germany would find ways to "destroy anti-Semitism in Germany forever."[26] For Merker, restitution "was a matter of simple justice and decency, but also part of an effort to reconstitute German-Jewish life in postwar Germany."[27] This approach included those Jews who did not reside in Germany. He also thought critically about the Communists' role regarding the situation of European Jewry. In 1944 he addressed the shortcomings of the German labor movement toward Jewish issues. He focused his criticism on August Bebel's 1894 famous paraphrase of anti-Semitism as "Socialism of the dumb,"[28] for anti-Semitism was "already at that time much more than that. It was an instrument of extreme reaction to educate the people into becoming dumb." Merker emphasized that it was necessary to press this issue, "to fight it in unity with all liberal forces," to attack anti-Semitism "already within the imperialist-capitalist era," and to make this fight an essential component of the struggle for democracy and socialism.[29] Like the German communists in Moscow, he expressed the responsibility of the German people for the Nazi crimes but, unlike them, he pointed out that the people "allowed the crimes of the ruling class against the Jewish people to take place."[30]

With similar vigor, Merker justified the creation of a Jewish state. This issue was supposed to be handled at the peace conference after the victory over the Nazis, "regardless of all previous principles, considerations and prejudices, in accord with the wishes of the Jews." In addition, the full civil rights of the Jews were to be restored in all countries from which they were expelled. The complete national equality of the Jews was to be recognized in all these countries.[31] "Though Merker did not say so explicitly, such views would require the communists to revise explicitly the denial of Jewish nationhood enshrined in Stalin's essay on the national question," Jeffrey Herf has noted.[32] On the eve of the foundation of the State of Israel, Merker wrote in the SED newspaper *Neues Deutschland* that "the establishment of a Jewish state within a part of Palestine, with progressive ideas and the socialist aspirations of its working-class movement, will not remain without consequences for the reactionary feudal Arab kings, princes, and muftis."

Merker emphasized that the Soviet Union will "even permit the *Aliyah*, the migration of Soviet Jews to Palestine. The leaders of Soviet Jewry from now are going to be in direct contact with the Jewish center in Palestine." As a Politburo member, Merker took the official position when he wrote that "the Jewish population [in and outside Israel] should get the sympathy and active assistance of all progressive forces. Especially the democratic forces in Germany should be obliged to show their sympathy and readiness to help."[33]

The stance taken by Merker was at this time by no means contrary to the position of the Stalinist regimes in Moscow and their East German comrades.[34] Yet, in 1949 the Soviet Union had changed its approach; at that point it favored "progressive" forces within the Arab sphere.[35] Thus, one's previous enthusiasm for Israel constituted a black mark in the records that were kept by the ZPKK and its regional organizations.

On November 22, 1952, Prague witnessed the opening of one of the most startling trials of the twentieth century with Rudolf Slánsky, former general secretary of the Czechoslovakian Communist Party and Stalin's erstwhile lieutenant, appearing as the principal defendant. The trial showed how much the Soviet secret apparatus had infiltrated, as Francois Fejtö pointed out, "the Eastern European communist parties and governments, robbing them of their sovereignty, paralyzing their nerve centers, and producing a kind of collective pathological condition, compounded of fear, mistrust, apathy and self-destructiveness from which it was to take the leaders and their peoples much time and trouble to recover.[36]

The defendants were subjected to all kinds of moral pressure and physical torture in order to convince them that there was no escape from their fate. They were informed by the police that the party had complete knowledge of their actions and demanded a full confession of guilt. The defendants were maltreated to such an extent that some of them believed they had fallen into the hands of fascist torturers, but they were also promised that the court would deal leniently with them if they made complete confessions.[37]

Of the 14 defendants, 11 were of Jewish origin. The organizers tried to show that this was no coincidence, and that the Jewish prisoners were predisposed to become instruments of American espionage and of "Zionist conspiracy." The testimonies at the trial provided the material for a sort of new "Protocols of the Elders of Zion"; the Jews, an international people with the State of Israel as its main base, were playing a key role in the American conspiracy against the Soviet Union and her allies. One of the aims of this conspiracy was defined as "to destroy the ties of friendship between Czechoslovakia and the Soviet Union, and to turn the country into a new Yugoslavia."[38]

The Communist allies of the Soviet Union, and her satellites in particular, were empowered to adopt the proclamation of the editorial of *Rudé*

Pravo (the Czechoslovakian party newspaper) on November 24, 1952. This proclamation stated that Zionism was the "number-one enemy" of the working class. It seems that one of the aims of the organizers of the trial was to justify the anti-Israeli and pro-Arab switch in Soviet foreign policy. Czechoslovakia, with Russian approval, had supplied the Israeli army with arms, ammunition, and even fighter planes. However, as of 1949 the USSR realized that American influence had prevailed in Israel over that of pro-Soviet elements. Moreover, Soviet "anti-Zionism" served as a cover for unacknowledged anti-Semitism. The Jewish victims of the Slánsky Trial remained, through their "cosmopolitan" background and their experience of living in different cultures, a factor of potential dissidence for the Stalinists, who sought to transform the party and the society into a monolithic body. Slánsky and ten other defendants were subsequently executed.[39] The specific feature of Stalinist anti-Semitism was to neutralize the internationalist tradition within the communist party, including the SED.

On December 2, 1952, parallel to the anti-Semitic Slánsky Trial and its associated atmosphere, Paul Merker was imprisoned. The official justification was provided by a Central Committee decision to "draw lessons from the case against the center of conspiracy."[40] This text documents the full subordination of the SED to Stalin. Merker was accused by the Central Committee of having promoted Zionist views during his years in exile, as well as having urged the compensation of those Jews whose property was stolen by the Nazis, only in order to allow U.S. capital to penetrate Germany. "This is the true origin of his Zionism,"[41] the SED leadership claimed, and even used the Nazi phrase "transfer of German *Volksvermögen*" [the country's fortune] in its condemnations of Merker. He was linked to the "Slánsky conspiracy" through his friendship with André Simone (Otto Katz), one of the defendants in Prague. A reason for indictment was that he had contaminated "the workers with the most reactionary bourgeois ideology" and with "the poison of chauvinism and cosmopolitanism." The resolution pointed to Merker's publications in Mexico, to his public efforts on behalf of financial restitution for the Jews, and to his support for Israel.[42] The resolution charged that Merker did not care about working-class Jews, but rather that he was "above all" concerned with "the wealthy Jews, so-called economic emigrants with whom Merker, André Simone, and other German emigrants in Mexico were in closest touch." Contacts with wealthy Jews in Mexico were the reasons for Merker's support for Zionism.[43] Stalin's death on March 5, 1953 and the subsequent rehabilitation of the imprisoned Jewish physicians prevented possible further repression in the GDR. Yet, Merker was secretly tried and sentenced in 1955 within the context of SED anti-Semitism.[44]

After his release from the Stasi prison in Berlin-Hohenschönhausen, Merker started his struggle for complete rehabilitation.[45] On June 1, 1956,

Merker submitted a 38-page statement on his "attitude toward the Jewish question" to the ZPKK. He wrote that his Soviet and German interrogators were convinced that he must have been an agent for the United States, Israel, or the "Zionist organization" because he had taken such a strong position on the Jewish cause. He noted that the interrogators found no evidence that he was Jewish. He wrote the they "repeatedly said that it was completely incomprehensible to them that a non-Jew, such as myself, would become active on behalf of the Jews unless he was paid by Jewish organizations, all of which, in the opinion of these examiners, were without exception, agents of the imperialist powers. Therefore, a non-Jew could be active on behalf of the Jews only as an agent of imperialism. For them, my engagement on behalf of the Jewish people . . . was by itself a sufficient proof that I must be an agent of imperialism and an enemy of the working class."[46]

Merker emphasized:

> I am neither Jewish, nor a Zionist, though it would be no crime to be either. I have never had the intent to flee to Palestine. I have not supported the efforts of zionism. I have . . . occasionally said that the feeling of a deepest bond and the desire for their own Jewish country emerged among the Jews of different countries after they had been plundered by Hitler fascism and had been most deeply humiliated and driven from their homelands, millions of them murdered, only because they were Jews. This feeling was the expression of people most deeply harmed and outraged. Moreover, Hitler fascism emerged among us. We [Germans] did not succeed through the actions of the working masses in preventing the establishment of its rule and hence its crimes. Therefore, we Germans in particular must not and ought not ignore or fight against what I call a reinforcement of Jewish national feeling."[47]

On July 21, 1956, the first chamber of the GDR supreme court declared laconically that "in the case against Merker, Paul Friedrich . . . the sentence by the supreme court of March 30 has been nullified. The accused is to be released."[48] Yet, Merker was not satisfied with this decision. He demanded complete political and legal rehabilitation, including compensation. After Merker sent a letter to the supreme court,[49] it was decided that 50,000 GDR marks would be transferred to him.[50] In response to Merker's inquiry, Walter Ulbricht replied on July 31, 1956, and referred to the twenty-eighth Central Committee meeting in July 1956: "The follow-up investigation concluded that most charges against you are political in nature and do not warrant a criminal trial. . . . With socialist greetings . . ."[51] Any further discussion within the party was usually stopped with the warning "no *Fehlerdiskussion!*" [discussion of wrong measures taken by the party], which was regarded as water on the mills of the class enemy.

Yet, Merker did not give up. On August 23, 1956, he wrote again to Ulbricht and inquired how his failings were to be understood as political in nature and thus did not require a criminal trial including sentencing. "Does the Central Committee maintain its charges against me and feel only compelled to concede that these charges do not justify a criminal trial, which nevertheless has taken place?"[52]

Merker defended his dignity as a communist, as he tirelessly insisted during and after the trial. He also emphasized that he defended the "interests of the party and its leadership against the Beria gang, which lifted itself above party and leadership, and which mistreated and ridiculed me because I refused to flee to West Germany and, instead, confronted them." As a "reward," Merker found himself being treated unjustly and shamefully by the GDR legal system. "And now, after this shamefulness had to be discontinued, I am still being treated as an outcast by the party leadership." The decision at the twenty-eighth Central Committee meeting was an attempt not to rectify injustice, but to trivialize it and to maintain it, albeit in a much reduced form.[53]

According to the decisions of the plenary twenty-eighth party meeting, Ulbricht explained that Merker's readmission "into the party had to be immediately arranged. Your release was regarded, by the party and the state authorities, as rehabilitation."[54] This is all the compensation that Merker received, unless one regards the piece of tin that was given to Merker shortly before his death in 1969—the *Vaterländischer Verdienstorden* medal—as sufficient recompense for the years of suffering.

The series of internal party investigations, imprisonment, professional difficulties, and degradations, as well as excommunications from the party, intensified during the winter of 1952 to 1953. The Jewish communities, just recently granted state subsidies, were now regarded as the Fifth Column of the capitalist-imperialist system. At the beginning of 1953, the offices of Jewish communities were searched by the Stasi and members of the communities were imprisoned and interrogated, as well as accused of being Zionists, "ready and able to work under orders of the American secret service." Within this context Merker was accused of encouraging the Jewish SED members to join Jewish communities. Merker rejected such charges; yet, they were often repeated.

Indeed, many East German Jews were materially supported by the U.S. Joint Distribution Committee; this was, however, well known and tolerated by the SED leadership for a long time. Suddenly, this support was viewed with suspicion. As early as December 1951, selected Jews were ordered to the Soviet Control Commission. They were asked questions such as, "Where do your instructions and directives come from? Do you get them in a similar fashion as the Catholic Church gets its instructions from Rome? . . . Don't you understand why 'Joint' sends its gifts of love to Germany?"[55]

After the end of 1952 the Stasi not only searched Jewish community offices but also confiscated their files. This led to great fear among many Jews. In January 1953 alone, over 400 Jews fled to the West, including Leo Zuckermann, who used to be Wilhelm Pieck's chief of staff, and Julius Meyer, leader of the Jewish community in East Berlin. Nathan Peter Levinson, an American rabbi who resided in Berlin, urged Galinski to call on the Jews of East Germany to leave for the West. Galinski, who was reluctant at first, conceded and announced a press conference. The Jewish library was taken from East to West Berlin across the still-open border. The leaders of the Jewish community in Leipzig, Erfurt, Halle, and Schwerin went to the West.[56] This period of suffering came to an end only after Stalin's death. Yet, as eyewitnesses, such as Heinz Brandt, reported, mistrust toward the state authorities remained for a while.[57] But then, at least, requests to return to East Germany were dealt with more swiftly, as Carl Jacob Danziger and Franz Loeser testified.[58]

There is nothing that can negate or trivialize the pressure on the Jewish community in the GDR, nor the persecutions of the Jewish Communists. But one should be aware of the fact that East Germany did not experience the excessive anti-Jewish hysteria of the Soviet Union or Czechoslovakia. There were no officially instigated or even tolerated pogroms in the GDR, despite contextually justified Jewish fears. On the contrary, *Neues Deutschland* reported on January 29, 1953, that the regional courts of Magdeburg, Gera, and Frankfurt an der Oder issued prison sentences, ranging from one to two years, for "the propagation of anti-Semitism and lies about our Jewish fellow citizens."[59] One should also note that there were no anti-Semitic elements connected to the working-class uprising of June 17, 1953. Thus, the old Nazi cliché of "Jewish Bolshevism" was not resurrected.[60]

The conflicts around June 17 pushed the problem of anti-Semitism of the SED into the background. It is indeed a paradox that the same Jewish Communists, who just six months earlier had feared state power, as well as the party and security apparatus, and most of all the will of the Soviet dictator, now came to regard the presence of state power as a warranty for their (relative) safety. Not everyone was able to push aside so quickly what had happened earlier. Alfred Kantorowicz, who was in the hospital on June 17, recorded in his diary: "Why did we, intellectuals and old socialists, not lead this movement? What did we do besides resist passively, complain, or relocate?"[61] Whether the demonstrating workers would have listened to state-supporting intellectuals is a different matter. Ulbricht and his people were even more firmly entrenched after June 17. This new constellation motivated many Jews, who remained in the GDR, to accept the realities and move closer to the regime. Afterward the SED was able to introduce a policy of tolerance toward the Jewish community and toward secular Jews. The memory of the Nazi genocide was disseminated, if somewhat one-sided, throughout society. The Jewish community was expected to comply with official policy, but was not forced to come out in open opposition to Israel. In the 1980s, this measured tolerance was replaced by active support of Jewish culture, including religious practices. The reasons for this remarkable shift are to be found in more general overtures towards the United States, increased prestige in the eyes of West German public opinion, and new freedoms resulting from changing Soviet policies (Gorbachev was decidedly against any form of anti-Semitism).

However, any attempt to come to terms with the anti-Semitic interlude in GDR policy from 1952 to 1953 would have required a free discussion of key questions in East German history. This was not possible until the fall of 1989. While it is true that the specifically Stalinist anti-Semitism disappeared after the dictator's death, it was revived once more at the beginning of 1968 in Poland. This recurrence shows, among other things, how incompletely the post-Stalinist state socialist societies were able to cleanse themselves from this terrible legacy.

Notes

1. This essay is based on my book, *Die SED und die Juden—zwischen Repression und Toleranz: Politische Entwicklungen bis 1967* (Berlin: Akademie Verlag, 1995). For the preparation and correction of this English text I am indebted to Axel Fair-Schulz, Diethelm Prowe, and Eleanor Yadin. For an earlier German version, see "Antisemitismus in der SED 1952/53. Verdrängung der Geschichte bis ans Ende," *Utopie kreativ* 85–86 (November-December 1997): 158–66.

2. For the Comintern's attitude towards Zionism and Jewish issues, see Jack Jacobs, *On Socialists and "The Jewish Question" after Marx* (New York: New York University Press, 1992); Mario Kessler, *Antisemitismus, Zionismus und Sozialismus* (Mainz: Decaton, 1993); Mario Kessler, *Zionismus und internationale Arbeiterbewegung 1897–1933* (Berlin: Akademie Verlag, 1994); Enzo Traverso, *The Marxists and the Jewish Question: The History of a Debate, 1843–1943* (Atlantic Highlands, NJ: Humanities Press, 1994); Shlomo Na'aman, *Marxismus und Zionismus* (Gerlingen: Bleicher, 1997).

3. Quoted from Lothar Berthold and Ernst Diehl, eds., *Revolutionäre deutsche Parteiprogramme. Vom Kommunistischen Manifest zum Programm des Sozialismus* (Berlin: Dietz, 1964), 193.

4. People who break labor contracts.

5. *Deutsche Volkszeitung* (July 3, 1945): 4.

6. *Deutsche Volkszeitung* (September 25, 1945): 3.

7. The Association, or *Vereinigung der Verfolgten des Naziregimes* (VVN), was set up in February 1947, but it ceased to exist in 1953. Cf. Elke Reuter and

Detlef Hansel, *Das kurze Leben der VVN von 1947 bis 1953* (Berlin: Edition Ost, 1997).

8. Cf. Richard L. Merritt, "Politics of Judaism in East Germany," unpublished manuscript (1988), 8; Stefan Küchler, "DDR-Geschichtsbilder: Zur Interpretation des Nationalsozialismus im Geschichtsunterricht der DDR," *International Textbook Research* 22 (2000): 31–48.

9. For details, see Kessler, *Die SED und die Juden,* 37.

10. The SED's leading body; it was succeeded by the *Politbüro* in 1949.

11. Cf. Thomas Schüler, "Das Wiedergutmachungsgesetz vom 14. September 1945," *Jahrbuch für Antisemitismusforschung,* vol. 2 (Frankfurt am Main: Campus, 1993): 118–38.

12. SAPMO-BArch, DY 30/2/2027/30, 3. The abbreviation stands for the Foundation for the Archives of the Parties and Mass Organizations of the GDR under the Federal Archives of Germany.

13. Cf. Angelika Timm, *Hammer, Zirkel, and Davidstern: Das gestörte Verhältnis der DDR zu Zionismus und Staat Israel* (Bonn: Bouvier, 1997), 66. See also Angelika Timm, *Alles umsonst? Verhandlungen zwischen der Claims Conference und der DDR über "Wiedergutmachung" und Entschädigung* (Berlin: Helle Panke, 1996), 8; and Mario Kessler, *Die SED und die Juden,* 37.

14. Schüler, "Wiedergutmachungsgesetz," 131.

15. Angelika Timm, "Assimilation of History: The GDR and the State of Israel," *The Jerusalem Journal of International Relations* 14 (1992): 38.

16. Quoted in Nora Goldenbogen, "Antisemitismus und 'Säuberungen' in Sachsen (1949–1953)," in *Arbeiterbewegung und Antisemitismus: Entwicklungslinien im 20. Jahrhundert,* ed. Mario Kessler (Bonn: Pahl-Rugenstein, 1993), 126.

17. Wolfgang Kiessling, *Partner im "Narrenparadies": Der Freundeskreis um Noel Field und Paul Merker* (Berlin: Dietz, 1994), 263; and Kessler, *Die SED und die Juden,* 70.

18. Abusch was a member of the SED Politburo.

19. Cf. Leo Bauer's brief reminiscences, "Die Partei hat immer recht," *Aus Politik und Zeitgeschichte* 27 (July 4, 1956): 405–13.

20. Cf. SAPMO-BArch, DY 30, IV 2/4/11, 9.

21. Wilhelm Pieck was the president of the GDR.

22. For Zuckerman's biography, see Wolfgang Kiessling, *Absturz in den Kalten Krieg* (Berlin: Helle Panke, 1999).

23. SAPMO-BArch, DY 30/2/4/111, 43.

24. Cf. Parts of Abusch's hitherto unpublished memoirs in Karin Hartewig, "Das Gedächtnis der Partei. Biographische und andere Bestände im Zentralen Parteiarchiv der SED in der Stiftung Archiv der Parteien und Massenorganisationen der DDR im Bundesarchiv," *Jahrbuch für Kommunismusforschung* (Berlin: Akademie Verlag, 1993), 312–23. Abusch's official memoir omits this incident. Cf. Alexander Abusch, *Mit offenem Visier: Memoiren II* (Berlin: Dietz, 1986).

25. Cf. Erica Wallach, *Licht um Mitternacht: Fünf Jahre in der Welt der Verfemten* (Munich: List, 1969).

26. Paul Merker, "Hitlers Antisemitismus und wir," *Freies Deutschland* 1 (October 1944): 11.

27. Jeffrey Herf, "East German Communists and the Jewish Question: The Case of Paul Merker," *Journal of Contemporary History* 29 (1994): 631.

28. August Bebel defined Anti-Semitism as "Sozialismus des dummen Kerls." This statement was given in a press interview. Cf. Hermann Bahr, ed., *Der Antisemitismus: Ein internationales Interview* (Königstein/Taunus: Jüdischer Verlag, 1979): 24. Reprint of the 1898 edition.

29. Paul Merker, *Deutschland: Sein oder Nicht-Sein?,* vol. 2 (Mexico, D. F.: El Libro Libre, 1944), 36.

30. Paul Merker, "Hitlers Antisemitismus," 11.

31. Ibid., 11.

32. Jeffrey Herf, *Divided Memory: The Nazi Past in the Two Germanys* (Cambridge, MA: Harvard University Press, 1997), 50.

33. Paul Merker, "Der neue Staat des jüdischen Volkes," *Neues Deutschland* (January 24, 1948).

34. For the SED's attitude toward the Arab-Jewish conflict in Palestine and the new State of Israel prior to 1949, see Martin W. Kloke, *Israel und die deutsche Linke: Zur Geschichte eines schwierigen Verhältnisses* (Frankfurt am Main: Haag & Herchen, 1990); Timm, *Hammer, Zirkel, Davidstern: Das gestörte Verhältnis der DDR zu Zionismus und Staat Israel,* (Bonn: Bouvier, 1997), 81; and Kessler, *Die SED und die Juden,* 47.

35. Cf. The contributions of Peter Brod and Arnold Krammer in Robert S. Wistrich, ed., *The Left against Zion: Communism, Israel, and the Middle East* (London: Frank Cass, 1979): 50–70; 71–86.

36. François Fejtö, *A History of People's Democracies: Eastern Europe Since Stalin* (Harmondsworth: Pelican Books, 1974), 14.

37. Cf. the moving report of one of the survivors. Arthur London, *Ich gestehe: Der Prozess um Rudolf Slánsky* (Berlin: Aufbau, 1991). Reprint of the 1970 West German edition. The film version, *L'Aveu,* was directed by Kostas Gavras, and starred Yves Montand and Simone Signoret.

38. Klement Gottwald on a party conference on December 16, 1952, as quoted in Fejtö, 18.

39. There is a vast amount of literature about the Slánsky Trial. Among the most recent publications are Karel Kaplan, "Der politische Prozess gegen R. Slánsky und Genossen," in *Der Spätstalinismus und die jüdische Frage,* ed. Leonid Luks (Cologne: Böhlau, 1998), 169–87; Karel Kaplan and Frantisek Svátek, "Die politischen Säuberungen in der KPC," in *Terror: Stalinistische Parteisäuberungen 1936–1953,* ed. Hermann Weber and Ulrich Mählert (Paderborn: Schöningh, 1998), 487–562.

40. The resolution "Lehren aus dem Prozess gegen das Verschwörerzentrum Slánsky" is published in *Dokumente der Sozialistischen Einheitspartei Deutschlands* IV (Berlin: Dietz, 1954), 199–219. Excerpts in Kessler, *Die SED und die Juden,* 153–55.

41. *Dokumente,* IV, 206.

42. Ibid., 203–4.

43. Ibid., 207.

44. The judgment is published in Jeffrey Herf, "Antisemitismus in der SED: Geheime Dokumente zum Fall Paul Merker aus SED- und MfS-Akten," *Vierteljahreshefte für Zeitgeschichte* 42 (1999): 643–50.

45. Documented in Kessler, *Die SED und die Juden*, 156–70.

46. SAPMO-BArch, NL 102/27, 31–32. Parts of the document can be found in Kessler, *Die SED und die Juden*, 157–70; full text in Wolfgang Kiessling, *Paul Merker in den Fängen der Staatssicherheitsorgane Stalins und Ulbrichts* (Berlin: Helle Panke, 1995), 27–68; English excerpts in Herf, *East German Communists and the Jewish Question*, 645.

47. SAPMO-BArch, NL 102/27, 46.

48. Ibid., 73.

49. Ibid., 76.

50. Ibid., 81.

51. Ibid., 84.

52. Ibid., 85.

53. Ibid., 87.

54. Ibid., 92.

55. Quoted from a manuscript by Rainer Hildebrand, "Vorbereitungen für gesteuerten Antisemitismus?" *YIVO Archives* (Spring 1953), New York, FAD-1, Box 25; also in Olaf Groehler and Mario Kessler, *Die SED-Politik, der Antifaschismus und die Juden: In der SBZ und der frühen DDR* (Berlin: Helle Panke, 1995), 16.

56. Cf. Lothar Mertens, *Davidstern unter Hammer und Zirkel: Die Jüdischen Gemeinden in der SBZ/DDR und ihre Behandlung durch Partei und Staat 1945–1990* (Hildesheim: Olms), 1997, 54–62.

57. Cf. Heinz Brandt, *Ein Traum, der nicht entführbar ist: Mein Weg zwischen Ost und West* (Munich: List, 1967), 192.

58. Carl Jacob Danziger, *Die Partei hat immer recht* (Stuttgart: Deutsche Verlags-Anstalt, 1976); Franz Loeser, *Die unglaubwürdige Gesellschaft: Quo vadis, DDR?* (Cologne: Bund-Verlag, 1984).

59. *Neues Deutschland* (January 29, 1953).

60. Two months after the Luxemburg Treaty, which clarified the reparation issue between Israel and West Germany, *Neues Deutschland* spoke of "a deal between West German and Israeli big capitalists." "Reparationen—für wen?," *Neues Deutschland* (November 25, 1952). The unsigned article came out only three days after parts of the Slánsky Trial were published in the same newspaper.

61. Alfred Kantorowicz, *Deutsches Tagebuch II* (Berlin: A. W. Mytze, 1980), 365.

CHAPTER EIGHT

READING "BETWEEN THE LINES"
Daniel Libeskind's Berlin Jewish Museum and the Shattered Symbiosis*

NOAH ISENBERG

Jewish museums in Germany do not just present and reconstruct Jewish history; they are simultaneously exhibits of contemporary history in their own right.

—Cilly Kugelmann

I

During the summer of 1989, just months prior to the collapse of the Berlin Wall, the American architect Daniel Libeskind was awarded first prize in the international design competition for the Berlin Jewish Museum. Initially conceived as a new annex to the Berlin Museum, the building was, in the words of the official guidelines of the competition, "to be devoted above all to a representation of Jewish history as an integral part of the city's history."[1] Of the 165 entries in the competition, Libeskind's design stood out for its unconventional style, its sheer innovation, and, perhaps most significant, its provocative rendering of the aesthetic interplay between Jewish history and the history of Berlin, between shared memories of the past and new ideas for the future. According to James Young, "Libeskind's [design] struck the jury as the most brilliant and complex, possibly as unbuildable."[2] In its final statement, the jury emphatically claimed, "This work is an opportunity and a challenge for Berlin!"[3]

In many respects, Libeskind was the perfect choice for the task. Born in Lodz, Poland, in 1946, the child of Holocaust survivors, he was reared in Israel and educated in the United States and Great Britain. At the time of the competition, he had already accumulated a vast array of international experience, having taught and lectured at over a dozen schools in seven different countries, and he had received numerous prestigious awards. His reputation as an architect, while more as a theoretician than as an actual builder, was steadily growing, so much so that his inclusion in the New York Museum of Modern Art's 1988 "Deconstructivist Architecture" exhibition placed him in the vanguard of contemporary architects. Upon winning the Jewish Museum competition, Libeskind relocated both his architecture studio and his principal residence from Los Angeles—where, until recently, he held a professorship at UCLA's school of architecture—to Germany's new capital (he was one of many "high-visibility outsiders," as Michael Wise calls them, including I. M. Pei, Sir Norman Foster, and others, imported to give Berlin its new face-lift).[4] There he was to pursue what many saw as a signature project, a building that would forever mark his transition from theory to praxis. At the time, he is said to have been issued a visa that stated bluntly: "Mr. Libeskind is admitted to Germany to work on and to *realize* the Jewish Museum project."[5]

Ten years and 120 million Deutsche Mark later, after having overcome a number of tough obstacles including intense resistance by Berlin's notoriously conservative building officials and the dramatic departure of the Museum's initial director, Amnon Barzel (or the "Israeli Rambo," as he was sometimes called in the popular press),[6] Libeskind did finally realize his project. The building currently stands—with its permanent collection now in place—as an independent museum, one that has drawn considerable attention since its initial opening in January 1999. Because the building itself is so remarkable, it was decided that it would be open to the public before the installation of the permanent collection; during its first year alone, over 160,000 people paid to visit the empty museum.[7] Guided tours, offered on a regular basis, proved extremely popular. As one contemporary critic has observed, "School children, students, building and architecture fans, and tourists wander through the zigzagged building . . . through the subterranean passages, narrow hallways and rooms, across bridges and through empty rooms—the so-called 'Voids' . . . and they marvel at the pure architecture."[8] Although the first exhibition did not open until early September 2001 (the final scheduled date, after a series of previous postponements), the building had already made a strong impact. In November 1999, Libeskind was awarded the coveted German Architecture Prize, and his Jewish museum project has been hailed as "the last architectural masterwork in twentieth-century Berlin, and its foremost building for the twenty-first."[9]

Libeskind's design, which he has dubbed "Between the Lines," emerges from four ideas and sources. The first has to do with two lines—German and Jewish—that interact in the project: "One is a straight line, but broken into many fragments; the other is a tortuous line, but continuing infinitely. These two lines develop architecturally and programmatically through a limited but definite dialogue. They also fall apart, become disengaged, and are seen as separated. In this way, they expose a void which runs through this museum and through architecture, a discontinuous void."[10] Libeskind posits the notion of an "invisible matrix or anamnesis of connections" that encompasses the ties between German and Jewish culture. These lines, grafted onto a map of Berlin using coordinates of former addresses of Jewish writers, musicians, artists, and scientists as well as those of their gentile counterparts, are meant to chart "a particular urban and cultural constellation of Universal History." To this Libeskind adds: "Great figures in the drama of Berlin who have acted as bearers of a great hope and anguish are traced into the lineaments of this museum. . . . Tragic premonition (Kleist), sublimated assimilation (Varnhagen), inadequate ideology (Benjamin), mad science (Hoffmann), displaced understanding (Schleiermacher), inaudible music (Schoenberg), last words (Celan): these constitute the critical dimensions which this work as discourse seeks to transgress."[11] The lines of the external design form an "irrational matrix" of zigzags, rifts, and fissures that resemble a compressed or distorted Star of David (one rather sharp-tongued critic in the *tageszeitung* compared it to an "*entgleisten ICE,*" or a derailed bullet train). [12] As his second major source, Libeskind claims Arnold Schoenberg's incomplete opera, "Moses und Aron." Composed during the late 1920s and early 1930s, it is a deep brooding work in which its evocation of loss—the dilemma of giving expression to the inexpressible—is said to have animated Libeskind's use of the void.[13] Then there is the *Gedenkbuch,* a vast inventory of the names of Holocaust victims, from which Libeskind derived further inspiration to infuse his project with the memory of those who perished in the Shoah. And, finally, as the fourth major source, there is Walter Benjamin's *Einbahnstraße,* or *One-Way Street,* of 1928, a suggestive though equally elusive text, the ideas in which have somehow found their way into Libeskind's greater aesthetic concerns.

In the following analysis, I would like to explore the intellectual foundations of Libeskind's work, investigating the ways in which he draws—often playfully and sometimes only superficially—on specific ideas and sources as a means of highlighting his "architecture of memory."[14] With regard to the fateful and ever-recurrent question of symbiosis, I wish to examine the aesthetic commentary (that is, the bearing it has on the symbiosis debate) as evoked in Libeskind's design. Finally, I would like to pose a challenge to Libeskind, to apply pressure to his conception of the museum, thereby pointing not only to its much-praised virtues, but also to some of its seemingly unexpected and unacknowledged shortcomings.

II

Before proceeding to a closer analysis of Libeskind's design, it is instructive to recall, if only briefly, the genesis of the Jewish Museum project. On January 24, 1933, just six days before Hitler was named chancellor of the German Reich, the first incarnation of the Berlin Jewish Museum, housed next to the Oranienburger Straße Synagogue, made its inauspicious debut. In retrospect, the opening, which was attended by such renowned figures from Weimar Germany as the museum's honorary president Max Liebermann, was "the last great Jewish cultural event in the German capital before its collapse."[15] Indeed, under these most unfavorable of circumstances, the museum would run its initial course within a mere five years. Having once been part of the Jewish Community of Berlin, and sponsored by the so-called Society of the Jewish Museum, the collection had already evolved during the first decades of the century (major donations, notably the Judaica holdings of Albert Wolf, were collected, maintained, and housed by the Jewish community's head librarian Moritz Stern, who oversaw the collection from 1917 to 1930). The first director of the Museum, art historian Karl Schwarz, declared the main task of the museum the presentation of "Jewish art and culture as *living* history."[16] As Michael Brenner has aptly pointed out in his book *The Renaissance of Jewish Culture in Weimar Germany,* this meant combining ritual objects, such as Passover Seder plates and menorahs, with more overtly modernist artworks, e.g., paintings by Jakob Steinhardt and Lesser Ury. The question of what constitutes "Jewish" art—beyond the standard defamation of völkisch ideologues who declared it "*undeutsch*" [un-German] and "*entartet*" [degenerate]—was one of the minefields that the Jewish Museum had to negotiate during its earliest years. Opening as it did in 1933, the Jewish Museum seems to have had a set political agenda in mind. As Young has suggested, "It is almost as if the museum had hoped to establish the institutional fact of an inextricably linked German-Jewish culture, each a permutation of the other, as a kind of challenge to the Nazis' assumption of an essential hostility between German and Jewish culture."[17] In other words, one might think of the Jewish Museum, at least in its first incarnation, as a bold attempt to prove, on a concrete and institutional level, the existence of a German-Jewish symbiosis. How else could Berlin's Jewish Museum make its debut on the eve of the Third Reich? As is now well known, such institutionally driven aspirations of symbiosis were put to a halt during the November pogrom of 1938, when the Nazis claimed the Jewish Museum among their numerous conquests.

After the war, and after the Shoah, the campaign for a new Jewish museum did not begin again until the late 1960s, during which time Heinz Galinski, then president of the (West) Berlin Jewish community, declared it a moral imperative to replace the museum that the Nazis had destroyed. According to Robin Ostow, Galinski was the first to insist that "the history of the Jewish people . . . be exhibited in the Berlin Museum."[18] Important to recall is the fact that the Berlin Museum had itself only been reopened in 1969 in the restored baroque Collegienhaus, next to which the result of Daniel Libeskind's design currently stands; it was West Berlin's effort to preserve its urban history after it had lost, due to the city's division in 1961, all ties to East Berlin's Märkisches Museum, the capital's original museum. A mere two years after its opening, in 1971, the Berlin Museum offered a large-scale exhibition titled "Leistung und Schicksal. 300 Jahre Jüdische Gemeinde zu Berlin: 1671–1971" [Achievement and Fate: 300 Years of Jewish Community in Berlin: 1671–1971]. The show, asserts Ostow, was little more than a tribute to famous Jews. And yet it still managed to "generate public discussion around the need for a Jewish museum in (West) Berlin, as part of the Berlin Museum."[19] By 1975, the [West] Berlin Senate had approved the establishment of a Jewish department in the Berlin Museum. The Senate described its rationale—notably consistent with Heinz Galinski's position—for integrating the Jewish department within the Berlin Museum as follows: "close association with the Berlin Museum in the shape of one of its departments protects the Jewish Museum from isolation and conveys an interwoven relationship with the whole Berlin cultural history."[20]

The push toward an integrationist model, or an "integratives Konzept," as Vera Bendt, who was hired as head of the Jewish department in 1979, would call it, was one that brought together Heinz Galinski, as chair of the Society for a Jewish Museum, and a widespread constituency of popular and official support from Berlin. There was, however, also a countermovement, led by a Berlin citizen's initiative called the Friends of the Jewish Museum, that insisted on having a separate building for the museum. The two sides squared off for nearly a half-decade, from 1982 to 1987, but in 1988 compromise was reached when the Berlin Senate voted in favor of what would somewhat confusingly be known as the "Erweiterung Berlin Museum mit der Abteilung Jüdisches Museum" [Extension of the Berlin Museum with the Jewish Museum Department]. In short, the resolution met the demands from both sides: the museum, according to its planners, was to be independent but also integrated into the Berlin Museum. Thus, when the formal announcement of the design competition was made in December 1988, the message that the planners conveyed was one that appealed to both goals. As the director of the Berlin Museum Rolf Bothe and the director of the Jewish Department Vera Bendt together declared: "The history of the Jews of

Berlin is so closely tied up with the history of the city that it is virtually impossible to separate the two; i.e., an autonomous Jewish Museum is necessary but almost inconceivable without the history of Berlin, in the same way as, conversely, a Berlin Museum of urban history would lose all meaning if it did not take its Jewish citizens into consideration."[21] Regardless of the apparent disagreement of the two sides—integration versus autonomy—both seemed to rely on an understanding of German-Jewish history and Berlin-Jewish history, in which the Jewish component is central, fundamental, and inextricable from its German counterpart. Yet, as we will in turn see, Libeskind's museum, first under the directorship of Barzel and now under that of W. Michael Blumenthal, has in fact become an entirely separate building with its own distinct identity.

III

Located at 14 Lindenstraße, in the Kreuzberg section of Berlin, the site of the museum lies amidst the remains of several past eras (see figure 8.1): the Friedrichstadt, the eighteenth-century district where the museum stands, was part of the westward expansion of the city under the first Prussian king, Friedrich Wilhelm I (the adjacent Berlin Museum, designed by Philipp Gerlach and constructed in 1735, reflects the baroque style of the period); then there are the late-nineteenth- and early-twentieth-century workers' and ethnic neighborhoods surrounding it (one can see the *Alexanderplatz,* old tenement houses, as well as gray public housing blocks from the 1960s and 1970s); and, finally, there is the area that once backed up onto the former East Berlin, now the heart of the city.

As architecture critic Herbert Muschamp has remarked, "A zigzag of concrete, steel and zinc, the building appears to reel through time from the Enlightenment to Prussian militarism, German Romanticism, Marxism, Fascism and on into the future."[22] Or, put differently, what Brian Ladd has recently termed the "Ghosts of Berlin," those urban traces that still very much define and even "haunt" the twentieth-century's fifth German capital, circulate within and around the general area of the museum.[23] And as Libeskind himself notes, "The Jewish Museum has a multivalent relation to its context. It acts as a lens magnifying the vectors of history in order to make the continuity of spaces visible."[24]

The exterior of the shiny zinc-clad building bears intersecting fissures that set the structure in kinetic motion (see figure 8.2). Evoking the oblique lines of a fragmented—or, rather, shattered—Star of David, the façade is adorned with more than 1,000 custom-made windows, nearly all of them of a different shape. This image of the dramatic exterior has become the official view of the building and has been widely reproduced as its stock repre-

Figure 8.1: Panorama. Photo courtesy of Bitter + Bredt, Berlin.

sentation.[25] As one winds around the building, it becomes clear that there is no main entrance or exit to the museum. In fact, in order to enter the building, one has to descend a set of stairs, which lead 18 feet below grade and are located within the main entrance to the neighboring Berlin Museum (see figure 8.3).

There is no external connection between the two museums, yet the subterranean passageway forges a latent connection between the old and new, between the history of Berlin and Jewish history in general. Libeskind has forcefully incorporated this layering of history and memory—of their disparate and interlocking strands—into his design. In the very layout of the exhibition floors, there is a suspension of levels that allows individual spaces to rise one over the other.

Libeskind explored a similar line of inquiry in his design for the Felix Nussbaum Museum in Osnabrück, a building that he finished—his first completed project, with its opening in July 1998—during the same time that he was at work on the Jewish museum. In the case of the Nussbaum Museum, which Libeskind has named the "museum without exit," visitors are made to feel that history cannot be escaped. The entrance consists of a single route: a stark steel bridge suspended above a newly unearthed brick

Figure 8.2: Exterior. Photo courtesy of Bitter + Bredt, Berlin.

bridge dating back to the seventeenth century. Crossing it, Libeskind has suggested, is like a journey during which "one feels the vulnerability of all those layers of history."[26] From the pathway, one moves into a labyrinth of contorted walls, winding corridors, and windowless spaces, illuminated only by triangular skylights high above.

Indeed, a number of these same elements—such as the evocation of labyrinthine space, the dramatic passageways, and heavy contrast lighting—can also be found in the Berlin Jewish Museum (see figure 8.4).

Figure 8.3: Entrance Stairwell. Photo courtesy of Bitter + Bredt, Berlin.

Figure 8.4: Intersecting Void. Photo courtesy of Bitter + Bredt, Berlin.

Here the open space, which will presumably serve as exhibition space, interacts with the negative space of the voids as well as with the radiant light cast from the windows above. Exhibition spaces stand alongside spaces that defy exhibition. (One critic has already remarked that "exhibits may feel superfluous" in such a museum, while another has called it a "curator's night-mare."[27]) With regard to the passageways and the voids, the design itself, il-luminated by the light seeping in through the jagged windows, serves as an exhibition in its own right. As Libeskind comments, "The windows are the physical manifestation of a matrix of connections pervading the site. These cuts are the actual topographical lines joining addresses of Germans and Jews immediately around the site and radiating outwards. The windows are the 'writing of the addresses by the walls of the Museum itself.'"[28]

Libeskind's will to inscribe his design with the memory of countless un-knowns ("invisible figures," as he calls them) in addition to that of the more eminent figures (e.g., Celan, Schoenberg, Benjamin, et al.) recalls Israeli sculptor Dani Karavan's 1994 monument to Walter Benjamin.[29] Karavan's work, built of steel and glass and located on a dramatic cliff in the Spanish bordertown of Portbou (where Benjamin committed suicide in September 1940), serves as a monument not only to the eminent German-Jewish writer and critic, but also to all who have similarly perished. As for its structure, it is not markedly different from the voids in Libeskind's Jewish museum de-sign—one must enter into the stark steel walls of the shaft and descend some 85 steps, during which time the concealed void opens to the natural light, glimmers of which one can already see from above. At the end of the pas-sageway, written upon a sheet of glass, are the words of one of Benjamin's fragmented commentaries on memory: "It is more difficult to honor the memory of the nameless than that of the famous. . . . Historical construc-tion is devoted to the memory of the nameless."[30]

In his design for the Jewish Museum, Libeskind "cites" Benjamin's *One-Way Street* in particular, as well as the historical rift that Benjamin's life sym-bolizes. According to Libeskind, "This aspect [i.e., the inspiration of Benjamin's *One-Way Street*] is incorporated into the continuous sequence of sixty sections along the zigzag, each of which represents on the 'Stations of the Star' described in the text of Benjamin's apocalypse of Berlin."[31] In a qua-simystical and portentous reading of Benjamin, Libeskind considers the Ger-man-Jewish critic among the many "deported archangels" who figure prominently in his architectural conception of the new Berlin as "an exem-plary spiritual capital of the 21st century" and a site for "re-membering the future."[32] To be sure, a prescient element of Benjamin's Berlin runs through *One-Way Street*: "Like ultraviolet rays, memory shows to each man in the book of life a script that invisibly and prophetically glosses the text."[33] Libe-skind's appropriation thus maintains a state of in-betweenness, of incomplete translation, of past and future, memory and prophecy. As a work that reflects the ruptured history of Germans and Jews, the Jewish Museum makes Ben-jamin an analog of the larger story. As Jacques Derrida has remarked, re-sponding to Libeskind's design, "I wonder what he [Benjamin] would have

Figure 8.5: Interior Void. Photo courtesy of Bitter + Bredt, Berlin.

thought about your project, remembering that he died during the war, on a border, committing suicide in a very strange situation."[34] Benjamin's life, and in particular his death, becomes an essential stand-in for an entire historical epoch—giving voice to the "nameless" in the case of Karavan's monument and setting the tone of a cultural museum in the case of Libeskind.[35]

Using a similar void to that of Karavan, Libeskind draws viewers into a shaft-like space, putting to a halt any sense of continuity that one might otherwise have. The voids interrupt the flow in such a way as to invite contemplation on the part of the viewer (see figure 8.5).

Libeskind points out that the building itself is shaped around the void, around the "space which nothing can ever fill again," yet it is also a space that viewers temporarily inhabit. As Andreas Huyssen notes, elaborating further on Libeskind's use of the void: "It is both conceptual and literal. And, clearly, it signifies: As void, it signifies absence, the absence of Berlin's Jews, most of whom perished in the Holocaust. As fractured void it signifies history without continuity—the history of Jews in Germany; of German Jews; and therefore also the history of Germany itself, which cannot be thought separate from Jewish history in Germany."[36]

In terms of the connection between Libeskind's design and Schoenberg's incomplete opera, *Moses und Aron,* it is precisely in the realm of the void that the two meet. Schoenberg's work has been termed "a drama of noncommunication," an aesthetic composition that seeks to overcome the gulf between language and music.[37] In a similar vein, Libeskind's design seeks to overcome the gulf between language and architecture. Like Schoenberg, he attempts to express the inexpressible (or, what in the opera is deemed the *Unvorstellbar,* or "unimaginable") in an aesthetic medium. Both wrestle with the biblical proscription against graven images—in Schoenberg's case, images of an inconceivable God and, in the case of Libeskind, the unimaginable horror—each attempting to render the invisible fleetingly palpable.[38] As Moses utters in Schoenberg's opera:

> Inconceivable because invisible;
> because immeasurable;
> because everlasting;
> because eternal;
> because omnipresent;
> because omnipotent.[39]

Libeskind's museum has been praised for its ability to make the inconceivable felt by its viewers. As architect Frank Gehry has noted, referring to the composition of the museum, "Libeskind expressed an emotion with a building, and that is the most difficult thing to do."[40]

At a lecture given in December 1998 at New York's Architectural League, Libeskind spoke of the need to create "functional links" between the viewer and the museum. Accordingly, the visitor can no longer be seen as "passive," but rather must actively engage in constructing the meaning of the space that he or she occupies. "I don't think it's necessary to make a museum only as a container for precious objects," Libeskind has commented elsewhere. "I think people want something which is no longer a dogmatic, didactic and artificial presentation, but an experience, a seamless excitement from the moment they enter until they leave. It has to be not just intellectual, but emotional, and it has to appeal to your senses."[41] The Berlin Jewish Museum seems to operate, as least in part, under this very principle. Consider, for instance, the Holocaust Tower, a massive concrete building offset from the rest of the museum (see figure 8.6).

This space, which is neither heated nor air conditioned, elicits an emotional response on the part of the viewer who enters into the void and thereby feels the radical absence within the stifling concrete walls of the hallowed shell. One might think of the effect of the Holocaust Tower as a form of "prosthetic memory," a sensory experience that serves to remind the viewer of the event that the space seeks to convey, and yet one that is nonetheless artificial.[42] In addition to this final void, there are also the two outdoor gardens, "homes of provocation and contemplation," as one critic has called them,[43] that demand intense interaction between the viewer and the museum: first, the Paul Celan Courtyard named after the renowned German-speaking Jewish poet, which surrounds the viewer with the exterior of the museum; and second, the Garden of Exile and Emigration, alternately referred to as the E. T. A. Hoffmann Garden, which takes the form of 49 hollowed columns, 7 by 7, of which 48 are filled with soil from Berlin and are to symbolize the year of Israel's birth as a national state, and the last, representative of Berlin, filled with soil from Jerusalem.

Because of Libeskind's emphasis on symbolic space—sometimes numerically encoded, other times geographic or philosophical—and the power of revelation, his work has been viewed as seemingly kabbalistic. The "Mystic of Lindenstrasse," as architecture critic Philip Noble has pronounced him, Libeskind has sought to illuminate concealed meaning in various forms. In a sketch from "Between the Lines," a mapping of the star matrix, we observe the mystical dimension. Noble explains it this way: "Rather than belaboring his ideas into life, a pitfall common in experimental architecture, his mystical bent allowed him to let meaning enter quietly into the Jewish Museum."[44] Not all critics have been equally taken with Libeskind's mysticism, which some have interpreted as gratuitous abstraction, pretentious self-indulgence, little more than conceptual folly.

And yet the most notable opposition that Libeskind's museum has come up against since the building's opening has not been in reaction to its architect's putative mysticism, but rather to the difficulty of filling a museum— that is, with art and cultural objects—when it is already so full of meaning. As *New York Times* Berlin bureau chief Roger Cohen has noted, "the build-

Figure 8.6: The Holocaust Tower. Photo courtesy of Bitter + Bredt, Berlin.

ing amounts to such an overpowering architectural sculpture that the biggest problem may prove to be ensuring that exhibits, when they are installed, are not crushed by the power of the rooms they fill."[45] No doubt the exhibition space will be marked by the uniqueness of the building itself, but this need not necessarily detract from the meaning of what is on display. Of more immediate concern is the problem of complementing the already dominant narrative of the museum with the narrative of the exhibition. The Museum's current director, W. Michael Blumenthal, has described his aims in a way that may, regrettably, not be altogether consonant with Libeskind's design: "I do not want young Germans to view Jews solely as victims. . . . I want to show that their own history was linked to a flowering Jewish intellectual, professional and cultural presence for many years."[46] Blumenthal makes no secret of his hopes for the depiction of a kind of "Golden Age" of German-Jewish history, or what he has referred to elsewhere as "the German-Jewish symbiotic relationship."[47] As Blumenthal recently commented in his director's column of the May 2000 Jewish Museum newsletter: "It is our duty to remind our fellow citizens of the creative people Jews were, people who played a decisive role in shaping and defining our culture. The diversity of Jewish life in Germany will find its expression in the permanent exhibition."[48] Granted, Libeskind's design is not presented merely as a memorial to Jewish victims—to be sure, he is adamant about not wanting it to be mistaken for such—but the shadows of the Holocaust loom large, very large, throughout. Indeed, some politicians have begun to wonder, with Libeskind's museum now standing, what need there will be for building the much-disputed Holocaust Memorial (Libeskind was one of four finalists for that project, which will now reportedly be undertaken by American architect Peter Eisenman, one of Libeskind's former mentors but with whom he has since parted ways).[49]

Although I do not wish to rehearse the terms of the debate over the Holocaust Memorial,[50] I think it is fair to say that Libeskind's design of the Jewish Museum does in fact offer a place for contemplation and reflection, yet without being built specifically for the purpose of memorialization. While the museum alludes to the flowering of German-Jewish culture—or what some have chosen to pronounce the German-Jewish symbiosis—the dreams of that era are represented as shattered, fragmented, and in disjointed pieces in Libeskind's design. As we might recall from his programmatic statement in "Between the Lines," the German and Jewish lines of Libeskind's design "fall apart, become disengaged, and are seen as separated."[51] Libeskind has been heralded for undercutting traditional narratives of German-Jewish history, disrupting such conceptions with his series of voids that define the museum's profoundly vertiginous character. This may indeed be a grand accomplishment. Yet, in my view, he has also replaced one narrative (the narrative of German-Jewish symbiosis) with yet another (a type of "master narrative"—or, rather, his very own personal rendition—of the Shoah).[52] Perhaps, then, his design is at odds with the task at hand for the curators of the museum. And perhaps, too, it defies what the organizers of the original competition had in mind. I certainly do not see Libeskind's museum as "devoted above all to a representation of Jewish history as an integral part of the city's history" (as the official guidelines had emphasized), unless of course

Jewish history can be reduced to the Holocaust.[53] This leads me to a final concern, one that I would like to address at some length before I offer a few concluding remarks.

IV

Earlier in my discussion, I suggested that Libeskind might be viewed as "the perfect choice" for the task of designing Berlin's Jewish Museum. There are, however, obvious risks in making such an assertion. As one critic has declared, relying quite unabashedly on misguided notions of ethnic essentialism, "This is the building Daniel Libeskind was born to build."[54] And Libeskind himself has similarly viewed the project as part of his personal history. "[It] is my biography," he told a reporter from the *Jerusalem Post,* "I was lucky to build it."[55] The problem with this is that the building may actually have much more to say about Libeskind than it does about the history of German Jewry. As his so-called signature project, the Jewish Museum has been inscribed with Libeskind's personal identity. The Holocaust narrative, very much a part of his own autobiography, thus overshadows the narrative of German-Jewish cultural history, that is, the supposed underlying narrative of the museum. Much like the position that Daniel Jonah Goldhagen assumed in Germany,[56] Libeskind's stance in relation to his predominantly non-Jewish audience is that of the "authentic" Jew who communicates in the voice of a child of Holocaust survivors. "I've been pursuing ideas that relate to the catastrophe of the twentieth century for a long time," he commented in 1998, at the same time that he was busy completing the Berlin Jewish Museum project, "and the Holocaust is not just an incidental topic to my interests as an architect and a human being."[57]

With such an acute awareness of the Shoah as a key component of his critical and aesthetic reflexes, it should come as no surprise that Libeskind's design for the Jewish Museum is centered around this event. "From the entrance," he explains, "one is faced with three roads: the road leading to the Holocaust tower which. . . . has no entrance except from the underground level; the road leading to the garden [of exile and emigration]; and the road leading to the main circulation stair and the void. The entire plane of the museum is tilted toward the void of the superstructure. The building is as complex as the history of Berlin."[58] Yet, while the building is arguably as complex as any representation of the Holocaust, or any representation of absence, might be, it nonetheless does not reflect equally well the complexity of Berlin's expansive history—which certainly is not comprised merely of absences and voids. Just as Libeskind claims that "the museum is tilted toward the void," so too is the museum's narrative tilted toward the Holocaust. "The Jewish Museum building is interesting," asserts the historian Julius Schoeps, "but it's a Holocaust sculpture, not a museum."[59] Schoeps maintains that the building is in essence "an American museum," and as such risks perpetuating what he scornfully calls "a Disneyland aesthetic."[60]

Schoeps's critical remarks on the American nature of the museum emerge from a contemporary historical context in which Jews living in Germany, or German Jews (as they are increasingly calling themselves once again), have begun to resent the shameless importation of American Jews—and American Jewish institutions—to assist the Germans (and, by extension, German Jews) in dealing with their past. This phenomenon, recently addressed in the Berlin-based Jewish newspaper, *Allgemeine Jüdische Wochenzeitung,* in a polemic titled "Der Onkel aus Amerika" [The Uncle from America],[61] is one that allows American Jews to feel righteous about their cause, German gentiles to sense relief at having "authentic" envoys to aid them in working through their past, and German Jews to remain by and large on the sidelines. With specific regard to the choice of Libeskind as architect of the Jewish Museum, it makes it practically impossible to criticize his design without risking being branded an antisemite—unless of course, like Schoeps, one is a Jew. An additional case in point is the Jewish critic and perennial *enfant terrible* of the German press, Henryk Broder, who has boldly asserted, with his trademark mordant sarcasm: "The Jews know that the museum is a crazy piece of junk [*megalomanischer Schrott*] meant to lighten the wounded souls of non-Jews, but they don't want to spoil the fun for the Germans who financed the whole thing."[62] For Broder, the Libeskind design, which he refers to elsewhere as "House of Nonsense," is a classic example of blind Jewish fetishism among Germans. Raising the tenor of debate still further, the cultural editor of Berlin's *Tagesspiegel,* Thomas Lackmann, has maintained in his book-length critique of the Jewish Museum (part satire, part polemic, part taboo), *Jewrassic Park,* that the entire Libeskind project thrived on Germany's climate of philosemitism. According to Lackmann, one of Libeskind's most effective means of garnering support was to operate under the motto: "All Germans are antisemites. Just not those who endorse my building plans."[63] For Lackmann, it is not only a matter of Jewish fetishism, but also of Holocaust manipulation.

German debates on the Holocaust have long involved American (Jewish) representatives, and, especially during the past decades the Americanized discourse on the Holocaust has left a notable impact on the German discourse.[64] Yet just when the question of a particular American instrumentalization of the Holocaust has come under intense scrutiny,[65] Germany still shows great eagerness to have American (Jewish) artists and architects, scholars and intellectuals guide them in their ongoing project to remember the Holocaust. In this regard, Libeskind has clearly benefited from the privileged status of Holocaust consciousness in today's Germany. Indeed, the fact that he conceived his museum design in such an unmistakable Holocaust vernacular must be duly recognized.

Paradoxically, Libeskind's biases recall, in an indirect way, some of the concerns faced by the Museum's planners in its first phase of existence in the 1930s. During the early decades of the twentieth century, German Jews managed to make their mark in nearly all branches of Berlin life: science, literature, politics, commerce, and the arts. Indeed, these were the much-celebrated (and vilified) years of the cosmopolitan city, now memorialized and preserved in scholarly and popular literature as well as in recent museum exhibitions.[66] Although Jews in the public sphere often acted largely as Germans, there was a growing fear of Jewish "over representation" (sometimes described as *Verjudung,* or "Jewification") "in the professions, in the media, in the intelligentsia."[67] The concurrent goal of symbiosis, however, tended to preclude any form of separatism or ethnic/religious exclusivity.[68] Thus, when the Jewish Museum opened in 1933, there was opposition among Jews who saw it as a deep blow to German-Jewish assimilation. As one detractor argued, establishing an autonomous "Jewish" museum "leads to a split, which is totally undesirable and from an academic point of view in no way justifiable. [Max] Liebermann, for example, is a European. He is a German, a Berlin artist. The fact that he belongs to a Jewish family is totally irrelevant with regards to the form and essence of his art."[69] To extract "Jewish" art from its German context, so the argument went, was to strip it of its universal appeal and reduce it to ethnic categorization by housing it in the Jewish Museum. By making today's Jewish Museum a Holocaust museum, or at least a museum that is fundamentally shaped around that event, Libeskind's design exacerbates that problem by favoring one chapter—admittedly, a very profound one—over the larger, more complex sweep of modern German-Jewish history.

What Libeskind has created in the Berlin Jewish Museum is visually and rhetorically different from its German *Collegienhaus* counterpart.[70] The interaction between the two histories and cultures remains subterranean, shattered, incomplete. One might argue that Libeskind's design represents a kind of aesthetic response to Dan Diner's notion of "negative symbiosis," if, as Diner claims, "the aftermath of mass murder has been the starting point for self-understanding [among German and Jews]."[71] But even there, the German side of this equation seems to be reduced to its Nazi past, just as the Jewish side is to the Holocaust, and little more. (The references, in Libeskind's design, to E. T. A. Hoffmann and other non-Jewish Germans appear merely ornamental, even token.) In his analysis of the museum, James Young has pointed to a "final historical irony" that the Libeskind building illustrates, now that it dwarfs the neighboring Berlin Museum; the Jewish Museum has over 80,000 square feet of exhibition space and another 43,000 square feet of "storage, office, and auditorium spaces," while the Berlin Museum has a mere 27,000 square feet of exhibition space. "Where the city planners had hoped to return Jewish memory to the house of Berlin history," writes Young, "it now seems certain that Berlin history will have to find its place in the larger haunted house of Jewish memory. The Jewish wing of the Berlin Museum will now be the prism through which the rest of the world will come to know Berlin's past."[72] A "prism" colored so dramatically by the Shoah, as I believe it to be, can hardly be an effective, let alone accurate, way for Berlin's history to be presented to the world. On this count, Libeskind's spectacular design of the Berlin Jewish Museum ultimately fails to deliver.

Notes

* Earlier versions of this essay were presented, in Fall 1999 and Spring 2000, at Indiana University, Harvard University, Dartmouth College, and the University of Minnesota. I would like to thank, in that same order: Michael Morgan; Bernd Widdig; Susannah Heschel and Gerd Gemünden; as well as Leslie Morris and Jack Zipes for their generous invitations. I have benefited immeasurably from the critical feedback received during those presentations.

1. Bernhard Schneider, *Daniel Libeskind: Jewish Museum of Berlin. Between the Lines* (Munich: Prestel, 1999), 19.
2. James E. Young, *At Memory's Edge: After-Images of the Holocaust in Contemporary Art and Architecture* (New Haven: Yale University Press, 2000), 163.
3. Cited in Schneider, *Daniel Libeskind*, 19.
4. See Michael Z. Wise, *Capital Dilemma: Germany's Search for a New Architecture of Democracy* (New York: Princeton Architectural Press, 1998), 156.
5. Cited in Andrew Patner, "Filling a Void," *Madison* (July-Aug. 1999): 103, emphasis added.
6. Cf. "Ein Zerwürfnis, kaum zu heilen; Der Streit um das Berliner Jüdische Museum," *Neue Züricher Zeitung* (October 17, 1997): 45.
7. These figures are provided in the official publication, *Jewish Museum Berlin* (May 2000): 3.
8. Rolf Lautenschäger, "Jüdisches Museum kommt jetzt in Etappen," *die tageszeitung* (April 8,1999): 19.
9. Schneider, *Daniel Libeskind*, 58.
10. Daniel Libeskind, "Between the Lines," *radix-matrix* (Munich: Prestel, 1997), 34.
11. Rolf Bothe and Vera Bendt, *Realisierungs Wettbewerb: Erweiterung Berlin Museum mit Abteilung Jüdisches Museum* (Berlin: Senatsverwaltung für Bau- und Wohnungswesen, 1990), 169. Cited in Young, *At Memory's Edge*, 167.
12. Ulrich Clewing, "Linien der Zerstörung," *die tageszeitung* (February 1, 1999): 15.
13. Philip Noble, "The Mystic of Lindenstrasse," *Metropolis* (January 1999): 79.

14. See Andreas Huyssen, "The Voids of Berlin," *Critical Inquiry* 24 (Autumn 1997): 57–81, esp. 72–81; and also my brief profile, "Scaling Daniel Libeskind's 'Architecture of Memory,'" *Forward* (January 1, 1999): 11–12.

15. Veronika Bendt, "Das Jüdische Museum: Eine Abteilung des Berlin Museums," *Berliner Forum* (June 1986): 8. See also her contribution (as "Vera" Bendt) "Das Jüdische Museum," *Wegweiser durch das jüdische Berlin* (Berlin: Nicolai, 1987): 200–209, as well as the more recent and more thorough volume by Martina Weinland and Kurt Winkler, *Das Jüdische Museum im Stadtmuseum Berlin* (Berlin: Nicolai, 1997). See also Michael Brenner's discussion in *The Renaissance of Jewish Culture in Weimar Germany* (New Haven: Yale University Press, 1996), 177–81; and James Young's account in *At Memory's Edge,* 155–62.

16. Cited in Brenner, *The Renaissance of Jewish Culture in Weimar Germany,* 179; emphasis in original.

17. Young, *At Memory's Edge,* 156.

18. See Robin Ostow, "(Re)Building German-Jewish History as a Museum: The Moral and National Division of Labour, or Seven Models of Jewish Cultural Integration in Germany," unpublished manuscript. I am indebted to Ostow for sharing with me her insightful analysis of the museum.

19. Ostow, "(Re)Building German-Jewish History as a Museum, 2.

20. Weinland and Winkler, 17, *Das Jüdische Museum;* cited in Young, *At Memory's Edge,* 161.

21. Rolf Bothe and Vera Bendt, "Ein eigenständiges Jüdisches Museum," in *Realisierungs Wettbewerb,* 159; cited in Young, *At Memory's Edge,* 162.

22. Herbert Muschamp, "Once Again, a City Rewards the Walker," *New York Times* (April 11, 1999): 39.

23. See Brian Ladd, *The Ghosts of Berlin: Confronting German History in the Urban Landscape* (Chicago: University of Chicago Press, 1997).

24. Cited in Schneider, *Daniel Libeskind,* 27.

25. It is printed on the cover of the museum's brochure and newsletter; it is a page in the 2000 calendar, distributed by the Press and Information Office of the Federal Government of Germany; and it is the image that is printed on postcards of the museum.

26. Cited in my "Scaling Daniel Libeskind's 'Architecture of Memory,'" 11.

27. See Ralph Rugoff, "Cathedrals for our Times," *Financial Times* (April 24, 1999): 6; and John Czaplicka, "Resonanzen in der Leere," *Berliner Zeitung* (January 23, 1999).

28. Cited in Schneider, *Daniel Libeskind,* 27.

29. For further discussion of Karavan's monument, see Noah Isenberg, *Between Redemption and Doom: The Strains of German-Jewish Modernism* (Lincoln: University of Nebraska Press, 1999), 139–45.

30. Walter Benjamin, *Gesammelte Schriften,* vol. 1.3, ed. Rolf Tiedemann and Hermann Schweppenhäuser (Frankfurt am Main: Suhrkamp, 1974), 1241. "Schwerer ist es, das Gedächtnis der Namenlosen zu ehren als das der Berühmten. . . . Dem Gedächstnis der Namenlosen ist die historische Konstruktion geweiht."

31. Libeskind, "Between the Lines," *radix-matrix,* 34.
32. Libeskind, "Out of Line, Berlin," *radix-matrix,* 26.
33. Walter Benjamin, *One-Way Street,* trans. Edmund Jephcott, *Selected Writings, Volume 1: 1913–1926,* ed. Marcus Bullock and Michael W. Jennings (Cambridge: Harvard University Press, 1996), 483.
34. Jacques Derrida, "Response to Daniel Libeskind," *radix-matrix,* 112. It is perhaps worth noting that Benjamin's life and work have themselves served as subject of at least one museum exhibition (December 28, 1990 to April 28, 1991, at the Martin-Gropius-Bau, Berlin). See the exhibition catalog *Bucklicht Männlein und Engel der Geschichte: Walter Benjamin, Theoretiker der Moderne,* ed. Werkbund-Archiv (Giessen: Annabas, 1990).
35. On the larger problem concerning the "uses" of Walter Benjamin, and the still-growing "Benjamin industry," see Noah Isenberg, "The Work of Walter Benjamin in the Age of Information," *New German Critique* 83 (Spring-Summer 2001, forthcoming).
36. Huyssen, "The Voids of Berlin," 78–79.
37. George Steiner, "Schoenberg's *Moses and Aron,*" *Language and Silence* (New York: Atheneum, 1986), 132.
38. Commenting on the significance of the biblical commandment in Schoenberg's work, Theodor W. Adorno has remarked, "this feature [i.e., the *Bilderverbot*] characterizes the idiom in which every one of Schoenberg's musical ideas is conceived." See Adorno, "Arnold Schoenberg, 1874–1951," *Prisms,* trans. Samuel and Shierry Weber (Cambridge, MA: MIT Press, 1981), 162. See also Charles Rosen, *Arnold Schoenberg* (Chicago: University of Chicago Press, 1996).
39. Cited in Steiner, "Schonberg's *Moses and Aron,*" 135.
40. Cited in Noble, "The Mystic of Lindenstrasse," 83.
41. Cited in Rugoff, "Cathedrals for our Times," 6.
42. On the concept of "prosthetic memory," see Alison Landsberg, "America, the Holocaust, and Mass Culture of Memory: Toward a Radical Politics of Empathy," *New German Critique* 71 (Spring-Summer 1997): 63–86, here 66. I am grateful to Lutz Koepnick for calling my attention to this idea in relation to Libeskind's design.
43. Patner, "Filling a Void," 104.
44. Noble, 85. Tour guides of the Berlin Jewish Museum are quick to give fanciful quasikabbalistic, numerological explanations of Libeskind's symbolic architecture. The one who guided a tour of the Fulbright German Studies Summer Seminar in June 2000, at which I happen to have been present, spoke passionately, if unconvincingly, about the 18 steps of the staircases representing "Chai" or life. He pointed out that Libeskind has 7 flights of stairs, each with 18 steps, and together they derive from an allegedly deep understanding of Jewish mysticism on the part of Libeskind.
45. Roger Cohen, "Fresh Perspectives on Past and Present," *New York Times* (March 14, 1999): E8.
46. Cited in Cohen, "Fresh Perspectives." See also W. Michael Blumenthal, "Streit um die Erinnerung," *Frankfurter Allgemeine Zeitung* (October 9,

1999): BS 2. Blumenthal had been working together with the former director of Washington's Holocaust Museum, Shaike Weinberg, to prepare for the official debut—unfortunately, however, on New Year's Day 2000, Weinberg passed away in a Tel Aviv hospital. See Michael S. Cullen, "Der Ausstellungsphilosoph," *Frankfurter Allgemeine Zeitung* (January 6, 2000): BS3. In the time since Weinberg's death, New Zealander anthropologist and museum curator Kenneth Gorbey, whose credits include the Te Papa Museum in Wellington (a high-tech "Event Park"—where, according to its Web site [www.tepapa.govt.nz], "dinosaurs roar into life"—devoted to the history of the Maori), has been named project director. He and his colleague Nigel Cox, also a New Zealander, were thus made responsible for picking up where Weinberg and the former deputy director, Tom Freudenheim, who departed (on less than ideal terms) from the museum in summer 2000, had left off. The rest remains a mystery.

47. Cited in the description of the museum in the 2000 calendar distributed by the Press and Information Office of the Federal Government.

48. W. Michael Blumenthal, "Greetings," *Jewish Museum Berlin* (May 2000): 3. See also his more extensive remarks on German-Jewish cultural ties in his "family" chronicle, *The Invisible Wall: Germans and Jews* (Washington, DC: Counterpoint, 1998), as well as my review, "Before Kristallnacht," *The Nation* (October 19, 1998): 34–35.

49. With the recent discussion of adding special rooms devoted to the documentation of the Holocaust, which according to Blumenthal will have the character of a memorial site [*Gedenkstätte*], there is renewed skepticism about the Holocaust component. Sibylle Quack, a member of the Holocaust Memorial Commission, has expressed her concern that the Jewish Museum not stand "in competition" to the Holocaust Memorial. See Rolf Lautenschläger, "Leerstelle füllt sich wieder," *die tageszeitung* (June 15, 2000): 19.

50. For a more thorough account of the debate, see Michael S. Cullen, ed., *Das Holocaust-Mahnmal: Dokumentation einer Debatte* (Zurich: Pendo, 1999).

51. Libeskind, "Between the Lines," 34.

52. Ironically, Libeskind calls the spaces of the Museum "open narratives." See Young, *At Memory's Edge*, 175.

53. Robin Ostow makes a similar point in her discussion of Libeskind's design. See Ostow, "(Re)Building German-Jewish History," 5.

54. See Jonathan Glancy, "The Hole in the Heart," *The Guardian* (January 27, 1999): 14. Architecture professor Don Hanlon (University of Wisconsin) has instead suggested that Libeskind's design be viewed as part of his architectural biography, i.e., as part of his professional trajectory from his training until now, and not as part of his personal background. (E-mail communication, 14 April 2000.)

55. See Jeff Barak, "Berlin's Jewish Museum," *The Jerusalem Post* (July 9, 1998): 28.

56. On the Goldhagen debate in Germany, see Robert R. Shandley, ed., *Unwilling Germans? The Goldhagen Debate,* trans. Jeremiah Riemer (Minneapolis: University of Minnesota Press, 1998).

57. Cited in Michael Wise, "Daniel Libeskind," *Art News* (November 1998): 135. In a presentation given to the Fulbright German Studies Summer Seminar, held at Humboldt University on June 20, 2000, Libeskind's wife and partner Nina Libeskind suggested that the Holocaust narrative was the most important component of the Jewish Museum project.

58. Daniel Libeskind, "1995 Raoul Wallenberg Lecture," cited in Young, *At Memory's Edge,* 174.

59. Cited in Roger Cohen, "A Jewish Museum Struggles to Be Born," *New York Times* (August 15, 2000): B3. Schoeps expressed a very similar sentiment in a personal exchange with me on June 22, 2000 at the Moses Mendelssohn Center, the institute for Jewish studies he directs, in Potsdam. As he put it, "it's not a museum, it's a Holocaust monument."

60. Other observers have pointed to a "haunted house" effect of Libeskind's design, an eerie sensation that the Holocaust tower, together with the monumental voids and sharp angles, tends to evoke. As theater critic Robert Brustein recently put it, "[the museum] tries to recreate the monstrous oppression of the camps by means of a skewed series of metallic corridors resembling those in *The Cabinet of Doctor Caligari.*" See Rober Brustein, "A Berlin Diary," *The New Republic* (July 24, 2000): 30.

61. Leibl Rosenberg, "Der Onkel aus Amerika: Eine Polemik gegen die Einmischung von US-Organisationen in deutschjüdische Angelegenheiten," *Allgemeine Jüdische Wochenzeitung* (May 25, 2000): 1.

62. Henryk M. Broder, "Nun weiter im Pogrom . . ." (article posted on his Web site: www.henryk-broder.de). See also his printed essay on the museum, "Kirche ohne Fenster," *Der Spiegel* (August 7, 2000).

63. Thomas Lackmann, *Jewrassic Park: Wie baut man (k)ein Jüdisches Museum in Berlin* (Berlin: Philo, 2000) 148.

64. See, for example, James Young's chapter on his involvement in the planning of the Berlin Holocaust Memorial, "Germany's Holocaust Memorial Problem—and Mine," in *At Memory's Edge,* 184–223. See also Jacob Heilbrunn, "Deutsche gegen Deutsche: Schluss mit den Stellvertreterdebatten," *Süddeutsche Zeitung* (August 26, 2000).

65. See Peter Novick, *The Holocaust in American Life* (Boston: Houghton Mifflin, 1999); Hilene Flanzbaum, ed., *The Americanization of the Holocaust* (Baltimore: Johns Hopkins University Press, 1999); Tim Cole, *Selling the Holocaust: From Auschwitz to Schindler, How History is Bought, Packaged and Sold* (New York: Routledge, 1999); and, most recently, Norman G. Finkelstein, *The Holocaust Industry: Reflections on the Exploitation of Jewish Suffering* (London: Verso, 2000).

66. See the recent exhibition catalog edited by Emily D. Bilski, *Berlin Metropolis: Jews and the New Culture, 1890–1918* (Berkeley: University of California Press, 1999). See also Paul Mendes-Flohr's essay contained in the same volume, "The Berlin Jew as Cosmopolitan" (14–31), as well as his book-length study, *German Jews: A Dual Identity* (New Haven: Yale University Press, 1999).

67. See Omer Bartov, "'Seit die Juden weg sind . . . ': Germany, History, and Representations of Absence," *A User's Guide to German Cultural Studies,* ed. Scott Denham et al., (Ann Arbor: University of Michigan Press, 1997) 209–26.

68. See Robert S. Wistrich, "Fateful Trap: The German-Jewish Symbiosis," *Tikkun* 5.2 (March-April 1990): 34–38.

69. Weinland and Winkler, *Das Jüdische Museum,* 10; cited in Young, *At Memory's Edge,* 157.

70. In the meantime, i.e., since W. Michael Blumenthal assumed the directorship of the Jewish Museum, the neighboring Berlin Museum (housed in the Collegienhaus) has been annexed by the Jewish Museum. The rooms there will be used for administrative offices, archives, and rotating exhibitions.

71. Dan Diner, "Negative Symbiose: Deutsche und Juden nach Auschwitz," *Babylon* 1 (1986): 9–20. See also my epilogue, "Beyond Symbiosis," in Isenberg, *Between Redemption and Doom,* 147–50.

72. Young, *At Memory's Edge,* 183.

Cultural Relations

CHAPTER NINE

THE CRITICAL EMBRACEMENT
OF GERMANY

Hans Mayer and Marcel Reich-Ranicki

JACK ZIPES

While it is more common to talk about a symbiosis (negative and positive), a rift, a rupture, or a trauma when examining relations between Germans and Jews since 1945, I want to address another aspect of the relationship by discussing how certain German-Jewish intellectuals returned to and critically embraced Germany after 1945 and, in the process, stamped postwar German culture in unusual ways.[1] Therefore, it is impossible to talk about Germans without talking about their relationship to Jews, and it is impossible to conceive of postwar German culture without a Jewish presence, even though many critics, Christian and Jewish, have denied and would like to continue denying or to repress this presence. In fact, if one wanted to be extremely provocative, one could argue that older German Jews of the prewar generations set the framework or parameters of crucial intellectual discussions about German culture following World War II. This influence was true even in the former East Germany, as it was definitely true in the West, and I want to discuss the memoirs and works of two notable male intellectuals, Hans Mayer and Marcel Reich-Ranicki, formidable Jewish critics in the cultural scene of Germany, to explore a paradox: both Mayer and Reich-Ranicki resist the label of German, and yet, they have done more than most German critics to reestablish the German humanistic tradition of literature in the postwar period, as well as the German-Jewish tradition of provocative criticism forged earlier in the century by Alfred Kerr, Alfred Polgar, Kurt Tucholksy, and others, more, that is, than any German critic of their generation or younger generations. In fact, the development of German literary criticism and literature in Germany from 1945 to 2000 is unthinkable without considering the contributions of Hans Mayer and Marcel Reich-Ranicki.

Why choose only Mayer and Reich-Ranicki to talk about how Jews of the returning generation set the groundwork for debates and concerns of German culture in the postwar years? Wouldn't it be more appropriate to analyze the immense influence of the Frankfurt School, especially the work of Theodor Adorno and Max Horkheimer? What about Ernst Bloch's effect on philosophy and politics, or even the controversial sociologist Alphons Silbermann? There are, in fact, a number of returning Jews to East and West Germany who had an influence on postwar German culture that was out of proportion to their numbers. In this regard, I believe that a more thorough social history of these returning émigrés and their influence in Germany is long overdue. I have chosen Mayer and Reich-Ranicki as short case histories because they have reached out successfully if not provocatively to the German public in the domain of literature, a domain that they have indelibly stamped with their modes of criticism and intense mission to recuperate the humanistic tradition of German culture. Though they—Mayer more than Reich-Ranicki—are often mentioned or used by Germanists in scholarly studies, their influence in academic circles is not crucial to their fame and significance, which barely extends over German borders and borders of Germanistik—another factor that demonstrates how germane and particular they are to German culture.[2] This may be due to the fact that they are not theoreticians but provocative and superb essayists with great formats that make them accessible to a larger educated reading public than just students and professors. Mayer is the more astute and original thinker with strong connections to the Frankfurt School, Bloch, and Marxist thought,[3] whereas Reich-Ranicki is a perceptive and frank if not opinionated commentator who has a vast knowledge of contemporary literature and a comprehensive understanding of the development of German literature since the Enlightenment.[4] Both have an uncanny sense for addressing problematic aspects of German literature and culture. Both have been active radio and television critics and even teamed together to develop one of the most popular radio talk shows about literature in the 1960s. They have often appeared on television, and Reich-Ranicki created the controversial *Literary Quartet* in 1988, a show that featured and still features Reich-Ranicki as the literary pope of Germany. Yet, with all their success, they remain skeptical about the role Jews can play in German culture and adamant about rejecting Germanness as part of their identity. This becomes evident in reading their memoirs and criticism that are concerned specifically with Germans and Jews, and I want to deal with these works by examining how Mayer and Reich-Ranicki personally engaged themselves, body and soul, in the postwar years to outdo or out-German Christian Germans and to become the major spokesmen for German literature in the public domain.

꽃　　꽃　　꽃　　꽃　　꽃

Mayer, born in Cologne in 1907, has written two large volumes about his life that he has entitled *Ein Deutscher auf Widerruf: Erinnerungen,* published in 1982 and 1984. The title itself is meant to provoke: "A Revocable German," or "A German to be Revoked" are two possible translations. The term *"auf Widerruf"* is generally a phrase linked with *"bis,"* that is *"bis auf Wider-ruf,"* meaning "until revoked." But Mayer leaves out the "bis," insisting on remaining "revocable," and his memoirs are calculated to address the necessity for his refusal to revoke the revocable situation. In fact, he wants his readers to grasp his two volumes not as an autobiography but as memoirs or remembrances about conditions that brought about his revocability and the revocability of many other Europeans who resisted the spread of fascism and communism. "Memoirs are a literary genre. One has to be clear about what they are to contain, whether they are pleasant or agonizing or not. Whoever does not consider this will fail because of the literary aspect. I had warning images as I began thinking about the idea to write a book with the title 'A Revocable German.'"[5]

These warning images were transformed by Mayer into an elegant and disturbing social history about the trials and tribulations of a secular Jewish intellectual whose devotion to German culture and to changing the world as a committed socialist led to the revocation of his German citizenship in 1938 and, in some sense, part of his identity. Mayer is forever the teacher, and he writes his memoirs to forge a social and political history of his times. He is indeed the key player in this history, but he is less concerned to write about his personal anxieties, desires, and conflicts than he is to situate himself against the shattering events that effected millions of people, particularly German Jews, and to explore why these events occurred. His books are, however, not books about the Holocaust or Holocaust books. Rather, they seek to explain how a single individual, destined to lead a particular privileged life as a secularized if not assimilated German Jew, was compelled to respond to forces that transformed him into an outsider who insists on being marginalized even if he is successful in contemporary Germany. Thus, the warning images become a warning to German readers, as images rooted in history.

Mayer selects the memories of his life to warn of, to remind himself why he wants to warn, and to understand what he calls the failure of the Enlightenment, very much in the tradition of Adorno and Horkheimer. Mayer sketches his early years as an only child in a wealthy German-Jewish environment in which he learned about expressionist art in his own house, became an expert piano player, and succeeded in his studies at the gymnasium. All the while, he recalls that the Jews of Cologne lived separately behind invisible ghetto walls even though the borders between Jews and Christians were fluid. In 1925 he began studying law at the University of Cologne, but his commitment to his studies was not very strong, and though he attended classes in Cologne and later in Berlin, he was more interested in the changing political and cultural events that were rocking Weimar Germany. Ernst Bloch's early writings on utopia, Kurt Tucholsky and the *Weltbühne,* and Georg Lukács's *Geschichte und Klassenbewußtsein* played an enormous role in his private education and drew him to critical thinking. By the winter semester of 1927 to 1928, he became heavily involved in a Marxist student group directed by Communist Party members. Indeed, Mayer states bluntly that the first evening with this group changed his life (*Ein Deutscher,* I, 98), for now he began to study Marx and Engels, dialectical materialism, and Hegel. By late 1928 he moved away from the Communists to join an independent socialist group, and he also made a major break with his family and led what he calls a double life: on the one hand, he was the member of a respectable middle-class Jewish family and, on the other, he was an active socialist who helped found a newspaper called *Der Rote Kämpfer* and joined a small political group that broke away from the Socialist Democratic Party in 1930. What is astonishing during this time up to 1933 is that Mayer was able to complete his law examinations, write a Ph.D. dissertation, and immerse himself in cultural and political activities in Cologne and Berlin. In the summer of 1933, however, he had to flee Berlin to escape arrest by the Nazis. His first destination was Strasbourg, then Paris, and finally Geneva, where he spent most of his forced exile years until 1945.

Mayer's memoirs move back and forth between the present (the early 1980s) and the past, and he is intent on providing background material for his readers about the people he meets and the living conditions of the times. Therefore, the second part of the first volume of his book presents a fascinating picture of the lives of political refugees in Paris and Switzerland from 1933 to the end of the war. There are accounts of illegal activities, the common front, research for the Institute for Social Research, and detailed depictions of such figures as Max Horkheimer, Carl Burckhardt, Georges Bataille, Robert Musil, Michael Teschno, and the communist group *Freies Deutschland.* Aside from writing political pieces for Swiss newspapers and doing hard labor in internment camps for German refugees, Mayer completed a major political and literary study of Georg Büchner, which was later to count as his *Habilitationsschrift* upon his appointment as professor for national literature at the University of Leipzig in 1948.

Immediately after the termination of the war, Mayer wanted to return to Germany and help rebuild a free Germany based on a socialist-planned economy and democratic civil rights. Since he had become very close to the communists in the Freies Deutschland movement in Switzerland, he decided to apply for membership in the Communist Party, but his membership was never approved because nobody could become a party member if he or she was working with an illegal group in a foreign country like Switzerland. Moreover, the Communists preferred that Mayer did not become an open member of the party so that he could work for them without being directly connected to the Communist Party and thus perhaps stigmatized.

Ironically, the Americans sent for him and brought him to Wiesbaden to work for the German-American press agency [Deutsch-Amerikanische Nachrichten Agentur] in October of 1945 and then for Radio Frankfurt in May of 1946 until the spring of 1948. What is interesting about Mayer's memoirs is that he does not comment about his parents and relatives who were killed in concentration camps and does not reflect upon the meaning that Auschwitz had for him except in indirect ways. Mayer attended the Nuremberg Trials briefly and includes a short commentary that he wrote for the radio in his book. He closes with the remarks: "What remains for us is the lesson: the necessity for a spiritual renewal as a rejection of that cult of blood and iron, a rejection of mockery of freedom, humanity, human rights and civil rights. What remains is the return to simple human decency. The judgment of Nuremberg is addressed to all of us" (vol. 1, 352).

Mayer sought to live and work according to this principle while repressing (at least in public) his feelings as a Jew and a homosexual, which were later to be addressed in his book *Außenseiter* [Outsiders] in 1975. The period in Leipzig from 1948 to 1964 until his departure for West Germany was perhaps the happiest and most meaningful in his life, and he looks back on it with great fondness despite the fact that he had to learn to use *Sklavensprache* [slave language]: "I had to learn it and practice it for fifteen years. When I met Bertolt Brecht in Berlin at the end of 1948, it became clear to me thanks to the example of my great colleague, who had to testify before the House Committee for un-American activities, that a slave language, which had to be ambiguous and can also include the opposite of the testimony, remains applicable in the most different forms of society—not only in a slave society" (vol. 1, 415–16). But Mayer did not have to use slave language constantly since his Marxist approach to literature and his critique of capitalism were very much in keeping with East German policies, especially in the early period of the German Democratic Republic. Mayer could and did embrace Germany with a vigor and dedication that many of the returning refugees, Jewish and Christian, possessed in an endeavor to rebuild the spiritual and cultural aspects of the nation. The University of Leipzig was a dynamic center of intellectual activity. Not only were the famous Romanist Werner Krauss and Germanist Karl Korsch there, but Ernst Bloch was soon to join the faculty, and Mayer was able to build one of the foremost centers for the study of both German and world literature. A brilliant orator and an innovative administrator, Mayer educated hundreds of students during his tenure in Leipzig, and he also created a name for himself nationally and internationally as one of the most perceptive Marxist critics of German literature from the Enlightenment to the present. Among his approximately 25 books published in both East and West Germany were: *Goethe in unserer Zeit* (1949), *Thomas Mann: Werk und Entwicklung* (1950), *Schiller und die Nation* (1953), *Von Lessing bis Thomas Mann: Wandlungen der bürgerlichen Literatur in Deutschland* (1959), *Bertolt Brecht und die Tradition* (1961), *Heinrich von Kleist. Der geschichtliche Augenblick* (1962), and *Zur deutschen Klassik und Romantik* (1963). Just these titles alone indicate Mayer's mission: a comprehensive reevaluation of the classical writers with a strong emphasis on the humanistic ideals that could be made useful for the cultural heritage that Mayer, as well as many other returning refugees, believed could be reestablished in East Germany.

The fourth part of his memoirs, "Leipzig oder die Alternative," depicts Mayer's engagement and conflicts in the German Democratic Republic in order to represent if not embody the idealistic German humanistic tradition in the public sphere of Europe.[6] Mayer took part in political party meetings and international conferences in Europe, knew and worked closely with most of the leading East German writers and intellectuals of his time, wrote for newspapers and magazines, and gave talks on the radio. Under the influence of Bloch, Mayer sought the anticipatory illumination [Vor-Schein] of the past to guide his work in the future and endeavored to establish categories in his literary criticism and studies of music, especially Wagner, that would expose the contradictions of bourgeois art and at the same time make this art relevant for the present. This utopian commitment to German culture was, however, tested constantly by the East German party functionaries and government. Many of Mayer's friends in Eastern Europe were arrested, harassed, and executed. By 1956, after the so-called Harich Affair, when several leading philosophers of the German Democratic Republic were incarcerated and sentenced to prison terms for conspiring against the government and when Ernst Bloch was dismissed from the university and almost sent to prison, Mayer became more aware than ever that his position was precarious despite his commitment to socialism. Nevertheless, he continued to work to change conditions within East Germany, especially in the cultural spheres, and he appeared to have more leeway than some other colleagues. In fact, when the Berlin Wall was built in the summer of 1961, he was in England and actually returned to East Germany to demonstrate his commitment to his friends and colleagues. However, Mayer refused to comply with the party edicts that fostered socialist realism and a critique of western literature as to-

tally decadent. Therefore, he came under attack more and more until one review in 1963 entitled "Eine Lehrmeinung zuviel" [A Superfluous Doctrine]
made him realize that the pact he had formed with East Germans had finally
been broken: "That disturbed me deeply. A bitter feeling returns to my
tongue, even today still as I write. Ever since I had gone to the 'Russians' in
October of 1948 to work as a professor and to help with the founding of a
changed social science and literary criticism, I had understood my work as a
pact. I wanted to remain the person who and what I was and only agree with
arguments that convinced me and wanted to have nothing to do with public applause that I secretly disapproved [of]" (vol. 2, 256).

By the summer of 1963, Mayer left East Germany and subsequently settled in Tübingen to be near his friends Ernst Bloch and Walter Jens. Then
in 1965 he received a professorship for German literature at the Technische
Universität Hannover and taught there until his retirement in 1972.
Though Mayer resumed his manifold activities as literary, music, and
drama critic and wrote for *Die Zeit, Der Spiegel*, and almost all the leading
newspapers in West Germany, became involved with the famous Gruppe
47 and most of the leading writers and intellectuals, in particular Theodor
Adorno, in important cultural debates, and traveled to the United States,
where some of his books and essays were translated into English,[7] there was
a spark missing in his embracement of German culture. The Enlightenment
heritage that he had sought to develop in East Germany along socialist lines
was now apparently a fruitless mission. Though he endeavored to develop
an innovative interdisciplinary center for the study of German literature in
Hannover in cooperation with other universities, he was unsuccessful because of bureaucratic resistance and the rise of the student movement.
Whereas East Germany had been somewhat of a provincial haven for him,
West Germany exposed him to more violent conflicts between the generations, anti-Semitism, racism, and a cultural industry that made a mockery
out of the classical German humanist tradition.

This does not mean that Mayer stopped embracing German culture
after his arrival in the West. Rather, he began to embrace and interpret the
legacy of the German Enlightenment in a more critical vein. For instance,
his provocative book, *Außenseiter* (1975), dealt with different literary types
of outsiders, Jews, and women, who represent the failure of the bourgeois
Enlightenment to bring about authentic equal rights. The concept for the
book was developed in the United States during the early 1970s, and
though it has been interpreted as autobiographical, Mayer insisted that he
was concerned mainly with tracing our continual interest in mythical figures and motifs into the modern period and how they have been reshaped
and reinterpreted. Yet, it is not by chance that the theme of marginalization
rose to the forefront of his interest in the 1970s when he was entering a new

phase of his life after retiring from the university. This was also a period when many Jewish writers began dealing more directly with topics concerned with the German-Jewish symbiosis, the Holocaust, and anti-Semitic acts of violence. After the immense effect of the Holocaust telecast in 1979, such events as the Fassbinder Scandal, the *Historiker-Debatte,* and desecration of cemeteries certainly played a role in Mayer's writing and changed attitude toward cultural and political developments in Germany. He does not deal with these problems in *Ein Deutscher auf Widerruf,* which was completed in 1984, but he does turn toward it in an interview with Herlinde Koelbl published in 1989 and in his book *Der Widerruf: Über Deutsche und Juden* (1994).

The interview with Koelbl is, aside from another interview conducted in 1978 with Hans Jürgen Schultz,[8] one of the most revealing statements about Mayer's feelings concerning his Jewishness and his relationship to the "Jewish Question" or German-Jewish symbiosis. Aside from providing more information about his Jewish background, he is extremely pessimistic about the results of his work and his critical embracement of Germany.

> The hopes and new beginnings from those times have been repressed and erased. In the West by the politics of the free market economy, in the East by the Stalinists. Enormous guilt has been piled on, and therefore, we must live today in terrible conditions that can only become worse. I also want to make clear that later, after I left Leipzig and became a tenured civil servant in the Federal Republic of Germany, I continually asked myself: Was it perhaps a mistake to have returned to Germany? But at that time it was certainly the right decision. For without this decision I would not have become what I am today. All that which I have written could only have been written here. . . . I believe, if I were twenty years younger, I would give up my residence in Germany again. I make no distinction between the Federal Republic and German Democratic Republic. When I say something like this, then the question arises immediately: Where do you want to go? And I have no answer to this question.[9]

Koelbl asks why Mayer's attitudes toward Germany and Germans have changed, and he bluntly replies:

> I believe it's because of the Germans. They have not changed. I continue to see today the people who made 1933 and the consequences possible. Everything is virtually still there. . . . I see all this more clearly because it's all been set free. The threshold of inhibitions has fallen. This is also naturally due to West German politics. The West German politics with the Federal Chancellor Helmut Kohl at the head of the government makes its calculations based on the assumption that the laws against hunting [Jews] have been lifted. One does not

have to take precautions anymore. The people follow the example of their superiors. And let's not forget Austria. I'm not objective here. I'm still the person
who cannot forget and is not allowed to forget. It makes no sense to reproach
me. There is a great deal in my life that cannot basically be reconciled—I've
been the winner of national awards in the German Democratic Republic, been
granted the highest awards of the Federal Republic, all the while I've had profound feelings of a revocable German. But my work originated out of this high
voltage relationship.[10]

It is indeed this paradoxical relationship that Mayer sees as the dilemma
of the Jews and the failure of the Enlightenment: the more the Jews became
assimilated and became just as German as the Germans, the more the Germans have rejected them. In his masterful study, *Der Widerruf: Über
Deutsche und Juden,* Mayer concludes his study of some of the key Jewish
writers, intellectuals, politicians, and artists in the German and Austrian tradition from the Enlightenment to the present by declaring:

> All reflection about the revocation of the co-existence and common working of
> the Germans with the German Jews must start on the day of the end of it and
> look back to the beginnings. Whoever understands or [wants to understand]
> the revocation of the winter of 1933 as the process of a universal anti-Enlight-
> enment must comprehend the historical process of German Enlightenment.
> The legal and social granting of equal rights to those Jews living in Germany
> with their German compatriots corresponded to a philosophical-political pos-
> tulate of the Enlightenment. Once again one could see that the Marxist talk
> about the comparatively insignificant meaning of individuals vis-à-vis the total
> significance of the people or masses everywhere in the past has been refuted by
> the facts. Indeed, Enlightenment thinking about a German-Jewish symbiosis
> was not the work of a mass movement but first a bold and endangered mind
> game of a few Germans on German soil and in the middle of the eighteenth
> century. There were two who were at the forefront: Gotthold Ephraim Lessing
> and Moses Mendelssohn. . . . Nevertheless, after approximately 250 years one
> must ask today whether the way of Moses Mendelssohn had to suffer heavy
> losses because much too much from the Jewish side had to be cast off as a bur-
> den. Whoever thinks today about the end of the German-Jewish symbiosis will
> have to ask himself/herself whether Mendelssohn's (and Lessing's) basic cate-
> gory of *assimilation,* which seemed almost unassailable for such a long time,
> did not belong to the causes of the revocation.[11]

Is it then possible to ask whether Mayer's Enlightenment project, his critical embracement of Germany after 1945, has contributed to his own personal disillusionment with Germany toward the end of his life? Was he naive
to think that he could perhaps restore some kind of basis for a German-
Jewish symbiosis? Not that this was his goal, but certainly his work after

1945 was predicated on the basis that he, as Jew, homosexual, Marxist, would be accepted equally in Germany along with other critics who sought to provide a changed cultural and political basis for a free Germany. Is it also possible that Mayer's critical embracement of Germany has had more of an effect than he realizes, and that what constitutes some of the more vibrant critical thinking in Germany is a result of his legacy, among others? After all, Marcel Reich-Ranicki includes him in his book about famous Jewish "troublemakers" and maintains that "even at his weakest times Mayer has more to say than most of Germanisten at their strongest."[12]

But before I comment further on Mayer's dilemma and the ramifications of his critical embracement of Germany, I want to turn to Reich-Ranicki, for he, like Mayer, embarked upon a project of restoring a critical tradition in Germany with the hope that he might make a difference in German cultural life after the Shoah. However, his path toward becoming what some of his critics have called (sarcastically and fondly) the literary pope of Germany was markedly different from Mayer's path, just as his important autobiography, *Mein Leben,* has a different tone and purpose than Mayer's memoirs. Reich-Ranicki sought to record how he developed a great love for Germany and German culture as a young man and then miraculously survived the Holocaust to become a thorn in the eyes of Germans and has remained a controversial figure to the present.

Born on June 2, 1920, in Wloclawek, a small Polish city close to the German-Russian border, Reich-Ranicki was influenced by the German cultural tradition from early childhood on. His mother Helene Auerbach came from Prussia, and his father David Reich, a businessman, was from the Russian part of Poland and spoke German. Indeed, Reich-Ranicki (he added Ranicki to his name later in life) was educated at a German elementary school until he was nine, when the family moved to Berlin, and just as he was about to leave Wloclawek, he clearly remembers one of his favorite teachers telling him: "You are going to travel, my son, into the land of culture,"[13] as his mother nodded her approval. Indeed, for the next nine years, until he was forced to leave Germany and go to Warsaw, Reich-Ranicki imbibed German culture with tremendous passion, and in his autobiography he describes his love affair with German literature in great detail. He attended two gymnasiums in Berlin, was the number one student in German, went to the theater, concerts, and the opera as often as he could, and wrote reviews for himself about everything he experienced. However, as soon as he received the *Abitur* in 1938, he was arrested by the Nazis as a foreigner and deported to Warsaw.

At first, Reich-Ranicki floundered in Warsaw because he had not learned a trade, and he had forgotten a good deal of his Polish. He took menial jobs and also began to give German lessons to Poles. When Warsaw became occupied by the Germans, he was compelled to live in the ghetto and was employed as a translator and interpreter by the Jewish Council. At the beginning of 1943 he became a member of the Jewish resistance and managed to escape the ghetto with his wife, Teofila Langnas, after their parents and relatives had been sent to concentration camps. Reich-Ranicki's account of the sordid and humiliating conditions of life in the ghetto is an important document of the barbarism of the Nazis and the valor of the Jews, especially because he worked in the offices of the council and was privy to major encounters with high-ranking officials on both the German and Jewish side. Moreover, he experienced the daily deprivation as most of the Jews did and worked with members of the resistance. Once he and his wife managed to get outside the ghetto, they were hidden by simple Polish peasants in a crude cellar for close to two years, an incident that Günter Grass fictionalized in his novel *Aus dem Tagebuch einer Schnecke* (1972). After they were liberated by the Russians, Reich-Ranicki and his wife made their way back to Warsaw, where he joined the Communist Party and began working for the Polish Foreign Ministry. In his autobiography, he makes it clear that he joined the Communist Party out of conviction and because he was grateful to the Russians for having liberated them. It was also at this time that he changed his name as he began working for the ministry in London from 1947 to 1949. "Even those Poles and English who could not speak one word of German were familiar with the term Reich. It reminded people too much of the 'Third Reich.' Was the name with which all my passports and visas had to be signed too German? Or perhaps too Jewish? At any rate, it was not Polish enough. I did not want to prolong things, agreed that the name had to be changed and chose the name Ranicki without thinking about it too much. I thought I would use it just for the time I was in England. But afterwards the name remained—my entire life" (*Mein Leben,* 324–5).

Reich-Ranicki's career in the government and party was, however, short-lived. He was obliged to resign his position and return to Warsaw, where he was imprisoned for a few months and dismissed from the party because he did not hold the correct ideological views. By 1950 he was allowed to resume work and became active in publishing as a freelance writer. Ironically, the dismissal from the party enabled him to turn his love for German culture into a profession. Although he continued to have difficulty with the party, he managed to make a living as a professional writer using Hans Mayer, Georg Lukács, Alexander Abusch, and Paul Rilla[14] as models, and soon he became the foremost critical commentator of modern and contemporary German literature in Poland. Aside from publishing reviews and articles in important Polish journals and newspapers as well as in East German publications, he wrote two important studies, *From the History of German Literature 1871–1954* (1955) and *The Narratives of Anna Seghers* (1957). In addition, he edited and wrote the introductions to various Polish editions of

German classical authors as well as to an anthology of German exile writings, and he translated the stage adaptation of Kafka's *The Castle* and Friedrich Dürrenmatt's *The Visit*. Despite this visible success, or perhaps because of it, Reich-Ranicki had continual problems with governmental authorities, and when anti-Semitism became more virulent in 1956, he decided that it was time to think about emigrating:

> I, too, was greatly irritated and uneasy about the anti-Semitic mood and the occasional infringements. I asked myself what I was doing in this country in which I had been born to be sure, but to which I had not returned voluntarily. Certainly I never forgot for a moment to whom I was thankful for being able to survive the Second World War. But what I had already felt as I had visited Berlin for the first time after the war became noticeably stronger ten years later. Despite the fact that I had published such a great deal in the Polish language (of course only on German literature time and again), Poland remained for me somewhat alien. Had it ever been my home country? I had long since stopped believing in communism. So did it make any sense to live here? (372–73)

In May of 1958, Reich-Ranicki answered this question by emigrating to West Germany, and thanks to his connections with numerous German writers, such as Heinrich Böll and Siegfried Lenz, and key people in the mass media, he was able to establish himself quickly on the German cultural scene. In fact, it is astonishing how fast he became famous if not notorious. After settling in Frankfurt am Main with his wife and son, Reich-Ranicki began writing reviews and essays for the *Frankfurter Allgemeine Zeitung* and *Die Welt* and became a permanent member of the weekly *Die Zeit* from 1973 to 1988, when he was hired by the *Frankfurter Allgemeine Zeitung* as literary critic, a post that he has held up to the present. Aside from participating in all the meetings of the Gruppe 47 from 1958 to 1967, he was also the speaker of the jury that awarded the Ingeborg Bachmann prize in Klagenfurt from 1977 to 1986, and he joined with Hans Mayer in organizing the popular radio talk show *Das Literarische Kaffehaus* in 1964, which Reich-Ranicki later transformed into the influential TV show *Das Literarische Quartett* in 1988. Like Mayer, Reich-Ranicki won numerous awards and published important books, mainly collections of his reviews, such as *Deutsche Literatur in West und Ost: Prosa seit 1945* (1963), *Wer schreibt, provoziert* (1965), *Lauter Verisse* (1970), *Über Ruhestörer: Juden in der deutschen Literatur* (1973), *Betrifft Goethe* (1982), *Zwischen Diktatur und Literatur* (1987), and *Die Anwälte der Literatur* (1994). Like Mayer but more provocative and less thorough, Reich-Ranicki focused all his efforts on reestablishing the great humanistic German literature tradition and becoming the spokesman for the renewal of this tradition on the contemporary scene. In his autobiography he attributes his astonishing success to his efforts to follow in the footsteps of such critics as Heine, Fontane, Kerr, Polgar, and Tucholsky. "They all worked for newspapers, and that stamped their style. They had the same target audience in mind—the general public. Of course, this is not, especially in Germany, where the commentary of literature lay, for it was mainly in the hands of academics and literary experts, and I have nothing to say against this. But the academics wrote mainly for other academics and the literary experts for other experts. Meanwhile the public was left holding an empty bag. Even without Heine and Fontane I would have written primarily for the readers and not for the literary guild. Just my temperament alone would have driven me to do this" (435). And also, his love for literature would have driven him, for Reich-Ranicki always had an intense love affair with German literature.

However, he also had a knack for making enemies, even among those writers who had befriended him, such as Böll and Grass, as well as Walter Jens and even Mayer. Reich-Ranicki was a compulsive writer, who felt himself to be on a mission in postwar Germany. But his mission, his critical embracement, was somewhat different than Mayer's. In discussing his work as part of the editorial staff in the feuilleton department at the *Frankfurter Allgemeine*, he writes:

> From early morning until late in the evening I worked—sometimes at the newspaper, other times at home. I hardly ever had a free weekend. And I rarely made use of whatever vacation was due to me and did not like to take vacations. I was industrious, incredibly industrious. But why? Nobody had expected it or demanded it from me. What I did, I did not always have to do, nor did I absolutely have to do it myself. I could delegate a great deal. Why then the great trouble, the constant strain? Because of the literature? Yes, certainly. Was it my ambition to continue, perhaps in a very demonstrative manner, the tradition of Jews in the history of German literary criticism to which I had long since adhered in a leading position and in great public view? Certainly. Did my passion have anything to do with my yearning for a home country, that home which I was lacking and which I had believed to have found in the German literature? Yes, and possibly in a much greater degree than I was even aware. (491–92)

In his autobiography, Reich-Ranicki is not afraid to raise very honest questions about his vanity, his difficult temperament, and his symbiotic relationship with Germany. In the final chapter of his autobiography, completed in 1999, Reich-Ranicki devotes his remarks to a consideration of the several incidents that were disturbing to Jews in Germany—the Fassbinder scandal; the Historians' Debate, prompted by his friend Joachim Fest, who hired him at the *Frankfurter Allgemeine;* and the more recent Martin Walser debacle in Frankfurt in 1998. While all these events made Reich-Ranicki feel uneasy, he also recalls how Willy Brandt knelt before the monument honoring Jews of the Warsaw Ghetto in 1970 and how he discussed this incident with Brandt later in a report that he wrote in 1990. "When I was finished with my short report, someone had tears in his eyes. Willy Brandt or I? I don't know any more. But I certainly know what I had thought when I had seen the photo of the kneeling Federal Chancellor in 1970: I thought to myself that my decision to return to Germany in 1958 and to settle in the Federal Republic of Germany was not false but correct. Fassbinder's play, the Historians' Debate, and the Walser Speech, altogether important symptoms of the mood of the times, have not changed my mind" (551).

Unlike Mayer, Reich-Ranicki would not revoke his decision to return to Germany after World War II. However, he does have some reservations. In an interview with Herlinde Koelbl published in 1989, he states, "I feel a strong attachment to German culture. . . . I only have one feeling that can interest you because it cannot be found every day. I said before that I am not a German, and I shall never be one. But I do not feel as if I were a guest in this country and not a foreigner. . . . I do not feel as if I were being tolerated in this country, but as someone who feels as if I had a claim to be in this country and has a complete right to participate in the cultural life of this country."[15]

Though his attitude toward Germany and his decision to remain in Germany are essentially positive, it is a different story when it comes to discussing the role that Jews have played, and to a certain extent his own role, in German culture.

> The Jews play no role in the culture of the Federal Republic of Germany. Don't imagine that. Naturally the Federal Republic has the most opera houses in the world and hires many conductors to work in them. Among them are Israelis and Jews from America. They conduct here because there happens to be a position free. But they do not belong strictly speaking to the German cultural life. . . . It is not worth it anymore to speak about the part played by the Jews in contemporary German culture. There is Peter Zadek, an emigrant, the Swiss Jew Lucien Bondy, the Hungarian Jew Ivan Nagel. They are already part of the older generation. Most of the writers, I mean the Jewish ones, did not return to Germany after 1945. Erich Fried remained in London, Peter Weiss in Sweden, Canetti in England, Hildesheimer also in Switzerland . . . You cannot pound literature out of the ground without a certain base in the population. There are no more Jews in this country. There are hardly more than 30,000, and most of them live only with one leg in Germany. Their children are being raised to emigrate.[16]

These are, of course, ridiculous and misleading statements even when they were made over ten years ago. Rafael Seligmann, an outspoken Jewish writer of the generation born after World War II, points out some of Reich-

Ranicki's misconceptions. "There is the theory that only those Jews who never felt anger or even hatred toward their tormentors came back to Germany, but this theory has been proven false. Equally fallacious is the assertion by postwar Germany's most renowned literary critic, the redoubtable Marcel Reich-Ranicki. This 'pontiff of German letters,' who happens to be Jewish, says that Jewish literature in postwar Germany is impossible because all the German Jewish writers are dead. As we have seen, a number of them returned to Germany after 1945. What keeps the Jewish writers, and for that matter German Jews in general, from expressing their anger and even their hate? The answer is banal: fear and shame."[17]

In fairness to Reich-Ranicki, he made his comments about Jewish culture in Germany in 1989, right about the time that there was a kind of renascence of Jewish writing in Germany and a rapid growth in the population. But even in 1989 his remarks were exaggerations. Certainly, very few Jews born in Germany today are contemplating packing their bags and leaving the country, and more and more Jews have become strident in their critiques of both Germans and Jews in united Germany. Whether Reich-Ranicki or for that matter Hans Mayer want to admit it, they paved the way for two if not three generations of Jews to play an important role in German cultural and political life. One need only think of critics like Henryk Broder, Maxim Biller, Dan Diner, Mischa Brumlik, Esther Dischereit, Seligmann, and others to realize that Germany is being embraced critically by Jews who lay claim to a right to speak without fear and shame.

I do not want to exaggerate the role these Jews are playing or the role that critics such as Mayer and Reich-Ranicki have played. There are indeed major differences between Jews of the older generation, who returned with an unusual longing to re-represent German culture to Germans and to the world, and the younger Jews who have grown up in the ruins of the German Enlightenment and with the Holocaust on their minds and as part of their identity. Neither Mayer nor Reich-Ranicki grew up with the Holocaust as part of their identity. Rather, they grew up with a great love for German culture that they continued to cultivate in their mission to salvage what was the best of the German tradition, as did many others, after the war. Neither Mayer nor Reich-Ranicki, though they lost their parents and many relatives in concentration camps, wanted to make the Holocaust part of their identity or public persona. In this regard there is a certain nobility in their stance as returning Jews because they refrained to make much out of their "alleged" Jewishness. Of course, one of the reasons they refused to do this is because they had stopped believing in the Jewish religion as young men and had turned toward socialism and secular humanism. But another reason is that they did not want to be categorized or stigmatized and wanted to keep the categories of identity open and fluid. By claiming to be neither German nor

Jewish writers, Mayer and Reich-Ranicki have made it difficult for their readers and critics to classify them. This is not to say that they reject their Jewishness, whatever that may be. Rather, they compel their audiences in the public sphere to spell out for themselves what their Jewishness is, what their stance is vis-à-vis Germany, and how they have come to be two famous, if not the most famous, literary critics in postwar Germany.

What is significant about Mayer's *Ein Deutscher auf Widerruf* and Reich-Ranicki's *Mein Leben* is not only their paradoxical position as Jews who have resisted definition as Germans and who seek to make German culture valid in the postwar period, but also the manner in which they explode the category of negative and positive symbiosis. By reflecting on their lives and their works, one can see that the relations between Germans and Jews from Mendelssohn's days, that is, from the period of Jewish emancipation to the present, have been multifaceted and so intertwined that it is impossible to separate Jewish from German and German from Jewish even today, and it is too simple to generalize and talk about a common Jewish attitude in the postwar period. The Nazis' endeavor to purify Germany and eradicate the Jews failed, and the Jewish endeavor of those Jews who returned to and were born in Germany to keep a distance from Germany has failed. It failed from the very beginning because many Jews refused to abandon German culture and an Enlightenment tradition in Germany. The acculturation process in both postwar Germanies demanded involvement and engagement of Jews, and the critical embrace of Mayer and Reich-Ranicki represents a particular form of engagement of older-generation Jews who, whether they desired this or not, came to represent part of the established German cultural hegemony of the postwar period. Ironically, many of the younger Jews have criticized or ignored their embracement, while many regard the accomplishments of Mayer and Reich-Ranicki with respect. Here, too, it is important to distinguish between Mayer and Reich-Ranicki, for Mayer has always commanded more serious consideration and played a more important role in scholarly circles while Reich-Ranicki has often played the role of an enfant terrible or cultural clown whose opinions are not always taken seriously by the German public.

In one of Mayer's last talks, "Deutsche Geschichte und Deutsche Aufklärung," delivered on June 6, 1999, in the Roman Palace on the Wartburg, Mayer used Adorno and Horkheimer's concept of the dialectics of the Enlightenment to comment on essential moments of German history that constitute what I would like to call the German dilemma. Mayer defined the dialectics of the Enlightenment in a succinct way: "In every freedom movement, historical freedom movement, there is already a germ of a sudden change into repression and restoration. Or the other way around. In each restoration, social restoration, oppression and repression, there is always the possibility in any moment—whether it is by many people, or just by individuals—of the revolt, the chance of emancipation."[18] After surveying key moments of German misery and freedom from the fourteenth century to the present, Mayer raised the question about the future of Germany, in particular after unification, and he concluded by stating that this question is still open, but that the problem of the Enlightenment and the bourgeois society remains with us. His ending is a warning and a call to responsibility.

Again there is a startling paradox in Mayer's stance in 1999: He as Jew and outsider still insisting on his revocability represents to the Germans in the name of the humanistic and critical side of German Enlightenment what their role in the twenty-first century should be. Reich-Ranicki would and did argue in a 1995 talk, "Die verkehrte Krone: Über Juden in der deutschen Literatur," that the German-Jewish cultural symbiosis, if it ever existed, has long since ended, and what has determined the particular Jewish contribution to German literature has been the extreme treatment they have been fated or destined to experience. Reich-Ranicki represents to the Germans a troublemaker, which he has wanted to be, and insists on a particular role of Jews in a German-Jewish symbiosis that he wants to deny.

There can be no summary to the lives and work of Mayer and Reich-Ranicki and the manner in which they have embraced German culture, identified themselves with it, and sought to distance themselves from such an identity. Mayer, who had been blind for the past four years, died on May 19, 2001, at the age of ninety-four, just as he completed a book about Willi Brandt and German politics; and of course, Reich-Ranicki at eighty-two, still vigorous, published a laudatory and somewhat snide obituary about Mayer.[19] Both Mayer and Reich-Ranicki have forged their marks on German postwar culture. Quarrelsome and troublesome, Mayer, even in his death, and Reich-Ranicki, still kicking, are unwilling to surrender Germany to the Germans.

Notes

1. Frank Hirschbach discusses some of the problems for returning Germans and German Jews in "Heimkehr in die Fremde: Zur Remigration deutscher Schriftsteller nach 1945" in *Fremdheitserfahrung und Fremdheitsdarstellung in dizidentalen Kulturen,* ed. Bernd Lenz and Hans Jürgen Lüsebrink (Passau: Wissenschaftsverlag Richard Rothe, 1999), 331–45.

2. This is not to say that they are not known outside of Germany. In particular, several of Mayer's works have been translated into English. To my knowledge, this is not the case with Reich-Ranicki. What is interesting is that they are household names in Germany, but they are not easily recognized as dominant figures of German culture in English-speaking countries. Their popularity remains well within circles of Germanistik.

3. For some of the many accounts of Mayer's achievements, see Inge Jens, ed. *Über Hans Mayer* (Frankfurt am Main: Suhrkamp, 1977); Gert Ueding, ed. *Materialien zu Hans Mayer "Außenseiter"* (Frankfurt am Main: Suhrkamp, 1978); Alfred Klein, Manfred Neuhaus, and Klaus Pezold, eds. *Hans Mayers Leipziger Jahre* (Leipzig: Rosa-Luxemburg Stiftung Sachsen, 1977).

4. For some of the many accounts of Reich-Ranicki's achievements, see Jens Jessen, ed., *Über Marcel Reich-Ranicki: Aufsätze und Kommentare* (Munich: Deutscher Taschenbuch Verlag, 1985); Peter Wapnewski, ed., *Betrifft Literatur: Über Marcel Reich-Ranicki* (Stuttgart: Deutsche Verlags-Anstalt, 1990); Franz Josef Czernin, *Marcel Reich-Ranicki: Eine Kritik* (Göttingen: Steidl, 1995).

5. Hans Mayer, *Ein Deutscher auf Widerruf: Erinnerungen,* vol. 2 (Frankfurt am Main: Suhrkamp, 1984), 384. Hereafter all page references will be cited in the text.

6. The best study of this period is Alfred Klein's *Unästhetische Feldzüge: Der siebenjährige Krieg gegen Hans Mayer, 1956–1963* (Leipzig: Faber und Faber, 1997).

7. Though Mayer does not mention this in his book, he helped inspire the founding of the American journal, *New German Critique,* and some of his essays appear in early issues of this periodical.

8. See Hans Jürgen Schultz, ed., *Mein Judentum* (Stuttgart: Kreuz Verlag, 1978), 248–60.

9. Herlinde Koelbl, *Jüdische Portraits: Photographien und Interviews* (Frankfurt am Main: Fischer, 1998), 254–55.

10. Ibid., 255.

11. Hans Mayer, *Der Widerruf: Über Deutsche und Juden* (Frankfurt am Main: Suhrkamp, 1996), 431–32.

12. Marcel Reich-Ranicki, *Über Ruhestörer: Juden in der deutschen Literatur,* rev. ed. (Stuttgart: Deutsche Verlags-Anstalt, 1989), 155.

13. Marcel Reich-Ranicki, *Mein Leben* (Stuttgart: Deutsche Verlags-Anstalt, 1999), 25.

14. See Volker Hage and Mathias Schreiber, *Marcel Reich-Ranicki: Ein biographisches Porträt* (Cologne: Kiepenheuer & Witsch, 1995), 67.

15. Herlinde Koelbl, ed., *Jüdische Portraits: Photographien und Interviews,* 273.

16. Ibid., 271–72

17. Rafael Seligmann, "What Keeps Jews in Germany Quiet?" in *Reemerging Jewish Culture in Germany: Life and Literature Since 1989,* ed. Sander L. Gilman and Karen Remmler (New York: New York University Press, 1994), 174.

18. Hans Mayer, *Deutsche Geschichte und deutsche Aufklärung: Gedanken auf der Wartburg* (Frankfurt am Main: Suhrkamp, 1999), 10.

19. Marcel Reich-Ranicki, "Eine Lebensgeschichte, die das Jahrhundert anklagt. Freund des Gesprächs, Virtuose der Polemik: Erinnerungen an Hans Mayer, *Frankfurter Allgemeine Zeitung* (May 21, 2001): Feulliton, 1. See also Lorenz Jäger, "Sag, was könnt' uns übrigbleiben? Abschied vom Mandarin: Zum

Tod von Hans Mayer, dem letzten Gelehrten mit geschichtlichem Auftrag," *Frankfurter Allgemeine Zeiting* (May 21, 2001): Feuilleton, 1; and a series of small obituaries by some of the leading writers and intellectuals from the former East German state: Christoph Hein, Christa Wolf, Sylvia Schlestedt, Adolf Dresen, and Friedrich Dieckmann, in *Freitag 22* (May 22, 2001): http://www.freitag.de. It is interesting to note that almost all of the major publications in Germany carried an obituary about Mayer emphasizing how he had stamped German culture in the postwar years while his death went virtually unnoticed in the United States.

CHAPTER TEN

RETURN TO GERMANY
German-Jewish Authors Seeking Address

PASCALE R. BOS

The Holocaust ended the life of European Jews as it had existed for centuries.[1] Jews were segregated, isolated, hunted down, and murdered in unprecedented fashion. Whereas the Shoah is commonly understood as having led to the *physical* destruction of the European Jewish community, what has been acknowledged explicitly only recently is how these events also brought about a traumatic *shift in identity* for surviving European Jews. Particularly the assimilated, middle-class Jews of Western and Central Europe had to confront and redefine their sense of belonging in Europe after 1945 as Jews and citizens.

This shift in identity and the ensuing process of redefinition was often torturous and complicated, especially in countries such as Austria and Germany, where Jewishness had been defined as a racially inferior trait and where national identity had come to exclude Jewishness. The political and legal failure of German-Jewishness as a viable national identity was thus underscored. As a result, the majority of German Jews in the first decades after 1945 saw themselves having to make a choice. They would either live as *Jews,* but no longer in Germany or Austria (or even Europe altogether), or renounce Jewishness and live as *Germans* in West or East Germany. Few survivors felt that they were able to continue living in Germany as *German Jews.* As such, it can be said that the Nazi era effectively ended the German-Jewish symbiosis in culture and identity.

Nevertheless, for a small group of German Jews, often those who had been most assimilated, and often those who had come from an (upper-) middle-class background and who had considered themselves "as German as the Germans," the question of identity remained unresolved and *at the center*. Because the Holocaust put Jews and Germans at opposite sides of the historical divide, Jews were no longer able to subsume themselves under a German identity. On the other hand, a return to Jewishness seemed impossible, as many had turned their back on Judaism generations earlier. Furthermore, the religious as well as the secular and the cultural Jewish communal structures that existed in Germany before 1933 had almost completely been destroyed. Even if one had wanted to, there was no German-Jewish world to turn to in the first several decades after the war.

The reconciliation of identity for this particular group, then, remained much desired but elusive. In fact, it seemed that to be a German Jew was now an *impossible* identity. The consequences of Nazi persecution proved permanent. Jean Améry, a highly assimilated Jewish-Viennese intellectual who fled to Belgium after 1938 and who survived both torture at the hands of the Gestapo and imprisonment at Auschwitz, would write in the mid-1960s:

> Suddenly, the past was buried and one no longer knew who one was. . . . My identity was bound to a plain German name and to the dialect of my immediate place of origin. But since the day when an official decree forbade me to wear the folk costume that I had worn almost exclusively from early childhood on, I no longer permitted myself the dialect. Then the name . . . no longer made sense either. . . . And my friends, too . . . were obliterated . . . everything that had filled my consciousness—from the history of my country, which was no longer mine, to the landscape images . . . —had become intolerable to me . . . I was a person who could no longer say "we" and who therefore said "I" merely out of habit, but not with the feeling of full possession of myself.[2]

Améry, whose name had been *Hans Maier* before 1938, never returned to Austria, for after seven years in exile and imprisonment, he no longer felt it was *his* home: "When my country lost its national independence on March 12, 1938 . . . it became totally alien to me" (55). It is not just that he lost his nationality, but rather, that German-Jewish and Austro-Jewish identity had been made retroactively unimaginable: "We . . . had to realize that it had never been ours. For us, whatever was linked with this land and its people was an existential misunderstanding" ("How Much," 50). Although the longing for his native country, its landscape, its language, would remain strong for Améry, he went back to Belgium after his liberation, where he committed suicide in 1978.

Few German and Austrian Jews would in fact return "home." For those who did so, the attempt to reconcile identity could no longer take the shape of a merger of two clearly and positively defined cultural poles (Germanness and Jewishness). Instead, the Holocaust now became the defining factor of one's identity. For as Dan Diner has argued, many came back because "through their proximity to the crime scene and the perpetrators, they can stay the most closely connected to their past . . . as if one can find back that which was lost in Germany, by way of the Germans."[3] Diner thus suggests that the life of German Jews is determined in a thoroughly negative fashion by their relationship with non-Jewish Germans and by the Holocaust, and has called this relationship a *negative symbiosis*.[4] *This* form of German-Jewish symbiosis is not based on a mutual and fruitful exchange, but refers to the fact that the self-conception of both Germans and Jews became interdependent because of the shared history of the Holocaust.

There is, however, also a different form of "return" to Germany. Some German and Austrian Jews would indeed come back to Germany, but not in order to try to return to that which was lost, but to publicly articulate a literary discourse that invited Germans into a dialogue about the Nazi past and to participate in the formulation of postwar German-Jewish relations. This discourse rethinks the pre-1933 situation of Jews in Germany and Austria and the shifts in identity that have ensued since then.

I discuss a number of such textual "returns," texts by German-Jewish authors who seek to actively engage questions of postwar German and Jewish identity and belonging. These are literary works that attempt to work through the events of the Nazi era not merely to describe the alienating effects of racial persecution, but also to try to call their German compatriots into some sort of a new relationship. This literature creates address: a German audience is appealed to explicitly and is drawn into a dialogue about the role of the Holocaust and of (German) Jews in contemporary German culture and national identity.

As examples of this kind of literary discourse I discuss German-Jewish novels and autobiographical works published after 1945 by Grete Weil and Ruth Klüger, both assimilated, middle-class Jewish women. Weil and Klüger, each in their own way, articulate poignantly the process by which they were "called into" estranging identities as Jews, and how they attempt to make sense of this in their postwar lives and within the postwar German context.

Born in 1906 and 1930 respectively, Weil and Klüger share a similar ethnic and class background but became active in Germany's postwar literary life in different decades, independent of each other. Both are survivors of Nazi persecution: Weil fled to the Netherlands in the early 1930s and lived in hiding for the last two years of the war; Klüger was deported from Vienna and survived several concentration camps. One important fact nevertheless distinguishes these authors from each other: while Weil resettled in Germany soon after the war and wrote and published in Germany, Klüger left Europe for the United States in 1949 and, apart from brief professional trips, would return *only* in the form of her publications. While she publishes texts in the German language in Germany, she maintains her residence in the United States. Still, her literature has been described by German critics as symbolic of the author's "return" to Germany. I describe her work instead as an attempt at a *critical intervention* into a German dialogue about Jews in Germany that seems to exclude living Jews.

Discussed together, Weil and Klüger's literature presents a fascinating case of a German-Jewish intervention in the postwar public sphere, as it attempts to engage readers who had been conditioned to treat them as *others*. By publishing these texts in the German language in the country where they were formerly persecuted, these authors moved their private, emotional, and psychological battle of exclusion from and persecution by the national community of their forebears to the public realm of these nations.

Grete Weil's Mythical Interventions

Grete Weil was born in 1906 in southern Germany in a well-to-do, strongly assimilated Jewish family of lawyers. Weil's relationship to Judaism was, as she herself suggests, "lukewarm and lax, without clear contours."[5] At the most, Jewishness meant having "two sets of roots," which she considered enriching, an advantage for her career as a writer. "Access to both . . . The triumphant rationality of the Enlightenment and the transcendental magical formula for the sole, invisible, omnipotent God."[6] It was the former, the German tradition of *Bildung,* however, with which Weil identified most strongly. "I feel closer to Antigone than to Ruth."[7] It thus came as a tremendous shock to her when, immediately after Hitler's rise to power in 1933, her husband was arrested and jailed. Having come to understand the danger of Nazism in a way that most other German Jews had not yet, they emigrated to Amsterdam after his release. Emigration was difficult in light of their mutual attachment to the German language and culture in both private and professional life. Weil described the ensuing years in exile as a process of profound losses: losses of country, language, security, and identity: "Emigration is not merely falling out of one's own social class into a lower one; emigration is plummeting into a bottomless chasm."[8]

By 1940, the Nazis had caught up with them in the Netherlands, and a year later Weil's husband was rounded up and deported to Mauthausen and killed. Weil worked briefly for the Jewish Council in Amsterdam, a position about which she felt highly ambivalent, as this situation created an uncomfortable alliance between the Council members and the Nazis: "Members of the Jewish Council are not required to leave. They are performing their work detail in Holland, the Germans explain cynically. Helping the Germans deport other Jews."[9] In 1943, she went into hiding.

When the war ended, Weil made immediate plans to return to Germany, for she needed to return to a country that was just as "damaged" as she was herself: "The ruins? They suited me, not only the German cities had been ruined by war, I had been, too."[10] But more importantly, now that the Nazis were gone, she felt that she was still, above all, German.[11] After her short, illegal return in 1947 and her permanent return in 1948,[12] she managed to acquire ownership of her father-in-law's pharmaceutical firm and gain financial independence. She remarried and spent the next 45 years writing, publishing seven books, all dealing with some aspect of her experience under the Nazis, all reflecting different attempts to come to terms with this past and to call her German audience into a dialogue about the Holocaust.[13]

Weil's success as an author in Germany would be a long time in the making, however, as her work was rather uncomfortable for the German audience. Even though she never propagated a sense of collective guilt and was nuanced in her judgment of the Germans, her work was still seen as a monument to Jews killed under the Nazis. She wrote about the most painful details of her life under Nazi persecution and about her personal transformation from a privileged woman raised with bourgeois Enlightenment values into an outsider who came to question these values and who became an outspoken critic of war and all forms of oppression. She wished to testify to her experiences and have her work form a part of a new, democratic, German consciousness. It would not be until the 1980s, however, that she would find a larger German audience for her work.

Although her later work is of particular interest to me, it is one of her earlier works, *Tramhalte Beethovenstraat* (originally published in 1964), that first gives us a glimpse of Weil's attempt to engage her German readers with the Holocaust. She does so by providing a perspective with which a German audience could identify. Based on her personal experience of witnessing from the window of her apartment in the Beethovenstraat in Amsterdam the nightly deportations of Jews in 1943, *Tramhalte* depicts the events in a third-person narrative from the perspective of a non-Jewish German war correspondent named Andreas. The text moves back and forth between the past of the 1940s and the present of the 1960s, as if to highlight the need to belatedly come to terms with the past. After the war, Andreas struggles with the possibility of bearing witness to the event, as he finds himself unable to articulate what he has seen as an *outsider*. While witnessing the deportations, Andreas first thought he was hallucinating. Even while now knowing that what he saw really occurred, he cannot find the right words to describe the events, since there is no frame of reference, nothing to compare it to. The events he witnessed and wants to testify to are unfathomable, unacceptable. Furthermore, as Andreas's narrative suggests, the inability to bear witness strikes those who were not in the concentration camps. Like Weil, the protagonist can only imagine what people experienced there, what brutalities took place, which forces were at work. As he has not witnessed this with his own eyes, however, he can not produce testimony about the Nazi murders. Nevertheless, he *needs* to write. He attempts to find a compromise: if he cannot write as an eyewitness to the genocide of the Jews, he can describe the circumstances leading up to these murders. He can bear witness to the process, if not to its results.

This question of how to bear witness to the Shoah if one was able to avoid deportation (and thus had not witnessed the "concentrationary universe," the pinnacle of Nazi genocide) would remain central in Weil's work. It not only described her own dilemma as a German Jew who lived first in exile, then in hiding, but was also symbolic for the perspective of Germans generally. If she and other Germans would attempt to come to terms with this past, it is precisely this bystander position and collaboration with the regime that they would have to analyze. What could, or should, one have done? How should one speak of it, now that it was all over? By writing about these questions as a German who is also a Jew, instead of from an exclusively Jewish (survivor) perspective, Weil attempted to address the Germans from within.

The lack of public engagement with the Nazi past and the question of responsibility in Germany in the first three decades after the war was in fact of great concern to Weil. Her return to her home country had been a deliberate choice, for not only did she consider herself still *German* (even though the Nazis clearly thought differently), but also she had returned to bear witness, to make a confrontation with the Nazi past possible, precisely in Germany. Weil's choice for a young, male, non-Jewish protagonist for *Tramhalte,* then, was an attempt to engage her readers—who as she assumed were mostly young non-Jewish Germans—with the question of German responsibility and accountability. She wanted to create a representation that Germans and Jews could share.[14] When the novel fell on deaf ears in Germany, Weil was so disappointed about the lack of an audience that she ceased to publish for over ten years.[15] If readers would not engage with her texts (or the past), what good would writing do?

While *Tramhalte* and the other two works of autobiographical fiction published in 1949 and 1968 did not sell well, when Weil began to write in a more personal voice in the 1980s, she did find an audience. Influenced by the social and cultural movements of the late 1960s and 1970s (in particular, feminism), she found a new, more strongly autobiographical voice and a more intimate tone for her writing. She published three autobiographical novels in close succession, while already nearing eighty years of age. In these works, too, Weil appeals to her German audience to rethink their own position during the Nazi years, a time that is now discussed in conjunction with contemporary political and social issues, such as left-wing terrorism. What is new is that Weil now also explicitly problematizes her own subject position as a German, a Jew, and a woman. She does so by means of a rewriting of mythical Greek female, and, increasingly, Jewish biblical figures.

Meine Schwester Antigone, the first work of this period, describes one day in the life of an older woman with a personal history very much like Weil's. The narrator is an aging German-Jewish writer who tries to come to terms with her past—the years of persecution, hiding and loss during the Nazi-era—while living in West Germany in the late 1970s. The narrative consists of an almost continual stream of consciousness, an inner monologue of about 18 hours, which follows the thoughts, memories, and associations and even a dream of the narrator. As the narrative moves back and forth from the present to thoughts and memories of the past, the text spans many decades.

The particular day in the life of this woman represents an acute crisis. Recently, she has lost her dog, and this loss has opened up a much older and deeper wound, that of the Nazi persecution. We soon learn that this wound represents an array of unsettling feelings of guilt, shame, and fear that have dominated the narrator's life since the war. Like Weil, the narrator fled from Germany to the Netherlands during the Nazi years, lost her husband, and survived in hiding, after working briefly for the Jewish Council. She returned to West Germany soon after the war, and remarried a non-Jew. Now that she has reached old age, she feels disconnected from life and from her emotions and at times feels so overwhelmed with guilt and hopelessness that she contemplates committing suicide.

These guilt feelings all seem to stem from her war experience and her feeling that she should have done more during the Nazi years, that she should have saved her husband, or other Jews. She wonders why she survived, an assimilated Jew from the German upper class, who had, up until Hitler's reign, never felt very Jewish. She struggles with her position of privilege: her class, her wealth, her connections. She had a chance to work for the Jewish Council and delay her own deportation, and she found safety in hiding when most others did not. But what else should she, or could she have done? What does her survival mean?

In order to find answers, the narrator looks, as she has done throughout her life, at the Greek myth of Antigone, which plays such a central role in the cultural imagination of German *Bildung,* and in her upbringing. While the text recounts a day filled with doing routine errands, the narrator tries to rewrite Sophocles's Antigone story into a novel. Antigone, the Greek princess born out of the incestuous marriage between Oedipus and Jocasta, resists the will of King Creon when she attempts to bury her brother Polynices, who is killed by his brother Eteocles in rivalry over the rule of the city Thebes. As a result, she is sentenced to death by being buried alive in a cave.

Had Antigone listened to her sister Ismene's advice and not resisted Creon's rule, she would have remained alive. In her attempt to fulfill the promise made to her brother to defend his honor, however, she ends up dead.[16]

The narrator identifies with the Antigone figure and she measures herself against this historical resistance fighter: "How do I see her? One day I think I have her, the next day the certainty eludes me. At times she is part of me, at other times my exact opposite. A dream over time, the image of what I wish to be but am not . . ." (14). The comparison between herself and her heroine, however, is a painful one. While the mythical Antigone risked her life for her beliefs, the protagonist did not. "I misinterpret the topic . . . of Antigone. I want to write about her, want to be her, but when the opportunity presents itself to take arms against hate, I leave the dead unburied" (192). Thus, even though she feels strongly connected with this mythical resistance figure and with her fate, she is aware that Antigone may actually be quite different from her. Still, the protagonist wants to understand her, to measure herself against her: "I want to write a book about a girl that does not let herself be written by me, measure my stubbornness against hers, see who will win out in the end."[17] The rewriting of her story is an attempt to make sense of Antigone's act of resistance. She wants to understand why Antigone was able to act, and whether her actions made any difference.

Two-thirds into the story, a "contemporary" Antigone enters the scene in the form of Marlene, a young girl affiliated with a German leftist terrorist group who, during this day, spends several hours at the protagonist's home, hiding from the police. The confrontation with this girl and with present-day terrorism brings up questions for the protagonist about the past, and about one's opportunity or obligation in life to resist or rebel. It is the encounter that makes the narrator rethink Antigone's actions, and her prominent role in the German humanist tradition of *Bildung*. "The sudden insight that my princess has much in common with Marlene and would be just as difficult to put up with. The thought is painful. I surmise that the flesh-and-blood Antigone, not the one I can call forth and send back into obscurity at will, would put quite a strain on my nerves" (128–29). Toward the end of the story, the narrator lets go of Antigone as her heroine, and seems to have reconciled herself with her own much more ambiguous historical position.

Weil's autobiographical reworking of her own and her husband's story of persecution under the Nazis in light of the archetypal dilemmas of the Sophocles drama results in a highly original kind of survivor narrative. At the same time, the format of the story allows a German audience to participate in the protagonist's dilemmas of living under the Nazis and her lack of resistance, and see these conflicts as universal, as human, rather than particular or Jewish. In fact, in order to facilitate this form of identification for the German reader, the text also introduces a completely separate narrative by a *different* author, a text that seems to have no relationship to the overall narrative of *Meine Schwester Antigone* and stands on its own in a separate chapter.

This text is the eyewitness account of a young German soldier who witnessed (and who was part of the army unit that took part in) the liquidation of Petrikau, a Jewish ghetto in Poland in 1943. Reprinted here almost in its entirety (almost 22 pages long in the German edition), the graphic and horrifying scenes of "ordinary" German soldiers doing the work of deporting and shooting thousands of Jewish men, women, and children leaves the reader stunned and confused. The text remains separate from the larger story—the narrator mentions it briefly and then it simply follows in its entirety.

While the account itself does not give us any clues as to how it fits with the rest of the narrative (apart from it representing an elaborate description of Nazi atrocity, something the narrator has witnessed, but to which she does not want to testify), the way the text is framed does give us some clues. The author of the testimony is introduced by the narrator as the brother of a friend, and as "an intellectual and a man of the theater" who was, "as we all were in those days, a pacifist and a leftist" (123). The implications for the reader are clear: this soldier, this man, was *one of us*. In fact, the narrator suggests, they had many acquaintances in common, "for we belonged to the same circles" (123). A note in the back of the book reads that the author of the account, Friedrich Hellmund, studied history and German literature and received his doctorate at age 21. He was killed in 1945 in Poland. Not only was he an "ordinary" German—not a Nazi—he was also highly educated. Clearly, this kind of educational background did not help him or the narrator to guard themselves against the ideological onslaught of the Nazis. "Neither you nor I was trained in obedience, but on the other hand no one has taught us to be wary of slogans, either. And so we allowed ourselves to be destroyed, you as a German soldier, I as one of the persecuted" (123). Both of them, she suggests, have failed (124). By speaking of a German *Wehrmacht* soldier and herself in the same breath, in allowing his traumatized description of the murders he witnessed (but in which he was also forced to participate) to stand next to her narrative of persecution and loss, the narrator allows her German readers to identify with all aspects of her text. The Holocaust, then, she seems to suggest, is not a story of Germans versus Jews, but one that asks difficult questions about responsibility and (in)action of all of us.

This is not to say that, beyond the Antigone story and the Petrikau account, *Meine Schwester Antigone* is not also a text that attempts to rearticulate the narrator's very specific identity crisis. While the text works as an intervention into the public discourse in Germany about the Holocaust in the late 1970s and early 1980s, it is also very much a text about loss of identity and the postwar desire of a German Jew to belong *somewhere*. At different points throughout the text, the narrator speaks in moving passages about the profoundly alienating experience of racial persecution. She was "made into" a Jew: "We are no longer what we were until only recently. At least not in the eyes of the others. But you cannot undergo change in the eyes of others without your own sense of changing as well" (146). Neither her sense of Germanness nor her previously "lukewarm" sense of Jewishness has remained intact. This process is traced throughout the novel.

Initially, while in exile in Amsterdam, the narrator becomes aware of the fact that she belongs to neither the Dutch, nor the Dutch Jews, nor the Germans (who are the occupiers) and wonders what this makes her: "I belong to neither group, belong to no one, am alone, without the faintest notion of what to do or where to go once the war is over" (60). The confrontation with other Jews is new and complex, and does not necessarily create for her a sense of solidarity:

> I meet a stratum of Jewish society I never encountered before: the petty bourgeoisie and proletariat . . . very Oriental, alien, suspicious toward outsiders . . . difficult to handle, and hard to take for me, who am not one of them, who am one of them, an assimilated Jew without religious ties who shares their fate, a fate that extends back thousands of years and forward into the immediate future. (74)

Jewish identity, in the religious and Zionist sense, remains alien to her, and her sense of Jewishness remains firmly tied to her social class and education. The confrontation is thus a difficult one, as she seeks to distinguish herself from other Jews, while the Nazis have assigned them all the same fate. This dramatic change in her self-understanding as well as in her rights as a German and as a Jew creates an intense and prolonged identity crisis. Stripped of her citizenship, her career, her social position, contact with her family and friends, her freedom, she had become a "Jew among Jews" (148). In her case, this marginalization was completely unexpected, and left her unprepared. "Our parents were convinced they had smoothed the path for us. In this modern, progressive world their children's Jewishness would never be used against them. We were rooted in that belief" (9).

When the war was over, neither her social position nor her sense of privilege and belonging was easily restored. The Nazi persecution changed everything, especially the sense of home and safety. "Fleeing. Fleeing home . . . in the end I learned all the tricks for survival and became the ideal victim of persecution. Still am. Yet no one is persecuting me now . . . the passport in my handbag is authentic—German, in fact, which sometimes strikes me as odd or ridiculous—and yet I am still fleeing" (107). In this sense, hers was the position of that of many assimilated Jews. For as Sidra DeKoven Ezrahi suggests, "The restoration of identity may prove more difficult for the assimilated Jew, deprived of national citizenship yet unattached to the Jewish collective, whose definition of self has no social reference."[18] (In the case of German and Austrian Jews, however, I argue that this process may be doubly complicated, for the perpetrators came from among one's own nation.) By "allowing" the Nazis to persecute the Jews, by having been unprepared, the narrator feels as if she has given up her sense of autonomy:

> Saying no is the only freedom that cannot be taken from you . . . I said yes, Yes I shall leave Germany, yes I am no longer a German, yes I shall give up my writing, yes I shall wear the yellow star . . . yes I shall make no effort to spring Waiki from the concentration camp, yes I shall answer to a name that is not my own . . . In this way I shall save my life while destroying myself [while doing away with myself]. (118)[19]

Ezrahi suggests that survivors who did not return or reconnect to a Jewish community after the war and thus missed out on an opportunity for collective mourning might have been more susceptible to feelings of guilt about surviving. Eventually, such feelings may lead to a state of "Emotional paralysis in which [the survivor] allows himself to be acted upon, but hardly ever acts. He has, as it were, lost his right to his own biography" (*By Words Alone*, 92).

It is tempting to take this loss of the narrator's ability to reclaim her biography as a German and as a Jew as an explanation for the highly complex narrative structure of *Meine Schwester Antigone*. For the text is so fragmented in its shifts via an inner monologue from the protagonist's present to her past, to her childhood, to life during the war, to postwar life in Germany, to the Antigone story, and then back to the present, that it is in fact rather confusing. The narrative is fragmented to such a degree that upon first reading it, it is difficult to interpret its meaning. Is this the story of "a day in the life of"? Is it an autobiographical novel in which the narrator thinks about her past and meanwhile attempts to rewrite the story of Antigone? Does the Antigone story stand by itself?

A structural analysis reveals that the retelling of Sophocles' Antigone story is embedded in the larger narrative, which in turn tells us the story of the protagonist's process of writing her own version of the Antigone story. In other words, the seemingly loose relationship between the primary and the embedded story turns out to be relevant to the development of the primary narrative. Throughout the narrative, the protagonist mirrors the Sophocles story with her own, and in so doing, rewrites both. But why is the text so fragmented, why does the narrator move back and forth in time, in her own story and in that of Antigone?

Dagmar Lorenz contends that the "simultaneity of all the different time periods in the consciousness of the narrator suggest that the past is everlasting."[20]

The seamless switching between the different time periods, in particular the war past and the present, reflects the fact that this particular past is very much present for the narrator. Leslie Adelson has argued that Weil's fragmentary style in this work underscores "the tormented quest for solutions that neither she nor her protagonist ever finds."[21] Indeed, it can be argued that the complexity of the narrative structure of the text suggests that *confronting* her past in this personal way is an arduous and ongoing task for the narrator. It is impossible to "own her biography," as Ezrahi suggests, to reassess her own position in a straightforward way.

This is, then, not a traditional kind of Holocaust memoir, but a complex novelistic working through of (German) mourning, guilt, and responsibility, as well as a narrative on the difficulties of reassessing postwar German and Jewish identity. It is ironically this search, rather than the solution itself, that makes Weil's work so engaging and that opens it up for a German audience willing to confront the questions of the Nazi past.

In contrast to her earlier work, *Meine Schwester Antigone* won much acclaim in Germany (in particular among an audience of women, ages 30 to 50).[22] Weil became a well-known literary figure; she was interviewed often; her earlier work was reprinted; and now it found a much wider audience. Apparently, the new more autobiographical form and more personal tone with its implied promise of an open dialogue attracted a new audience.

This belated interest in her work and the German war history in turn stimulated Weil to write more. In 1983, Weil's *Generationen* was published. This work, too, is autobiographical and highly personal, but seems even more so than *Meine Schwester Antigone* as most of the narrative plays itself out in the present. The narrative recounts a period in the protagonist's life in which she lives together with two women (one 15 years younger than herself, one 40 years younger) with whom she enters a complicated, triangulated relationship. The narrative consists of short fragments in which the tumultuous relationship is examined in every detail. The protagonist's aging process, the German politics of the period, and once again, her own war-shaped past, are other recurring themes in this work.

Generationen also seems to be a critique of her own work's reception and the workings of the literary system in Germany, however. For during the same time period in which the relationship between the three women unfolds, one also learns that the protagonist is writing a novel, which turns out to be a book very much like *Meine Schwester Antigone*. At the end of *Generationen,* we find out that this work has been received well by the German audience and sells well, and that the author has become a celebrated literary figure in Germany. The narrator feels intense ambivalence toward this fame, however. Why did it come so late? What does her audience want from her? In the epilogue the narrator once more returns to the Antigone story, and writes one more scenario for her heroine. This scenario closely resembles the narrator's (and Weil's) present life: Antigone has lived to old age, and quite suddenly finds herself living among a new generation that does want to know what has happened in Thebes (read: Auschwitz, Mauthausen). They show interest, but instead of getting closer to her, they objectify her: she has become a "case" (140). This then becomes the new dilemma for the narrator: how to share one's life through literature, how to testify to one's experiences under Nazism, while remaining true to her self.

Then in 1988, after a period of rather serious illness, a sixth book, *Der Brautpreis* was published. This story, even more than *Meine Schwester Antigone* or *Generationen,* relies on a retelling of its intertext for its story. This time, however, in a dramatic move away from her reliance on literary examples that represented German *Bildung,* the story used stems from the *Tanach,* the Old Testament. The narrator, whose name this time is Grete, tells the story of Michal, King David's first wife. Michal, portrayed here as an old woman, becomes the narrator of her own (past) life story, looking back on her life once David has passed away. Interspersed with this narrative, in alternating chapters, but far less prominent in this text than in others, we again get Weil's personal story. The fact that the narrator now uses the first name of—and seems to fully be identified as—the author, blurs the distinction between Grete the author, Grete the narrator, and Grete the protagonist and character even further than in her previous work.

In this work Weil uses the Michal story to explore the roles of women under the Jewish patriarchal system, not unlike some of her work on the Antigone myth. Dagmar Lorenz has thus pointed to a strong similarity between the texts. This time, Judaism as autonomous culture is examined. Here, too, Weil points to the brutality and the oppression of those who are weaker, including women, just as she highlighted this in her analysis of Antigone's Greece.[23] This similarity is less self-evident than it seems, however. Weil's preoccupation with Antigone was clearly linked to the prominent place Greek mythology held in her cultivated prewar German upbringing. The choice for Michal, a minor character in the *Tanach,* is far less obvious, and suggests a deliberate choice for a new, *Jewish* subject matter for Weil.

Furthermore, the way this Michal figure operates in this text is vastly different from Weil's use of Antigone. Not only does Michal function as a character whose story is recounted here in its entirety from beginning to end, but because Michal also functions as her own narrator, without intervention from "Grete," her narrative takes on a great degree of independence and coherence. It is only at the very end that Grete explicitly mentions that she, of course, is the narrator of Michal's story (236). On the other hand, the separation of the two voices also reveals there to be a greater distance between

Grete and Michal than between the narrator and Antigone. Michal's story *can* be told in its entirety, while it remains difficult to tell Antigone's, for her meaning, her story, is so overdetermined for the narrator, and so strongly tied to her own story.

So, who is Michal, and what story does *Der Brautpreis* tell about her? In the *Tanach,* Michal is a relatively minor figure in I Samuel and II Samuel, known only as the first wife of King David, and is perhaps best remembered by the bride-price she receives from David: the foreskins of two hundred murdered (or at least castrated) Philistines.[24] This is double the bride-price that was set by her father, King Saul. David does not get killed. Rather, he gets to marry Michal and soon reveals himself to be a fearsome and ambitious warrior. He is so successful that Saul worries about a takeover and thus he attempts to kill David. David survives Saul's murder attempts by fleeing town with the help of Michal and remains on the run for several years. While David has fled, in a—for the *Tanach*—highly unusual decision, Saul marries Michal off a second time, to another man, Palthi, even though she is still married to David. (The ancient Jewish law of adultery prohibited intercourse between a man and another man's wife. It did not prohibit intercourse between a married man and an unmarried woman. The man could also get married more than once).[25] While away from Michal, David, in turn, marries six more wives.[26]

We only hear of Michal again when Saul and his son Jonathan have been killed in battle, and David has just become king of the tribe of Judah. David now demands Michal back, for having her back will help David establish the legitimacy he needs to become leader of all of Israel. His desire for Michal is thus motivated by political opportunism, not love. Of Michal's return to David, we know only that her second husband weeps when she leaves. Michal reenters the story some time later, when David has brought the Holy Ark to Jerusalem and "Michal daughter of Saul looked out of the window and saw King David leaping and whirling before the Lord; and she despised him for it" (II Samuel 6:16). When Michal confronts David about his behavior, they have an angry exchange, and this is the end of their relationship, the chapter ends with the verse "So to her dying day, Michal, daughter of Saul, had no children" (II Samuel 6:23). From this we conclude that Michal and David were never intimate, even though Michal would live at David's palace the rest of her life.

This, then, is the story of Michal, insofar as she plays a role in the story of David and as can be read about her in the *Tanach.* If one were to combine all the passages in which she is mentioned, they would barely make up a full page. Her story is entirely subordinated to that of David's. The only way in which Michal stands out in the Jewish tradition is that "she is the only woman in the Hebrew Bible whose love for a man is recorded."[27]

(Nowhere else is the love of a woman for a man described from the woman's perspective.)[28] Perhaps it was this detail that drew Weil to explore Michal's story in more depth. Because even though we hear of Michal's love for David at the beginning of this saga, we know nothing of her feelings and thoughts in regard to all the other events that will later so dramatically affect her life.

Weil focuses precisely on this missing perspective: What did Michal think when David brought her the bloody foreskins as a dowry? How did she feel when her father tried to murder her husband? What did it mean to her to be married off again, in defiance of the Seventh Commandment against adultery? How did she respond when David took her back, and now to be one of many wives, her place in this marital hierarchy having been changed? And, finally, what did it mean to her to remain childless, and perhaps more importantly, without love the rest of her life?

In *Der Brautpreis* Michal narrates her own story as an old woman. Most remarkable about the retelling are not the changes added to what we know from the original (many are not that great, although some are notable), but the fact that we now hear the story from Michal's perspective. This female perspective is missing entirely from the *Tanach*, as a Jewish feminist critique has pointed out.[29] Furthermore, Michal's view on her life reveals itself to be an outspoken feminist one. In this story, Michal rebels.

Michal's rebellion is directed not just against the men surrounding her, but also against what she perceives as the restrictions of the Jewish religion. She rebels against the way women such as herself are treated in ancient Israel. She points out that women are objects, possessions to be traded, raped, and exchanged by men (59). Michal's story tells us of her increasing defiance against this God, whom she describes as cruel and unpredictable, and against the use of this deity to justify every war, killing, and disaster. As Jewish law, practice, and faith were closely linked to a Jewish patriarchal tradition in biblical days, Michal's critique of religious practices is also a critique of the male dominance in, and misuse of, Judaism. Her criticism of male privilege is aimed at the Jewish religious practice in which this sense of male entitlement is rooted. Michal's critique of Jewish religious practices is nevertheless ambivalent, as she simultaneously reveals that she, after all, still believes in Jahwe. What she objects to most in the Jewish practice of her day is how this God is used as a justification to enter into war.

The project Weil engages in here by providing Michal with a voice can be seen as part of a larger feminist critique of the Jewish patriarchal tradition that has emerged since the late 1970s. What is important to note, however, is that this kind of serious (scholarly) critique was launched from within Jewish circles. Thus Weil's engagement with this kind of criticism needs to be seen as rather remarkable. For while some critics have argued that this project is a variation of her work on Antigone, Antigone was part of Weil's particular upbringing, and Michal was not. In fact, even her familiarity with the figure of David came about not through Torah study, but through *art:* Michelangelo's sculpture and Rembrandt's painting. This, too, is typical of the upper-class *Bildung* Weil received, which was decidedly more German than Jewish. Her work on Michal, then, seems a deliberate move away from the German material she was familiar with and toward a concerted effort to explore Jewishness. Weil uses the Michal story to explore the roles of women in Jewish biblical history while also examining what Jewishness, a Jewish identity, means for herself.

What makes this rewriting of Michal's story interesting, in fact, is precisely the complexity of the narrator's critique of Judaism. Michal's attitude suggests more a protest against male dominance than against Jewish tradition itself. Jewishness might have to be reinterpreted in a more modern and more emancipated way, and this would be possible if it were not for the men, Michal suggests. The text posits a mostly *positive* engagement with the Jewish (biblical) tradition, which can also be seen in the chapters that are Grete's personal narrative.

What she recounts here is her personal story of exile, war, and her return to Germany, but now with a specific emphasis on her sense of Jewishness, which remained in the background in her earlier works. She traces the transition of living under an imposed (racial) Jewish identity to living one that she claims herself. For initially, at the end of the war, Grete wanted to return to Germany and to being German. She wanted to get rid of this tainted identity which had been imposed upon her: "I don't want to hear the word Jew anymore" (37). Soon she realized, however, that Jewishness had in fact become of central importance to her self-understanding, and to the other people's understanding of her. "[I] still very often heard the word 'Jew,' which I had not wanted to hear anymore after the war, used it myself, it had become a compulsion . . . to profess the fact . . . As a Jew, I had been persecuted, as a Jew . . . my husband had been murdered. I couldn't put being Jewish aside, like a dress that had become old-fashioned" (51). Through the experience of persecution, Jewishness had become central to her identity, even though it took on a very different shape from that with which she had once associated it.

Still, precisely because it was imposed from the outside in such a problematic fashion, Jewishness remains complicated. For a Jewish identity, one either has to believe in God or feel a connection to the land of Israel, Grete argues, and "Neither the one nor the other is present in me, never was present" (127). Instead she suggests that "What remains is that I have experienced, as a Jew, what suffering means. So probably the single rudiment of an identity, mutual suffering and fate" (127). Her life remains determined, then, not by Jewish faith, or by Jewish culture, or Jewish national identity, but by the Jewish genocide. Her identity has become that of "the survivor who has not forgotten, cannot forget, and does not want to forget" (124).

On the other hand, her identity as a survivor has indeed brought her back to Jewish culture, and hence, to the story she is now trying to tell, of David and Michal. She does so out of " . . . curiosity and the conjecture that not only the myths and the history of the Greeks are worth knowing, but those of the Jews as well" (128). She becomes interested in Judaism as a culture, as text. In turn, writing the Michal project eventually makes her more strongly identified as a Jew: "Have I become more Jewish since I've been involved with David and Michal? Yes, surely, something has started that was not there before" (128). In order to write this story, Weil in fact visits Israel for the first time. This does not mean, however, that the identification with Michal leads to a similar degree of affinity as with Antigone: "For me, she was never a sister, like Antigone, admired and envied for her courage. No deep relationship between me and this woman who was pushed around and often misused by men" (128–29). What she feels instead is:

> " . . . sympathy and compassion . . . She and I, bound together by our belonging to a people that is not really one people at all but always wanted to be one: two Jewish women" (129).

Michal, then, more than Antigone, formed a personal and a literary *exercise* for Weil: This was an exercise in which the narrator could place herself as a Jewish survivor in Germany and as a Jew within a much larger and older Jewish history and culture. In the end, she seems to have embraced her Jewishness.

Whereas her earlier work thus functioned as an intervention in the German public sphere in which the Nazi past continually needed to be invoked and made present, in which Weil sought address, in this later work she seems less concerned with engaging in a dialogue as a German with other Germans. Instead, she asserts herself here with a *Jewish* text written in German in Germany. It should be seen as a sign of success for her earlier project that by this time, her German audience no longer seemed to mind. *Der Brautpreis* found much acclaim, and it was reprinted four times in the course of just a few months. In 1988, Weil received the "Geschwister-Scholl-Preis" for it, and it was translated in several languages, including English.[30]

Klüger's "German Address"

While Grete Weil's return to Germany was both literary and actual, and her project to draw the German audience into a dialogue about the Holocaust and German Jewish life in contemporary Germany relatively straightforward, the case of Ruth Klüger is a far more complex one. Most well known for her 1992 autobiographical text *weiter leben: eine Jugend* [Living On: A Childhood] published in German in Germany, Klüger is an American Holocaust scholar and university professor of German who left Germany in 1948 after surviving the Shoah. The text then, properly, seemed to be the address of an *American* to the Germans. Or was it? Right from the start of *weiter leben,* the narrator makes it clear that she speaks *both* as an Austro-German Jewish survivor and as an American academic, but that she means to address a German audience as an (Austro-) German Jew, not as an American citizen.

Interestingly enough, Klüger's memoir was received in 1992 with glowing reviews in Germany as a *German* book and became a bestseller. It immediately became canonized as the best of a new German-Jewish literary tradition. This makes for a fascinating but somewhat problematic form of displacement. After all, Klüger left Germany after the war as a survivor of a regime that defined her as a part of a subhuman species and set out to kill her and her family. With *weiter leben,* Klüger was said to "have returned" and was heralded as an important postwar *German* author.[31] Yet, upon a closer reading of the text, the German appropriation of this outsider's Holocaust memoir as *German* will show itself to be highly inappropriate and ironic.

This text, then, presents an interesting case. For not only does it figure in interesting ways in 1990s (postreunification) Germany's cultural debates about German Jews and the Nazi past, it also complicates the Holocaust memoir as a genre. While the circumstances of its publication are thus remarkable, the text itself, too, is unusual, both in its inception and in its address.

On the face of it, *weiter leben* is a straightforward Holocaust memoir. It recounts the author's life in four parts: "Wien" (her prewar life, 1931–1942), "Die Lager" (Theresienstadt, Auschwitz-Birkenau, and Christianstadt/Gross-Rosen), "Flucht/Bayern" (her escape from a death march with her mother and her postwar life in Germany until 1948), and "New York" (her first decade in the United States). It ends with an epilogue (entitled "Göttingen") that recounts the author's return to Germany in the late 1980s for a work assignment (directing a study-abroad program for her university in the United States). The structure of the text is such, however, that even as *weiter leben* provides the autobiographical narrative of survival, emigration, and success in America, it also contains a *meta-discourse* on (German-Jewish) Holocaust experience and Holocaust literature. As a result, the text has an unusually sophisticated narrative structure that is fragmented through the narrator's comments in the present, and through the associative use of flashbacks and foreshadowing. *Weiter leben's* unique quality is located, then, precisely in the fact that it also turns a critical eye toward itself to self-consciously deconstruct its own testimony and the psychological, historical, and literary discourses that have surrounded this kind of literature for the last 25 years.

In some ways, this text "does it all," for it provides testimony while commenting on the impossibility of testimony, and it problematizes the recall of memory, the constructed nature of survivor narratives, and the function of writing. It invites a dialogue with its German readers while commenting on the difficulty of this dialogue; it uses the insights of many different academic disciplines as well as from works of art and literature as intertexts, only to criticize many of these forms of theoretical and artistic discourse. In so doing, the text in part reflects the remarkable professional and intellectual journey of its author, which differs in many respects from most survivor-authors.[32] The text relies on representing Klüger as a well-read intellectual, a professor of German literature (at the University of California at Irvine, now retired); equally at home with German literature as with the research on Holocaust history, psychology, literature, and the critical discourses on memory and the memorialization of the Holocaust. Before she published *weiter leben,* Klüger had already written critically on several aspects of Holocaust studies. This book then reflects in its make-up—a memoir of a childhood under the Nazis, but also a critical analysis of, and an answer to, several theoretical discourses on the Holocaust—Klüger's considerable literary talent, combined with her familiarity with a form of critical scholarly analysis that does not seek to please or appease.

The fact that the narrative of *weiter leben* is filled with intertexts and commentary on other Holocaust memoirs and analyses, however, does not mean that Klüger's work only seeks to serve as a correction of postwar popular and academic discourse on the Holocaust, in which case she might have been better off publishing her work in English in the United States. After all, a great deal of academic discourse on the Holocaust is produced in North America. By writing in the German language and publishing in Germany, Klüger also explicitly seeks a *German* address. After all, few German Jewish survivors would come to write or publish their memoirs in German and publish them *in* Germany.[33] By not publishing in the United States, which has a considerable market for (English-language) Holocaust memoirs, Klüger made a conscious choice to be part of a German and not just American literary landscape.

Strangely enough, even though Klüger's memoir is a story of oppression, isolation, murder, and of a difficult reentry into the postwar world, a story without a happy ending, most German critics still proceeded to interpret the work as a triumph, as a success story.[34] The focus in these critics' analyses falls on Klüger's prewar life as a Jewish girl in Vienna, on her miraculous selection, and on her postwar success as a *Germanistin.* Little mention is made of all the instances of hopelessness, the deep break her persecution by the Nazis and the camp experiences have formed with her former life and identity, or of her sharp critique of the Holocaust as a *German* crime and of

Germans' inability to deal with the Holocaust and its survivors in a way that does not reify them, nor minimize or appropriate survivors' experience. Instead, her achievement as a postwar academic is hailed by critics in order to foreground a single historical fact: that Klüger managed to become highly successful professionally, and more importantly, that she has "returned to Germany," after all.

Martin Walser, for instance (who is depicted by Klüger in *weiter leben* as her German youth friend Christoph), suggests that her work is a "Sprachwunder," a miracle of language with which she has achieved a return to Germany. He thereby explicitly ignores that she chose *not* to return: "regardless of where she now resides . . . it is not the passport which tells where one belongs, but language . . . Ruth Klüger has returned to the German language, and in a masterful way."[35] What occurs here is an interesting negation of the historical context. For the Nazis it was precisely through the taking away of German citizenship, one's passport, that they managed to undo German Jews of their German identity. For the Nazis, it made absolutely no difference whether your language was German, if you were not of the "proper" race. The fact that Ruth Klüger no longer has an Austrian or German passport but carries American citizenship is thus no mere coincidence, and does not reflect her own choice. Her "return" to Germany in the German language is then not at all irrespective of where she now resides, but both in spite of and because of her postwar life in the United States.

Not unlike Weil, Klüger seeks to reconnect through her work with Germans and Germany for she, too, because of her particular class background and *Bildung*, still identifies culturally with a German Enlightenment tradition. Perhaps this is what makes her text so quintessentially German. Nevertheless, her text shows again and again that reconnecting to this particular tradition of German-Jewish symbiosis after the Shoah is problematic. For a discerning reader, Klüger's text never implies a facile return of any kind, in language or otherwise. These kinds of reviews, however, were common, even though Klüger suggests that this return is in fact *not possible*. Instead, then, of picking up on the complex reading suggestions Klüger offers, critics have used this book to appease themselves:

> Klügers highly idiosyncratic discourse on Auschwitz has been generally misheard or misread. One applauds without holding back, there where one recognizes one's self, and skips energetically those passages where difference manifests itself as true difference, there where . . . it really cannot be integrated into one's own imagination.[36]

Many German critics have sought to identify with Klüger in this work, and have thus avoided a confrontation with their own possible complicity, and their responsibility to come to terms with the Nazi past.[37] But what, in fact, may then have been the text's intention?

By writing in German and publishing in Germany, Klüger opens a dialogue with Germans and engages in the public German debate on the Nazi past and the Holocaust. The Germans she addresses are friends (mostly not Jewish) and acquaintances, writers and thinkers, as well as her audience of strangers. Thus she engages in a conflict-laden, textual dialogue about the German attempts to come to terms with the past, the tendency to misunderstand or minimize the experience of the Jews, and the possibility of postwar German-Jewish life. She seeks to engage in a dialogue about the Nazi past, about what has been done by the Germans to the Jews, in order to bring about the possibility for a conversation between Germans and Jews *in the present*. For until this dialogue about the past takes place, Germans and Jews do not meet sufficient common ground to function together in a German present or future, she suggests.

A great deal of the narrative in *weiter leben* that deals with German-Jewish interaction suggests, then, precisely *what is wrong* with this relationship as it is today. Take, for instance, Klüger's use of the character Gisela throughout the text. Gisela embodies everything that is problematic about the relationship between Germans and Jews after the war. She is full of judgments, diminishes the suffering of Jews, denies German guilt, and exudes an ambivalence about the past and her parents' generation, which Klüger suggests is all too common among certain Germans. Most of her interjections are deeply offensive to Klüger. For example, Gisela suggests that Theresienstadt could not have been so bad for Klüger, and that although Auschwitz must have been horrible, "yes, after everything that she had heard, said Gisela, that must have been bad," Klüger really did not spend too much time there.[38]

Although Klüger is open to discussing useful comparisons, Gisela instead equates her own German postwar experience with that of Klüger and comes up with absurd and insulting parallels: "I had it relatively good, I was able to emigrate to America, and I was spared the German postwar misery. Compared to her mother, who lost her husband at the Russian front, my mother, who married twice more in America, had been very lucky" (92). Once again, the historical context disappears completely.

The roots of the conflict between the "average" Germans such as Gisela and Klüger need to be sought, suggests Klüger, in the fundamental difference in experience of Germans and of Jews. The points of view of Germans and of Jews were incommensurable, a discrepancy that showed itself as soon as the war was over. Although Germans and Jews share memories of these postwar years, the content of the memories differs based on their perspective: "Memory connects us, memory separates us" (218). This gap between Germans and Jews is still present today. She realizes, for instance, that while "you may and can speak about your war experiences, dear friends, I cannot. My childhood falls into the black hole of this discrepancy" (109).

It is this silence she is trying to overcome in this book. She writes to create a bridge because, "if there is no bridge at all from my memories to yours, why am I even writing this?" (110). She suggests that in order to build a bridge to each other's experience, one needs to compare, not mythologize or silence the Holocaust.[39] Finding an address, however, remains difficult:

> People do not want to hear about it, or only in a certain pose, with a certain attitude, not as a partner in dialogue, but as one who subjects himself to an unpleasant task, with a kind of reverence which easily reverses itself into irritation. For the objects one reveres, like the ones one hates, one tends to keep far away from oneself. (110)

Or people do not want to listen at all, as they argue that they "already know everything." Or people seek to diminish the "strangeness" they encounter in her, in her story, and seek to identify with her and her past, which in turn denies that a real gap of experience remains present between their position and hers.

This is the challenge, then, that *weiter leben* presents and that German critics have overlooked in their too simple affirmation of the text's reference at the cost of recognizing its narrative quests. In their reading of this book, they have not seen it as an opportunity to communicate from their own position with the "other" this book represents. Instead, they have identified with Klüger, made her one of them, even though Klüger explicitly admonishes them not to do so:

> You should not identify with me, I would much prefer if you did not; and when I seem *Artfremd* [of a different species or race] I will accept that . . . and . . . apologize for it. But at least allow yourself to be agitated, don't hide, don't say beforehand: that has nothing to do with you . . . you already have . . . absolved your task of complicity and compassion. Become militant, seek the dialogue. (141)

Even as Klüger seeks to engage and enrage her German readers in *weiter leben,* and as she seeks to unsettle them with her sharp criticism of German discourse surrounding the Holocaust, it is significant that she still offers openings for a dialogue. She has just one condition: that each one faces one's *own* past. These critical warnings and comments in the text are nevertheless ignored by the German critique. Thus, what takes place is not a German encounter, in the present, with one who is Jewish. Instead, Klüger's publication in Germany is itself used as evidence that the gap has *already* been bridged between Jews and

Germans, and that they can welcome her back as a German. Her Jewishness is thus seen as something of the past, as related solely to the Holocaust, not as a difference that still exists as a real, viable form of identity.

Even though the German response is inadequate, the fact that Germans do feel that the war is a past they have to come to terms with somehow is what allows Klüger to address them. In contrast, Austrians have avoided a confrontation with the past for so long (they consider it unnecessary) that there is no postwar basis for a German-Jewish dialogue to which Klüger can appeal. A reception of her work there, her *address,* is not possible. Klüger suggests that she has in fact cut all her connections to Austria. Her memories of Vienna remain solely those of the war, and they have not been replaced by a postwar possibility for new Jewish life. Her only connection with Austria is with its language.

Klüger's choice then, to seek a *German,* not an Austrian, or even an Anglo-American address for the personal act of witness, needs to be considered as central to the text's interpretation, even though the early reception of this aspect of the work in particular may have been inadequate and too simplistic.

Conclusion

Shoshana Felman and Dori Laub argue in their study on testimony that the Holocaust as a reality was traumatic precisely in that it extinguished *the very possibility of address,* the possibility of appealing to another person outside of the reality of one's own experience of persecution.[40] This in turn convinced some survivors "that their experiences were no longer communicable, even to themselves, and therefore perhaps never took place" (28). The situation in which the survivor now *reclaims the position of speaking or writing witness,* in which he or she creates address, is crucial, as it enables a degree of psychological reintegration.

I have discussed several German-Jewish autobiographical texts here, not only to show how these texts indeed seek address (and in Weil's case, how this address may have indeed been meaningful to her), but also to show how difficult it is to compose such an address both as a German and as a Jew. As highly assimilated Jews, both Weil and Klüger struggle with articulating Jewishness beyond their experience of Nazi persecution. At the same time, both struggle as women in their attempt to rearticulate Jewishness into something more positive, more meaningful. In turn, their German audience still has a hard time reading their "return" as German-Jewish, rather than just German.

At the same time, these authors do succeed through their publications in reinserting themselves as German-Jewish survivor-authors into the German language and culture from which they had been forcefully removed by the Nazis. They return in the form of their textual address and seek to move a dialogue about Germans and Jews as well as Jews in Germany beyond the postwar stalemate. In creating such "address" for their stories, these authors are doing more than salvaging their own identities. They are consciously engaged in postwar Germany and Austria's processes of historical and social redefinition as well: Through their literature they seek to create room for themselves as German or Austrian Jews to exist within these post-Holocaust national communities.

How one should interpret this kind of "reentry" into the national consciousness of these nations, however, remains open to debate. In part the effect of these texts depends on how one reads the reception of the authors and their literature. Does one consider the literature and its reception to be a continuation of a German-Jewish symbiosis, or conversely, of a negative symbiosis, as Dan Diner has characterized the postwar relationship between German Jews and other Germans? Or is it something altogether new and different?

Notes

1. There was and is no term for the Nazi genocide of the Jews in 1933–1945 in either the English or the German language. Thus, initially one sometimes used the Hebrew terms *Churban* (in Hebrew, or *churbm* in Yiddish) and Shoah (*sho'ah* in Hebrew), which pre-1945 were used to refer to the destruction of the First and Second Temples. Since the 1960s, the term Holocaust (from the Greek *holokauston,* meaning "whole burnt" or sacrifice by fire) has been most commonly used in the United States. Neither of the most commonly used terms today, Holocaust and Shoah, are entirely satisfactory as they both carry religious connotations, which I deem inappropriate. Whereas these are the names most customarily used in public as well as academic discourse on this subject, however, I have decided to employ them both, interchangeably. It is interesting that for most Europeans, both terms were publicly introduced through foreign media events. *Holocaust* became common usage only after the American television series with the same name was shown around Europe in 1978, and *Shoah* was introduced through Claude Lanzmann's documentary of the same name, which was widely shown in Europe on television around 1985. On the importance of this naming of the Nazi genocide of the Jews, see James Young, *Writing and Rewriting the Holocaust: Narrative and the Consequences of Interpretation* (Bloomington: University of Indiana Press, 1988).

2. Jean Améry, "How Much Home Does a Person Need?" *At The Mind's Limits: Contemplations by a Survivor on Auschwitz and Its Realities,* trans. Sidney Rosenfeld and Stella P. Rosenfeld (New York: Shocken Books, 1990), 43–44.

3. Dan Diner, "Negative Symbiose: Deutsche und Juden nach Auschwitz," *Jüdisches Leben in Deutschland seit 1945,* ed. Micha Brumlik, Micha, Doron

Kiesel, Cilly Kugelmann, and Julius H. Schoeps (Frankfurt: Jüdischer Verlag bei Athenäum, 1986), 255. My translation.

4. "Since Auschwitz—what a sad joke—one can truly speak of a German-Jewish symbiosis, a negative one, however. For both Germans and Jews the fact of the mass murder has become the starting point of one's self-understanding, a kind of contradictory union—whether they want it or not." Diner, "Negative Symbiose," 243. My translation.

5. Grete Weil, *My Sister, My Antigone,* trans. Krishna Winston (New York: Avon Books, 1984), 146. I quote from this edition when possible, but when I feel the translation is lacking, I provide my own translation of the German text: Grete Weil, *Meine Schwester Antigone* (Frankfurt am Main: Fischer, 1982).

6. Weil, *My Sister,* 147.

7. Weil, *My Sister,* 147.

8. Weil, *My Sister,* 147.

9. Weil, *My Sister,* 84. In an early scene in *Ans Ende der Welt,* Weil's first published book, a Jewish family imprisoned in the Schouwburg has a conversation with the German-Jewish typist of the Jewish Council. The portrait of the typist suggests a critical self-portrait of Weil. The family, upset about their impending deportation, and irritated about the lackluster response of the typist, confronts her with the fact that she, too, is a Jew. "Only for the duration of the war," the woman answers, completely seriously . . . "afterwards I will be a human again." In turn, the Jewish family confronts her with the hypocrisy of her position as an employee of the Joodse Raad: "That is easy for you to say, miss, sitting here at your safe post. When the Jewish Council has sent all other Jews to Poland, their employees might have the chance to experience these fortunate times, in which one may just be a human. For us ordinary mortals, the outlook is significantly more grim" (*Ans Ende der Welt,* 13). My translation. In Weil's other work the Joodse Raad and her employment there is discussed repeatedly and always in ambivalent terms. Weil, *Ans Ende der Welt* (Frankfurt am Main: Fischer Taschenbuch Verlag, 1987).

10. Weil, *Der Brautpreis* (Frankfurt am Main: Fischer Taschenbuch Verlag, 1991), 138. Translation comes from *The Bride Price,* trans. John Barrett (Boston: David R. Godine, 1991), 103.

11. "Whether I like it or not—and very often I don't like it—I am a German." As quoted in Laureen Nussbaum and Uwe Meyer, "Grete Weil: unbequem, zum Denken zwingend," *Exilforschung* 11 (1993): 159. My translation. See also a very similar statement in Weil's writing in *Der Brautpreis,* 165.

12. Weil had to return illegally because she no longer possessed a German passport, deprived as she was of her German citizenship. Weil, *Generationen* (Frankfurt am Main: Fischer Taschenbuch Verlag, 1985), 88.

13. Grete Weil's works, in order of original publication dates: *Ans Ende der Welt* (Frankfurt am Main: Fischer Taschenbuch Verlag, 1987); first published by Verlag Volk und Welt in East Berlin in 1949. *Tramhalte Beethovenstraat*

(Frankfurt am Main: Fischer Taschenbuch Verlag, 1983); first published by Limes Verlag in Wiesbaden in 1963. *Happy, sagte der Onkel* (Frankfurt am Main: Fischer Taschenbuch Verlag, 1982); first published by Limes Verlag in Wiesbaden in 1968. *Meine Schwester Antigone* (Frankfurt am Main: Fischer Taschenbuch Verlag, 1982); first published by Benziger Verlag in Zürich and Köln in 1980. *Generationen* (Frankfurt am Main: Fischer Taschenbuchverlag, 1985); first published with Benziger Verlag, Zürich and Cologne, 1983. *Der Brautpreis* (Frankfurt am Main: Fischer Taschenbuch Verlag, 1991); first published by Verlag Nagel & Kimche AG in Zürich and Frauenfeld, 1988. *Spätfolgen: Erzählungen* (Zürich: Nagel & Kimche, 1992).

14. Nussbaum and Meyer, "Grete Weil," 160–61.

15. In contrast, in the Netherlands it did receive a positive response, and so would all of Weil's later works. This prompted a German critic to remark in 1991 that Weil had in fact now become "the most read German (female) author" in the Netherlands (Alexander von Bormann as quoted by Nussbaum and Meyer, "Grete Weil," 168, my translation). In order to fully understand the contrast in the reception of Weil's work in the two countries, one would have to take into account the very different legacy of the war in Germany and the Netherlands, and the way in which these countries have chosen (were able to choose) to memorialize the past. Clearly, as "victim of the Nazis," the Dutch had less difficulty accepting the literature of a German Jew in the Netherlands, hunted down by the Nazi invader—even though Weil suggests that many Dutch citizens' behavior toward the Jews during the war was less than admirable.

16. When I discuss the Antigone "master text," not the one the narrator invents, I base my description on Heinrich Weinstock's Sophocles translation (Sophocles, *Die Tragödien,* trans. Heinrich Weinstock (Stuttgart: Kröner Verlag, 1962), as well as those of Friedrich Hölderlin (Hölderlin, *Die Trauerspiele des Sophocles* (1804; Frankfurt am Main: Stroemfeld/Roter Stern, 1986), and the interpretation of Gustav Schwab (Schwab, *Griekse mythen en sagen,* trans. J. K. van den Brink (Utrecht: Het Spectrum, 1956), as all these versions are mentioned explicitly in *Meine Schwester Antigone* as the texts on which the narrator bases her Antigone character.

17. Weil, *Meine Schwester Antigone,* 17, my translation. Krishna Winston's translation in the Avon edition: "I should like to write a book about a girl, a book which does not want to let me write it. I should like to compare her stubbornness with my own and see who finally gains the upper hand." Weil, *My Sister,* 1.

18. Sidra DeKoven Ezrahi, *By Words Alone: The Holocaust in Literature* (Chicago: University of Chicago Press, 1980), 73.

19. The translation of this passage in the Winston translation hardly does justice to the text, and I therefore offer my own alternative translation for the ending of the quote between brackets. The German reads: "Ich sagte nicht nein—Neinsagen, die einzige unzerstörbare Freiheit . . . ich sagte ja. Ja, ich verlasse Deutschland, ja, ich bin keine Deutsche mehr . . . ja, ich nähe mir

auf die Kleider den gelben Stern . . . ja, ich nehme einen fremden Namen an, ja, ich mache keinen Versuch, Waiki aus dem KZ mit Gewalt zu befreien . . . So rette ich mein Leben, so schaffe ich mich selber ab." Weil, *Meine Schwester Antigone,* 88.

20. Dagmar C. G. Lorenz, *Verfolgung bis zum Massenmord: Holocaust-Diskurse in deutscher Sprache aus der Sicht der Verfolgten* (New York: Peter Lang, 1992), 169.
21. Leslie Adelson, "1971 *Ein Sommer in der Woche der Itke K.* by American born author Jeanette Lander is published," *Yale Companion to Jewish Writing and Thought in German Culture, 1096–1996,* ed. Sander L. Gilman and Jack Zipes (New Haven: Yale University Press, 1997), 751.
22. Grete Weil suggests this herself, in an interview with Adriaan van Dis. See van Dis, "Nee zeggen is de enige onverwoestbare vrijheid," *NRC Handelsblad* Cultureel Supplement (November 12,1982): 3.
23. Lorenz, *Verfolgung bis zum Massenmord,* 262.
24. I made use here of *Tanakh: A New Translation of the Holy Scriptures According to the Hebrew Text* (Philadelphia: The Jewish Publication Society, 1985).
25. Judith Romney Wegner, *Chattel or Person? The Status of Women in the Mishnah* (New York: Oxford University Press, 1988), 13. Wegner points out that the Tenth Commandment, which "forbids an Israelite to covet his neighbor's possessions: wife, slave, cattle, or anything else that belongs to his neighbor," as well as the prohibition of adultery, bear "the inescapable connotation of [women as] property of an owner" (13). "A daughter is likewise perceived as the property of the father; he collects bride-price from the man who marries her or from one who seduces or rapes her whether or not the violator marries the girl. The bride-price compensated for the loss of the daughter's virginity, treated as the father's economic asset" (13).
26. Adultery was defined as a sexual act between a man and a married woman. Wegner explains that "a girl or woman who may have become espoused to a given man cannot marry another until the first man divorces her . . . a girl or a woman who mistakenly consummates marriage with one man when she is promised to another counts as an adulteress, and her children will be illegitimate . . . worse still, she cultically pollutes the man who has intercourse with her" (29). Jewish men, up to this point in time at least, were allowed by Jewish law to have more than one wife at any given moment, as is evident from David's multiple marriages in which he procured over six wives at the same time. Wegner suggests, "The polygynous system of the Mishnah involves a pervasive double standard. Though a man has the *exclusive* right to his wife's sexuality, the wife's right to the husband's sexual function is never *exclusive.* She cannot legally preclude her husband from taking additional wives or having sexual relations with unmarried women. By contrast, she can neither have more than one husband nor indulge in sexual relations with other men" (220–21). Wegner explains that "the key to differential treatment of women in Mishnah lies specifically in the sexuality factor. . . . Whenever some man has a proprietary interest in the sexual and reproduc-

tive function of a specified girl or woman, the Mishnah's framers treat the woman as that man's chattel in all matters that affect his ownership or her sexuality" (19). It all comes down to the point that a man owns the biological function of the woman at hand and thus controls the woman's life to a greater or lesser degree. Wegner, *Chattel or Person?*, 29, 220–21, and 19.

27. Joseph Telushkin, *Biblical Literacy: The Most Important People, Events, and Ideas of the Hebrew Bible* (New York: William Morrow and Company, 1997), 212.

28. Except for in *The Song of Songs,* which also describes love from a woman's perspective. This character does not have a name, however. Telushkin, *Biblical Literary,* 212.

29. Since the 1970s, a number of works have been published in the United States in particular that deal with the role of Jewish women in ancient and in modern religious practice. There are also a number of texts that explore specifically the question of Jewish women's status in ancient Israel, as well as in the *Tanach* and in Rabbinic Commentary. Written by Jewish theologians and (Jewish) women's studies scholars, most of this work is undertaken by women. See among others, Elizabeth Koltun, ed., *The Jewish Woman: New Perspectives* (New York: Schocken Books, 1976), Susannah Heschel, ed., *On Being a Jewish Feminist* (New York: Schocken Press, 1983), Rachel Biale, *Women and Jewish Law: An Exploration of Women's Issues in Halakhic Sources* (New York: Schocken, 1984), Carol Meyers, *Discovering Eve: Ancient Israelite Women in Context* (New York: Oxford University Press, 1988), Judith Plaskow, *Standing Again at Sinai: Judaism from a Feminist Perspective* (San Francisco: Harper, 1990) and Wegner, *Chattel or Person?*.

30. This needs to be seen as a somewhat exceptional accomplishment, as up to that point, few of Weil's works had been translated into English, since there seemed to be no interest in the United States for a survivor who wrote about the war but *who remained in Germany by her own choice.* In part it could be argued, though, that marketing was to blame for Weil's lack of recognition in the American market, as well. *Meine Schwester Antigone* came out in the United States only in a cheap pocket book edition with a mediocre translation. As mentioned earlier, however, translated into a good Dutch translation (under Weil's supervision), and published with a major Dutch press, almost every work by Weil sold well in the Netherlands. Most likely then, both marketing and political factors influenced the ebb and flow of her literary career outside of Germany.

31. Marcel Reich-Ranicki mentioned in his literary magazine on ZDF television, *Das literarische Quartett* on January 14, 1993, that *weiter leben* counted "as the best work that has been published in the German language in the last two, three, four years." As quoted in Stephen Braese and Holger Gehle, "Von 'deutschen Freunden:' Ruth Klüger's 'weiter leben. Eine Jugend' in der deutschen Rezeption" *Der Deutschunterricht* 47.6 (1995): 76. My translation.

32. Klüger's ascendance in the American academic world is rather unique among survivors, and is in part due to the convergence of some uncommon demographic factors. Few Jews Klüger's age made it out of Germany alive or

through the concentration camps. Because she survived precisely at the age that she was young enough to enter an American university as a first-time student after the war, she was perhaps better able to restart her life in the United States and integrate more fully into its academic and professional structure. In contrast, survivors who were older than she usually did not enter university but entered the work force, or had children right away. (If some did reenter academia, they had already been socialized in a German university system, which differed from that of North America, which in turn often worked to their disadvantage.)

33. Often, the relation to the language and to German identity had become extremely ambivalent, and the majority of German Jews elected after the war to do away with both. If they indeed wrote and published their memoirs, they almost always did so in the English language with American publishing houses. In turn, this switch in language almost always also signals a shift in identity. A well known example is Gerda Klein, author of *All But My Life* (New York: Hill and Wang, 1957). Born in 1924 in Bielitz, Poland (formerly a part of Austria, many Jews of this region therefore spoke German) Klein was liberated by American soldiers in Volary in Czechoslovakia after her stay in six different camps and married the (German-Jewish, now turned American) officer who aided in her liberation. She left with him for America in 1946. Her memoir has been very successful in the United States. Hers thus became an American story, as she never returned to Europe, nor wrote in German again. Gerda Klein describes the use of the English language as helpful in establishing a new life: "I also found that language can become a buffer, a filter for emotions, a free zone to which I can safely retreat" (255). In turn, the use of German had become extremely problematic: "[German] has its lyrical beauty, but for me the Nazis succeeded in perverting it into the strident, staccato cadences that implied and expressed ominous threats. It was in those tones that my parents' terrible death warrant had been decreed" (256). When soon after establishing a life in America she was asked to speak in a radio interview in German, the following incident occurred: "I became petrified. To speak German on the radio was something completely out of my province. Hitler, Goebbels, and their cohorts had spoken on the radio, and to me this made it forever theirs. . . . A paralyzing fear gripped me, and the walls of safety that English had built around me came tumbling down . . . I could not go on" (255).

34. As Stephan Braese and Holger Gehle point out in their comprehensive analysis of this reception, Braese and Gehle, "Von 'deutschen Freunden,'" 76–83.

35. Walser, "Ruth Klüger zur Begrüssung," *Das Kulturjournal* Bayerischer Rundfunk (radio broadcast) presented by Peter Hamm, September 27, 1992. Reprinted in Braese and Gehle, "Von 'deutschen Freunden,'" 84–85. My translation.

36. My translation. Irene Heidelberger-Leonard, *Ruth Klüger: weiter leben. Eine Jugend,* Oldenbourg Interpretationen, vol. 81 (München: R. Oldenbourg, 1996): 88.

37. Braese and Gehle, "The German dialogue-engagement circumvents the problem of Jewish life since Auschwitz . . . the dialogue intended by Klüger has become a German monologue" (80). My translation. They suggest that the analyses from Martin Walser and Andreas Isenschmidt and "almost every review" read the book this way (80–83).

38. Klüger, *weiter leben,* 92. My translation. All of the following citations from *weiter leben* are translated by me.

39. Thus, she applauds the use of the word "Holocaust," however imprecise and problematic its connotation may be, as it is useful in conversation with Germans who were not there. Before this word was used in Germany, the events existed as "Event, but not this expression, and therefore also not the notion. . . . As long as we just have a word somewhere that can be used without circumlocution and extra clauses" (233). As there was no word that covered the whole array of Nazi crimes against the Jews, there could not be (and needed not to be) any discussion about it.

40. Shoshana Felman and Dori Laub, *Testimony: Crises of Witnessing in Literature, Psychoanalysis, and History* (New York: Routledge, 1992), 82.

CHAPTER ELEVEN

THE JANUS-FACED JEW

Nathan and Shylock on the Postwar German Stage

ANAT FEINBERG

The scene: a succession of gray bulwarks and fortifications representing Jerusalem, which seems neither exotic, magical, nor holy, but rather mundane and ahistorical. Gotthold Ephraim Lessing's Nathan, a Jew in modern garb with a skullcap on his head, is tired of being wise. The play will not take place, announces Lessing's eponymous protagonist, who grapples yet again with the text. The vitriolic polemics over the (im)possibility of a performance and the equally difficult issue of what it means to be a Jew in post-Holocaust Germany involve all the figures of Lessing's *Nathan the Wise,* as well as, surprisingly, Shylock. Shakespeare's Jew, in black clothes and a ubiquitous bowler hat, is Nathan's counterpart, even his alter-ego. The suitcase in Shylock's hand has the same metonymic function as the cart in which Nathan stores his belongings. Both are wandering Jews, scarred and vulnerable; acknowledged at best, and at worst, ostracized. At one point during a passionate argument, Shylock cynically mocks Nathan: "You are the good conscience of the anti-Semites," insinuating that his fellow Jew deserves a prize for good will and tolerance. This is one of many ironic twists in Elmar Goerden's theater project *Lessing's Dream of Nathan the Wise,* staged in Stuttgart in February 1999.[1] Premiered only four months after Martin Walser's highly controversial speech on the emerging cult and culture of remembrance in Germany,[2] the young director's presentation is a collage of fractured voices and stage images from the past and the present, merging the traumatic experiences of Shylock, Nathan, Jud Süß, and Fassbinder's Rich Jew. Goerden stages a rehearsal that fails, an attempted performance of *Nathan the Wise* that miscarries. It fails because Lessing can offer, as it were, only a disjointed work with no adequate ending, certainly no reconciliation; because Nathan remains the other, as much of an outsider as his predecessor, Shylock. It fails because the Jew's arguments are misunderstood, challenged, distorted. It fails because the memory-laden past constantly erupts into the present, into the dream world of the theater and into our own reality.

A glance at the history of German theater after 1945 suffices to establish the pivotal role of Lessing's *Nathan the Wise* and Shakespeare's *Merchant of Venice* in the theatric confrontation with the collective past—that is, with the Holocaust—and with the reemergence of Jewish life on German soil. I propose to trace and examine the changing functions Nathan and Shylock, the Janus-faced stage Jew, served and affected. The transformations will be discussed within the wider context of postwar German theater—mainly the West German theater—and the still evolving "cultural memory" [*kulturelles Gedächtnis*], to use the term coined by Jan and Aleida Assmann.[3]

Tellingly, it was Lessing's canonical plea for tolerance that was chosen for the reopening of the Deutsches Theater in Berlin on September 7, 1945, only four months after the end of the war. This first postwar production of *Nathan* is characteristic of most other stagings of the play during the 1950s. There was virtually no allusion to the immediate past and certainly no attempt to reappraise the classic play in the context of the Holocaust. Director Fritz Wisten presented the audience of ravaged Berlin with a fairy tale [*Märchen*][4] set in the exotic Orient. His colleague Willi Schmidt recalls that Wisten made sure there would be "nothing gloomy about the performance, but rather an atmosphere of sublime gaiety, something of an oriental fairy tale, a mixture of talmudic wisdom, melancholy, experience in worldly affairs and knowledge of human nature [*Menschenkenntnis*]."[5] Paul Wegener's Nathan, in a gray-and-burgundy gown and a cap, was a dignified, aged man who avoided pathos or sentimentality, and was imposing in his serenity. The surprising moment of this prematurely conciliatory production came at the very end. Wisten chose to forgo Lessing's tableau of harmony, closing instead with Nathan standing apart, lonely, absorbed in his thoughts, while the brightly clad others partake in the happy ending. This had been done before, namely in the *Nathan* production of the *Jüdischer Kulturbund,* produced for and by the ostracized Jews in October 1933,[6] and this twist on the play became one of the striking hallmarks of many productions.

It is ironic that the director of the first postwar *Nathan,* Fritz Wisten, born Moritz Weinstein, was a Jewish survivor of a Nazi concentration camp and that the production was staged in the playhouse closely linked with Jewish theater-master Max Reinhardt. Wisten's avoidance of any direct allusion to the Holocaust—a directorial concept that in fact marked many *Nathan* productions immediately after the war—derives at least partly from his hope of continuing the thread of the glorious prewar stage tradition.

The cast included actors who had been well known before 1933, first and foremost Paul Wegener (Nathan), who did not jump on the Nazi bandwagon to promote his artistic career. Nathan's Muhammadan friend, the dervish, was played by Alfred Balthoff, a Jewish survivor who, like Wisten, was active in the theater of the Jewish *Kulturbund,* while the role of Daja, Nathan's garrulous housekeeper, was acted by the acclaimed expressionist Gerda Müller, who had just returned from self-imposed exile. Indeed, dissidents and emigrants featured in many of the early *Nathan* productions, and the storms of applause reported in nearly all the reviews were no doubt a token of acknowledgment and gratitude for those who chose to return and possibly to forgive.

Holocaust survivor Marcel Reich-Ranicki, a Polish Jew who later became Germany's leading literary critic, happened to be in Berlin when the play opened. He was curious to find out how German spectators reacted to *Nathan,* but as it turned out, the audience of the performance he watched was made up of "officers in uniform . . . , mostly Jews." Years later he still remembers that Wegener/Nathan tried hard to avoid "anything Jewish" in his gestures and intonation. Apparently, he was afraid it could be misunderstood as anti-Semitism."[7] It did not take director Fritz Wisten too long to realize how naive he had been: "The con-men are still alive," he wrote in 1947, "I believed in the liquidation [*sic*] of anti-Semitism. A superstition!"[8]

Surely, the best known, the Nathan of the earlier years, was Ernst Deutsch, a Prague Jew. One of the prominent actors in Berlin during the 1920s, Deutsch emigrated in 1933, had a modest career in Hollywood, and was among the first to return. By the time he settled back in Germany in 1951, *Nathan* had become a regular feature in the repertoire of the mainstream theater.[9] Erich Ponto, who played the lead in Dresden (July 1945) and subsequently in other cities,[10] is said to have brought out the magnificence of the play and its language after a twelve-year ban. In Frankfurt (1947) Otto Rouvel presented a young, sprightly, and unassuming Nathan, whereas in Munich (1946) Hellmuth Renar eschewed the clichéd portrayal of the Jew ("Bilderbuch-Juden der alten Schablone"[11]), foregrounding the expressive and reflective energy of the text.

Ernst Deutsch towered over these Nathans. In productions under various directors[12] between 1954 and 1967, he enacted the noble, long-suffering, and yet magnanimous victim; a sagacious, physically impressive Jew, with (despite?) side locks, prayer cap, and jewels, blessed with a redeeming sense of humor and good will. For spectators and critics alike, Deutsch did not act the role of Nathan, he was Nathan. "He made the role existentially his own," wrote Paul Hübner; and the leading critic of the day, Friedrich Luft, contended that "this is the Nathan of our era."[13] One does not have the feeling that a prominent guest plays this star role, writes a Viennese critic of the production at the Burgtheater in 1962 (this time under Jewish director Leopold Lindtberg!), adding: "Nathan has finally returned home."[14]

Clearly, for spectators Deutsch and Nathan were one; the actor and the role were intertwined. In a Germany nearly devoid of Jews, Deutsch/Nathan embodied the ideal Jew, if ever there was one, the Jew Germans might even be willing to tolerate: wise, enlightened, "the incarnation of humanism."[15] And though Auschwitz came to mind in his recollections of how Christians murdered his wife and children, Deutsch's Nathan was not out to seek revenge, punish, or point an accusing finger. Indeed, in retrospect it appears that Jewish directors and actors such as Wisten and Deutsch, far from emphasizing contemporary relevance and provoking a genuine encounter with the recent past, played into the hands of postwar Germans by encouraging suppression and amnesiac indulgence, appeasing guilty consciences and pacifying political responsibility.

Statistic records reveal that the stage version of *The Diary of Anne Frank* and *Nathan* were the box-office hits of the 1956 to 1957 season in Germany, with *Nathan* enjoying even more performances in East than in West Germany. During the same period, a handful of contemporary plays challenging the past had difficulties getting staged. The reason is obvious: *Anne Frank* and *Nathan* were successful because they voiced no accusation and called for no vendetta. The one offered—like Kurt Maetzig's popular film melodrama *Marriage under the Shadow* [(Ehe im Schatten), 1947]—the heart-wrenching story of a young victim with whom spectators could empathize; the other, a classic, was a commendable plea for tolerance and understanding.

Deutsch's Nathan cast a shadow over the Nathan of the 1960s. Leo Nyssen's review of the 1960 Bochum production is typical: "Any other actor will be hard put to play Nathan, in relation to the imprint Ernst Deutsch . . . has made upon this humanitarian figure."[16] The Nathan of the Bochum production, played by Claus Clausen, is characteristic of most 1960s productions of the play. Avoiding pathos, ingenious and genial, he is half hero, half realistic character. Time and again spectators were offered a broadminded, kind-hearted, and amenable Nathan, whom they received with standing ovations, applauding the leading actor as well as the image of a forgiving Jew he presented. Friedrich Domin's Nathan (Munich 1957) was a good-humored, avuncular story-teller,[17] as conciliatory as the Nathans created by Ernst Seiltgen (Cologne 1963), Kurt Ehrhardt (Bad Hersfeld 1965) and Mathias Wieman (Munich 1965). Few and far between are any captious remarks from theater critics about this undemanding, snug, "*gemütlicher*" Nathan.[18]

This carefree, conciliatory interpretation of *Nathan* is perplexing. After all, this was the period when, for the first time since the Holocaust, Jewish graves were being desecrated (Cologne 1959); for months the public intently followed the Eichmann trial in Jerusalem (1961) and the Auschwitz trial in Frankfurt (1963–1965). Indeed, those were the heydays of the so-called documentary theater: playwrights like Rolf Hochhuth, Peter Weiss, and Heinar Kipphardt sought to debunk the myths and the premises upon which postwar society rested. Erwin Piscator, one of the foremost political directors from the Weimar period, returned to stage many of these plays and to raise disturbing questions about the past. Dispelling the self-indulgent excuse that the Germans had been overpowered by demons, and stressing the guilt of bystanders as well as active Nazis, these playwrights (often assisted by Piscator) forced spectators for the first time to confront Auschwitz, or, more precisely, to consider how and what made Auschwitz possible. There is an ironic parallel here: the sense of victimization was avoided in the productions of *Nathan* during the 1960s by deliberately avoiding the context of diasporic Jewish condition, particularly the Holocaust; in a similar fashion, the docudramatists sidestepped the issue of the victimization of the Jew by focusing on the workings of the system that made the unprecedented Nazi crimes possible.

Again, statistical records are revealing. *Nathan* features at the very top of the performance list in the seasons of 1960 to 1962 (ranking second and fourth on the list) and enjoys a steady popularity in the following seasons (less in the GDR than in the FRG). It ranks fifth during 1965 and 1966, the season when Peter Weiss's *Investigation* premiered to notably fewer performances than *Nathan*. A second look at the 1961 to 1962 season reveals that while *Nathan* was fourth on the list, it was surpassed by another play about a 'Jew' as an outsider—the premiere of Max Frisch's *Andorra*.

Consider this phenomenon: less than a generation after the unprecedented attempt by the Germans to eliminate the Jewish people, two of the dramatic spectacles that capture the highest popularity among the Germans are about Jews. And there is something quite striking about the portrayal of these Jews: they are neutralized in a sense, stripped of their Jewish attributes, made into abstractions or personifications of a humanistic quest. Nathan becomes the existential Other, "a Jew without a people in the dream-realm of humanity,"[19] whereas Andri, the scapegoat in Frisch's parable is not even Jewish in the first place. An imaginary phantom Jew is fabricated in a country that had recently made brutal attempts to rid itself entirely of its Jews. Notably, during the years in question, the 1960s, the survivors, a negligible minority, were keeping a low profile. Jews were virtually unknown to many Germans. Director Volker Canaris (born in 1942) attests that he first encountered Jews in the form of dramatic characters. "The first Jews I knew were Nathan and Shylock," he writes in response to Hans Mahnke's perturbing, almost anti-Semitic rendering of Shylock in Peter Zadek's controversial production of *The Merchant of Venice* (Bochum 1972).[20]

For obvious reasons, theater practitioners turned to Nathan, the upholder of tolerance and common sense, not to Shylock, the gruesome, vindictive villain. A Jew as a vicious perpetrator was inconceivable and impossible to dramatize publicly. Statistics record the reluctance of German directors to stage the play: there was a single production of only four performances in 1949to 1950. In the 1950s, there were two to four productions yearly; not surprisingly, Ernst Deutsch's Shylock (Berlin 1963) was the best-known rendering in the years immediately after the war. Director Boleslaw Barlog recalls:

> [Ernst Deutsch's] friendly, unresentful attitude towards Werner Krauss, who was incriminated due to his Nazi past [and played Shylock in the notoriously anti-Semitic production in Vienna 1943] was moving. [Deutsch] couldn't understand that the thematics [of *The Merchant of Venice*] was a taboo due to the outrageous deeds of the thousand-year Reich. Neither could the protest of the Jewish community in Berlin, represented by its president, Heinz Galinski, influence him. Deutsch unshakably believed in the rectifying effect of his own personality, and he refused to realize that the facts of the plot itself remain unbearable, particularly for Jewish citizens, after the gruesome experiences of the preceding years.[21]

When Barlog turned down Deutsch's offer to produce the play, Deutsch approached Erwin Piscator, whose original and deliberately irritating *Nathan,* in line with the political theater he championed, premiered in Marburg in 1952. Deutsch portrayed Shylock as "a noble Jew,"[22] a man more sinned against than sinning. "A human being is driven to inhumanity, and this is his tragedy," maintains Volker Canaris. Only five years later, television viewers could watch the celebrated Jewish actor/director Fritz Kortner, a returned exile, in the role of Shylock. His was an angry old man, in a black robe, cap and beard, who was caught between misery and cruelty, dignity and grief.[23]

No doubt the most daring *Merchant*—despite the little attention it received—was the one staged in Ulm in 1961 by another Jewish returned exile, the 35-year-old Peter Zadek. Against the background of a Venetian carnival "here on stage stood a Shylock [Norbert Kappen] who became a 'devil' because he has been treated by the others as one," in the words of critic Hellmuth Karasek, who reproached Zadek for presenting an anti-Semitic *Merchant.* Zadek, whose later productions of the play (1972 and 1988) were no less provocative, replied that his Jewishness entitled him to adopt such an interpretation, and that in any case he found German philo-Semitism unbearable.[24]

Zadek played the devil's advocate even more explicitly in his 1972 production of the *Merchant.* Unscrupulous, vile, and hideous, Shylock (Hans

Mahnke) had nothing in common with Nathan, but smacked of the stereotypical image of *Jud Süß*.[25] In fact, Zadek's Shylock seemed like an amalgamation of all anti-Semitic stereotypes: ugly and sinister, with a dwindled goat-beard and blinking beady eyes, he slobbered, shuffled his feet, lisped and spoke distorted German with a "Jewish" accent. During the trial scene, he anxiously awaited revenge, the knife ready in his hand. In the face of those who claimed that Shylock had been wronged and ill-treated, Zadek introduced Shylock as a "potential murderer" whose gruesome deed was fortunately averted at the last moment.[26] Can a Jew do evil, even murder? Yes, insinuated Zadek, as did that spectator of Kortner's televised Shylock who in the wake of the heated debate entitled "Could Shylock be evil?" [*Darf Shylock böse sein?*] stated that "the Jew is capable of monstrous acts, like every other human being too. Good and bad deeds alike."[27]

Many critics and viewers felt that Zadek was impertinently violating taboos, that his approach was—in the words of critic Joachim Kaiser—a "scandalous distortion."[28] Yet Zadek himself apparently felt that only by shocking the audience into understanding the dangers of discrimination could residual anti-Semitism truly be challenged. This was his stand during the world-wide oil crisis spurred by the conflict in the Middle East, which gave rise in West Germany to an upsurge of a new kind of anti-Semitism, a left-wing anti-Semitism associated with anti-Israel propaganda.

On the whole, German interest in Jewish matters receded in the 1970s, and there was a corresponding decrease in stagings of Nathan and Shylock.[29] A few ahistorical productions of the convivial Nathan ("*Nathan der Lustige*"[30]) were staged, but for three seasons (1975 to 1978) Shylock was entirely absent. The surprising finding to my mind is the growing number—relatively speaking—of Jewish theater artists who were attracted to the deprecatory, unloved Jew, Shylock. Moreover: Only Imo Moskowicz, a Jewish survivor and Gründgens's assistant after the war, chose to stage the benign Jew, Nathan, in a production (Frankfurt 1971) that—attuned to the prevailing spirit of Lessing productions of the time—underlined the fantastic, utopian facets of the comedy.[31] For others, the mellow, suave, almost insipid Nathan seemed anachronistic, irrelevant. It was Shylock, the perplexing baddy, whom the Nazis had (mis)used for their anti-Jewish propaganda, who now kindled the imagination of Jewish directors. Peter Zadek's staging is a radical example of this trend, which was to gather momentum in the following years. Two years after Zadek's deliberately shocking Shylock, Conny Hannes Mayer, a Viennese Jew, sought to underscore the paradoxical makings of Shylock while justifying his pursuit of vengeance in the Venetian ghetto.[32] In Cologne 1979, Arie Zinger—who had done some of his practical training with Zadek and was introduced by reviewers as an Israeli—directed a Shylock (Hermann Lause) who, not representative of diasporic suffering, had a real personal grievance. Zinger's point of departure was his conviction that the play "was not anti-Semitic, it was realistic," even though Shylock was "an extreme, radical" figure.[33] Many rehearsal hours were spent discussing how German actors could impersonate Shylock after what their people had recently done; one of the crucial decisions was whether or not to present the Jew together with the ubiquitous clichés, which so tellingly expose "society's relationship to the outsider."[34]

Zinger's unsettling production was premiered only a few months after the memorable *Improvisations on Shylock,* directed by George Tabori (Munich 1978). Hungarian-born, Jewish, holder of a British passport and one of the most intriguing theater artists in postwar German theater, 64-year-old Tabori considered the performance a challenge for himself and for the twelve actors, most of whom were children during the war. Focusing on Shylock at the expense of all other characters, Tabori collectivized the victim experience foregrounding the Jewish trope of the maltreated, downtrodden, and persecuted victim, "a rock [whose] injuries are 6,000 years old."[35] At the same time, he multiplied the figure, enabling each actor to respond to the fictitious Jew in a personal manner. Related to the multivalent depiction of Shylock is the temporal overlap, the conflation of past(s) and present. The "rock of injuries" is an ahistorical metaphor of Jewish suffering in a performance historicized through innumerable references to the Holocaust.

The performance sought to taunt and disconcert, to shock, even to offend and injure—in short, to get under one's skin. And it definitely did this. Spectators wept (and had to be consoled), expressing anguish and consternation to the troupe. Among the critical voices heard was the self-righteous argument that "the only honest way of playing *The Merchant of Venice* today, is not to play it at all."[36] It was precisely against this attitude, a type of "false piety,"[37] that Tabori resolved to conduct his *Improvisations.* Not to perform the play after Auschwitz is much the same as to turn one's back on the past, to encourage amnesia, to add insult to injury. For Tabori, theater-making is by definition an act of demystification, an assault against taboos; in the case of the *Merchant* it is also the studied stripping away of the false masks of self-exoneration and self-righteousness.

Back to statistical records: *Nathan* productions outnumbered the *Merchant* in the period discussed, the mid-1970s, as well as in the following seasons. And yet, it seems that Shylock gradually eclipsed the preeminent Nathan, not least through the original stagings of Jewish iconoclasts like Zadek and Tabori. Their work placed Shylock at center stage, as the quintessential Jew whose drama was charged with contemporary relevance. For it was in the figure of Shylock that the Jew was given his narrative, his identity, both of which were effaced in depictions of Nathan.

Precisely at this time, additional Jewish reassessments contested Nathan's predominance. Reviewing a production of Lessing's play in 1969, Friedrich Torberg denounced Lessing's philo-Semitism, maintaining that tolerance that is gained at the price of self-abnegation is no tolerance at all. Subversively, he contended that "Lessing accepts the Jew as a German, as a human being, even as a Christian—as everything, but not as a Jew."[38] No less radical was Hans Mayer's evaluation of Nathan and Shylock in his seminal study *Außenseiter* ([Outsiders], 1975). Mayer, himself a Holocaust survivor, examined the process of acculturation and its price, and argued that Lessing's Jew must renounce his existential otherness to become a member of German bourgeoisie. For Mayer, it is Shylock, "the man without forename, the Jew of Venice," who is "the phenotype of the failed Jewish acculturation."[39] One is reminded of Ernst Simon in 1929, echoing Heine's sympathy for Shylock: "Shylock is more of a Jew than Nathan. . . . We should own up to this tragic brother Shylock instead of casting him off apologetically. . . . We should dispense with the faint apparition of a Jew, Nathan."[40] Small wonder that theater scholar Andrej Wirth, having watched yet another of those trivial Nathans, calls for a "moratorium for this alibi play."[41]

Both *Nathan* and the *Merchant* were in extraordinary demand in the season of 1979 to 1980, the year that marks the beginning of the third phase in post-Holocaust theater. The tremendous impact on German television viewers of the American film—some say soap opera—"Holocaust," in January 1979, brought with it a reawakening of interest in the fate of Jews during the Third Reich. The mini-series, criticized by many for trivializing the extermination of the Jews, "opened the floodgates. It seems as if for the first time an entire nation dared to remember and to look at its own past . . . this time from the perspective of the victims," according to film expert Anton Kaes.[42] Following the screening with its accompanying discussions and enormous media coverage, numerous documentaries and case studies on the Holocaust emerged while the theaters uncovered and premiered plays by Jewish authors. Established playwrights like Erwin Sylvanus and Heinar Kipphardt addressed the past once again,[43] and young authors, refusing to wriggle out of responsibility in the name of "the grace of belated birth" [*Gnade der späten Geburt*], confronted on the stage a past they had not experienced.[44] In truth, this Hollywood import, so vehemently berated, had a very powerful effect in Germany, ushering in a phase characterized by *Erinnerung* [memory/memorization], according to Aleida Assmann in her recent study of the Germans and their relationship to the past.[45]

The 1980s and 1990s are marked by a twofold trajectory. On the one hand, there was a vigorous culture of memory [*Erinnerungskultur*]—revisiting authentic sites, erecting memorials, producing symbols, and rituals. On the other hand, there was "the massive warding off of memory,"[46] the wish, often triggered by the surfeit of memory, to put an end to the "permanent presentation" and the "instrumentalization of our shame," as Martin Walser formulated it in his polemic speech, suggesting that Auschwitz has become "a means of intimidation," always ready to be used as a "moral bludgeon." These opposing attitudes are inextricably related, and there can be no doubt that the excess of memory, the ubiquity of Holocaust discourse, prompted antagonistic reactions.

The theater was part of this ongoing impassioned discourse, mostly affected by topical debates and public sentiment, rarely initiating them. One of the few cases in which the stage propelled a heated controversy that went far beyond artistic considerations, was the attempt to premiere Rainer Fassbinder's play *Der Müll, die Stadt und der Tod* [The Garbage, the City and Death] in 1985.

The staging of Fassbinder's work in autumn of 1985 was preceded by two momentous political events. The first was the official ceremony on May 5 in the cemetery of Bitburg which contains graves of SS-Waffen soldiers. Headed by Chancellor Helmut Kohl and U. S. President Ronald Reagan, this much disputed occasion epitomized Kohl's version of *Vergangenheitsbewältigung* [overcoming the past]. Only three days later, the German president Richard von Weiszecker gave a memorable speech, advocating *Vergangenheitsbewahrung,* preserving the past, instead of forgiving and forgetting.

Germany was plunged into an intensive discussion of the culture of remembrance and the politicization of memory, which culminated the following year in the *Historikerstreit* (The Historians' Debate). The Fassbinder premiere, the second momentous event, came in the midst of all this, in October 1985. The denial of the play's anti-Semitic content suggests the Germans' craving to unburden themselves of the past and their yearning for a normalization in their relationship with the Jews, a normalization that implies, among other things, the right to depict Jews and Jewish life while ignoring the Holocaust, severing the present from the past. The attempt to stage the play, nearly ten years after its inception, ended as a political-cultural scandal when the stage was besieged by Jewish protestors with hundreds more outside, voicing their remonstrance. This was the first time since 1945 that Jews in Germany, those "invisible Jews," made a public protest; and the first manifestation of a *"geteilte Erinnerung"* (the adjective *"geteilte"* connotes both shared and divided) between Jews and non-Jews in Germany.[47] Whether due to genuine conviction, in line with political correctness, or simply in response to the Jewish protest and the pressures of public opinion, the decision was made: There was no place for Fassbinder's antagonist, the nameless Rich Jew, couched as he was in abusive traditional clichés, no stage for a victim turned wrong-doer.

During these political events and the Fassbinder scandal, the noble, long-suffering, and ever-forgiving Nathan continued to predominate in the minds of many. Not surprisingly, the play ranked high and steady among theater successes of the 1980s, enjoying particular popularity in the season of 1985 to 1986 (second in spectators' ranking). But what kind of *Nathan* were spectators offered? As it turns out, a whole series of productions avoided the real issue; instead they trivialized the drama, contributing to the wide-spreading folklorization of Judaism while seeking to dazzle though theatric sleights-of-hand. Among these productions are Claus Peymann's 1981 *Nathan,* brilliant and playful, acknowledging "the mendacity of reconciliation"[48] yet lacking any reference to either the past or the present;[49] Hansgünther Heyme's new wave production (1982), settled somewhere between "a disco and a boutique," with a stooped and perspiring Nathan embracing heaps of money, parading his murdered family members as puppets; Fritz Marquardt's black-and-white performance on a huge chessboard-like stage (1984); and Nathan as a realistic self-made man in caftan, in Hans Gratzer's 1990 production.

As for Shylock, it was again Peter Zadek who set the tenor, with his third staging of *The Merchant of Venice.* This was not only the most intriguing interpretation of the play in the 1980s, it was also immensely influential on Shylock productions in the following decade. Zadek had made a name for himself as an enfant terrible: He was one of the very few Jews who spoke in favor of staging Fassbinder's play ("surely it is anti-Semitic. . . . That's precisely why it should be performed"[50]); he also incensed both Jews and gentiles with his spectacular revue of Jehoshua Sobol's *Ghetto,* which depicts the Jews as complex and flawed human beings, not just victims.[51]

Zadek's third Shylock was neither a devilish avenger nor an obnoxious *Stürmer*-Jew. In fact, he had no recognizable Jewish attributes whatsoever. Like any other ambitious man in a Venetian society of yuppies, he was pragmatic, dispassionate, self-controlled. Far from an outcast, he was an insider in chic modern clothes, speaking business with his peers, as cool and unaffected as any of them. In fact, Shylock is so well assimilated, acts so much like a Venetian, that judge Portia mistakes him for Antonio. At the end, Shylock accepts the verdict with good sportsmanship; he had taken the usual risk, only this time he lost.

What a long way Zadek had come since his 1961 production! Through his three very disparate productions over the course of three decades, Zadek freed Shylock from both anti-Semitic and philo-Semitic fetters. Ironically, here was once again a Jewish director who gave vent to German hopes: Normalization was possible, Zadek's Shylock insinuated. Commenting on his approach, Zadek explained: "The Jew is no longer the victim, but the perpetrator. . . . It is no longer the image the Germans liked to have of Jews. . . . It is easier to handle victims, one can also be nicer to victims." Typically subversive, he added: "I hope I have contributed with my production to changing the image because I too would rather be considered a perpetrator and a cynic than a victim."[52]

The concept of Shylock as member of a capitalist society—"the economic model," in the words of Hans-Peter Bayerdörfer[53]—characterizes most productions of *The Merchant of Venice* that followed. Time and again spectators witnessed the internecine struggle between business rivals, set in a decadent contemporary milieu. Rock music accompanied Kurt Hübner's production (1989); Antonio and his buddies enter with cellular phones, back from a tennis club (Hübner, 1992) or sit around a billiard table, a somewhat jaded band, in Annegret Ritzel's staging (1994). Shylock's Jewishness lost its explosiveness. "A Shylock beyond Auschwitz," wrote one critic, and another quipped, "Citizen Shylock, brother Shylock."[54] There is little to set Shylock apart from the others (all too often appearing like Mafiosi): He is as genteel and canny as they are, at times more intelligent, quick-witted, animated, or even more likeable.

Some scholars have claimed that the further in time the Holocaust recedes, the more concrete it becomes;[55] but there is little evidence to support such a claim in the stagings of Nathan and Shylock. Admittedly, the plays maintained their popularity through the years; particularly in the case of *Nathan,* which ranks among the top ten (as far as spectators' numbers are concerned) between 1990 and 1996, that is, after the *Wende,* or the fall of the Berlin Wall. However, productions of both works no longer draw explicit connections to diasporic history of anti-Semitism and to the Holocaust in particular, as was done in preceding decades. Theaters in the five new *Bundesländer,* previously the German Democratic Republic or East Germany, are not particularly keen on staging either of the plays, as statistic records evince. Neither the encounter with new historic narratives so varied and different from the official, single-minded one coerced by the GDR, nor the ever-fresh accounts, documentaries, and films about the Holocaust (Victor Klemperer's Diary, 1995, Spielberg's *Schindler's List,* 1994, the Goldhagen debate, 1996, the ongoing controversy over the memorial for the perished Jews in Berlin) seem to have engendered a special interest in these plays in what was formerly East Germany. One exceptional attempt to interlace Shylock's story with memories of a traumatic past was the production of *The Merchant of Venice* in Weimar 1995—a place associated with Goethe as well as with the nearby Buchenwald concentration camp. The production was structured as a play-within-a-play: Shylock's drama was performed by Jewish inmates of the camp and by their Nazi guards.[56] Does it come as a surprise that it was a Jewish director, the Israeli Hanan Snir, who was responsible for this provocative and deeply disturbing performance?

Along with the odd productions—*Nathan* as psychodrama (Zurmühle 1993), Shylock as everyman and *Biedermann* [57] (Beier, 1994)—questions were raised more often than before about the very performability of the two plays and their relevance.[58] The 1990s witnessed a number of experimental performances focusing on Nathan and Shylock that, far from being faithful [*werktreu*] stagings, seek to deconstruct the texts in order to recontextualize them. Theater subversive George Tabori provided an idiosyncratic answer in a production he tellingly entitled *Nathan's Death* (1991), a highly original albeit artistically debatable variation on Lessing's appeal for tolerance. "Tabori's interest lies in exploring the dialectics of good intentions," maintains Barbara Fischer.[59] Indeed, his interpretation goes against the grain of Lessing's play by placing it under the dark shadow of the Holocaust; it is a piece with no reconciliation, in which evil has the upper hand ("Tabori's Satan the Wise," summarized one critic[60]).

Equally disconcerting and artistically flawed was the project directed by Anselm Weber in Hamburg in 1994. Weber chose to couple Lessing's *Nathan* with Marlowe's *Jew of Malta,* a play rarely produced in Germany because of the anti-Semitic coloring of the eponymous protagonist, Barabas. The noble Jew, Nathan, in waistcoat and tie, perspiring anxiously as he delivers the famous ring parable, and the diabolical Jew Barabas, a slapstick master, "with an Al Capone outfit"[61] come across as man and his shadow. Whenever Nathan muses or hesitates, in comes the resourceful knave Barabas. "Both are artists, dreamers. Both are geniuses. Nathan—God's genius, Barabas—Machiavelli's genius," maintains critic Gerhard Stadelmaier.[62] Are the fairy-tale Jew, the victim, and the demonic Jew (the perpetrator) supposed to constitute the "total" Jew, a Janus-faced figure, conspicuously ambiguous? So it seems. The concocted synthetic Jew in Weber's willful, dogmatic production is not only simplistic and crude, but also downright pernicious.[63]

Finally, I would like to return to Elmar Goerden's experimental exploration *Lessing's Dream of Nathan the Wise.* On the threshold of the emerging Berlin Republic and the upcoming millennium, nearly a half-century after the Holocaust, Goerden ("I come from a Jewish family"[64]) reflects in his "project" on the major stage Jews: Nathan, Shylock, Jud Süß, and Fassbinder's Rich Jew. This is an all-inclusive settling of accounts with the past and the present, that provokes the spectator and sends him home perplexed and disconcerted. The supposed rehearsal of Lessing's play fails, as has the symbiosis between Jews and Germans. And the violation of taboos cannot bring Jews and Germans together, well intended and philo-Semitic as these gestures may be. Historic wrongs and past insults cannot be rectified: The Holocaust created a decisive breach in the fabric of relations between Germans and Jews.

More than five decades of productions of Nathan and Shylock show that the (re)presentation of these paradigmatic stage Jews is still a delicate and tortuous undertaking. Ignoring or denying the Jewish attributes of the two is no less problematic than treating them with kid-gloves, not to mention the problems with anti-Semitic stagings. Tellingly, Nathan and Shylock are stripped of their Otherness, their Jewishness, particularly in the 1980s and 1990s—a time when German Jews, for years allegedly "invisible Jews," became visible and audible, voicing their stance on political and cultural matters, protesting against the inexorable erosion of memory. As far as the theater is concerned, it is fascinating to trace the preponderance of Jewish actors and especially Jewish directors among post-Holocaust interpreters of Nathan and Shylock. This includes not only celebrities of the prewar stage who chose to return—like Deutsch and Kortner—but also members of the so-called Second Generation: directors such as Benjamin Korn, Arie Zinger or Jossi Wieler.[65] Between these two generations lies the stage work of two outstanding directors, Zadek and Tabori, who studiously set out to violate the taboos that burden and strain the relationship between Jews and Germans, in hope of clearing the ground for a genuine dialogue.

Notes

1. Elmar Goerden, *Lessings Traum von Nathan der Weise: Ein Projekt* (Stuttgart: Schauspiel Staatstheater Stuttgart, Programmbuch 50, Spielzeit, 1998–1998). Interestingly, Goerden is the author of an academic article entitled "Der Andere: Fragmente einer Bühnengeschichte Shylocks im deutschen und englischen Theater des 18. und 19. Jahrhunderts," *Theatralia Judaica: Emanzipation und Antisemitismus als Moment der Theatergeschichte. Von der Lessing-Zeit bis zur Shoah,* ed. Hans-Peter Bayerdörfer (Tübingen: Niemeyer, 1992), 129–61.

2. Martin Walser's acceptance speech of the German Book Trade Peace Prize was delivered in Frankfurt on October 11, 1998. For analyses of the speech and discussion of its repercussions, see Frank Schirrmacher, ed., *Die Walser-Bubis Debatte* (Frankfurt am Main: Suhrkamp, 1999); Moshe Zuckermann, *Gedenken und Kulturindustrie. Ein Essay zur neuen deutschen Normalität* (Berlin: Philo, 1999); Gerd Wiegel and Johannes Klotz, eds., *Geistige Brandstiftung? Die Walser-Bubis Debatte* (Cologne: PappyRossa, 1999); Joachim Rohloff, *Ich bin das Volk. Martin Walser und die Berliner Republik* (Hamburg: KVV Konkret, 1999).

3. See Jan Assmann, *Das kulturelle Gedächtnis: Schrift, Erinnerung und politische Identität in frühen Hochkulturen* (Munich: Beck, 1997). Of special value to my paper is Aleida Assmann and Ute Frevert, *Geschichtsvergessenheit Geschichtsversessenheit: Vom Umgang mit deutschen Vergangenheiten nach 1945* (Stuttgart: Deutsche Verlags-Anstalt, 1999). For further reading see, for instance, Peter Reichel, *Politik mit der Erinnerung* (Munich: Hanser, 1995).

4. See Paul Wiegler's review in the *Allgemeine Zeitung* (Berlin, September 9, 1945). See also Diedrich Diedrichsen and Bärbel Rudin, eds., *Lessing im*

Spiegel der Theaterkritik 1945–1979 (Berlin: Gesellschaft für Theatergeschichte, 1980); Jo-Jacqueline Eckardt, *Lessing's "Nathan the Wise" and the Critics, 1779–1991* (Columbia, SC: Camden House, 1993); and Henning Rischbieter, "'Nathan'—Als Märchen," in *Theater Heute* 3 (1983): 24–29. A short survey is given also by Ferdinand Piedmont in "Unterdrückt und rehabilitiert: Zur Theatergeschichte von Lessings *Nathan der Weise* von der zwanziger Jahren bis zur Gegenwart," *Lessing Yearbook* 19 (1987): 85–94. The most recent contributions to *Nathan* scholarship are Astrid Oesmann, "Nathan der Weise: Suffering Lessing's 'Erziehung,'" *The German Review* 2 (1999): 131–45; and Barbara Fischer, *Nathans Ende? Von Lessing bis Tabori* (Göttingen: Wallstein, 2000).

5. Willi Schmidt, "Rückkehr zu Nathan, dem Weisen," *Fritz Wisten: Drei Leben für das Theater,* ed. Jörg Gronius (Berlin: Akademie der Künste, 1990), 106–13.

6. The production was directed by Karl Loewenberg with Kurt Katsch as Nathan. See Barbara Fischer, *Nathans Ende?,* 125–42. Cf. Paul Mendes-Flohr, *German Jews: A Dual Identity* (New Haven: Yale University Press, 1999). See also Rebecca Rovit, "Collaboration on Survival, 1933–1938: Reassessing the Role of the *Jüdischer Kulturbund,*" *Theater in the Third Reich, the Prewar Years,* ed. Glen W. Gadberry (Westport, CT: Greenwood, 1995), 141–56; and Eike Geisel and H. M. Broder, *Premiere und Pogrom: Der jüdische Kulturbund 1933–1941* (Berlin: Siedler, 1992).

7. Marcel Reich-Ranicki, *Mein Leben* (Stuttgart: Deutsche Velags-Anstalt, 1999), 318–19.

8. Cf. Gronius, *Fritz Wisten: Drei Leben für das Theater,* 52.

9. I have relied on statistical records produced and partly published (under the title "Was spielten die Theater?") by the Deutscher Bühnenverein in Cologne.

10. Erich Ponto played Nathan in Dresden and Hamburg (1945), Munich (1946), and Frankfurt (1947).

11. Cf. Alfred Dahlmann's review in *Süddeutsche Zeitung* (May 21, 1946).

12. For example, Karl-Heinz Stroux in Berlin and in Düsseldorf, Leopold Lindtberg in Vienna, Boleslaw Barlog in Berlin.

13. See Paul Hübner's review in *Rheinische Post* (September 10, 1956), and Friedrich Luft's review in *Die Welt* (April 21, 1955).

14. Elisabeth Pablé in *Illustrierte Kronen-Zeitung* (May 12, 1962).

15. Cf. Günther Grack in *Der Tagesspiegel* (January 13, 1962).

16. See Leo Nyssen's review in *Theater Heute* 3 (1960): 31–32.

17. See Walther Kiaulehn in *Münchner Merkur* (November 23, 1957).

18. Exemplary of the critical voices is Wolfgang Drews in his review of *Nathan* at the Bayerisches Staatstheater in *Münchner Merkur* (October 29, 1965).

19. Walter Jens, "Nathan der Weise und der Sicht von Auschwitz," *Kanzel und Katheder: Reden,* (Munich: Kindler, 1984), 45.

20. Volker Canaris, "Die ersten Juden, die ich kannte, waren Nathan und Shylock," *Theater Heute* 2 (1973): 20–24.

21. Boleslaw Barlog, *Theater lebenslänglich* (Munich: Knaur, 1981), 116.

22. Peter Zadek, *My Way: Eine Autobiographie, 1926–1969* (Cologne: Kiepenheuer & Witsch, 1998), 315.

23. See Volker Canaris, "Die ersten Juden."

24. Zadek, *My Way,* 317.

25. Interestingly, *Jud Süß* appeared on the postwar German stage in the 1980s. Veit Harlan's film, serving the vicious propaganda of the Nazi regime, was not easily forgotten. In 1983, Dieter Munck directed an open air dramatization of the *Jud Süß* story in the marketplace in Bonn. See *Theater Heute* 8 (1983): 41. Five years later, in 1988, during the time of the *Historikerstreit,* Hansjörg Utzerath directed Paul Kornfeld's prewar drama *Jud Süß* in Nürnberg (the play was premiered in Berlin, 1930, under director Leopold Jessner). In Esslingen, Wolfram Mehring directed Albert Dulks's *Lea,* another stage version (dating back to 1848!) of the Süß story. The dramatized version of Lion Feuchtwanger's novel was, interestingly, never produced on the postwar stage. The first postwar dramatization of *Jud Süß,* artistically poor and full of clichés, was penned by Klaus Pohl, and was premiered in Stuttgart in December 1999. See my review entitled "Zwiespältig," *Die deutsche Bühne* 1 (2000): 48.

26. Zadek, *My Way,* 318.

27. Cf. Gerd von Mallinckrodt's letter in *Theater Heute* 4 (1969): 57.

28. Cf. *Theater Heute* 13 (1974): 12.

29. Cf. Anat Feinberg, Wiedergutmachung im Progamm: jüdisches Schicksal im deutschen Nachkriegsdrama (Cologne: Prometh, 1988), 47 ff.

30. See Gerhard Stadelmaier, *Lessing auf der Bühne: Ein Klassiker im Theateralltag (1968–1974)* (Tübingen: Niemeyer, 1980), 97–108. Stadelmaier provides a discussion of *Nathan* production in the GDR on pages 147 to 156.

31. The production received bad reviews. See, for instance, Peter Iden's critique in *Theater Heute* 4 (1971): 12.

32. See Christoph Müller's review in *Theater Heute* 10 (1974): 59–60.

33. See Günther Rühle, "Wie zeigt man auf Wunden?," *Theater Heute* 12 (1979): 6–9.

34. Ibid.

35. Andrea Welker and Tina Berger, eds., '*Ich wollte meine Tochter läge tot zu meinen Füßen und hätte die Juwelen in den Ohren': Improvisationen über Shakespeares Shylock* (Munich: Hanser, 1979), 70. For a detailed account of the production see Anat Feinberg, *Embodied Memory: The Theater of George Tabori* (Iowa City: University of Iowa Press, 1999), 209–24.

36. Cf. Feinberg, *Embodied Memory,* 224.

37. Ibid., 224.

38. Friedrich Torberg's review was published in *Christ und Welt* (April 16, 1969). I am quoting with my own translation, from Ludwig W. Kahn's article "The Changing Image of the Jew: Nathan the Wise and Shylock," an article that treats the two plays as literary texts, in Mark Gelber, ed., *Identity and Ethos: A Festschrift for Sol Liptzin on the Occasion of his 85th Birthday* (New York: Peter Lang, 1986), 244.

39. Hans Mayer, *Außenseiter* (Frankfurt am Main: Suhrkamp, 1975), 315.

40. Ernst Simon's opinion is cited—with my translation—from Kahn, "The Changing Image of the Jew," 249. Heine wrote about Shylock in "Shakespeares Mädchen und Frauen," first published in 1839.

41. Andrej Wirth, "Doesn't Matter," *Theater Heute* 7 (1983): 45.

42. Anton Kaes, "The American television series *Holocaust* is shown in West Germany," in *Yale Companion to Jewish Writing and Thought in German Culture,* ed. Sander L. Gilman and Jack Zipes (New Haven: Yale University Press, 1997): 786–87.

43. Erwin Sylvanus, whose play *Korczak and the Children* was one of the earlier plays to address the Holocaust, wrote *Exile—A Journey to the* Heimat, which premiered in the season of 1980 to 1981. Heinar Kipphardt's problematic play *Brother Eichmann* premiered after his death in 1983. Cf. Feinberg, *Wiedergutmachung,* 60 ff.

44. The most impressive of these is Thomas Strittmatter's play *Viehjud Levi* (Cattle-Jew Levi) which premiered in the season of 1983 to 1984. For this play and the others see Feinberg, *Wiedergutmachung,* 50ff.

45. In this matter, I disagree with Aleida Assmann. The third phase begins for her as late as 1985. See Assmann, *Geschichtsvergessenheit,* 144.

46. Assmann, *Geschichtsvergessenheit,* 45.

47. The notion was coined by Salomon Korn. See his study *Geteilte Erinnerung: Beiträge zur "deutsch-jüdischen" Gegenwart* (Berlin: Philo, 1999).

48. George Tabori, "Ein Goi bleibt immer ein Goi . . . ," in *Unterammergau oder Die guten Deutschen* (Frankfurt am Main: Suhrkamp, 1981), 34.

49. Illuminating is Gerhard Stadelmaier's disappointed review "Lessings unmenschliche Märchenmenschlichkeit," *Theater Heute* 5 (1981): 38–39, ending with the author's wish to see what George Tabori would have made out of the drama.

50. Peter Zadek, "Aufführen!," *Die Zeit* (September 13, 1985).

51. Cf. Feinberg, *Wiedergutmachung,* 58–59.

52. Zadek, *My Way,* 321–22. (My translation). Zadek maintained that the change in his stance has something to do with his ambivalent attitude toward Israel. See also his interview with Olivier Ortolani in *Theater Heute* 7 (1990): 23.

53. Hans-Peter Bayerdörfer, "Shylock auf der deutschen Bühne nach der Shoah," in *Shylock? Zinsverbot und Geldverleih in jüdischer und christlicher Tradition,* ed., Johannes Heil and Bernd Wacker (Frankfurt am Main: Fink, 1997): 261–80.

54. Eckhard Franke, "Grosse Stoffe, kleine Münze," *Theater Heute* 11 (1994): 21; and Benjamin Henrichs, "Kein Messer im Fleisch," *Die Zeit* (October 7, 1994). Henrichs implicitly refers to Kipphardt's *Brother Eichmann.*

55. See Aleida Assmann, *Geschichtsvergessenheit,* 29. Historian Reinhart Koselleck's stance is different, when speaking of the change from a *"gegenwärtige Vergangenheit"* to a *"reine Vergangenheit,"* in "Nachwort," in Charlotte Beradt, *Das Dritte Reich des Traums* (Frankfurt am Main: Suhrkamp, 1994), 117–32.

56. The idea is less original than it may seem at first. George Tabori directed a production entitled *The Merchant of Venice as Performed in Theresienstadt* at the Berkshire Theater Festival in Stockbridge, Massachusetts, in 1966. Likewise, he initially thought of presenting his *Improvisations on Shylock* on the grounds of the Dachau concentration camp. For details see Feinberg, *Embodied Memory,* 209–24.

57. Cf. Benjamin Henrichs, "Kein Messer."

58. Noteworthy are likewise two books by Dietrich Schwanitz. The first, an original study of Shylock and Jewish history in Germany is available in *Shylock: Von Shakespeare bis zum Nürnberger Prozeß* (Hamburg: Krämer, 1989). The second is entitled *Das Shylock-Syndrom oder die Dramaturgie der Barbarei* (Frankfurt am Main: Eichborn, 1997).

59. Barbara Fischer, *Nathans Ende?,* 152.

60. Gerhard Stadelmaier, "Satan der Weise," *Frankfurter Allgemeine Zeitung* (November 16, 1991). Also see Franz Wille's review in *Theater Heute* 12 (1991): 2–5.

61. Gerhard Stadelmaier, "Tut nichts, der Jude wird verkannt," *Frankfurter Allgemeine Zeitung* (October 10, 1994).

62. Ibid.

63. Cf. Benjamin Henrichs, "Lessings Schlaf, Marlowes Schweiß," *Die Zeit* (October 14, 1994).

64. Cf. Helga Stöhr-Strauch, "Nathan der Weise trifft Shylock," *Stuttgarter Nachrichten,* (February 19, 1999).

65. Arie Zinger directed the *Merchant* in Cologne 1978; Benjamin Korn directed *Nathan* in Hamburg 1981; Jossi Wieler directed *Nathan* (1991) and the *Merchant* (1992) in Basel, both with the same actor, Norbert Schwientek, in the role of the Jew.

CHAPTER TWELVE

FRITZ KORTNER'S LAST ILLUSION

ROBERT SHANDLEY

Directed by Josef von Baky, *Der Ruf* (1948) was based on a screenplay written by Fritz Kortner, a German-Jewish actor, who had always struggled with the identity designators of Germanness and Jewishness. The film, which was released in America as *The Last Illusion,* is driven by the psychological tension inherent in the discourse of German-Jewish coexistence. It underscores the pull between a Jewish heritage that had, before Hitler, been in danger of fading into the wash of modernity and a German process of identification that had simultaneously become stronger. The Shoah changed this discourse irrevocably. Thus, more than anything else, *The Last Illusion* presents a story of a man's attempt to create an image of himself as a German and a Jew in post-Holocaust (West) Germany. As the first cinematic intervention in the new and volatile postwar German-Jewish interaction, *The Last Illusion* set up the terms of discussion with which subsequent German filmmaking will necessarily have to contend.

The varied genealogy of the German-Jewish symbiosis contains at least one consistent trait that can be traced in *The Last Illusion:* It arises not as reportage of Jewish and German cultures, but more often as a response to a rift in the relations between German gentiles and German Jews. The illusion of symbiosis takes on its most sophisticated form in philosopher Hermann Cohen's *Deutschtum und Judentum* [*Germanness and Jewishness,* 1915].[1] In Cohen's text the discourse of coexistence and codependency of the cultures emerges as a response to the outbreak of World War I, a war that saw Jews serving and dying in battle next to their gentile compatriots, while encountering increasing anti-Semitism in the trenches. Symbiosis functions for Cohen as an ideal organizing principle for what he hoped would be a victorious and cosmopolitan

German empire, one that would include and recognize Jews as integral to it. This fantasy of belonging to a triumphant nationalist narrative must be read as more than mere denial of reality. It is an attempt on the part of thinkers such as Cohen, Martin Buber, Franz Rosenzweig, and Gershom Scholem, among others, to reconcile their own cultural assimilation with a cultural difference both that they felt and that was projected onto them. Symbiosis reads as a precarious performance of identity formation under the conditions of modernity.

In the years between the end of the war in 1945 and the founding of the two German states in 1949, Germany proved itself to be an even darker, more contentious stage to maintain a discourse about symbiosis. With both the delusion of integration and the promise of modernity in ruins, the question arises why someone would even bother to consider revisiting the symbiosis question after Auschwitz. Furthermore, the German-Jewish community that had generated and sustained the discourse had been either murdered or driven away. But while it was certainly reasonable to believe that the coexistence fantasy had been emptied of all of its promise, for many of those who had fled into exile in the 1930s and sought to return after the war, symbiosis was a way of organizing a confused identity structure that for varying reasons they wished to maintain. Furthermore, symbiosis discourse had always contained, among other things, a conciliatory impulse as well as a generous portion of moral righteousness, carrots and sticks that would prove necessary for survival in postwar Germany. In *The Last Illusion,* these tensions play themselves out actively in the same cultural spheres in which anti-Semitism had flourished.

The opening sequence cuts to a black man in a well-appointed servant's uniform walking to the side entrance of a small but elegant home. Emma, a woman with a thick German accent, greets the man called Homer at the door. Their exchange is a mixture of German and English. Preparations for a party are underway. The film makes light of who the 'we' are who are celebrating. Homer, answering the phone, says: "We are throwing a party . . . fifteen years in this country . . . No, no not me. It's an awful long time since we came." Meanwhile Emma talks about "over there" where she was "*glücklich*" [happy], noting that there is a difference between "glücklich" and "happy." She does not understand why one celebrates being away from home so long. "Those were the days," she says in German, "under Wilhelm . . . things went well for us while we still had him." The beverage deliverer Ludwig arrives. He speaks English with Homer and German with Emma. She goes on about how the Americans need a Kaiser too. Ludwig notes that his people had to look back a bit further to find a time when they "had it good," perhaps under King David.

Thus, the dominant topic of the opening sequence is the determination of ethnic specificity. Each of these three minor figures speaks of a collective "we." Homer refers to the "we" of African Americans; Emma, the Germans; and Ludwig, the Jews. Another man with a German accent, David, enters, seconding Ludwig's claim, noting that "ever since then, we have been in trouble." Although Ludwig is clearly a native speaker of German, it is obvious he does not share Emma's opinion about when times were good.

Enter Fränkl, a German with a thick Swabian accent. He and David engage in a discussion about Goethe. Fränkl notes that all of that talk of hope in Goethe was too much for him after the Nazis and their thousand-year Reich came marching in. But, now that the war is over and he is a little older, he likes the idea that Goethe slept with a 19-year-old at the age of 74. Both men turn to Homer. "Do you know Goethe?" "Yes, sir. He was a writer I suppose. A writer for the movies." The men answer: "He would not have debased himself. Decades saved him from that humiliation." This is not only a sideswipe at Hollywood. It is an attempt to portray the situation of these intellectuals in exile, who were forced into the American system of reification. Goethe, according to them, was beyond this. Indeed, Goethe still calls them to their Germanness.

All of the characters speak about "the Professor." When we finally see Mauthner, he is sitting listening to his young student, Mary, with whom he is said to be in love, play the piano while Homer sings a ballad about America. The whole scene is a mixture of celebration about the joys of America and the pull that *Heimat* [homeland] still has on all of the exiles. Mauthner announces to David that he is considering accepting a call [*der Ruf*] to return to his old post as a professor in Germany. David notes that Los Angeles is a place you go to, not from, and is puzzled why Mauthner would want to go back to evil Germany when he could remain in sunny California with beautiful young Mary. Mauthner replies that in both cases it is about a love affair.

Thus the film establishes early on that this is about a German emigrant's sense of place in postwar America and Germany. The utopian promise of the German-Jewish symbiosis expresses a search for both an emotional and a physical *Heimat* for these characters, a sense of longing for the mythic place from which one comes.

The film confronts the representation of both Germanness and Jewishness, with the Germanness being the larger category. While we are sure which of the characters are Germans, there is no reason not to assume that they are all also Jews, with the exception of Emma. Yet, it will still be necessary for the film to establish a specifically Jewish identity for Mauthner. How it goes about this task differentiates the film radically from other films of the era. Mauthner never once refers to himself as a Jew. While Kortner's own public persona would have been enough of a clue for many spectators in 1948, *The Last Illusion* nevertheless provides a differentiated set of anchors of identity that the spectator must be able to add up.

Perhaps the most convincing sign of Mauthner's Jewishness is the reaction of his friends to his idea of accepting the position from his old university. David, who appears to be his closest friend, is shocked and bewildered by the idea. "They are man-eaters, yes, man-eaters, cannibals over there." Mauthner's fiery response to this comment indicates that he is going to confront generalizations wherever he sees them. "There is neither a people made up entirely of criminals, nor is there one made up entirely of heroes." He even becomes conciliatory when he claims, "I do not know how I would have behaved had I been allowed to stay there." Much like his friends who reject Germany while still being called to their Germanness, Mauthner's Jewish identity at this point is being thrust upon him by his friends to such an extent that he counters it with a veiled defense of barbarism. This is the battle the film will depict throughout, one of his trying to reclaim a German identity while others confront him with his Jewish one. When he arrives in Germany, anti-Semitism establishes the latter completely at the cost of the former.

Apart from this film, it is striking how early postwar German cinema generally avoids or ignores German-Jewish relations. This cinematic wave of "rubble films" took place between 1946 and 1948 in Germany, and the films were marked by their mise en scene as war-torn Germany. In their best manifestations, they are some of the most honest confrontations with the Nazi legacy to be found in German film history. At their worst, they are apologetic and self-pitying, turning Germans into the ultimate victims of World War II. Many of the films give thematic priority to the concerns of everyday life in immediate postwar Germany, such as the black market, unemployment among returning soldiers, and the rampant spread of venereal disease. Within the category of rubble films there are films that thematize the persecution of Jews under Nazism. But only one film from the period portrays Jewish camp survivors—*Long is the Road* (1948). Made through the cooperative efforts of a Yiddish theater group comprised of camp survivors and non-Jewish German filmmakers, it contains the first feature film depiction of the transports to Auschwitz. It also documents a true story of persecution, survival and life in the displaced persons camps. But, although the film is partially done in German, it is not a film intended for the general German audience. Rather, it is an appeal to German Jews living abroad for support of Jewish displaced persons. *The Last Illusion* is the only other rubble film to depict a Jew in postwar Germany.[2] This time the Jew is a returned exile. So, although it can be said that the rubble films do address the Nazi past, they are still quite tentative about German-Jewish questions. In most rubble films, neither the extent of the genocide nor the possibility of surviving it had entered the postwar German cinematic imagination.

Why was it so difficult for filmmakers, even those inclined to face the Nazi crimes, to imagine the lives of Jews in Germany after 1945? Is it due to a residual genocidal anti-Semitism, seeking to deny the failure of the final solution to reach its goals? Or, is it simply shock that anyone could have escaped the horrors that they would have seen depicted in *The Death Mills,* the documentary on the camps many Germans were forced to watch? Or were Germans simply so obsessed with their own misery and "victimization" at the end of the war that they failed to direct any of their imaginative capacity to the plights of others? The last possibility would explain why, in the only other rubble film to depict a camp survivor, *The Murderers Are Among Us* (1946), the survivor turns out to be non-Jewish.[3]

Between *The Last Illusion* and Alexander Kluge's *Yesterday's Girl* (1964), no other German filmmaker portrayed the possibility of German Jews in postwar Germany. In Konrad Wolf's autobiographical film *I was Nineteen,* Wolf returns to Germany as a part of the Soviet Red Army, but without making his Jewishness explicit. The most plausible explanation for this is that, after the war, non-Jewish Germans simply presumed that the illusion of continued coexistence and cultural exchange had been shattered once and for all. Furthermore, in order to present Jews in the narrative of postwar Germany, one had to portray a range of possible reactions to them. This would require accepting rage, vengeance fantasies, and moral condemnation of Germans as a part of the story. Given the obsession of rubble films with *German* suffering in the wake of the war, the possibility of this cognitive switch would require much more drastic intellectual transformations. The hegemonic filmic discourse of the 1950s in both East and West Germany allowed little if any room for such discussions.

The Last Illusion is, therefore, all the more remarkable and unique in its endeavor to investigate the possibility of a German-Jewish identity after Auschwitz. Nevertheless, *The Last Illusion* still easily fits into the rubble film category. It is, in many ways, a *Heimkehrerfilm,* that is, a film depicting the war veteran's return to his home, only this time it is a refugee instead of a soldier. The diegesis remains solely in the postwar situation as the characters work through the implications and remnants of National Socialism in and for war-torn Germany. It contains many of the anxieties that define other German films of the era, namely the fear of excessive American influence, the tendency to view all female sexuality as a form of betrayal, and the depiction of postwar Berlin as a corrupted space.

Josef von Baky, the Hungarian born film director whose most famous work was the Universum Film AG extravaganza, *Münchhausen,* directed the film. Yet, his work was overshadowed by the film's screenwriter and star, Fritz Kortner. *The Last Illusion* is a thinly-veiled version of Kortner's own story of exile and return.[4] He fled Germany on January 30, 1933, just as the Nazis came to power. He emigrated first to his native Austria, then to England, and finally to the United States. He worked in Hollywood during the war and returned to Berlin in December of 1947. The bombastic, gruff, and uncompromising character he plays in *The Last Illusion* matches reports of his own personality. It is how others describe him and how he comes off in interviews. Kortner's personality and identity prepared him well to pose the question of a German-Jewish dialogue after Nazism.

The film's screenplay is Kortner's own response to over 20 years of battles. As early as the 1920s, he had been prey to anti-Semitic attacks. In 1928, theater critic Bar Kochba, writing a review of the Hermann Ungar play, "The Red General," in the right-wing journal, *Der Angriff,* shows to what degree Kortner was reviled by the Nazis. "Cohn-Kortner played the red Pokamjenski. He was so perfect as a Jew, that he is to be recommended as the ideal illustration for the handbook of anti-Semitism."[5] In 1930, Kochba again employs Kortner as the screen for his anti-Semitic fantasy. "The wretchedness, which in the course of centuries Jewry has produced, is excellently expressed in this Cohn."[6] As this quote indicates, Kortner served the Nazis as a symbol of the degradation of German culture through Jewish influence. They reviled him so much that, even five years after fleeing into exile, the *Völkischer Beobachter* ran a piece entitled "Hier Jude—Hier Lude," in which an anonymous author conjures up a memory of Kortner as the prime example of the degeneracy that had dominated the German stage. The article concludes with the haunting remark: "How quickly the good will of the Germans has forgotten this ghost of the past. If they finally answer the Jewish question for good, it is an old debt that will finally be repaid."[7] This article, written within weeks of Kristallnacht, uses the memory of the exiled Fritz Kortner to justify the persecution of Jews.

All of this merely indicates that Kortner was more than just a popular actor who had been forced to leave Germany. He was one whose memory could be invoked negatively by Nazis even after he was gone. Because of this—and due to his own proclivity to take on his opponents instead of avoiding them—he would not be able to return without confronting directly the ideology that had used him as its ultimate "other." *The Last Illusion*'s reception brings into relief both the role of film in general and Kortner's role specifically in early postwar German culture. His return to Germany from "sunny Californian exile" in December 1947 was a media event equaled only by Thomas Mann's brief return the following year. In both cases they were treated as stars who could, if they so chose, relegitimate and rejuvenate the cultural and intellectual life of the nation. Kortner is asked in newspaper editorials to use his appearance to open the possibilities of the public sphere. In fact, at first glance, the degree to which Kortner's presence is demanded in the theater obscures its intentions. That which the Nazi press had used against him for years was to be reworked into a positive form. Ilse Rewald writes a letter to the editor in the *Tagesspiegel* that "Kortner would be exactly the energy we need to transform our theater scene from a tight circle into an opportunity for a public life." An important and extraordinarily talented personality can, in fact, do much to invigorate a cultural scene. But Rewald's letter contains an embedded message that reveals why, of all the talented actors on earth, only Fritz Kornter will do. She writes, "If he has returned from America, can we not assume that he has done so for no other reason than to help us free ourselves of our guilt?"[8] Kortner's presence was to breathe life back into the symbiosis discourse. This time, however, the positions are switched. Non-Jewish Germans find themselves in the position of needing to justify why Jews would want to participate in German public life.

However cynically we might view the German hope that the most respected and, at the same time, most reviled Jewish actor of his time would recommit himself to the Berlin acting scene, the point remains that Kortner returned. If the Germans had to justify why it is that they needed Kortner, Kortner, too, had to account for his own return to a place that had driven him away. Rumors began to spread that he had returned because he had been offered large sums of money to perform in Germany. Given the lack of capital in the country at the time, this rumor, which he denies, seems animated by the general anti-Semitic stereotyping that Kortner had endured his whole life. When asked directly in numerous interviews about his return, Kortner made it clear that language was the thing that brought him home. As an actor in Hollywood with a thick German accent, his opportunities were limited. For that same reason, he chose not to go to Israel. His career and his success were tied to his mastery of German, an idiosyncratic pronunciation of which had been his trademark.

Kortner was obviously not alone among German-Jewish immigrants who sought to return to Germany. However, the caesura from previous German-Jewish history that the Holocaust presented forced these refugees from Nazism to justify how and why they could return to Germany. In *The Last Illusion* and its reception we can find the basic tenets of a new incarnation of the German-Jewish symbiosis.

This film received more prerelease publicity than any film of the era. There were reports that Kortner was writing a screenplay, that Josef von Baky had signed on to direct the film, in which Kortner would star, and that U. S. Ambassador Richard Murphy's daughter Rosemary would star in the ingenue role. The tone of the reports was positive and excited. During the film's shooting an article appeared in the Viennese journal *Mein Film* entitled "Fritz Kortner dreht einen Kampfilm." This headline carries on a narrative from before 1933 of Kortner as provocateur. In describing Kortner's character in *The Last Illusion,* the article states: "Once again the character is timelessly Jewish, just as the artist has been playing for years, and portrayed with great humanity."[9] The article cites Kortner's ability to portray a sympathetic Jew as an accomplishment, and then goes on to mention, before anything else, the many different Jewish roles, from Shylock to Dreyfus, the actor had played. Numerous reviews commended the film as a moral event that "holds the mirror to today's world."[10] A review from Düsseldorf starts out with a description of Kortner's face. "A deeply drawn nose makes him look as though he were not European. His lower jaw jets forward and betrays a desire to attack."[11] The image of Kortner's Jewish body from before the war still held valence a decade or two later, although in this article it is supposedly being given a positive value. Interestingly, the descriptions of Kortner or of his characters differ little from those in the 1920s or 1930s. They are merely inverted into a philo-Semitic tone.

Kortner's screenplay is a confrontation with the ways he had been treated in the past and his setting down of the conditions under which he would continue to function in the present. As a test case for the problems and possibilities of Jewish reimmigration and reintegration in postwar Germany, he did not create an accommodating and affable figure who would make symbiosis easy. He gives the spectator every chance to play out anti-Semitic fantasies by creating a character who appeals to almost all of the negative stereotypes that had been attributed to Jewishness in general and to him specifically. His character, Mauthner, is an old man who is chasing after a young girl and who has had a history of doing so in the past. He is an outsider who has been chosen over a non-Jewish German for a professorship. He becomes a compilation of all of the Jews around him, at once the stereotypical Jewish hysterical male and the orthodox Jew. He identifies himself with Heinrich Heine, whom he quotes. More importantly, Mauthner is not always portrayed as likeable. But the film insists rigorously that just because you cannot like him as an individual does not mean you are allowed to hate him as a signifier of a group. The film's rejection of him is simultaneously a rejection of Enlightenment values.

The first half-hour of *The Last Illusion* constructs this composite figure of the Jew, who is then hailed back to his Germanness. This carefully constructed Jew is called back home to educate the young in Germany. If he were just being called back to his university position as an act of reparation, the film would not be able to sustain a credible narrative for more than 20 minutes. Nor would Mauthner necessarily have to be a Jew. But, as is evident in the culture of the rubble film, Jewishness is equivalent to moral authority. This is not subtle in this film. Mauthner is a moral philosopher. He is called back to his German university post specifically to redeem German culture.

The climax of the film is Mauthner's opening lecture at the university on "The Learnability of Virtue." The speech is Mauthner's ultimate performance of his belief in traditional *Bildung,* that is, yet another German myth about the primacy of humanistic culture. Not only do his words fall on deaf ears but a hateful brawl erupts shortly but after his lecture, suggesting to Mauthner that his faith in humanism is misplaced. He dies at the end of the film of heartbreak. His mortal disappointment lies not in the fact that he is rejected as a Jew in postwar Germany, but that the place to which he has returned has lost that which called him back to it. The attacks on his Jewishness hits something even more vital in him, namely his identity, which he wishes to label "German" and which is grounded in humanist idealism.

Visually the film paints an entirely different picture of Germany than do the other rubble films. This Germany is filmed as dark and enclosed. The vast spaces provided by the ruins are eschewed for a claustrophobic film constructed almost entirely of medium and medium-close shots. Germany is not its buildings, countryside, city crowds, or any other location shot. It is an institution filmed in tight studio shots. The film's frequent use of close-ups establishes its emphasis on private rather than public attitudes. The only sequence with multiple long shots is Mauthner's lecture, thus coupling his public rejection with the private ones he encounters. The rubble the film attempts to portray is emotional and not only German. The ruins represented are the human remains on all sides of the war, its former soldiers, its civilian support system, the underground opposition, and those forced into exile. The film achieves this effect with facial shots used whenever a character is confronted with the contradictions of his or her past. Pans of large groups move quickly to characters in small groups. The film sutures the spectator into the narrative with conventional editing, in order to give the illusion that these disparate groups could somehow belong together.

Because the film has adhered strictly to the conventions of cinematic realism, the last sequence disrupts the narrative all the more. This transformation occurs in an almost illogical sequence shift. In one sequence Emma, the maid, who has accompanied Mauthner on his return to Germany, is talking to the convalescing Mauthner about returning to America. The scene is brightly lit and is a medium shot from above. It then blends into a close-up side view of Mauthner's face with his eyes closed. As the camera pulls back we see that the room is dark and the other characters express concern. The film provides no explanation for this change in the state of Mauthner's health, nor does it provide any conventional clues such as jarring background music or a contemporal diegesis. The next quiet, dark sequence is a transition to the film's concluding segment. The cinematic style morphs from classical realism to a sort of psychological realism found most often in Weimar-era German film. In the end, Mauthner dies with the Oedipal image of his son in the arms of his ex-wife.

Mauthner returns to Germany in hopes of finding a country seeking to rebuild its great humanist traditions. He subjects his homeland to an aptitude test, using the relative existence of anti-Semitism as the marker of humanity's progress in Germany. Instead of finding rich belief in the fundamentals of Enlightenment thinking, he finds a land filled with the same prejudices, pettiness, and deceit that he had left many years before. He had hoped that he could return idealism to a defeated community. Instead the community defeats his idealism. He is called home only to realize that the *Heimat* of German-Jewish symbiosis is an illusory space.

The film shows, at least as far as Kortner is concerned, the new conditions under which symbiosis might work. *The Last Illusion* proposes what must have been a radical idea at the time, namely that any continuing German-Jewish symbiosis in the wake of the Shoah must necessarily place Germanness and Jewishness on equal footing. There would be no folding of one into the other. Kortner needed Germany in order to continue his acting career. But, as his media reception indicates, Germany needed him too. In fact, the film reclaims Hermann Cohen's old argument that Judaism could provide and had, in fact, always provided the moral foundation Germany needed to survive.

The return of cultural figures from exile, particularly Jewish ones, served as markers of Germany's progress toward legitimacy. Such as in the case of Thomas Mann, Kortner's return also played into the increasing Cold War politics. He had become an American citizen and his initial return had been paid for by the American military government in Germany, as were his wages for *The Last Illusion*. The film, shot both in English and German, was meant to be shown in America as a sign of increasing German trustworthiness. Thus, we must view the event of his return both through the refractors of German guilt and through Cold War hegemonic strategies. Although Kortner states in interviews that the film is meant to show Americans how far Germany had come since the war, it is unclear to me how it would do that.

The Last Illusion advances ambivalent messages about the status of German-Jewish relations after Auschwitz. To be sure, the character of Mauthner offers a moral model, one grounded in pure Enlightenment principles of reason and *Bildung*. But that model suffers a defeat, one that animates the film's tragic ending. The possibility of a peaceful and productive German-Jewish symbiosis emerges as *the last illusion* to which the English title refers. And yet, even in that tragic end, the film holds out some hope that the forces of reason might prevail. Kortner's own choice to continue to live and work in Germany for many more years seems to be evidence that he still argued for a German-Jewish coexistence. His own demeanor suggests that he did not demand that it be a friendly one.

Finally, it is in the reception of *The Last Illusion* that we can see the traces it leaves behind. Critical and popular response to the film was overwhelmingly positive. Its reception carried on a trend of the era to view German-made films as moral events. This and many of the other rubble films would serve as one of the initial models of the confrontational "events" that would multiply in the coming years and decades. The controversy around Fassbinder's *The City, Garbage and Death* and the Historians' Debate in the 1980s or even the Goldhagen or Walser debates in the 1990s would become much louder examples. However, *The Last Illusion,* like almost every other film of the rubble era, was quickly forgotten. The big "moral event" was not assimilated into everyday practice. It would seem that the construction of great moral events actively inhibits their acceptance into everyday attitudes. This schism is the great unlearned lesson of *The Last Illusion.*

Notes

1. See *Deutschtum und Judentum mit grundlegenden Betrachtungen über Staat und Internationalismus* (Giessen: Töpelmann, 1915).

2. It is arguable that the character Mondschein in Wolfgang Staudte's *The Murderers are Among Us* (1946) is meant to be Jewish. That reading, however, is only possible in terms of the film's historical unconscious. There are no overt utterances as such.

3. Although the film itself leaves relatively ambiguous the reasons for her incarceration, the screenplay presents the unlikely scenario that she was taken away because her father was a communist.

4. For information about Kortner's life, see his autobiography, *Aller Tage Abend* (Munich: Kindler, 1959) and the two biographies, Klaus Völker, *Fritz Kortner: Schauspieler und Regisseur* (Berlin: Hentrich, 1993); and Peter Schütze, *Fritz Kortner* (Reinbek bei Hamburg: Rowohlt, 1994).

5. Quoted in Matthias Brand, *Fritz Kortner in der Weimarer Republik: Annäherungsversuche und die Entwicklung eines jüdischen Schauspielers in Deutschland* (Rheinfelden: Schäuble, 1981), 187.

6. Ibid., 264.

7. "Hier Jude—Hier Lude," *Völkischer Beobachter* (November 27, 1938).

8. *Tagesspiegel* (January 18, 1948).

9. "Fritz Kortner dreht einen Kampfilm," *Mein Film* (October 29, 1948).

10. *Nacht Express* (April 21, 1949).

11. Düsseldorf, "Fritz Kortner hat das Wort," *Rhein Echo* (June 6, 1949).

CHAPTER THIRTEEN

COMIC VISION AND "NEGATIVE SYMBIOSIS" IN MAXIM BILLER'S *HARLEM HOLOCAUST* AND RAFAEL SELIGMANN'S *DER MUSTERJUDE**

RITA BASHAW

"Negative symbiosis" is Dan Diner's term for the complicated set of dynamics that has influenced how Jews and Germans relate to one another and to their past since Auschwitz.[1] One of Diner's most significant contentions is that the memory of Auschwitz will exert an even stronger influence in determining the future consciousness of both collective groups (German perpetrators and Jewish victims). That is, the strategies that both employ either to circumvent or to come to terms with the memory of the genocide ultimately conflict and encourage a pattern of ritualized attitudes and behaviors that hamper open dialogue. Germans, for example, have sought to reduce their feelings of shame and guilt by observing the tenets of philo-Semitism and constructing their own narratives of victimization. Jews have legitimized their presence in Germany by assuming the role of moral watchdog, continually invoking the memory of the Holocaust in an effort to prevent such an act from ever happening again. As the decades pass, Germans attempt the predictable—if dubious—project of normalizing their history, which is read by Jews as a willful act of forgetting. Diner is not alone in observing that this state of affairs conceivably contributes to an anti-Semitism *because of,* not despite, Auschwitz.[2]

Two contemporary German-Jewish authors, Maxim Biller and Rafael Seligmann, address this sobering pitfall of modern German-Jewish relationships. In a broad sense, the controversy that their writings engender reflects the separation between the attitudes of a younger generation of postwar German

Jews and the norms espoused by the *Jüdische Gemeinde* (the official organ of Jewish representation that receives political and financial support from the government). Specifically, a gap exists between the *Gemeinde* leadership, which traditionally has been composed of German Jews, and the mass of its members, who feel estranged from what they consider to be the *Gemeinde*'s conservative political and social agenda. More often than not, *Gemeinde* membership is more diverse than its leadership: It is largely immigrant (most often from Eastern Europe), younger (with no direct experience of the Shoah), and often lacks knowledge of Jewish culture and religion. In addition, a significant number of German Jews do not officially register with the *Gemeinde*. Many Jews thus find themselves placed on the margins of a certain set of expectations regarding what it "means" to be Jewish in Germany. That these expectations are held not only by the *Gemeinde* but also by German society should be clear, for "negative symbiosis" entails, on the German side, a continued investment in philo-Semitic attitudes and behaviors.

Biller and Seligmann thematize this divergence of contemporary German-Jewish life from earlier models of German Jewry. They do so via a comic vision that transgresses or unexpectedly broadens conventional wisdom regarding German and Jewish identity and relationships; for example, both authors parody the ritualized remembrance of Auschwitz and upset the "German perpetrator vs. Jewish victim" equation. Our detection of these transgressions freely depends upon our knowledge of certain fields and discourses, such as our familiarity with German literary traditions, historical narratives, and trends in popular culture and politics. What is interesting is that our awareness of these comic transgressions may not necessarily result in laughter—especially when the material in question deals with a particularly grotesque juxtaposition or gallows humor. Maxim Biller's *Harlem Holocaust* (1990) and Rafael Seligmann's *Der Musterjude* [The Model Jew, 1997] are two examples of texts that raise the ire of many Jewish *and* German readers, for the former group perceives these texts as questioning their status as victims and moral superiors and the latter take affront at the charge that philo-Semitism is motivated by opportunism and latent anti-Semitic tendencies.

Nonetheless, as readers we are moved in some way—be it to laughter, horror, or their ambivalent mix—and it is this affective disposition that enables our sense or understanding of Biller and Seligmann's critique. The comic experience thus entails a process by which we *detect* and ultimately *reject* a transgression—a violation of shared social expectations presented as a normal and otherwise unobjectionable occurrence—in favor of a deeper awareness of German culture and society. Certain comic experiences are thus more than the expression of an eccentric subjectivity. They signify and also grant us a moment of understanding and intellectual insight about not only why a particular image is comical, but also why conventional understanding of some larger implied concept or event is misleading or inappropriate. Finally, while the *aperçus* of comic vision does afford our imagination a sense of pleasure, they also cultivate the mind by stimulating metaphysical reflection.[3] In other words, comic vision provokes us to examine the expectations that lead us to resist the ludicrous tendencies that Biller and Seligmann present in their texts.

My discussion of *Harlem Holocaust* and *Der Musterjude* focuses on the comic perspective that I perceive to structure them. In brief, I argue that if there are moments of intellection and understanding involved with certain comic experiences, then the significance of these texts lies in Biller and Seligmann's critique of the "negative symbiosis" that they depict as characteristic of contemporary German-Jewish relationships.

Maxim Biller, *Harlem Holocaust*

Maxim Biller, born of Russian parents in Prague in 1960, emigrated to the Federal Republic with his parents in 1970. He was on the staff of the German magazine *Tempo* and has become a controversial columnist and prose fiction writer. Biller has published three volumes of short stories, *Wenn ich einmal reich und tot bin* [When I am finally rich and dead, 1990], *Die Tempojahre* [The Tempo Years, 1991], *Land der Väter und Verräter* [Land of Fathers and Traitors, 1994], and most recently, a novel, *Die Tochter* [The Daughter, 2000]. *Harlem Holocaust* first appeared in the collection *Wenn ich einmal reich und tot bin* and was then republished on its own in 1998. It is a short story of some 50 pages; its main characters are three: Efraim Rosenhain, Ina Polarker, and Gerhard "Gary" Warszawski.

Warszawski is the only one of the three who is Jewish; he is also not German but American. He grew up in New York City, the child of German-Jewish refugees who fled Germany before World War II. As a 17-year-old, he despised his very *German* Jewish parents; he escaped their atmosphere of nostalgia and sentimentality by taking the subway to East Harlem, where he discovered jazz. Warszawski romanticized American blacks as "his" Jews until the day he met a family relative who had survived the Holocaust. Warszawski credits this Saul-like experience with his initiation as a writer and his identity as a Jew. When we meet him in the story, Warszawski is approximately 60 years of age, a linguistics professor on leave from Columbia University, courtesy of a writer's fellowship. Whereas his novels fall on deaf ears in the United States, they sell well in Germany. Consequently, he is spending his leave in Munich; more specifically, he has moved in with Ina in her apartment.

Ina Polarker, perhaps in her early thirties, is a journalist who "discovered" Warszawski and introduced him to German readers via the reviews and cultural columns she writes for a major German daily paper. In turn, Warszawski seduced Ina the first evening they met; more accurately, he attacked her in an elevator while it was stalled between floors of the *English House*, justifying his use of a condom (decorated with blue and white Stars of David) with an agitated, breathless lecture on the highlights of over 2,000 years of Jewish triumph over exile, suffering, and genocide. After surviving such diabolical odds, why should any Jew risk weakening his immune system and die a comparatively banal death? After Warszawski's return to New York, Ina and Efraim become lovers. Their relationship deteriorates approximately six months later, when Warszawski returns to Munich on the writer's fellowship. Ina aborts her child and leaves Efraim for Warszawski. It is at this point that we meet her in the story: a trophy girlfriend who neglects her own interests and career to remain, mute and supportive, at Warszawski's side.

Finally, there is Efraim, who, despite his name, is not Jewish. Rather, his name signifies his mother's attempt at reparation. As Efraim tells it, his family's resistance to Hitler was limited. His maternal grandfather did find Hitler vulgar and was thus prompted to rescue an Expressionist collection from Göring's waiting clutches—not that this counts as "resistance," for it is hardly on par with hiding Jews or printing leaflets. However, compared to Efraim's paternal grandfather and uncle—the former wrote for an anti-Semitic paper and the latter tortured communists, Jews, and homosexuals at Gestapo headquarters—it does count for something. Efraim, who appears to be Ina's age, first met Warszawski some years previously, when he was employed as the latter's German-language translator. Most importantly, however, Efraim is our narrator, and it is with him that the key to our story lies. Do we believe Efraim's account or not? Is Warszawski really the villain—that cynical, self-serving, rapacious, horny opportunist, clever enough but hardly creative— that Efraim makes him out to be? Has a monster truly bewitched Ina, that beautiful and now intellectually wilted flower of German womanhood? Is Efraim really a victim, a naive, long-suffering, and unrecognized talent?

We might find ourselves tentatively agreeing with this assessment were it not for one detail that is at first easy enough to overlook: Efraim's strange affliction. As Efraim mentions at the story's outset, he has since puberty increasingly suffered from dizzy spells, migraines, and fragmented, blurred vision. These symptoms appear periodically, are treated with medication, and then disappear. They stem from no physical malady but are an inherited condition, Efraim muses, that appeared only when he became an adult and, as he puts it, "my sensitivity, my craving for guilt and atonement could fully develop. . . ."[4] Strange and disturbing as this information is, it passes soon enough. We entertain suspicions when we learn that these symptoms strike Efraim with full force after Eve Lurie, his German-Jewish girlfriend, breaks up with him, but Efraim's recollection here is brief. Upon Warszawski's return to Munich, however, Efraim's symptoms reappear. By the end of the story they crescendo: Efraim experiences multiple delusions as he staggers from a luncheon meeting with Warszawski and Ina out onto the street and into the *Englischer Garten,* where he ostensibly falls asleep in the arms of a drunk. These events are followed by a laconic "editor's remarks," written by one Hermann Warschauer, professor at Columbia University. Warschauer indicates the text we have just read was the manuscript of one "Friedrich" Rosenhain, who apparently sent Warschauer his work immediately before his own suicide. Warschauer credits the work with being "the document of a self-destructive talent and the great German malady."[5]

It is difficult to ascertain what exactly does take place in *Harlem Holocaust,* for the revelations of the epilogue throw a pall of doubt over Efraim's narrative. Does Efraim's manuscript present "real" occurrences or merely the fanciful creations of a struggling, desperate mind? To what extent does Efraim's distorted vision corrupt *all* of his descriptions? Biller's surprise ending in effect implicates readers for failing to perceive Efraim's mental instability and dubious philo-Semitism. In other words, our initial laughter and disbelief at Efraim's more lurid exaggerations is not enough to make up for a complacent acceptance of Efraim's perspective of events. Some readers may assert that Biller baits them unfairly, for his charge comes at the close of a fantastic and comic piece, a context that predisposes readers to accept unusual elements of plot and narrative. Yet many comic experiences operate via the principle of the unexpected, by suggesting similarities within an unlikely juxtaposition. In this case, the grotesque engenders an ambivalent emotional reaction (laughter *and* horror exist in tension with one another[6]) to a conflict that lacks resolution. *Harlem Holocaust* is grotesque beyond its exaggerated parody of stereotypes of contemporary German and Jewish identity in that its sudden disclosure regarding the narrator exploits readers' shame and shock in an attempt to provoke a moment of radical consciousness. That is, *Harlem Holocaust* presents, in metaphorical form, Biller's contention that certain historical attitudes, such as the deception involved in German narratives of victimization vis-à-vis others—particularly Jews and other "foreigners"—*continue* to inform how certain Germans conceptualize Jewish identity and relate to Jews today.[7]

Efraim's "*große deutsche Krankheit*" is the *dis*-ease that negative symbiosis necessarily produces as Germans and Jews are compelled to relate to one another and their past in mechanistic and ultimately self-destructive ways. For example, consider that, as an adult, the only extended period in which Efraim does not experience hallucinations, migraines, and dizzy spells is during his relationship with Ina, that is, when no Jews are present. In contrast, his relationships with Eve and Warszawski leave him unhappy, frustrated, wracked by guilt, and impotent to change his situation, for Jews are the ones who hold an inviolable monopoly on moral superiority and victim status.

The first time Efraim attempts to sympathize with Eve when she begins one of her frequent tirades against Eastern European Jews (Eve is an upper-class German Jew; Chaim, her ex-husband, is from Poland), she slaps him in the face and snarls, "Only I may do that!"[8] Efraim continues:

> Her slap made me dizzy. Instead of making a retort, I choked and coughed. What response could I possibly offer someone like her? After all, Eve, who had a slender, neurotic appearance, declared to me three times a day how she immediately felt the full horror upon arriving in Germany, and how, when a capital "K" appeared in a street or shop sign, she instantly placed a mental "Z" next to it . . . [9]

Eve eventually breaks up with Efraim because she finds it impossible to continue to live, sleep, and eat with a *German.* Efraim cannot fault Eve, he tell us; she was right. He meekly accepts his typecast role as a mutilated piece of German history.

Additionally, consider that Warszawski's short stories and novels all apparently repeat what Efraim calls the closet, or *Kleiderschrank,* scene. Leo Schneider, the relative whose story of the Holocaust changed Warszawski's life, escaped deportation to Poland by hiding in a closet. How well this corresponds to what Warszawski reproduces in his fiction is unclear, for Efraim quotes from a passage that has Leo not only hiding in the closet but also frantically masturbating. Overcome by the smell of his sister (her clothes are in the closet and remind him of how he used to play with her underwear and watch her bathe), Leo begins to masturbate, climaxing once the house is sealed and he manages to burst out of the closet. Efraim broadly hints that Warszawski manufactures a crass eroticism in order to better sell his Holocaust novels. When we recall that Warszawski's books sell only in Germany, Efraim is implicitly suggesting that Americans have too much sense to buy such trash.

Americans should not feel flattered, however. The condition of being both Jewish *and* American not only renders Warszawski's superior moral status virtually unassailable but also makes him doubly repugnant to Efraim, for the latter perceives in Warszawski but the crassest of both kinds of stereotypes (he calls Warszawski a *"Literatur-Kissinger"*).[10] And yet, Warszawski gets his way: he bullies his publisher, he bullies his audience at readings, and when, as always, no representatives from Munich's Jewish community attend his weekly Saturday luncheons at *Klub Maon,* he exclaims, "They're all collaborators anyhow!" and begins one of his familiar tirades.[11] So Efraim, Ina, and Warszawski sit alone, week after week, at their Saturday luncheons. As the trio orders and eats, Warszawski basically mauls Ina (shoves her, bumps her, sticks his hands up her skirt and then sniffs them obtrusively afterwards), needles Efraim, and harasses the waitstaff. Once, after a book reading, Warszawski became so inebriated that he urinated from Ina's balcony while alternately singing the Star-Spangled Banner and a Hitler Youth song. Yet Efraim, who holds Warszawski responsible for stealing his girlfriend and murdering their child (Ina's abortion), remains unable to confront Warszawski directly; he can only assassinate the latter's character to us.

Warszawski's egregious behavior violates to an absurd degree at least two commonplace social expectations: that Jewish identity center on the remembrance of experiences of victimization and genocide and that this remembrance be solemn and unique.[12] Warszawski instrumentalizes his Jewish identity as he sees fit: to profit from the Shoah-business by writing bad books about the Holocaust, to malign Efraim and other Germans when it suits him, to commit acts of sexual aggression while cloaked in a mantle of moral superiority. Warszawski's "remembrance" goes so far that he holds lectures on the history of Jewish suffering and victimization at the same moment he puts a condom—emblazoned with Stars of David—over his member. Via this grotesque imagery we experience at least two levels of comic incongruity: first, that nasty sex is understood as an opportune moment for Holocaust "remembrance"; second, that this claim of Jewish victimization occurs at a moment when Warszawski is underscored as a *perpetrator*. Moreover, each of Warszawski's novels, purportedly about the Holocaust, feature the image of a masturbating boy hiding in the closet while his family is deported. This suggests the existence of a significant erotic dimension to the German reading public's fetish for texts of Holocaust remembrance.

The person and actions of Efraim Rosenhain disrupt a related expectation: that philo-Semitism represents the antithesis of, and in effect dismantles, the ideology of anti-Semitism. A literal embodiment of philo-Semitism—recall his family history and the significance of his name vis-à-vis this history—Efraim nonetheless delivers a narrative replete with anti-Semitic images and editorializing. More strikingly, Efraim cannot deal with real Jews; his encounters with Eve and Warszawski render him physically and mentally ill. Biller thus satirically parodies the results of the strange equation where Germans promote their own victimization in order to redeem themselves from their historic role as perpetrators. This occurs in stereotypically gendered ways. Ina's masochistic tendencies displace her from the public to the private sphere, where she submits to Warszawski's sexual aggression and domestic needs at the cost of her own self-determination and independence. Efraim, meanwhile, channels his hatred and competitive jealousy (recall that Efraim is an unsuccessful novelist) into his vitriolic narrative and eventual suicide. When Ina and Efraim's child is aborted, so are the chances of their future happiness. German attempts to disengage from their history and the reminders of that history (contemporary Jews) are misguided and inherently unstable.

Yet, at the other extreme, philo-Semitism—which would seem to serve as a legitimate guide for conduct toward promoting a respectful remembrance of the Holocaust and some attempt at a compensation for its horrors—is revealed to project a set of stereotypes that, like anti-Semitism, excludes Jews from the category of "German." It demands that Germans continually simulate expressions of shame and guilt and ultimately results in destructive behavior (Ina's abortion and professional death, Efraim's suicide).

The relevant comic experiences portrayed by Biller contain a cognitive moment because they necessitate an intellectual awareness of how socially expected behavior (in both word and deed) is flouted in face of what seems completely normal and otherwise unobjectionable, that is, it requires that we perceive a violation of shared social expectations despite an appearance to the contrary. Although the images presented by Biller in *Harlem Holocaust* are anything but unobjectionable, they are presented as events that are not unusual. This underscores not only the important comic element in *Harlem Holocaust,* but also provokes us to examine the expectations that lead us to resist the ludicrous tendencies of Warszawski, Efraim, and Ina. In spite of its tendency to distract the mindful reader with distorted and distasteful images, *Harlem Holocaust* critiques the negative symbiosis that determines the concepts, norms, and commonplace expectations regarding contemporary German and Jewish identity. It takes grotesque delight in stating that a Shoah-based identity is outmoded, produces a false sense of security, and cripples the future of all parties involved.

Rafael Seligmann, Der Musterjude

Rafael Seligmann, born in 1947 in Israel, moved with his parents, who were German Jews, to Munich in 1957. His first novel, *Rubensteins Versteigerung* [Rubenstein's Auction, 1989] is credited with being the first contemporary German-Jewish novel of the postwar period. He then published *Die jiddische Mamme* [The Jewish Mother, 1990], *Der Musterjude* [The Model Jew, 1997], *Schalom, meine Liebe* [Shalom, my Love, 1998, adapted from the TV film of the same name], and most recently, *Der Milchmann* [The Milkman, 1999]. Seligmann holds a doctorate in political science and was a lecturer at Munich University. His nonfiction publications include his dissertation, *Israels Sicherheitspolitik* [Israel's Security Policies, 1982], *Mit Beschränkter Hoffnung: Juden, Deutsche, Israelis* (With Limited Hope: Jews, Germans, Israelis, 1991), and *Das deutsch-jüdische Verhältnis: Bestandsaufnahme und Perspektiven* [The German-Jewish Relationship: A Stock-Taking and Perspectives, 1995].

Der Musterjude's main characters are Manfred Bernstein, also known as Moische, the central character and "model Jew" of the novel's title; Heiner Keller, Moische's "friend" from earlier school days; and Hanna Bernstein,

Moische's mother. The novel teems with other characters—a succession of Moische's girlfriends and professional colleagues comes to mind—but the relationships between these three frame much of the novel. Events are related by an omniscient narrator.

The story opens with Moische experiencing a crisis: it is his fortieth birthday. To say Moische is unhappy is putting it mildly; as he sees it, he is wasting his life slaving away in his mother's struggling jeans shop (Germans and Turks now give the once largely Jewish textile trade a run for its money). Moische feels completely unappreciated, significantly underpaid, and endlessly thwarted by his mother and by fate in regards to his true vocation in life: journalism. Moische is convinced that he is an inspired and talented writer whose journalistic ambitions were cruelly suffocated 17 years ago. At that time Moische was an intern with the newspaper *Aufbau* in New York. He returned to Munich on what he thought was a temporary visit when his father died. His mother, however, manipulated his feelings of guilt and familial obligation until he promised to stay with her.

Hanna epitomizes a role that Seligmann analyzed in a prior novel, that of the "Jewish mother." Hanna loves Moische, her only child, her one triumph over the German murderers. No matter that he is immature, irresponsible, has no head for business, and is disrespectful to her both in public and in private, in short, a failure who runs away from any type of unpleasant problem—Hanna dotes on her son. For her part, Hanna is a survivor. She not only survived Auschwitz, where she saw members of her family killed before her eyes, but she did so while managing to retain her dignity and inviolable sense of self. When we meet Hanna in the novel, her main goal in life is to get Moische away from his non-Jewish girlfriends and instead see him married to a nice Jewish girl for, as she herself often tells him, a Jewish wife will ensure that he one day amounts to something. By extension, he will then finally be able to take care of the mother who endured years of toil for his sake.

Seligmann's comic depiction of contemporary German-Jewish life is itself embedded within a satire of the German print media industry. In brief, Moische is propelled by a series of coincidences to become the darling of German journalism and editor-in-chief of a major German daily, *Germany Today*, only to crash and find himself, at the novel's end, once again reliant upon his mother and her jeans shop. Heiner Keller is important here because he projects stereotypical philo-Semitic attitudes and behavior and thus serves as Moische's foil. To be sure, Heiner shares this role with the other non-Jewish Germans in the novel, but Heiner's presence is the most constant. It is also Heiner who unwittingly—and unwillingly—enables Moische's initial journalistic breakthrough and, when he realizes that Moische's success cannot be checked, reconciles with his "friend" in order to profit from his rise to fame.

Der Musterjude presents a number of comic contradictions: Moische's belief that journalism represents a search for truth is undercut by his own pandering to sensationalist issues in the interests of raising profits; and the German fascination for things Jewish is revealed as a self-serving and even erotic fetish that makes periodic appearances without, however, representing any meaningful critical engagement with German history and contemporary politics. Yet these are but two permutations of the same comic vision. In Seligmann's eyes, contemporary German-Jewish relationships are characterized by a negative symbiosis, the dynamics of which promote certain attitudes and behaviors that ultimately bear negative consequences for the future of both parties involved. Consider, for example, the character of Heiner Keller.

Heiner's pained behavior and tastes are absurd because Seligmann parodies them as mechanical extensions of a bizarre logic. Consider how Heiner patronizes *Klub Maon* precisely because it is a Jewish restaurant and being there on the Sabbath makes him feel almost Jewish himself. Dining at Maon presents Heiner with an ideal opportunity to engage in reparations and Holocaust remembrance for a relative pittance, both in financial and emotional terms. It is much easier for Heiner to relate to dead or dying Jews— the elderly clientele of Maon whom he observes from a distance and finds exotic—than it is for Heiner to interact with Moische as a peer. Heiner finds it difficult to relate to Moische because Moische does not fulfill Heiner's expectations of what being Jewish "means." Moische disappoints Heiner when he reveals that he does not speak Hebrew, is not a Zionist, and prefers the *Schelling Salon,* a local Bavarian pub that Hitler chose to frequent, to *Klub Maon,* an institution that Moische disparagingly refers to as "the Jewish old people's home."[13] Moische furthermore abruptly dismisses Heiner's musings regarding *shtetl* life as sentimental kitsch and philo-Semitic rhetoric.

Heiner can never forget that Moische is Jewish, a fact that leads him to accord Moische a superior moral position despite the latter's boorish and egregious behavior. Heiner's internal censor chafes at this restriction, especially as Moische selectively flouts the standards of negative symbiosis that govern Heiner's own identity and structure his relationship to Jews. Case in point: When Heiner recognizes his feelings of disgust and boredom during one of Moische's rambling exercises in self-pity, he is shocked. Could Daniel Goldhagen be correct in his assertion that all Germans are anti-Semites? "*Nein!,*" Heiner decides, "*I don't even hate Moische.*"[14] That Heiner automatically evaluates his momentary frustration within the context of the latest sensational theory regarding murderous German anti-Semitism constitutes a dishonest and absurd juxtaposition that underscores the artificial nature of the equations "German equals perpetrator" and "Jew equals victim." *Der Musterjude* depicts numerous instances in which Germans perceive Moische as benefiting from a kind of fool's freedom or moral license to conduct and express himself with relative impunity. In these scenes, then, Seligmann thematizes that philo-Semitism reduces German-Jewish relationships to a set of behaviors and thoughts that exist at a surface level only. In some ways, philo-Semitism contributes to an anti-Semitism *because of,* not despite, Auschwitz—a grotesque incongruity indeed. His pronounced taste for *gefillte fish* and Israeli white wine aside, Heiner repeatedly demonstrates that philo-Semitism cannot dismantle latent anti-Semitic prejudices. Thus, he can outwardly respect Maon and patronize it frequently, only to later disparage it as a "Jew restaurant"[15]; he can call Moische his old school chum and, later, when Moische makes use of an inconsistent logic in conversation, curse him under his breath, "This Jew is like an eel."[16] Again, because Heiner identifies Moische primarily in terms of the latter's Jewishness, a category that Heiner associates with exotic difference, what he dislikes and resents in Moische's personality—his vanity, opportunism, unwillingness to accept responsibility, and so on—then become "Jewish" traits, even though they are shared by the population at large.

Negative symbiosis affects Moische as well, albeit in a different way. Caught as he is between Jews like Hanna and Germans like Heiner, it is no wonder that Moische's personality presents a bundle of contradictions. On the one hand, Hanna raises him to neither forget nor forgive the Germans for the Holocaust; on the other is the indisputable fact that he was born and raised in Germany, speaks German as his native tongue, and is in Germany to stay. As a young man, Moische rebels against the contradiction of physically living in Germany while remaining isolated in a ghetto of fear and hatred of Germans. He first flees to Israel, only to discover the hypocrisy behind the Zionist stance of friends and family in Germany. Moische then goes to New York City. As in Israel, here the existence of a thriving Jewish community ensures that he no longer feels like a museum piece. Even better, Moische feels able to fashion his Jewish identity as he sees fit: an awareness and observation of cultural and historic tradition *without* an obligatory focus on the Holocaust. Yet Moische returns to Munich, where he must navigate the contortions required by the prevailing patterns according to which Jews and Germans define themselves and relate to one another. The costs are evident: feelings of shame, guilt, fear, and anger, and a crippled ability to establish meaningful relationships with others. Because Moische is ambitious and opportunistic, he uses all the cards available to him, including, in his case, that "fatal weapon . . . the Germans' bad conscience regarding the Jews."[17] Yet its dynamics are beyond his control. Once Moische is promoted to editor of his own newspaper (by virtue of the sensationalism and profits his exploitation of German-Jewish themes creates), he believes that he can dump the "baggage" of his Jewish identity by shifting his attention to more sober issues, such as federal tax policies:

I'll expose these corrupt tax policies to the point where the finance minister won't know which end is up! Moische burst out laughing. That's how I'll become Germany's most important writer. I'll finally be rid of this Jewish ballast.[18]

Moische's ego has caused him to forget his place: He is Jewish, and in Germany he can neither transcend this fact nor define for himself what it means. Moische's problem is that he wants to be a *German* Jew. Seligmann is noted for having stated that Germany has gotten the Jews it deserves. The great incongruity of *Der Musterjude* is that those Jews are like Moische. The novel closes with Moische's cry to his German girlfriend, Cordula:

> "You!" Moische cried out. "You! And Heiner Keller and Knut Reydt and Georg Wimmler and all the other Germans . . ." Moische clenched his fists. "You all! You all make me into a Jew. Into your model Jew!"[19]

Conclusions

It is difficult to draw significant generalizations from the isolated texts by Maxim Biller and Rafael Seligmann that I have examined here. With that said, Biller's comic vision utilizes a deeper, more complicated grotesque humor whereas Seligmann presents more of a situational comedy with journalistic overtones. Indeed, *Der Musterjude* reads like a comic fictional case study of themes Seligmann analyzes in *Mit Beschränkter Hoffnung: Juden, Deutsche, Israelis* and *Das deutsch-jüdische Verhältnis: Bestandsaufnahme und Perspektiven*. *Der Musterjude* contains passages that digress from the immediate story and situate Jewish history within a broader historical and sociological context. For example, Seligmann's introduction of Hanna Bernstein is instrumentalized as a lesson regarding the situation and conditions facing Jews in displaced persons camps after the war. Whereas both authors parody common pitfalls in contemporary German-Jewish relationships, Biller employs a non-Jewish German protagonist (Efraim Rosenhain) and Seligmann focuses on a Jewish German (Moische Bernstein).

This difference aside, *Harlem Holocaust* and *Der Musterjude* have much in common. Their reliance on an intellectual and reflective moment as part and parcel of their comedic structure resonates with texts by authors such as Heinrich Heine, Kurt Tucholsky, and, more recently, Edgar Hilsenrath, Jakov Lind, and George Tabori. In this sense Biller and Seligmann continue a particularly vibrant strand within the tradition of German-Jewish writing, one that emphasizes both provocative and comic narratives.

Where Biller and Seligmann differ from these authors is, of course, in their content, which focuses on contemporary, that is, post-Shoah, German-Jewish life. Part of this is due to their relative youth; both are members of the first generation of post-Holocaust Jewish writers in Germany. But there is more to it than that: Fiction about *contemporary* Jewish life in Germany has existed only since circa 1989 (the publication date of Seligmann's *Rubinsteins Versteigerung*). Since then there has been a flowering of literature devoted to the various aspects of this topic. Here again Seligmann and Biller are unique, however, in that they apparently seek out controversial topics and address them with a provocative humor. Whether the issue at hand is to suggest the erotic and commercial dimensions of the phrase "there's no business like Shoah-business," to demonstrate the deception involved in German narratives of victimization, or to underscore the unstable and insidious nature of German philo-Semitism, both Biller and Seligmann rely on an aggressive and controversial comic structure to convey their point. They strongly suggest that the dishonesty and denial involved on both sides in fulfilling the philo-Semitic norms that replaced open anti-Semitism in the postwar period may entail side effects worse than the disease. Theirs is a controversial and troubling claim.

In this light, the disgust or annoyance that we feel for Warszawski, Moische, Efraim, and their sensationalist accounts contains an additional cognitive element. Not only do we have to be aware of the expectations and norms behind a negative German-Jewish symbiosis, but our negative emotional reactions leave us thinking about whether this symbiosis is at all natural or inevitable. Do all Jews and Germans recognize their personal histories as attached to the Holocaust? Has this remembrance diminished their ability to identify a life plan of their own? Must contemporary Jews and Germans incorporate their inescapable ties to the Holocaust into every mundane aspect of their lives? More importantly, does not the sort of philo-Semitic remembrance illustrated by Efraim and his family—or by Heiner Keller—demonstrate the insidiousness of anti-Semitism? It is one thing to remember. It is another to live life in the present with the demand that everything current be reduced to the past.

Notes

* Sincere thanks to Jeffery D. Smith for his thoughtful reflections on multiple drafts of this essay. Unless otherwise indicated, all translations from the original German are my own.

1. Dan Diner, "Negative Symbiose: Deutsche und Juden nach Auschwitz," *Babylon* 1 (1986): 9–20.

2. See, for example, Henryk Broder, *Der ewige Antisemit: Über Sinn und Funktion eines beständigen Gefühls.* (Fischer: Frankfurt am Main, 1986); and Micha Brumlik, "Zur Identität Juden in der Bundesrepublik," *Junge Juden in Deutschland: Protokoll einer Tagung,* ed. Ellen Presser and Bernhard

Schoßig (Munich: Jugend und Kulturzentrum der Israelitischen Kultusgemeinde München, 1991), 11–21.

3. Cf. Marie Collins Swabey, *Comic Laughter: A Philosophical Essay* (New Haven: Yale University Press, 1961).

4. In the original: "meine Empfindsamkeit, meine Gier nach Schuld und Entsühnung vollends entfalten konnte . . ." (9). Maxim Biller, *Harlem Holocaust* (Cologne: Kiepenheuer & Witsch, [1990]1998).

5. In the original: "das Dokument eines selbstzerstörerischen Talents und der großen deutschen Krankheit" (61).

6. Here I am influenced by Noël Carroll's discussion in "Horror and Humor," *The Journal of Aesthetics and Art Criticism* 57:2 (Spring 1999): 145–60.

7. Recall how Efraim depicts the shift from anti- to philo-Semitism within the three generations of his own family.

8. In the original: "Das darf nur ich!" (11).

9. In German, "KZ" is short for "Konzentrationslager" or "concentration camp." In the original: "Mir wurde von dem Schlag schwindlig. Statt ihr die Meinung zu sagen, verschluckte ich mich und hustete mich frei. Was konnte ich einer wie ihr schon entgegnen? Diese Eve, die eine schmale, neurotische Figur hatte, erklärte mir doch dreimal am Tag, sie habe, als sie nach Deutschland kam, sofort den ganzen Horror gespürt, und wenn in einem Straßenschild oder einer Ladenschrift ein K als Versal auftauchte, habe sie sich das Z sogleich dazu gedacht . . ." (11–12).

10. Biller, *Harlem Holocaust,* 15. Efraim's conflation of anti-Semitism and anti-Americanism is an interesting point. Both attitudes constitute ideological reactions to modernity and evidence structural and metaphorical similarities. See, for example, Dan Diner, *America in the Eyes of the Germans: An Essay on Anti-Americanism,* trans. A. Brown (Princeton: Markus Wiener, 1996), 20.

11. In the original: "Das sind doch alle Kollaborateure!" (16–17).

12. I derive these expectations from the discussions in, respectively, Diner, "Negative Symbiose," and Terence des Pres, "Holocaust Laughter?," in *Writing and the Holocaust,* ed. Berel Lang (New York: Holmes & Meier, 1988): 216–33.

13. Rafael Seligmann, *Der Musterjude* (Munich: DTV, 1987). In the original: "das Jüdische Altersheim" (Seligmann, *Der Musterjude* [Classen: Hildesheim, 1997], 16).

14. In the original: "Ich hasse nicht mal diesen Moische" (19).

15. In the original: "Judenlokal" (18).

16. In the original: "Dieser Jude war wie ein Aal" (20).

17. In the original: "tödliche Waffe . . . das schlechte deutsche Judengewissen" (96).

18. In the original: "Ich werde den Steuerschwindel entlarven, daß dem Finanzminister Hören und Sehen vergehen wird! Moische lachte unwillkürlich auf. Dadurch werde ich Deutschlands wichtigster Schreiber. Ich werde den Judenballast endgültig los" (233).

19. In the original: "Du!" schrei Moische. "Du! Und Heiner Keller und Knut Reydt und Georg Wimmler und all die anderen Deutschen . . ." Moische ballte die Fäuste. "Ihr! Ihr macht mich zum Juden. Zu eurem Musterjuden!" (390, ellipses in original).

CHAPTER FOURTEEN

GERMAN AND AUSTRIAN JEWISH WOMEN'S WRITING AT THE MILLENNIUM

DAGMAR LORENZ

Only a relatively small number of authors participate in today's German-Jewish literary culture, which is remarkably productive and versatile. The critical, often polemical Jewish discourse that has emerged in the past two decades may even seem incongruous with the diverse backgrounds and affiliations of its representatives, some of whom, such as Barbara Honigmann, were not raised Jewish, and others, such as Esther Dischereit and Katja Behrens, who established their Jewish identity through matrilineage. At the turn of the millennium, more than 50 years after the Shoah, the concepts of the Jewish intellectual and Jewish writing in the German language continue to be problematic. This is due in part to the fact that the representatives of today's Jewish literary culture do not form a particular group in Germany and Austria. Although they are aware of one another, they do not belong to a particular community, religious or otherwise, and they hold divergent political views.

Among the most visible Jewish women authors are the Viennese filmmaker and journalist Ruth Beckermann and the prose writers Esther Dischereit, a native of West Germany, and Barbara Honigmann, a native of the GDR who lives in Strasbourg, France. Their publications have shaped contemporary German-Jewish writing to the same extent as those of Henryk Broder, a journalist and *Spiegel* reporter, the novelist Rafael Seligmann, the poet and prose writer Robert Schindel, and the historian Doron Rabinovici, one of the foremost activists against the current Austrian government. The works of these authors have established Jewish positions in opposition to the dominant cultural discourse in Germany and Austria. It is important to keep in mind that all of these authors participate in the larger German and Austrian cultural milieu. It would be impossible for them to work in isolation from political allies, friends, and associates within the cultural and political establishment of their country of residence. Even authors such as Lea Fleischmann and Barbara Honigmann, who do not currently live in Germany, remain connected to the German-speaking public for whom they write and with whom they interact. Jewish-identified authors writing in German not only contribute to but are involved in the current debates about Jewishness in Germany and the German literary landscape.

Ruth Beckermann articulates the dilemma arising from possible conflicts of interest and the need to protect her integrity in conjunction with her film *Jenseits des Krieges* [East of War, 1996], which required the collaboration of former Nazi soldiers with whom she conducted interviews during the exhibit *Vernichtungskrieg—Verbrechen der Wehrmacht* [War of Annihilation— The Crimes of the German Armed Forces]: "I became very aggressive when my interviewees deviated from the topic of the crimes of the German military. I realized that working this way upset me and was not very productive. I had to take two emotional steps back, so-to-speak."[1] Having one's point of view and morale undermined by working in a hostile environment is a risk Jewish critics of German and Austrian society have to take. In addition to being directly attacked for their point of view, the validity of their analysis and their right to assume a Jewish position is not infrequently called into question. Doubt may be cast upon their Jewishness and the opportunistic motives attributed to their writing.

In addition, there is the dilemma of the disrupted continuity of Jewish life in Central Europe. As Matti Bunzl has pointed out in the case of Vienna, Jewish identity in the German-speaking context after the Holocaust is discursive, constructed from historical Jewish texts and survivors' narratives rather than an "organic" evolution from an community.[2] Precisely because of this history, the Jewish experience among intellectuals writing in German differs from the experience of Jews who grew up in communities unaffected by the Shoah, and there is little comparison between Jewish life in Germany and Israel. In the course of the more than 50 years of post-Shoah German and Austrian history, however, common topoi and attitudes have evolved in conjunction with the ongoing public debates. The presence of new non-Christian minority populations in Germany and Austria has affected the situation of Jews in these countries. So have changes in the way identity and cultural affiliation are conceptualized in response to new social and intellectual realities. The prospects for Jewish life in the increasingly diverse society of postunification Germany are in certain ways better than in 1945. The alternative of either rebuilding or abandoning the destroyed communities has been recognized as false. The more practical issue concerns how to establish new forms of existence and coexistence, particularly in view of the immigration of Jews from the former Eastern Bloc countries to Germany and Austria.

The reactions with which writers and intellectuals identified as Jewish had met in post-Shoah Germany are reflected in the articulation of shared core experiences early in the reemerging Jewish discourse. The discussion of these experiences provided the basis to explore Jewish specificity as distinct from the dominant culture. In the late 1970s and 1980s Jewish themes and characters, references to historical details and customs, and Jewish writing of earlier epochs expressed a connectedness to pre-Shoah Jewish culture and an awareness of its residues in the present. Fleischmann and Beckermann were among the authors who set forth secular Jewish points of view in their polemical confrontations with German and Austrian society. They examined their post-Shoah environment in conjunction with events that had direct bearing on Jewish concerns, such as the Eichmann Trial, Reagan's visit to Bitburg, the Historians' Debate, the Waldheim scandal, the controversies about restitution for Holocaust victims, and the success of Jörg Haider in Austria. Jewish positions were also shaped in response to everyday attitudes projected by the majority of Germans and Austrians that were perceived by Jewish-identified authors as offensive or harmful.

The Nazi era became the focus of attention among non-Jews during the 1960s student movement and the debates, sparked by the New Left, about the Nazi legacy in the Federal Republic. Outraged by the fact that contemporary and political history had been excluded from the curricula in West German schools during the 1950s and 1960s and by the complacency they observed all around them, the descendants of the Nazi generation began to ask questions about their parents' involvement in the totalitarian regime. The rhetoric of the New Left was informed by the Critical theory of the Frankfurt School as well as the language of antifascism practiced in the German Democratic Republic. Terms such as *Vergangenheitsbewältigung* [overcoming the past] and *Trauerarbeit* [mourning work][3] were coined in reference to German society, which was still caught up in the trauma of the lost war and absorbed in the effort of rebuilding a collapsed economy. The refusal to confront the Nazi past and to come to terms with the destruction and self-destruction by making amends was a central topic in the 1970s. Although Jews born in the 1940s and 1950s had taken part in the student movement and considered an alliance with the New Left possible, many of them came to realize that post-Nazi antifascism primarily concerned former perpetrators and their descendants. Foregrounding the issues of guilt, responsibility, and the continuation of Nazi patterns in the 1950s, the discourse of political radicalism excluded the experience of the Jewish victims, whom the New Left considered not the primary targets of Nazi genocide, but rather incidental victims of the class struggle. With a fascist bourgeoisie and an abstract proletariat cast as the major historical players, Jewish Holocaust survivors were themselves no less marginal to the new radical discourse than they had been to German and Austrian issues prior to the young Germans' ideological soul-searching.

Disappointment with the New Left brought to the fore new Jewish voices that emphasized the survivor experience and the specificity of Jewish culture and history. Many of the women among them appropriated concepts of the women's movement of the 1970s, although they had found German feminists by and large unresponsive to Jewish concerns.[4] Gradually, there emerged a postmodern body of literature by women, Jewish in its concerns and themes and German according to its historical reference points and language. Katja Behrens, Barbara Honigmann, and Jeannette Lander were among the authors who combined feminist and Jewish issues. They focused on matrilineal themes and the importance of the mother-daughter or mother-child relationship for Jewish survival.

Examining works by women authors who were instrumental in establishing the German-Jewish discourse in the wake of 1968 reveals how the recent attempts at normalizing German history and the simultaneous development of multicultural societies in Germany and Austria have affected intellectuals who began writing from the margins. The publications of these writers as reflections of social change suggest that the Federal Republic and Austria are still uncomfortable places for the daughters of Shoah victims and former exiles.[5] At the same time, compared to the 1970s and 1980s, Jewish writing in the 1990s gives the appearance of greater self-confidence, obvious from greater diversity and freedom of expression.[6] It seems that the intellectual basis established prior to German unification has allowed authors to expand their literary range and to adopt forms appropriate to their new experiences. Formal experimentation has given way to storytelling or critical prose, as shown by the clarity of expression and the directness of the narratives of authors formerly considered examples of esoteric postmodern writing, for example the works of Barbara Honigmann and Esther Dischereit. Certain aspects of earlier Jewish writing have remained unchanged: Jewish women's texts in German originate in numerous countries, including France, Israel, Austria, the Federal Republic of Germany, and the United States, and their complex cultural and linguistic references position them outside the confines of traditional national literatures. It continues to be difficult, if not impossible, to define Jewishness within the German-speaking context. Discussions regarding whether an author such as Irene Dische can be read as part of the German-Jewish context provide one case in point. (Dische is a U.S. citizen who has lived in Berlin on a tourist visa since 1980.) Similar discussions surround women authors such as Barbara Honigmann and Lea Fleischmann, who have embraced the Jewish faith and write about religious aspects of their Jewish heritage.[7]

Irene Dische writes in English about the interaction of Germans and Jews, but the most positive reception of her narratives is primarily in German translation. Similarly, the most recent publications of Anna Mitgutsch (Mitgutsch is a relatively recent convert to Judaism), notably her work *Abschied von Jerusalem* [Departure from Jerusalem, 1995],[8] the works of Katja Behrens and Esther Dischereit, which emphasize Jewish matrilineal issues, and the films of Ruth Beckermann, the daughter of a Viennese exile who returned to her native city, are read and discussed as part of German-Jewish discourse. Included in today's reception of Jewish women's writing are also works that have been published well after they were written, due to the circumstances of World War II. For example Veza Canetti's prewar works began to be published by her late husband, the Nobel Prize winner Elias Canetti, in the late 1980s. *Die Schildkröten* [The Turtles], a novel about Jewish life in pre-Nazi Vienna, appeared for the first time in 1999.[9] Veza Canetti's minimalist style, her nontraditional representation of Viennese suburban society in the 1930s, and her ingenious cast of characters place her pre-Shoah novel alongside current publications. Canetti's style blends into the contemporary scene extremely well because some writers of the post-Shoah generation, such as Ruth Beckermann and Barbara Honigmann, were inspired and informed by the interwar avant-garde.

Recently Henryk Broder has commented on the "Germanization" of the Holocaust in the Federal Republic. He cites the current debates about memorials, Holocaust education, and state-subsidized contacts with survivors,[10] all of which are conducted concomitantly with attempts at revising German history, minimizing the Nazi crimes, and relativizing the Holocaust. The support for the two seemingly opposing trends, memorialization and revisionism, within the German public has had a neutralizing effect. At the same time as the still empty Jewish Museum in Berlin, praised by some critics as the ultimate Holocaust memorial, attracts thousands of visitors, the leading historian in the 1980s Historians' Debate, Ernst Nolte, was awarded the prestigious Adenauer Prize. Similar incongruities have occurred in Austria as well. In 1986, the year of the Waldheim scandal, the Jewish author Erich Fried was honored at the University of Vienna, and the former Austrian chancellors Bruno Kreisky and Fred Sinowatz took part in the "Fest for Erich Fried." At the same time Kurt Waldheim, a politician with proven links to the Nazi regime, conducted a successful presidential campaign during which, ironically, a broad-based confrontation with Austria's Nazi past became unavoidable. In contrast to the smoother handling of controversies involving the Nazi past in the Federal Republic, the Austrians have generally dealt with the problem of collaboration with the Hitler regime and responsibility for the genocide in a heavy-handed way. Such was the case in the spring of 2000 when, under massive public protest, a government was inaugurated that included Jörg Haider's right-wing Freedom Party as the coalition partner of the OeVP [Austrian People's Party]. Throughout the history of the postwar republics in Germany and Austria, Jewish-identified intellectuals and authors have taken an active role by observing and exposing the balancing acts characteristic of the Federal Republic and the distortions of facts typical of Austrian media strategies.

More than five decades after the Shoah and one decade after German unification, the debates about the moral and material obligations on the part of the heirs to the Nazi regime continue. New information about profits reaped from state-sanctioned expropriation, extortion, slave labor, and murder continues to emerge. At a time when the numbers of surviving victims and perpetrators are dwindling, their children and grandchildren have moved to the forefront of the debates. A wealth of information about the Shoah and German-Jewish history has been made available and introduced into school curricula and media programming to foster more enlightened public attitudes about the Holocaust and National Socialism. Nonetheless, Barbara Honigmann writes that living in Germany precludes living as a Jew among Jews.[11] Not only is the Jewish population in Germany and Austria extremely small, even compared to the only approximately 1 percent of the pre-Shoah era, but also Jewishness and Jewish identity are configured in widely diverse ways, and authors identified as Jewish by the reading public may or may not be members of traditional Jewish secular or religious organizations. Some authors base their Jewish identity on their family background, others on a conscious decision. Anna Mitgutsch, for example, converted to Judaism because she was aware that her grandmother was Jewish. Residing in Linz, she is unequivocally an Austrian author and was read as such at the beginning of her career. Lea Fleischmann, the daughter of Polish Holocaust survivors, grew up Jewish in Germany and is now an Israeli citizen. However, she writes in German. Such multiple religious, cultural, and linguistic identities often converge in an author's biography as well as in her texts. These identities mirror the complex history of Jewish migration before and after the Shoah. Jeannette Lander, the daughter of European Jews, grew up in the United States, and is a speaker of Yiddish and English. She moved to Germany, married a German, and lives in the Federal Republic. After she published her early multilingual novel *Ein Sommer in der Woche der Itke K.* [A Summer in the Week of Itke K.], she has written in German.[12] Conversely, Irene Dische was reared as a Catholic in New York and does not identify herself as Jewish. However, her narratives revolve around the topic of displaced Jewish identities about which she writes from an insider's perspective. She focuses on Jewish immigrants and their children who, having escaped from Nazi Germany, brought their assimilated German-Jewish culture to the United States. Many of her protagonists are still emotionally and legally involved with Germany and interact with today's Germans. Dische's satirical representation of Germans and Americans with fascistic propensities, her intimate knowledge of German-Jewish exile history, and her familiarity with the New York German-Jewish exile community place her in the context of other contemporary Jewish satirists, such as Edgar Hilsenrath and Rafael Seligmann.

When Lea Fleischmann moved to Israel in 1979, she left as her legacy a passionately critical manifesto, *Dies ist nicht mein Land. Eine Jüdin verläßt die Bundesrepublik* [This is not my country. A Jewish woman leaves the Federal Republic]. In her account as to why she decided to leave the Federal Republic of Germany, she criticizes the striking lack of German guilt about the Holocaust. After settling in Jerusalem, Fleischmann continued to write for the German public. Her most recent publications are devoted to the goal of familiarizing Germans with Judaism and Jewish traditions.[13] Having lived in Paris for several years, Ruth Beckermann returned to Vienna. Her astute analysis of the relationship between Austrians and Jews and Jewish life in Vienna won critical acclaim in the late 1980s. In the 1990s she continued to examine the legacy of Word War II. Her film and the book *Jenseits des Krieges* [East of War], which consist of interviews with veterans who attended the Wehrmacht exhibition, explore the mental and emotional residue of Hitler's genocidal war from the point of view of a daughter of survivors trying to understand the perpetrators' frame of mind.[14] Katja Behrens focused in her earlier novel, *Die dreizehnte Fee* [The Thirteenth Fairy, 1983],[15] on the fragmented post-assimilation, post-Shoah existence of women of Jewish descent in West Germany. Embedded in her most recent novel *Die Vagantin* [The Wandering Minstrel, 1997] is a critical historical perspective.[16] *Die dreizehnte Fee* was a stocktaking of Jewish life in West Germany. The protagonists are situated on the fringes of postwar society, impoverished and neglected at a time when average Germans enjoy the comforts of the economic miracle and are intent to put the past behind them. In *Die Vagantin,* Behrens explores identity problems and double marginality through the character of a Turkish-German girl who is estranged from both German and Turkish culture. Behrens's focus on the non-Jewish Other in this work suggests that groups even more disenfranchised than the Jews have emerged in the new Germany. A parallel plot set during the age of the crusades traces the roots of the hatred of Jews and Muslims back to medieval Christian culture and reveals how deeply entrenched xenophobia is in the Central European tradition. In her latest novel, Barbara Honigmann explores various forms of Jewish experience. The central character of *Soharas Reise* [Sohara's Journey, 1996] is a woman from Algeria now living in Strasbourg. Sohara exists at the crossroads between Jewish and secular Western, Sephardic, and Ashkenazi culture. Her fate brings into focus an identity other than Ashkenazi Jewish experience: North African women like Sohara are strangers to the French as well as to Westernized Jewish society.[17]

After German unification, nonfiction by Jewish women authors who began their careers in the 1970s and 1980s reveals that the relationship between Jews and non-Jews in German-speaking societies continues to be tenuous. The authors revisit issues already raised in earlier decades—issues of identity and memory, guilt and compensation, tolerance and coexistence— indicating that none of these problems has been resolved. They address these issues from a more global point of view. The scope of Honigmann's *Am Sonntag spielt der Rabbi Fußball* [On Sunday the Rabi Plays Soccer, 1998] includes minority issues in France, the United States, Israel, and the fate of exiles from Nazi Germany, and contains observations on German high culture, contemporary fashions, and the aftermath of the former GDR. The ease with which Honigmann touches on all these issues reveals that she does not consider them separate but part of her contemporary reference system.

In the writing of Jewish women, the Nazi past and the Shoah continue to play an important role as touchstones of Jewish identity that expose the rift between Jews and non-Jews. Even a literary text that does not center on the Nazi era usually introduces the memory of the 1930s and 1940s through certain characters, such as the Holocaust survivor Mrs. Kahn in *Soharas Reise,* or deliberations about the Nazi legacy in Jeannette Lander's *Robert,* a novel about the relationship between a man of Jewish descent and an East German woman.[18] Foregrounding the problem of communication across cultural barriers, both authors refer to the Shoah as the ultimate enigma; Honigmann focuses on the problems between different Jewish traditions, Lander between the "Ossies" and the "Wessies."

The works of the 1990s build on texts of the 1980s that examined German-Jewish history and the Shoah from a more subjective point of view. A personal and at the same time political stocktaking is presented in Ruth Beckermann's *Unzugehörig* [Unrelated, 1989], a critical account about growing up Jewish in postwar Vienna and a survey of postwar Austrian history from a Jewish perspective. Barbara Honigmann's *Eine Liebe aus Nichts* [A Love out of Nothing, 1991] examined the author/narrator's relationship with her father and uncovered the suppression of Jewish life in the GDR. Revealing that Jewish Socialists such as her father Georg Honigmann supported GDR anti-Judaism (although he was the target of continued anti-Semitism), Barbara Honigmann rejected the internalized anti-Semitism characteristic of members in her parents' generation and opted for a Jewish life.[19] These examples show that Holocaust and pre-Holocaust history continues to be fundamental to post-Shoah Central European Jewish identity despite the fact that political, historical, and religious topics and concerns have emerged as a result of the changing situation in the authors' countries of residence. The new developments are reflected in Jewish women's writing of the 1990s and are contextualized within twentieth-century German-Jewish history. The particular conceptualization of history in these authors' texts is obvious from only a few examples. For example, among Jewish authors the Waldheim scandal and the Gulf War were more immediately discussed than German unification—the effects of which are thematized by other authors as well, but without the same urgency.[20] In her deliberately controversial essays, *Übungen jüdisch zu sein* [Exercises in Being Jewish, 1998], Esther Dischereit examines the prevalent political attitudes in today's Germany and exposes the customary rhetoric of avoidance and minimalization in conjunction with issues concerning German-Jewish relations. In *Am Sonntag spielt der Rabbi Fußball* Barbara Honigmann reflects upon her life in Strasbourg and her continued relationship with Germany, and she tries to come to terms with the legacy of the state where she spent her formative years, the GDR.[21] Compared to her earlier works, here she views the German situation from a greater distance and with a more distinctly articulated political awareness, which is also present in Dischereit's latest publications. Honigmann places Jewish issues into a global context.[22]

While critical interaction with the German-speaking mainstream culture has remained foremost for some authors, living a Jewish life has become the main concern for others. In 1979 in *Dies ist nicht mein Land*, Lea Fleischmann emphasized her disenchantment with everyday German life in her decision to leave the Federal Republic. On the other hand, Barbara Honigmann explains her relocation to Strasbourg after the birth of her first son as an affirmation of her Jewishness: "The Germans have lost any concept of what Jews are. All they know is that there is a terrible history between them, and every Jew who turned up reminded them of this history which continues to hurt and gets on their nerves."[23] For both authors, studying Torah with other women became a key to recasting their identity.[24]

Over the decades the memory of pre-Nazi German-Jewish culture and the Shoah is becoming increasingly abstract, not only for non-Jews but also for the descendants of survivors. Those who experienced the 1930s and 1940s will soon have died, and while the memory of the post-Shoah generations is sometimes derived from oral and written accounts and recorded narratives, more frequently it is constructed from media events, documentaries, exhibits, and history books. The distancing process is bound to occur in the absence of eyewitnesses, and it is also precipitated by the widespread pressures in German-speaking countries to lay the past to rest and normalize Nazi history. Aware that it is impossible to recreate the communities of the past or to forge new Jewish traditions unencumbered by twentieth-century history, the intellectuals who opt to live as Jews within Germany and Austria negotiate the legacy of the past while adjusting to the present. Their reality includes a unified Germany over-shadowed by social and economic problems and an Austrian Republic with an ever-more-visible right-wing potential. Both states are latently anti-Semitic; in light of predicate European unity, both face a yet undetermined future.

In the 1980s, films and literary works by Jewish women writers expressed the desire for a new start.[25] Jeannette Lander's novel *Robert* ends with the joy over a child from the union of "one-sixth Jewish protagonist" and his younger lover. The private celebration of Honigmann's Sohara over her re-turn to her home in Strasbourg and her new life as single matriarch of her family displays a certain optimism. However, the optimism is coupled with the awareness of increasingly complex relationships and social structures. The authors leave their endings open, and the personal success of their pro-tagonists in negotiating their multiple roles is indicative of a revitalized Jew-ish community. With Lander's protagonist entering into a union with a German non-Jew, his Jewish heritage is likely to be a minor factor for his child. The positive experiences Honigmann's narrator shares with her Sephardic friends in *Damals, dann und danach* [At that time, Then, and After, 1999] can be juxtaposed with her pessimism regarding the situation of Jews in Germany and Russia. Apparently Honigmann feels that a renewal of Jewish life must come from outside the European context.

The works of most of the established authors show a cosmopolitan sense of being in the world at the turn of the millennium. Jeannette Lander's nov-els *Im Jahrhundert der Herren* [In the Century of the Men, 1993] and *Eine unterbrochene Reise* [An Interrupted Journey, 1996] are set outside the Ger-man-speaking sphere and explore mechanisms of oppression and exploita-tion that affect women, children, and low-status males. Lander shows the potential for liberation on a political and personal level as well as the toll that the search for freedom takes on the individual.[26] In *Robert,* the setting of which is contemporary Germany, Jewish elements play only a back-ground role. *Überbleibsel* [Remnant] is an experimental prose work that combines the theme of memory with the mundane activity of cooking, thereby exploring the cultural significance of memory conveyed through recipes and the almost automatic performance of everyday tasks tradition-ally undertaken by women.[27] By revealing how closely her culinary prefer-ences and her expertise as a cook are connected to her Jewish family background and to cultural information transmitted to her by her mother, how reenacting her mother's movements and using her mother's kitchen tools calls forth stories and memories, Lander reveals that the past is pre-sent in her everyday life. In the process of remembering she recalls and re-constructs her Jewish heritage and her parents' stories. In her everyday activities both her Jewishness and her parents' stories are immediately available to her, not as part of a culture of remembrance but as an integral part of her consciousness. Being the daughter of a Jewish mother is not an issue for Lander, but rather a fact that requires no explanation. Through the example of food and food preparation, Lander shows how her primary identity has become amplified by acquired traits derived from other cultures to which she was exposed in different phases of her life, including the United States, Germany, and Sri Lanka. All of these have left traces in her food preferences and her cooking. Lander's highly personal text provides insight into the preservation and transmission of cultural information from one generation to the next and suggests simple ways of cultural rapprochement. By making initially foreign substances appeal to the senses and then ingesting them, their foreignness is reduced and one's own self enriched. From the point of view of traditional Jewish gender roles, Lander configures cooking and hospitality as integral parts of her identity. Through domestic activities an open, cosmopolitan attitude can be achieved without invalidating one's own origins and heritage. The text also has a feminist dimension in that it reassesses the importance of traditional women's work and stresses the talent and intelligence necessary to perform it well.

Similarly, Barbara Honigmann's recent publications take new directions. Having begun her career with the close examination of her immediate environment, including her body, her family, and her life as a young mother, she now reaches beyond herself and her culture of origin. As stated earlier, *Soharas Reise* is told from the point of view of a Sephardic woman who sees Ashkenazi Jews and Central European Jewish history from the outside. Thus the narrative reveals new aspects of Jewish life. Sohara, raised in the confining women's sphere of North African society, is portrayed as a woman in transition. A mother of six, she is forced to take charge of her own and her children's lives counter to the conventions of her patriarchal culture. Accustomed to being dependent on male patronage, welfare, and charity, unaccustomed to Western life, Sohara displays ingenuity and courage as she wins back her children after her husband kidnaps and tries to keep them in England. Defying cultural, religious, and linguistic barriers, Sohara prevails by enlisting the help of other Jews. Her reunited family will have to face the future without a father, but as a family nonetheless. The theme of Jewish unity and mutual help in conjunction with the theme of motherhood as the foundation of a culture whose integrity is threatened in the modern world points to the validity of traditional Jewish values. Sohara's disregard for material goods, her indifference to Western neatness and efficiency, and her ignorance of technology are combined with her unerring sense of what children require to prosper physically and emotionally. Her way of life is presented as a corrective to the fast pace of the 1990s. In that sense, Honigmann's Sephardic mother represents a positive utopian model, an alternative to the direction taken by the dominant culture under the auspices of the global economy.

Just as changes can be noted in Hongimann's work, Esther Dischereit's *Übungen jüdisch zu sein* represents a shift in the writing of an author known for her complex narrative prose and her radio plays. The essays in this volume explore events that shaped Dischereit's relationship to Germany and called forth her Jewish responses. Aware of the fundamental differences in citizen status and background, Dischereit underscores that she shares the characteristic of a multi-identity with "other others" in Germany, such as Sinti, Roma, and Turks. The stocktaking, similar to that in Honigmann's *Damals, dann und danach,* is in part a personal survey of her growing consciousness as a Jewish woman, and in part a counterhistory correcting the official versions of German post-Shoah history. Like Lander, Dischereit discovers cultural messages in mundane activities, for example, the house-cleaning she was told to participate in as a child on Fridays rather than Saturdays. She discusses an aversion to certain expressions in contemporary German speech that reflect Nazi usage and observes the difficulties Germans have saying the words Jew and Jewish. Dischereit recalls the profound effect certain persons and events, for example, Nelly Sachs's Nobel Prize, had on her mother, who was ashamed of her Jewishness. Acknowledging the significance that the example of Sachs and the writing of Jeannette Lander hold for herself, she places her own work within the tradition of German women's writing. Through her criticism of reconfigurations of the term Holocaust in expressions such as "nuclear holocaust" following the Chernobyl incident, Dischereit expresses her sensitivity to attempts to relativize Jewish suffering. While Dischereit's exploration of what it means to be Jewish in the 1990s culminates in a call for Jewish pluralism that prescribes neither particular religious orientations, nor dietary and sexual codes, nor specific political convictions, the Holocaust is basic to her understanding of German-Jewish identity. Dischereit does not identify herself through an allegiance with Israel. She does not know Hebrew and considers High German her literary medium. In her own terms, her sense of identity is *"defizitär,"* that is, it is an identity constructed *ex negativo.* Her Jewish identity is based on a variety of historical, cultural, and emotional factors that result in particular views and attitudes.

Dischereit's openness is able to accommodate idiosyncratic expressions of Jewishness and corresponds with the new, less self-conscious approach Jeannette Lander developed with regard to the issue of Jewish identity. The inclusive and expansive expression of the Jewish experience in the works of German-Jewish women writers reflects a political reality that is taking Germany beyond its national boundaries into the supranational community of Europe. This process, now well under way, dismantles the polarity of Germans and Jews and may, hopefully, result in a European community in which Jews are not limited to an antagonistic role nor to the position of outsider. At the turn of the millennium Jewish concerns continue to be discussed in the German language, which continues to be a viable medium for the shaping of Jewish discursive identities. Even though the German language may be at the point of becoming a minor language as a result of globalization and the tightening of the English-dominated communication networks, it is still historically entwined with and a part of contemporary Jewish life. The authors engaged in German-Jewish writing today may or may not reside in German-speaking countries, but they interact with the German and Austrian public and participate in the literary and critical discourses in Central Europe.

Notes

1. "Ich wurde sehr aggressiv, wenn meine Gesprächspartner vom Thema 'Verbrechen der Wehrmacht' abwichen. Ich sah, daß diese Arbeitsweise mich nur aufregte und nicht viel brachte. Ich mußte innerlich sozusagen zwei Schritte zurücktreten." (*Jenseits des Krieges* [Vienna: Döcker, 1998].) Unless otherwise indicated, all translations in this essay are my own.

2. Matti Bunzl, "Counter-Memory and Modes of Resistance: The Uses of Fin-de-Siècle Vienna for Present-Day Austrian Jews," in *Transforming the Center, Eroding the Margins. Essays on Ethnic and Cultural Boundaries in German-Speaking Countries,* ed. Dagmar C. G. Lorenz and Renate Posthofen (Columbia, SC: Camden House, 1998): 185–99.

3. See Alexander and Margarete Mitscherlich, *The Inability to Mourn,* trans. Beverly R. Placzek (New York: Grove Press, 1975).

4. In her critical assessment of anti-Semitism and the Left, Esther Dischereit takes issue with the emphasis of gender in conjunction with the Holocaust at the expense of the victims' human and Jewish identity. Esther Dischereit, "Die Linke und der Antisemitismus." *Übungen jüdisch zu sein* (Frankfurt am Main: Suhrkamp, 1998), 155–93.

5. Dagmar C. G. Lorenz, *Keepers of the Motherland* (Lincoln: University of Nebraska Press, 1996), xviii-xix.

6. See the discussions in Sander Gilman and Karen Remmler, eds. *Reemerging Jewish Culture in Germany: Life and Literature since 1989* (New York: New York University Press, 1994).

7. Guy Stern, "Barbara Honigmann: A Preliminary Assessment." *Bridging the Abyss: Reflections on Jewish Suffering, Anti-Semitism, and Exile,* ed. Amy Colin and Elisabeth Strenger (Munich: Fink, 1994), 304.

8. Anna Mitgutsch, *Abschied von Jerusalem* (Berlin: Rowohlt, 1995).

9. Veza Canetti, *Die Schildkröten* (Munich: Hanser, 1999).

10. Henryk M. Broder, "Die Germanisierung des Holocaust," *Volk und Wahn* (Munich: Goldmann, 1998), 214–28.

11. Honigmann, Barbara, *Damals, dann und Danach* (Munich: Hanser, 1999).

12. Jeannette Lander, *Ein Sommer in der Woche der Itke K.* (Frankfurt am Main: Suhrkamp, 1971).

13. Lea Fleischmann, *Dies ist nicht mein Land: Eine Jüdin verläßt die Bundesrepublik* (Hamburg: Hoffmann & Campe, 1980). For example, *Schabbat. Das Judentum für Nichtjuden verständlich gemacht* (Munich: Heyne, 1994) and *Rabbi Nachman und die Thora. Das Judentum für Nichtjuden verständlich gemacht* (Munich: Scherz, 2000).

14. Ruth Beckermann, dir., *Jenseits des Krieges* (Vienna: filmladen, 1997). *Jenseits des Krieges* (Vienna: Döcker Verlag, 1998).

15. See Katja Behrens, *Die dreizehnte Fee* (Düsseldorf: Claassen, 1983).

16. Katja Behrens, *Die Vagantin* (Frankfurt am Main: Fischer, 1997).

17. Barbara Honigmann, *Soharas Reise* (Reinbeck: Rowohlt, 1996).

18. Jeannette Lander, *Robert* (Berlin: Aufbau, 1998), for example, 55–56.

19. Ruth Beckermann, *Unzugehörig* (Vienna: Löcker, 1989); Barbara Honigmann, *Eine Liebe aus Nichts* (Berlin: Rowohlt, 1991).

20. See for example Lea Fleischmann, *Gas: Tagebuch einer Bedrohung; Israel während des Golfkrieges* (Göttingen: Steidl, 1991).

21. Barbara Honigmann, *Am Sonntag spielt der Rabbi Fußball* (Heidelberg: Wunderhorn, 1998).

22. Honigmann became known through *Roman von einem Kinde* (Darmstadt: Luchterhand, 1986), an eclectic postmodern examination of Jewish issues and motherhood; Dischereit through *Joëmis Tisch* (Frankfurt am Main: Suhrkamp, 1988) and *Merryn* (Frankfurt am Main: Suhrkamp, 1992), both thematizing the fragmented and marginal existence of protagonists profoundly effected by recent German history.

23. Barbara Honigmann, *Damals, dann und Danach* (Munich: Hanser, 1999), 15–16. "Die Deutschen wissen gar nicht mehr, was Juden sind, wissen nur daß da eine schreckliche Geschichte zwischen ihnen liegt, und jeder Jude, der auftauchte, erinnerte sie an diese Geschichte, die immer noch weh tut und auf die Nerven geht."

24. See Honigmann, "Meine sephardischen Freundinnen," *Damals, dann und danach,* 63–81; Fleischmann, "Vom Club Voltaire zum 'Or Sameach,' *Sabbath,* 54–60.

25. For example in Lea Fleischmann's *Dies ist nicht mein Land,* Nadja Seelich's film *Kieselsteine,* dir. Lukas Stepanik (Cinéart: Filmverleih Hans Peter Hofmann, 1982), and Ruth Beckermann, *Unzugehörig* (Vienna: Löcker, 1989). All these works suggest that it is possible and necessary to break free from the non-Jewish mainstream as well as from the conservative Jewish minority in Germany or Austria and the restrictions imposed by the conditioning of either environment.

26. Jeannette Lander, *Im Jahrhundert der Herren* (Berlin: Aufbau, 1993) and *Eine unterbrochene Reise* (Berlin: Aufbau, 1996).

27. Jeannette Lander, *Überbleibsel. Eine kleine Erotik der Küche* (Berlin: Aufbau, 1995).

POSTMEMORY, POSTMEMOIR

L E S L I E   M O R R I S

On the eighth page of Sarah Kofman's book *Smothered Words*, the late French philosopher's provocative meditation on the necessity and impossibility of narration and memory, is a one-page list, reproduced from Serge Klarsfeld's *Memorial to the Jews Deported from France 1942–1944* (1983), of deportees from Drancy to Auschwitz. Lodged between the names Simone Klempen and Grange Kohn is the name of Kofman's father, Berek Kofman. The sudden appearance (eruption) of the list of names in Kofman's text is a leitmotif for this essay on postmemory and postmemoir. The list as it appears in *Smothered Words* is a trace of the documentary and archival in Holocaust memoirs; yet, in the context of a book that posits speech as "choking," as sticking in the throat and causing suffocation—the "smothered words" of the title—this list of deportees (with her father's name embedded within it) stands as a poetic moment defined by the sudden, the arbitrary, the "unlost" in the landscape of mourning and loss that defines the genre of the Holocaust narrative.[1]

The title of my essay—the final one in this book devoted to the topic of the German-Jewish symbiosis—does not contain the word "symbiosis." Rather, "postmemory" and "postmemoir" signal the impossibility of this term, moving it beyond Dan Diner's critical formulation of a "negative symbiosis." The "postmemoirs" I will discuss allow neither for the possibility of a (former or present) symbiosis between Germans and Jews, nor for the possibility of "pure" or even "real" memoir. Instead, as the memory of the Holocaust circulates beyond the actual bounds of lived, remembered experience (and beyond the geographical where the "real" took place), it seeps into the imaginary of other cultures (and other geographical spaces) as postmemory and as postmemoir. Thus the German-Jewish symbiosis is recast as the newly refigured presence of Germans and Jews in texts that probe the contours of memory and the contours of the act of writing and, most significantly, in texts that move beyond the borders of Germany. Describing the protests in Paris in 1968 when Daniel Cohn-Bendit was denied permission to return to France and the crowds chanted in unison, "We are all German Jews," Alain Finkielkraut suggests his notion of the imaginary Jews who have "taken up residence in fiction" and as "spectators who project their desires, their frustrations, onto a panting plot they will never live."[2] The "postmemoirs" that I examine in this essay are all concerned with this engraving of the imaginary; they are all memoirs that, as Finkielkraut suggests, insist on the imaginary space (the only possible space) in which we might conceive of a "German-Jewish symbiosis." Rather than focusing on the figuration and representation through myth and memory of the so-called German-Jewish symbiosis, I propose instead to examine the remnants and the echoes and the ruin of the symbiosis in texts that push at the borders between fact and fiction, documentary and memoir: Wolfgang Koeppen's *Jakob Littners Aufzeichnungen aus einem Erdloch,* Sarah Kofman's *Rue Ordener, Rue Labat* and *Paroles Suffoquées,* Helen Fremont's *After Long Silence,* Timothy Ryback's *The Last Survivor,* Benjamin Wilkomirski's *Fragments,* and Helen Demidenko's *The Hand that Signed the Paper.*

These texts are rooted not in memory or lived experience, but rather in "postmemory," which I draw on to explore the prevalence of the museal in marking Holocaust remembrance in Germany[3] The many (perhaps even compulsive) acts of remembrance and commemoration in Germany in the past decade are as concerned with the mediated nature of memory as they are with both uncovering and challenging an "authentic" experience of the Holocaust that can then be represented through art or literature. I want to stress that post-Holocaust art in Germany and the United States emerges from the reservoir of memory, or postmemory, that circulates between America and Germany, a shared memory of the Holocaust that perhaps situates the "origin" metonymically as Auschwitz but that has created a chain of signification that moves beyond the borders—metaphorical and geographic—of Auschwitz. The exchange of memories and of memoir is enacted in the spaces that lie beyond the borders of Germany (or Auschwitz), in the ruins of Auschwitz that are now part of the cultural imaginary of L.A. and New York.

The "post" is the space conceptualized by post-Holocaust art in general. In addition to challenging the division between copy and original, between lived and imagined experience, memoirs such as those by Koeppen/Littner and Wilkomirski express a "crisis of memoir"; they are all, in one way or another, hybrid forms of memoir, some false memoirs, some even exposed as fakes. Like the spectator's desire for the reproduction of art that can substitute for, exceed, and challenge our desire for the original, the post-Holocaust texts (literary and visual) that I am interested in take up recent challenges to the notion of the original in art. Holocaust remembrance in these texts is a postmemory that "after Auschwitz" cannot be traced back to an originary moment of the Holocaust itself, but rather circulates—in the present—as representation, as melancholia, as elegiac repetition. Challenging the viability and possibility of history, knowledge, and subjectivity, these memoirs as post-memoirs are marked by metareflection about the Holocaust, memory, and the limits of art. Furthermore, in their attempt to problematize the limits of representing the Holocaust, they become elegies to the past viability of Holocaust representation. Thus Kofman's list of deportees in *Smothered Words* from Klarsfeld's "memorial" book (which he described as the only memorial for the 80,000 Jews deported from France who had no grave) stands not only as testimony or "evidence" of the deported, but also as tombstone, as inscription in a work that is itself an homage to three dead men (Robert Antelme, Maurice Blanchot, and her father, Berek Kofman): it is not Kofman's own, transparent memory of the Shoah, but rather postmemory—memory that is transmitted, mediated, reproduced, and ultimately then suffocated and smothered.

Postmemories have been called by Andrea Liss "the imprints that photographic imagery of the Shoah have created within the post-Auschwitz generation."[4] Postmemory takes as a given that the nature of memory itself is mediated, never transparent, an "imprint," as Liss terms it, of its prior representations. This notion of postmemory insists on the impossibility of a transparent relationship to the past and to language, announcing itself instead as artifact, as mediated between the various layers and levels of memory—experiential *and* textual. Postmemory, as I am using the term, is memory that cannot be traced back to the Urtext of experience, but rather unfolds as part of an ongoing process of intertextuality, translation, metonymic substitution, and a constant interrogation of the nature of the original. Memoirs as postmemoirs—such as those by Wilkomirski, Demidenko, and Ryback—all point to their own status (and failed status) as memoir, thus signaling their participation in the elegiac mourning for the loss of viability of poetic and narrative form.

As the memory of the Holocaust becomes less and less traceable to the originary moment, as it is replaced by postmemory, the relationship between German and Jew—the historical memory and the metaphorical constructions linking the two—becomes refigured. Thus I maintain that the task is no longer to adhere to a precise taxonomy of "memoir" (or even the German-Jewish memoir), but rather to reflect on how the proliferation of memoirs today circles around the Holocaust and the elusive notion of German and Jewish identity.[5] The booming business in memoirs is matched by the self-reflexive, autobiographical gesture in books that barely skirt the topic of history and memory. For the first time in a long career as a poetry critic, for instance, Marjorie Perloff begins her recent book *Wittgenstein's Ladder* with a reflection about her experience as a Viennese Jew; her "return" (as she calls it) to Vienna is signaled with the obligatory nod to the presence of the memoir embedded within her otherwise unselfreflexive reading of Ludwig Wittgenstein, Ingeborg Bachmann, and Thomas Bernhard.[6] Even Carl Schorske's recent *Thinking with History* devotes an entire chapter to the interplay between his personal history and his work as a historian,[7] and the English translation of Wolfgang Benz's *The Holocaust* markets the "personal" by the addition of a subtitle absent in the original German title: *A German Historian Examines the Genocide.*

Amid the proliferation of actual Holocaust memoirs and the recourse, in academic scholarship, to the realm of the personal to "ground" the motivation for the scholarship, the more interesting—if by now rather expected and routine—questions that have emerged concern the contested nature of memory and the elusiveness of identity. While there are still memoirs being published that seek to capture history "wie es eigentlich gewesen ist," there is now a corpus of texts that challenge the very undertaking of writing history (personal or political) and that highlight the difficulties inherent in any attempt at representation of the Holocaust. Thus the discursive space of "the Holocaust" now encompasses texts that explore the uncertainty of authorship, experience, and identity and the slippage not only between national and ethnic identities, but also between fact and fiction, between trauma and recovery, between Jew and non-Jew, and between victim and perpetrator.

I return now to Kofman's reproduced list to keep in mind the interplay between the remembered and the real, the reproduced and the original, the lost and the unlost in Holocaust postmemoirs. The page that Kofman inserts from Klarsfeld's memorial book that bears her father's name is a reconstruction of the original lists, which were found, heavily damaged, after the war, often with holes in the onion-skin paper and hard to decipher. It has become a trope of Holocaust memoirs to alert the reader, at the beginning, to the fallibility and precariousness of memory and narrative—one need only think, for instance, of Primo Levi's axiomatic first sentence of *The Drowned and the Saved:* "Human memory is a marvelous and fallacious instrument," or even Marguerite Duras's putative discovery of the found text—her own, yet one she does not recall writing—at the start of *The War.* Kofman's book goes beyond this gesture of self-reflexivity, creating a text that is part memoir, part poetic meditation, part philosophical treatise, and part elegy and homage, with the near constant refrain of the two paradoxical questions that frame the text: "How can it not be said? And how can it be said?" *Smothered Words* is postmemoir as it invokes not *her* memory of the camps, but those of Robert Antelme, who in the foreword to his memoir *The Human Race,* describes the gap between "the words at our disposal and that experience which, in the case of most of us, was still going forward within our bodies."[8] Kofman's text stands as ruin containing the scattered fragments of Antelme's memoir, Blanchot's work, the sudden inclusion of the page from Serge Klarsfeld's memorial/book, and the never-written text by her father, his imagined, forever fictive memories, of whom all she has left, as she tells us at the opening of her memoir *Rue Ordener, Rue Labat,* is the fountain pen with which he never wrote his story. Furthermore, the repetitive invocation of Antelme and Blanchot in the text constitutes yet another form of "choking" and suffocation—they are the text and the memory that bring Kofman's own text into being, yet at the same time they are the words that suffocate her words, that prevent her from writing "with her own pen." The reproduced list of deportees that contains Kofman's father's name appears suddenly, without warning, in *Smothered Words;* as a page from Klarsfeld's book that is itself a memorial, the list bears witness to the disaster yet at the same time chokes, smothers the memoir she is trying to write. The failed document that leads to the failed memoir is the *ruin* within the narrative, the memory that leads to Kofman's central paradox of writing: "How can it not be said? And how can it be said?" Kofman's memoir as ruin—the scattered fragments, quotations, the motif of smothering—becomes the medium for expressing the limits of representation and, as Kofman says, "the rupture which left nothing intact."[9]

Other recent memoirs and postmemoirs are concerned with a similar obduracy of memory and experience. The experience of genocide that lies at the center of all of these texts struggles with its representation, a battle between original and copy, with the form of the memoir—in contrast to that of fiction or imaginative writing—standing as a shield against "fictionalization." And yet the presence, in these attempts at representation, of already mediated memories drawn from visual and narrative accounts of the genocide, what Hirsch and Liss first termed postmemories, constitutes the elegiac within postmemoir. The elegiac mode that underlies these memoirs is based on tropes of repetition within the text that is the marker of the elegiac (and not of redemption). The repetition creates familiarity within the closed system of the memoir/text—the repetition that governs our reading of Kofman's (or rather, Klarsfeld's) list of names, the repetition (iteration) of archival material and also the repetition of names that points to particular deaths amid the enormity of genocide. As the poet Amy Clampitt writes, in her elegy for John Lennon, "Grief / is original, but it / repeats itself; there's nothing / more original that it can do."[10]

It is precisely the repetition of grief that constitutes its originality and that forbids entry into the symbolic realm of the redemptive, which lies beyond repetition and concepts of origin: This is, I maintain, the aesthetic challenge of Holocaust memoirs. Like the waylaid wedding guest of Coleridge's "Rime of the Ancient Mariner," we as readers of memoirs are "arrested" by the memoirist's imperative to remember, to narrate, to bear witness, and simultaneously are made aware of the suddenness and arbitrariness of the act of narration. Coleridge's Mariner stops the wedding guest he encounters by chance, assaulting him with his tale. The narrative onslaught that follows and that forms the basis of the poem is analogous to the apparent suddenness of remembering (or, perhaps, the suddenness of forgetting or of dissembling— for example, Duras's claim to have found the manuscript and to have forgotten that she even wrote it). It is, to return to Kofman for a moment, analogous to the suddenness within the text of the list of deportees that, despite its instant legibility (we know immediately what it signifies, and further inspection quickly reveals her father's name), nonetheless leaves us aware of its inexplicability while at the same time pointing (without pointing) to the text's struggle with the tasks of witnessing and representing grief and trauma. This is what constitutes the poetic of Kofman's list—a list of "facts" that are ultimately more elusive than documentary, as they also contain the layers of documentation from the Klarsfeld memorial book.[11] The list, an eruption in an already fragmented, ruptured text, is the elegy for a unified and perhaps transcendent mode of testifying, it is another layer in a text suffused with textual and historical layers. As such, "the poetic" does not stand outside of, or in opposition to, "history"; the poetic evocation of loss and absence through Kofman's list is as much a part of the discursive spaces of the Holocaust and of history and, as such, recalls Giorgio Agamben's statement that it is testimony that "founds the possibility of the poem."[12]

The memoirs and postmemoirs by Koeppen, Wilkomirski, Demidenko, and Fremont claim to enact the suddenness and the arbitrariness of narration; they are all imbued with the Mariner's obsessive need to stop all potential listeners in their tracks. And they all, in one way or another, point to the limits of language and of art in recounting atrocity and to the possibility for misleading and, as Dan Pagis suggests in his poem "Autobiography," for creating boredom for the listener.[13] Yet unlike Primo Levi, whom Giorgio Agamben claims as a "pure" witness, the survivor who is driven—like the Ancient Mariner with whom Levi identifies—to tell his tale tirelessly, the authors of these postmemoirs are driven to tell not their tale, but someone else's, under the guise of authentic subjectivity.[14]

The proliferation of memoir in recent years (which is "choking" the book market) has created a paradoxical situation—the more that is written, the more that becomes undone and challenged, the more the blurring between fact and fiction, between history (as "posthistory") and memory (or postmemory) takes place. I propose reading into the limits of memoir (the cases where the breakdown of form and the breakdown between fact and fiction become the text of the memoir) a space for the poetic, for silence that is not mere "unspeakability" but the medium for the paradoxical task of witnessing, what Agamben identifies as the space of the poem in which the "true" witness cannot bear witness. The paradoxical nature of testimony—Sarah Kofman's "How can it not be said? And how can it be said?"—is analogous to what Anne Carson locates as the space that holds the words that are "wasted" and lost, a poetic repository then of the "unlost." The enormous expanse of text that can be classified as "Holocaust" memoir, in which memory battles against silence, and the sparser texts of poetry that begin and sometimes end with silence are not as far apart in textual space as might at first appear.

The memoir that Sarah Kofman wrote after *Smothered Words*, *Rue Ordener Rue Labat* (1994, trans. 1996), begins with this space of the poetic and of the unlost as she reflects on the one object from her father that she possesses: his fountain pen, "Of him all I have left is the fountain pen. I took it one day from my mother's purse, where she kept it along with some other souvenirs of my father. I used it all through school. It 'failed' me before I could bring myself to give it up. I still have it, patched up with Scotch tape; it is right in front of me on my desk and makes me write, write. Maybe all my books have been the detours required to bring me to write about 'that.'"[15] Kofman's speculative "maybe," her suggestion that all her books, before this one "memoir," are detours, contains yet another elision—the "that" which is metonymic for the fountain pen (i.e., writing, the father, the phallus, death). The fountain pen that remains after her father was picked up with 13,000 other French Jews, on July 16, 1942, herded to the Velodrome D'hiver and from there to Drancy, becomes in Kofman's memoir the defining moment of the text, it is the remnant that then itself "failed" and yet which brings her to the writing, finally, of her story. The pen, patched with scotch tape and sitting on her desk, moves her to "write, write"—and yet is not, significantly, the instrument of her writing. Her previous texts are now seen as "detours" that have brought her to the writing of "this" (significantly, elided), "detours" that, I propose, join her project of writing this memoir with Celan's description of the poem as a "detour," as being "en route," thus situating her memoir on yet another level as poetic text—as echo of Celan—exploring the viability of post-Holocaust aesthetics and poetics.

Kofman's invocation of the pen at the start of *Rue Ordener, Rue Labat*— the pen that denotes absence and death, the pen with which her father most decidedly did not write his story, the pen that lies broken, in ruins, and that is not the instrument of her story either—situates her concern with writing and with language and recalls Roland Barthes's idea of intransitive writing, of "writing-oneself" in the "middle voice." Barthes draws on the linguistic definition of the middle voice as being neither active nor passive, but rather as the voice in which "the subject affects himself, he always remains inside the action, even if that action involves an object."[16] For Barthes, the middle voice corresponds to the "modern state" of the verb "to write": "to write is today to make oneself the center of action of speech, it is to effect writing by affecting oneself, to make action and affection coincide, to leave the *scriptor* inside the writing, not as a psychological subject . . . but as the agent of the action."[17] At the end of the passage about her father's pen, Kofman stammers: "it is right in front of me on my desk and makes me write, write." Kofman's evocation of the pen as totem (yet broken) that propels her writing (echoed twice, "write, write") is analogous to Barthes's notion of intransitive writing. It is not that Kofman (and others, such as Antelme and Levi) is writing herself "out of history" by writing intransitively; rather, they enact a writing about the Holocaust that is synonymous with their position as historical subjects and at the same time inscribe already known representations of history (that is, the imprints" that Liss describes) into this writing. This is the suggestion, prompted by Barthes's essay, taken up by Berel Lang, who calls for an antirepresentational writing about the Holocaust that would be intransitive, analogous, for instance, to the telling of the story of Exodus at Passover: "As the Haggadah places every Jew at Sinai, instructed to recount the events of the Exodus as though they had been part of his own life, the presence of all Jews is also fixed within the events of the genocide—those born after it as well as those who died in it or who lived despite it."[18] Citing literary forms such as the chronicle, the diary, and the memoir as exemplary of intransitive writing, Lang asserts that "all Jews should tell the story of the genocide as if he or she had passed through it,"[19] thus insisting on a midrashic narrative of presence in which all Jews tell the story literally, in the *present.*[20] The narrator is thus present in his or her own narration, and imagines him or herself back into history in order to make history present.[21]

I draw on Barthes's notion of the middle voice to help read Kofman's stammered "write, write," and, in the wake of the scandal and debates about authorship and authenticity that have followed the publication (and demise) of Wilkomirski's *Fragments,* to highlight the problems inherent in memoir writing and in "writing the self." Wilkomirski begins his book by asserting that he has no mother tongue, but rather his linguistic origin ("*sprachlicher Ursprung*") is the Yiddish of his brother Mordechai and the fragments of language gleaned from the camps. This is, of course, different from Antelme's assertions about the gap between "the words at our disposal" and the experience still carried by the body, yet it too situates language (or its absence) and writing (or, as in the case of Antelme, its near impossibility) as expressions of trauma. Yet what might Barthes's notion of the middle voice add to a reading of a text such as *Fragments,* where the writing subject is subsequently unmasked as a fraud, or, as LaCapra has suggested, where Wilkomirski's identity confusion was caused by a "displaced or secondary" traumatization?[22] There is, to be sure, a distinction to be made between an intransitive writing enacted from a writing subject who is what he is, and that of a subject, such as Wilkomirski, about whom we cannot be so certain.[23]

An earlier text, Wolfgang Koeppen's *Jakob Littners Aufzeichnungen aus einem Erdloch,* [Jakob Littner's Notes from a Hole in the Earth] raises similar issues as Wilkomirski's book. The first book in the publishing company Suhrkamp Verlag's new imprint Jüdischer Verlag in 1992, *Jakob Littners Aufzeichnungen aus einem Erdloch* is the reissue of a book published in 1948 with the Munich Kluger Verlag under the "pseudonym" (according to the book's jacket) of Jakob Littner (under the original title *Aufzeichnungen aus einem Erdloch*). The fuller story turns out to be the following: Littner, born in Budapest in 1883, moved with his wife in 1912 to Munich, where he worked as a stamp trader. He was registered as living in Munich from 1911 to 1939 and then from 1945 to 1947, when he emigrated to the United States. Because of his father's citizenship, he became a Polish citizen in 1919 (his father born in Oswiecim) and was thus subject to the deportation laws for all Polish Jews in 1938. His memoir begins with the deportation. Two weeks later he was able to escape to Krakow, where he witnessed the German *Angriff* on September 1, 1939, which forms the basis for the first part of his memoir. From Krakow he continued to flee further east via Lemberg and Tarnopol to Zaleczyki am Dnjepr, where he observed the arrival of Soviet troops on September 13. Most of his memoir consists of descriptions of the small town Zbaraz, in the region of Tarnopol (now in the Ukraine), where he fled in 1940. In April 1943, following the round-up and murder of hundreds of Jews in Zbaraz, Littner paid a Polish baker to hide him in his cellar; shortly before the ghetto in Zbaraz was liquidated, he made it safely to this cellar, where he remained hidden for nine months. His "underground exile" ("Verbannung unter der Erde") was, as he describes it, a period of "productive inwardness."[24] After the war, Littner returned to Munich and tried to find a publisher for his memoir, *Mein Weg durch die Nacht* (November 9, 1945), which we now know consisted of 183 pages (longer than Koeppen's text), detailing the deaths of Jews murdered in the Polish-Ukrainian Zbaraz. He was unable to get a publisher to print it. According to the story, Kluger Verlag then asked Koeppen if he would rework the manuscript. Koeppen claimed that the memoir consisted of little more than "three pieces of paper" and that he drew largely on the publisher's recounting of Littner's tale. Recent scholarship has revealed that in fact Koeppen borrowed much more freely from Littner's manuscript than he had previously admitted and that the Littner text is a rich and compelling document in its own right.[25] Koeppen—who in 1992 had not published a novel in nearly 40 years— finally claimed "authorship" for the book in that year.

In his foreword to the 1992 edition, Koeppen recounts that the publisher, Herbert Kluger, had met a man, Jakob Littner, who wanted to "bear witness" to what he had experienced and was looking for an author to tell his tale for him. In exchange, Littner, now in the United States, where he emigrated in 1947, sent Koeppen two care packages every month. Koeppen ends his foreword: "I ate canned American food and wrote about the suffering of a German Jew. And so it became my story."[26] Unlike Wilkomirski, who takes on the Jewish identity of a child survivor and writes as "imaginary survivor," Koeppen's seamless appropriation of Littner's identity and life story is conscious and not perceived, at least initially, as deceptive. The justification Koeppen gives remains entirely on the level of narrative: "And so it became my story." And yet Koeppen's appropriation of Littner's story masks his far darker and untold story as "inner émigré" that begins with his membership in the *Reichschriftitumskammer* and continues with various acts of conscious hiding and deception. This untold story becomes one more narrative layer in the Littner story, as Koeppen initially hides his past behind the story of Jakob Littner and then, in 1992, asserts that Littner's story became his story.

Another cause célèbre of contested authorship and falsified identity is Helen Demidenko's *The Hand that Signed the Paper*. Demidenko's novel, published in Australia in 1993 to great critical acclaim (it won the Australian Vogel prize in 1993 and the Gold Medal of the Australian Literature Society), raised similar questions as Wilkomirski's *Fragments* about the purpose and nature of memoir writing, after it was uncovered that Helen Demidenko was not the daughter of an illiterate Ukrainian taxi driver, as she claimed, but in fact Helen Darville, the daughter of a Brisbane couple who had emigrated to Australia from England. Darville's exploration of the (fictive) tale of the narrator's uncle, a Ukrainian brought to trial for war crimes, approaches the issue of memory and narrative from the perspective of the perpetrators, not the victims; however, in the end, Demidenko's text raises the same questions as the Koeppen and Wilkomirski memoirs: Does it matter?[27] Is the text altered by the divulging of the "true" identity? Certainly, in all of these cases, the scandal surrounding the "uncovering" of the "hoax" have made the texts—as texts—more interesting than they might otherwise have been. This was the question raised with the Wilkomirski affair, as the book had been welcomed with rave reviews when it first appeared, and then excoriated in the German press in particular after the uncertainties of Wilkomirski's identity began to emerge. Wilkomirski, as we now know, is really Bruno Dösseker, born not in Riga, as he claims in the book, but instead in Switzerland and adopted soon after birth by a Protestant couple. Yet the question that emerges with the Wilkomirski case is, again, about the interplay between imaginative and historical writing. Not only does the breakdown of form point to the postmodern mantra of the historicity of narrative and the narrativity of history, but even more significantly, both the Koeppen and the Wilkomirski cases, in their apparently blatant disregard for the "author," raise the question of what happens to truth claims when they are made by a fictive, invented Jewish subject. And, to return to Barthes: How does an invented Jewish subject write himself? What constitutes the middle voice when the writing subject is cloaking himself in artifice in order to write memoir? Can we, as LaCapra has recently asked, make truth claims in the middle voice?[28] Is Barthes's model of intransitive writing (as it is taken up first by Lang and White and later by LaCapra) predicated on a writing subject who is then unitary, "authentic," not to mention "Jewish"? In these "false" memoirs, the assumed Jewish identity (in the case of Wilkomirski and, in an entirely different but nonetheless analogous way, with Koeppen) results in an *assumed* retelling of the tale—no longer memoir, not quite fiction, but perhaps postmemoir. Yet as many have pointed out, the story as *story* remains the same, even after the unmasking (or partial unmasking) of Wilkomirski's identity—but the story of the story has not; it has, certainly in the case of Wilkomirski, become more interesting than the story itself.

In all of these cases, the reception of the text, after the falsified identity of the author has been revealed, has hinged on the authenticity of the author. Another text that raises the specter of the false memoir is Timothy Ryback's *The Last Survivor: In Search of Martin Zaidenstadt*. Ryback begins his book with the same quote from the "Ancient Mariner" as Primo Levi begins *Moments of Reprieve* ("Since then, at an uncertain hour / That agony returns / And till my ghastly tale is told / This heart within me burns"), thus inserting his text, through the invocation of Coleridge, into the body of Holocaust memoir literature. The book is a journalist's attempt to tell the story of Martin Zaidenstadt, an 87-year-old survivor who stands in front of the crematorium in Dachau and tells tourists that he is a survivor of Dachau and that he has been coming to the camp every day for the past 53 years. Ryback's book captures both the failures of Martin's memory and the uncertainty of Martin's "true" identity.[29] Ostensibly interned in Dachau from 1942 until the liberation, Martin married a German woman and stayed in the town of Dachau after the war ended. In the early 1990s, he started going to the camp and standing vigil in front of the crematorium in order to tell tourists that, contrary to historians' insistence, the gas chambers at Dachau were indeed used. No records exist of Martin's internment in Dachau, and when Ryback embarked on a search to find documents proving that Martin was from the town in Poland he claims to be from, he also could not find "proof." The figure of Martin Zaidenstadt[30] evokes the elusiveness of "evidence" or the explanation of why he is standing vigil in front of the ovens at Dachau, and, finally, the elusiveness of the nature of bearing witness.

Unlike Wilkomirski's and Demidenko's memoirs, Helen Fremont's *After Long Silence* is not based in "false" memory, but instead charts the author's attempt to reconstruct out of the rubble of "wartime lies" the "truth" about her family's history. Reared by two Polish parents as Catholics, Fremont and her sister, a psychoanalyst specializing in trauma victims, embark on a quest to learn the "truth" about their parents, who, we discover in the course of the book, were Polish Jews who lost their entire families in the war. The story Fremont tells is of her and her sister's recovery of their parents' true story, and within that is the tale of her mother and her mother's sister. Yet the picture of the two young girls on the cover is not the author and her sister, nor the author's mother and aunt, but rather a photograph by Roman Vishniac of two young girls in the ghetto. The photograph with which the memoir begins thus establishes this memoir as postmemoir, as engaged with memories from the corpus of Holocaust images, with the photograph guiding the reader back to the buried past of Fremont's parents that is, at the same time, immediately familiar to the reader through the Vishniac photograph.

Fremont's memoir seeks not only to recover family memory, but also to claim the immediacy of family stories as memory and not postmemory, to bring her family's story from the iconic imprint of the Holocaust (e.g., Roman Vishniac) and into her own personal sphere.[31] In this way, Fremont represents an important shift from the primacy of mediated postmemories in America to the family narrative. On the surface, *After Long Silence* seems to have absolutely nothing to say about Germans and Jews. Yet at the same time it expresses what I propose as the "new" symbiosis—not the symbiosis between German and Jews, but between American Jews and Germans. A pivotal event in this refiguration was Cynthia Ozick's letter in *Harper's* more than ten years ago in response to an invitation from the German government to address a group on the subject of Jews in Germany.[32] In the letter subsequently printed in *Harper's*, Ozick states her refusal to go to Germany, claiming that the absence of Jews in Germany is precisely the point with which Germans must grapple. Ozick's letter marks the beginning of a new discourse in the United States about Germans and Jews, insisting that Germans face the absence of Jews in Germany and no longer "import" an American Jew. Yet despite Ozick's cogent explanation for her refusal to go to Germany, the discourse about Germany in mainstream American-Jewish culture constructs an imaginary Germany replete with imaginary Germans (perpetrators).[33]

This "imaginary German," like Finkielkraut's "imaginary Jew," has now "taken up residence" in fiction by German authors such as Ursula Hegi and Bernhard Schlink, whose popularity in the United States attests to the ongoing symbiosis not between Germans and Jews, but between Germans and American Jews.[34] In an essay on "the end of history," Michael Geyer addresses the ties between Jewish identity in America and German identity that looks to Jewish American culture. Geyer suggests that the "surfeit of memory" in Germany today "expresses a rather curious, and largely unreflected, sensibility of living while becoming part of the past. In the United States, this sense of a lived present slipping away into the past—for individuals an awareness of aging, for nations a matter of becoming history—remains largely muted, private and on the whole unspoken."[35] This "muted" and private sense of history with which Geyer characterizes the United States' relationship to the past appears in contemporary fiction and memoirs (the two merging, without boundaries), of which Fremont's book is exemplary.

The imaginary within Germany that constructs Jews (either as part of a former symbiosis, or with nostalgia or, simply, fetishized reverence) as well as the American imaginary that is replete with the imaginary German, is the realm not of memory and memoir, but rather of postmemory and postmemoir. These texts—in some cases falsified, in other cases inexact and uncertain—are all poised between fact and fiction; experience and imagination; the immediacy of lived, remembered experience and mediated, transmitted, imagined memory, the memory as it is handed down in image, text, voice. The postmemoir is as inexact and liminal and poetic and sudden as the list of deportees in Kofman's book—it is there as trace and as echo and also as fact.

Notes

1. For an elaboration of the idea of the "unlost," see Anne Carson, *Economy of the Unlost: Reading Simonides of Keos with Paul Celan* (Princeton: Princeton University Press, 1999). Carson's study of Simonides and Celan begins with the question: "What exactly is lost to us when words are wasted? And where is the human store to which such goods are gathered?" Carson 3.

2. Alain Finkielkraut, *The Imaginary Jew* (Lincoln: University of Nebraska Press, 1992), 15.

3. I draw here primarily on Marianne Hirsch's definition of the term in *Family Frames: Photography, Narrative and Postmemory* (Cambridge, MA: Harvard University Press, 1997).

4. Andrea Liss, *Trespassing Through Shadows. Memory, Photography, and the Holocaust* (Minneapolis: University of Minnesota Press, 1998), 86.

5. This proliferation of memoir includes not only Holocaust memoirs, but AIDS memoirs, memoirs of childhood abuse, etc.

6. Marjorie Perloff. *Wittgenstein's Ladder: Poetic Language and the Strangeness of the Ordinary.* (Chicago: University of Chicago Press, 1996).

7. Schorske's reflections are hardly intimate, and suggest as well a rather perfunctory attempt to reflect on his life and work: "When my mother, who unlike my father, was Jewish, encountered unpleasant social prejudice during my high-school years, I acquired a second marginal identity. Perhaps this sense of marginality, imposed by history, enhanced history's fascination for

me and shaped my attitude toward it, at once wary and engagé." Carl Schorske, *Thinking with History* (Princeton: Princeton University Press, 1998), 19.

8. Robert Antelme, *The Human Race*. Trans. Jeffrey Haight and Annie Mahler (Marlboro, VT: Marlboro Press, 1992), 3. It is from Antelme that Kofman finds her metaphor of choking and smothering: "No sooner would we begin to tell our story than we would be choking over it" (3).

9. Kofman, *Smothered Words*, 15.

10. Amy Clampitt, "The Dakota," *The Kingfisher* (New York: Knopf, 1983), 23. The markedly elegiac quality to much of contemporary American poetry is, I believe, a displacement of the Shoah into a more generalized expression of grief and mourning. I would not categorize these poems as "Holocaust" poems per se, but rather as poetic texts that circle around the dominant discourse of mourning.

11. I am reminded here of Dan Pagis's poem "Autobiography," in which he suggests a similar relationship between facticity and boredom: "I won't mention names / out of consideration for the reader, / since at first the details horrify / though finally they're a bore." Dan Pagis, *The Selected Poetry*. Trans. Stephen Mitchell (Berkeley: University of California Press, 1989), 5.

12. Giorgio Agamben. *Remnants of Auschwitz. The Witness and the Archive* (New York: Zone Books, 1999). 36.

13. See Pagis, *The Selected Poetry*, 5.

14. Agamben acknowledges, however, the "lacuna" of testimony that Levi himself identifies and that "calls into question the very meaning of testimony and, along with it, the identity and reliability of the witnesses" (Agamben, *Remnants of Auschwitz*, 33). Agamben then cites Levi's definition of who "the true witnesses" are: "I must repeat: we, the survivors, are not the true witnesses. We survivors are not only an exiguous but also an anomalous minority: we are those who by their prevarications or abilities or good luck did not touch bottom. Those who did so, those who saw the Gorgon, have not returned to tell about it or have returned mute, but they are the Muslims, the submerged, the complete witnesses, the ones whose deposition would have a general significance. The destruction brought to an end, the job completed, was not told by anyone, just as no one ever returned to describe his own death. We speak in their stead, by proxy." Levi as cited by Agamben, *Remnants of Auschwitz*, 33–34.

15. Sarah Kofman, *Rue Ordener, Rue Labat* (Lincoln, University of Nebraska Press, 1996), 3.

16. Roland Barthes, "To Write: An Intransitive Verb?," *The Rustle of Language*, trans. Richard Howard (New York: Hill and Wang, 1986), 18.

17. Barthes, "To Write," 18.

18. Berel Lang, *Act and Idea in the Nazi Genocide* (Chicago: University of Chicago Press, 1990), xiii.

19. Lang, *Act and Idea in the Nazi Genocide*, xiii.

20. See Sara Horowitz. *Voicing the Void. Muteness and Memory in Holocaust Fiction,* (Albany: SUNY Press, 1997), 22–24. Horowitz takes up Lang's idea that links discourse about the genocide with midrash, where texts about the Holocaust can be seen—like midrash itself—as interpretive narrative that is capable of holding contradictory truth claims about the moral act of writing the genocide.

21. Hayden White concurs with Lang not that the Holocaust lies beyond representation and is not representable, but rather that writing of and about the Holocaust must, as Lang suggests, be enacted by Barthes's notion of the middle voice, thus proscribing any writing about the Holocaust that would be marked by non mediation. See Hayden White, "Historical Emplotment and the Problem of Truth," in *Probing the Limits of Representation. Nazism and the "Final Solution,"* ed. Saul Friedländer (Cambridge, MA: Harvard University Press, 1992), 53.

22. See Dominick LaCapra, *Writing History, Writing Trauma* (Baltimore: Johns Hopkins University Press 2001), 34. Although LaCapra cites displaced traumatization as one possible explanation for Wilkomirski's deception, at the same time he states that a reading of *Fragments* as "undecidable with respect to its status as fiction or memoir" is unacceptable.

23. Berel Lang argues that the distinction between fact and fiction should be "viewed not in aesthetic or cognitive terms at all . . . but as based on a moral foundation." For an interesting discussion of the moral dimension of the debate about fact vs. fiction, see Berel Lang, *Holocaust Representation: Art Within the Limits of History and Ethics* (Baltimore: Johns Hopkins University Press, 2000), 74.

24. Reinhard Zachau, "Das Originalmanuskript zu Wolfgang Koeppens *Jakob Littners Aufzeichnungen aus einem Erdloch.*" *Colloquia Germanica* 32 (1999): 124.

25. See *Colloquia Germanica* 32 (1999), in which, in addition to Zachau's useful study of the original Littner text, three excerpts from Littner's original manuscript are published.

26. "Ich aß amerkanische Konserven und schrieb die Leidensgeschichte eines deutschen Juden. Da wurde es meine Geschichte." Wolfgang Koeppen. *Jakob Littners Aufzeichnungen aus einem Erdloch* (Frankfurt: Jüdischer Verlag, 1992), 6.

27. See Berel Lang's discussion of Demidenko in *Holocaust Representation,* 75–77.

28. See LaCapra *Writing History, Writing Trauma,* 19–20. LaCapra cites Bernhard Schlink's *The Reader* as illustrative of writing in the middle voice. See LaCapra, 201–203.

29. An additional layer in the text is Ryback's position as an American of Austrian descent, who claims a distant relative in the SS and a grandfather who, although in the United States, was a Nazi sympathizer.

30. Martin Zaidenstadt is the subject of a new documentary film, *Martin,* written and directed by Ra'anan Alexandrowicz, that premiered at the New York Museum of Modern Art in April 2000.

31. It is interesting that this sphere of the personal is also marked by the buried narrative thread in *After Long Silence* about Fremont's identity as a lesbian, thus linking the "passing" as non-Jew (by her parents) to the passing as a heterosexual. Fremont makes the implicit claim that in order to discover the truth about her Jewishness, she must also "reveal" the truth about her sexual identity. It is at the moment that Fremont inserts this narrative of sexual and ethnic wholeness that the book, I feel, is most problematic; rather than allowing for the ambiguity and complexity of Jewish identity, by "coming out" as a lesbian (and by linking her lesbian and Jewish identities in a matrix of "revelation" and non-passing), Fremont thus imposes a more redemptive, unitary notion of Jewishness than her family history necessarily demands.

32. See Cynthia Ozick, "Why I Won't Go to Germany," *Harper's* (February 1989): 16–19.

33. Symptomatic of this is Walter Abish's sensationalized Germans in his novel *How German Is It*—the Germans *all* Americans love to hate—the German who, when hypnotized at the end of the novel, raises his right hand in a Hitler salute. Walter Abish, *How German is It?* (New York: New Directions, 1980).

34. Contemporary Jewish writing in Germany is heavily inflected with American Jewish fiction; significantly, the most popular American writers in Germany are Philip Roth, Saul Bellow, and more recently, Louis Begley, whose first novel, *Wartime Lies* is a paradigmatic example of the blurring of the distinctions between the autobiographical and the fictional. For the "new" symbiosis between Germans and American Jews, see Maxim Biller's *Harlem Holocaust* (Cologne: Kiepenheuer und Witsch, 1998). Another interesting example is Holly Jane Rahlens' *Becky Bernstein Goes Berlin* (Munich: Piper, 1996), first written in English by Rahlens but only marketed in German.

35. Michael Geyer, "Germany, or the Twentieth Century as History." South Atlantic Quarterly 96 (Fall 1997): 664.

BIBLIOGRAPHY

Abish, Walter. *How German Is It?* New York: New Directions, 1980.

Abusch, Alexander. *Mit offenem Visier: Memoiren II.* Berlin: Dietz, 1986.

Adelson, Leslie. "1971 *Ein Sommer in der Woche der Itke K.* by American born author Jeanette Lander is published." In *Yale Companion to Jewish Writing and Thought in German Culture, 1096–1996.* Ed. Sander L. Gillman and Jack Zipes. New Haven: Yale University Press, 1997. 749–58.

Adorno, Theodor. *Prisms.* Trans. Samuel and Shierry Weber. Cambridge, MA: MIT Press, 1981.

———. *Soziologischer Schriften II, Gesammelte Schriften,* Vol. 9.2. Frankfurt am Main: Suhrkamp, 1975. 258–61.

Agamben, Giorgio. *Remnants of Auschwitz: The Witness and the Archive.* New York: Zone Books, 1999.

Améry, Jean. "How Much Home Does a Person Need?" In *At the Mind's Limits: Contemplations by a Survivor on Auschwitz and its Realities.* Trans. Sidney Rosenfeld and Stella P. Rosenfeld. New York: Schocken Books, 1990. 43–44.

Andreas-Friedrich, Ruth. *Schauplatz Berlin. Tagebuchaufzeichnungen 1945 bis 1948.* Frankfurt am Main: Suhrkamp, 1984.

Antelme, Robert. *The Human Race.* Trans. Jeffrey Haight and Annie Mahler. Marlboro, VT: Marlboro Press, 1992.

"Antisemitismus in der SED 1952/53. Verdrängung der Geschichte bis ans Ende." *Utopie kreativ* 85–86 (November-December 1997).

Arendt, Hannah. "The Aftermath of Nazi Rule: Report from Germany." *Commentary* 10 (1950): 342–43.

Assmann, Aleida and Ute Frevert. *Geschichtsvergessenheit-Geschichtsversessenheit: Vom Umgang mit deutschen Vergangenheiten nach 1945.* Stuttgart: Deutsche Verlags-Anstalt, 1999.

Assmann, Jan. *Das kulturelle Gedächtnis: Schrift, Erinnerung und politische Identität in frühen Hochkulturen.* Munich: Beck, 1997.

Bach Jr., Julian. *American's Germany: An Account of the Occupation.* New York: Random House, 1946.

Bahr, Hermann, ed. *Der Antisemitismus: Ein internationales Interview.* Königstein/Tannus: Jüdischer Verlag, [1894]1979.

Bal, Mieke. *Narratology: Introduction to the Theory of Narrative.* Trans. Christine van Boheemen. 2nd ed. Toronto: University of Toronto Press, 1997.

Baldwin, Peter, ed. *Reworking the Past: Hitler, the Holocaust, and the Historians' Debate.* Boston: Beacon: 1990.

Barak, Jeff. "Berlin's Jewish Museum." *The Jerusalem Post* (July 9, 1998).

Barenboim, Daniel. "Germans, Jews, and Music." *The New York Review of Books* xlviii (March 29, 2001): 50–51.

Barlog, Boleslaw. *Theater lebenslänglich.* Munich: Knaur, 1981.

Barthes, Roland. "To Write: An Intransitive Verb?" *The Rustle of Language.* Trans. Richard Howard. New York: Hill and Wang, 1986.

Bartov, Omer. "'Seit die Juden weg sind . . . ': Germany, History, and Representations of Absence." *A User's Guide to German Cultural Studies.* Ed. Scott Denham et al. Ann Arbor: University of Michigan Press, 1997. 209–26.

Bauer, Leo. "Die Partei hat immer recht." *Aus Politik und Zeitgeschichte* (July 4, 1956): B27, 405–13.

Bauer, Yehudah. *Flight and Rescue: Bricha.* New York: Random House, 1970.

Bayerdörfer, Hans-Peter. "Shylock auf der deutschen Bühne nach der Shoah." In *Shylock? Zinsverbot und Geldverlieh in jüdischer und christlicher Tradition.* Ed. Johannes Heil and Bernard Wacker. Frankfurt am Main: Fink, 1997. 261–80.

Beck, Gad. *und gad ging zu david: die erinnerungen des gad beck 1923 bis 1945.* Ed. Frank Heibert. Berlin: edition diá zebra literaturverlag, 1995. (English title: *An Underground Life: The Memoirs of a Gay Jew in Nazi Germany.* Madison: University of Wisconsin Press, 1999.)

Beck-Gernsheim, Elisabeth. *Juden, Deutsche und andere Erinnerungslandschaften.* Frankfurt am Main: Suhrkamp, 1999.

Beckermann, Ruth. *Jenseits des Krieges.* Wien: Löcker, 1998.

———. *Unzugehörig.* Wien: Löcker, 1989.

Behrens, Katja. *Die dreizehnte Fee.* Düsseldorf: Claassen, 1983.

———. *Die Vagantin.* Frankfurt am Main: Fischer. 1997.

Bendt, Veronika. "Das Jüdische Museum: Eine Abteilung des Berlin Museums." *Berliner Forum* (June 1986): 8.

———. *Wegweiser durch das jüdische Berlin.* Berlin: Nicolai, 1987.

Benjamin, Walter. *Gesammelte Schriften.* Vol 1.3. Ed. Rolf Tiedemann and Hermann Schweppenhäuser. Frankfurt am Main: Suhrkamp, 1974.

Benjamin, Walter. *One Way Street.* Trans. Edmund Jephcott, *Selected Writings, Volume 1: 1913–1926,* ed. Marcus Bullok and Michael W. Jennings (Cambridge: Harvard University Press, 1996), 483.

Benz, Wolfgang, ed. *Antisemitismus in Deutschland. Zur Aktualität eines Vorurteils.* Munich: DTV, 1995.

Berger, Tina and Andrea Welker, eds. *"Ich wollte meine Tochter läge tot zu meinen Füßen und hätte die Juwelen in den Ohren": Improvisationen über Shakespeares Shylock.* Munich: Hanser, 1979.

Bergmann, Werner and Rainer Erb. *Berlin: Kampf um Freiheit und Selbstverwaltung 1945–1946.* Senat Berlin: Heinz Spitzing, 1961.

———. *Antisemitismus in der Bundesrepublik Deutschland. Ergebnisse der empirischen Forshung von 1946 bis 1989.* Opladen: Leske und Budrich, 1991.

———. "Wie antisemitish sind die Deutschen?" In *Antisemitismus in Deutschland.* Munich, DTV, 1995. 47–63.

Berthold, Lothar and Ernst Diehl, eds. *Revolutionäre deutsche Parteiprogramme. Vom Kommunistischen Manifest zum Programm des Sozialismus.* Berlin: Dietz, 1964.

Biale, Rachel. *Women and Jewish Law: An Exploration of Women's Issues in Halakhic Sources.* New York: Schocken, 1984.

Biller, Maxim. *Wenn ich einmal rich und tot bin.* Cologne: Kiepenhauer & Witsch, 1990.

———. *Die Temporjahre.* Munich: DTV, 1991.

———. *Land der Väter und Verräter.* Cologne: Kiepenhauer and Witsch, 1994.

———. *Harlem Holocaust.* 1990. Cologne: Kiepenhauer & Witsch, 1998.

———. *Die Tochter.* Cologne: Kiepenhauer & Witsch, 2000.

Bilski, Emily D., ed. *Berlin Metropolis: Jews and the New Culture, 1890–1918.* Berkeley: University of California Press, 1999.

Blanchot, Maurice. *The Writing of the Disaster.* Trans. Ann Smock. Lincoln: University of Nebraska Press, 1986.

Blumenthal, W. Michael. *The Invisible Wall: Germans and Jews.* Washington, DC: Counterpoint, 1998.

———. "Greetings." "Streit um die Erinnerung." *Frankfurter Allgemeine Zeitung* (October 9, 1999): 2.

———. *Jewish Museum Berlin* (May 2000): 5760–63.

Bodemann, Y. Michal. "Reconstructions of History: From Jewish Memory to Nationalized Commemoration of Kristallnacht in Germany." *Jews, Germans, Memory: Reconstructions of Jewish Life in Germany.* Ann Arbor: University of Michigan Press, 1996.

Bornemann, John and Jeffrey M. Peck. *Sojourners: The Return of German Jews and the Question of Identity.* Lincoln: University of Nebraska Press, 1995.

Bothe, Rolf and Vera Bendt. *Realisierungs Wettbewerb: Erweiterung Berlin Museum mit Abteilung Jüdisches Museum.* Berlin: Senatsverwaltung für Bau- und Wohungswesen, 1990.

Botting, Douglas. *In the Ruins of the Reich. Germany 1945–1949.* London: Allen and Unwin, 1985.

Boveri, Margret. *Tage des Überlebens Berlin 1945.* Munich: Piper, 1968.

Braese, Stephan and Holger Gehle. "Von 'deutschen Freunden': Ruth Klüger's 'weiter leben. Eine Jugend' in der deutschen Rezeption." *Der Deutschunterricht* 47.6 (1995): 76–87.

Brand, Matthias. *Fritz Kortner in der Weimarer Republik: Annäherungsversuche und die Entwicklung eines jüdischen Schauspielers in Deutschland.* Rheinfelden: Schäuble, 1981.

Brandt, Heinz. *Ein Traum, der nicht entführbar ist: Mein Weg zwischen Ost und West.* München: List, 1967.

Brandt, Leon. *Menschen ohne Schatten: Juden zwischen Untergang und Untergrund 1938 bis 1945.* Berlin: Oberbaum Verlag, 1984.

Brenner, Michael. *After the Holocaust: Rebuilding Jewish Lives in Postwar Germany.* Princeton: Princeton University Press, 1997.

———. "East European and German Jews in Postwar Germany, 1945–50." In *Jews, Germans, Memory: Reconstructions of Jewish Life in Germany.* Ed. Y. Michal Bodemann. Ann Arbor: University of Michigan Press, 1996.

———. *The Renaissance of Jewish Culture in Weimar Germany.* New Haven: Yale University Press, 1996.

Brenner, Michael and Stefan Rohrbacher, eds. *Wissenschaft vom Judentum: Annäherungen nach dem Holocaust.* Göttingen: Vandenhoeck & Ruprecht, 2000.

Brod, Peter and Arnold Krammer. *The Left against Zion: Communism, Israel, and the Middle East.* Ed. Robert S. Wistrich. London: Frank Cass, 1979, 50–70, 71–86.

Broder, Henryk M. *Der ewige Antisemit: Über Sinn und Funktion eines beständigen Gefühls.* Fischer: Frankfurt am Main, 1986.

———. *Volk und Wahn.* Munich: Goldmann, 1998.

———. "Die Juden zuerst." *Der Spiegel.* (July 13, 1998): 29.

Brumlik, Micha. "Zur Identität Juden in der Bundesrepublik." In *Junge Juden in Deutschland: Protokoll einer Tagung.* Ed. Ellen Presser and Bernhard Schoßig. Munich: Jugend und Kulturzentrum der Israelitischen Kultursgemeinde München, 1991.

———. *Kein Weg als Deutscher und Jude. Eine bundesrepublikanische Erfahrung.* Munich: Luchterhand, 1996.

Brumlik, Micha, ed. *Zuhause, keine Heimat? Junge Juden und ihre Zukunft in Deutschland.* Gerlingen: Bleicher, 1998.

Brumlik, Micha, Doron Kiesel, Cilly Kugelmann, and Julius H. Schoeps, eds. *Jüdisches Leben in Deutschland seit 1945.* Frankfurt: Jüdischer Verlag bei Athenäum, 1986.

Brustein, Robert. "A Berlin Diary." *The New Republic* (July 24, 2000): 30.

Bunzl, Matti. "Counter-Memory and Modes of Resistance: The Uses of Fin-de-Siècle Vienna for Present-Day Austrian Jews." In *Transforming the Center, Eroding the Margins. Essays on Ethnic and Cultural Boundaries in German-Speaking Countries.* Ed. Dagmar C. G. Lorenz and Renate Posthofen. Columbia, SC: Camden House, 1998.

Canaris, Voker. "Die ersten Juden, die ich kannte, waren Nathen und Shylock." *Theater Heute* 2 (1973): 22–24.

Canetti, Veza. *Die Schildkröten.* Munich: Hanser, 1999.

Carroll, Noël. "Horror and Humor." *The Journal of Aesthetics and Art Criticism* 57:2 (Spring 1999): 145–60.

Carson, Anne. *Economy of the Unlost: Reading Simonides of Keos with Paul Celan.* Princeton: Princeton University Press, 1999.

Caruth, Cathy, ed. *Trauma: Explorations in Memory.* Baltimore: Johns Hopkins University Press, 1995.

———. *Unclaimed Experience: Trauma, Narrative, and History.* Baltimore: Johns Hopkins University Press, 1996.

Cheah, Pheng and Bruce Robbins, eds. *Cosmopolitics. Thinking and Feeling beyond the Nation.* Minneapolis: University of Minnesota Press, 1998.

Clewing, Ulrich. "Linien der Zerstörung." *die tageszeitung* (February 1, 1999).

Cocks, Joan. "A New Cosmopolitanism? V. S. Naipauls and Edward Said." *Constellations* 7.1 (2000): 57.

Cohen, Roger. "Fresh Perspectives of Past and Present." *New York Times* (March 14, 1999): E8.

———. "A Jewish Museum Struggles to Be Born." *New York Times* (August 15, 2000): B3.

Cole, Tim. *Selling the Holocaust: From Auschwitz to Schindler: How History is Bought, Packaged and Sold.* New York: Routledge, 1999.

Cullen, Michael S, ed. *Das Holocaust-Mahnmal: Dokumentation einer Debatte.* Zurich: Pendo, 1999.

———. "Der Ausstellungsphilosoph." *Frankfurter Allgemeine Zeitung* (January 6, 2000): BS3.

Czaplicka, John. "Resonanzen in der Leere." *Berliner Zeitung* (January 23, 1999).

Czernin, Franz Josef. *Marcel Reich-Ranicki: Eine Kritik.* Göttingen: Steidl, 1995.

Danziger, Carl Jacob. *Die Partei hat immer recht.* Stuttgart: Deutsche Verlags-Anstalt, 1976.

Davidson, Eugene. *The Death and Life of Germany. An Account of the American Occupation.* New York: Alfred A. Knopf, 1959.

Demidenko, Helen. *The Hand that Signed the Paper.* St. Leonards, New South Wales: Allen & Unwin, 1994.

Des Pres, Terence. "Holocaust Laughter?" In *Writing and the Holocaust.* Ed. Berel Lang. New York: Holmes and Meier, 1988.

Deutschkron, Inge. *Ich trug den gelben Stern.* Munich: Deutscher Taschenbuch Verlag, 1987.

Diedrichsen, Diedrich and Bärbel Ruden, eds. *Lessing im Spiegel der Theaterkritik 1945- 1979.* Berlin: Gesellschaft für Theatergeschichte, 1980.

Diner, Dan. "Negative Symbiose: Deutsche und Juden nach Auschwitz." *Babylon* 1 (1986): 9–20.

———. *America in the Eyes of the Germans: An Essay on Anti-Americanism.* Trans. A. Brown. Princeton: Markus Wiener, 1996.

Dis, Adriaan van. "Nee zeggen is de enige onverwoestbare vrijheid." *NRC Handelsblad* (November 12, 1982): Cultureel Supplement, 3.

Dischereit, Esther. *Joëmis Tisch.* Frankfurt am Main: Suhrkamp, 1988.

———. *Merryn.* Frankfurt am Main: Suhrkamp, 1992.

———. *Übungen jüdisch zu sein.* Frankfurt am Main: Suhrkamp, 1998.

Dos Passos, John. *Tour of Duty.* Boston: Houghton Mifflin, 1946.

Drews, Wolfgang. "Nathan." *Münchner Merker* (October 29, 1965).

Eckardt, Jo-Jacqueline. *Lessing's "Nathan the Wise" and the Critics, 1779–1991.* Columbia, SC: Camden House, 1993.

Eshel, Amir. "Jewish Memories, German Futures: Recent Debates about the Past." Bloomington: The Robert A. and Sandra S. Borns Jewish Studies Program, Indiana University, 2001.

Ezrahi, Sidra DeKoven. *By Words Alone: The Holocaust in Literature.* Chicago: University of Chicago Press, 1980.

Fabian, Hans-Erich. "D.P." *Der Weg* 2 (February 1947).

———. "Liquidationsgemeinden?" *Der Weg* 2 (May 1947).

Fassbinder ohne Endung. Eine Dokumentation anlässlich der Uraufführung von Rainer Werner Fassbinders Theaterstück "Der Müll, die Stadt und der Tod" im Kammerspiel von Schauspiel Frankfurt am 31. Oktober 1985. Frankfurt am Main, 1985.

Feinberg, Anat. *Wiedergutmachung im Programm: jüdisches Schicksal im deutschen Nachkriegsdrama.* Cologne: Prometh, 1988.

————. *Embodied Memory: The Theatre of George Tabori.* Iowa City: University of Iowa Press, 1999.

Fejtö, François. *A History of People's Democracies: Eastern Europe Since Stalin.* Harmondsworth: Pelican Books, 1974.

Felman, Shoshana, and Dori Laub. *Testimony: Crises of Witnessing in Literature, Psychoanalysis, and History.* New York: Routledge, 1992.

Felstiner, John. *Paul Celan: Poet, Survivor, Jew.* New Haven: Yale University Press, 1995.

Finkelstein, Norman G. *The Holocaust Industry: Reflections on the Exploitation of Jewish Suffering.* London: Verso, 2000.

Finkielkraut, Alain. *The Imaginary Jew.* Lincoln: University of Nebraska Press, 1992.

Fischer, Barbara. *Nathans Ende? Von Lessing bis Tabori.* Göttingen: Wallstein, 2000.

Fischer, Erika. *Aimée und Jaguar. Eine Liebesgeschichte, Berlin 1943.* Cologne: Kiepenheuer and Witsch, 1994.

Flanzbaum, Hilene, ed. *The Americanization of the Holocaust.* Baltimore: Johns Hopkins University Press, 1999.

Fleischmann, Lea. *Dies ist nicht mein Land: Eine Jüdin verläßt die Bundesrepublik.* Hamburg: Hoffmann & Campe, 1980.

————. *Gas: Tagebuch einer Bedrohung: Israel während des Golfkrieges.* Göttingen: Steidl, 1991.

————. *Schabbat. Das Judentum für Nichtjuden verständlich gemacht.* Munich: Heyne, 1994.

————. *Rabbi Nachman und die Thora. Das Judentum für Nichtjuden verständlich gemacht.* Munich: Scherz, 2000.

Fontheim, Ernst-Günter. "Befreite Juden." *Der Weg* 1 (September 6, 1946).

————. "Lagerleben." *Der Weg* 1 (August 30, 1946).

Foschepoth, Joseph. *Im Schatten der Vergangenheit. Die Anfänge der Gesellschaft für Christlich-Jüdische Zusammenarbeit.* Göttingen: Vandenhoeck und Ruprecht, 1993.

Fremont, Helen. *After Long Silence: A Memoir.* New York: Delacorte, 1999.

Freund, Elisabeth. *Als Zwangsarbeiterin 1941 in Berlin: Die Aufzeichnungen der Volkswirtin Elisabeth Freund.* Ed. Carola Sachse. Berlin: Akademie Verlag, 1996.

Friedländer, Saul, ed. *Probing the Limits of Representation: Nazism and the "Final Solution."* Cambridge, MA: Harvard University Press, 1992.

"Fritz Kortner dreht einen Kampfilm." *Mein Film.* (October 29,1948).

"Fritz Kortner hat das Wort." *Rhein Echo* (June 6, 1949).

Gadberry, Glen W. *Theatre in the Third Reich, the Prewar Years.* Westport, CT: Greenwood, 1995.

Geisel, Eike and Henryk Broder. *Premiere und Progrom: Der jüdische Kulturbund 1933- 1941.* Berlin: Siedler, 1992.

Gelber, Mark, ed. *Identity and Ethos: A Festschrift for Sol Liptzin on the Occasion of his 85th Birthday.* New York: Peter Lang, 1986.

Geyer, Michael. "Germany, or The Twentieth Century as History." *The South Atlantic Quarterly* 96 (Fall 1997): 664ff.

Gillis, John R., ed. *Commemorations: The Politics of National Identity.* Princeton: Princeton University Press, 1994.

Gilman, Sander. L. "America and the Newest Jewish Writing in German." *The German Quarterly* 73 (Spring 2000): 151–62.

Gilman, Sander L. and Karen Remmler, ed. *Reemerging Jewish Culture in Germany: Life and Literature Since 1989.* New York: New York University Press, 1994.

Gilman, Sander L. and Jack Zipes, eds. *Yale Companion to Jewish Writing and Thought in German Culture, 1096–1996.* New Haven: Yale University Press, 1997.

Ginzel, Günter Bernd. "Phasen der Etablierung einer jüdischen Gemeinde in der Kölner Trümmerlandschaft 1945–1949." In *Köln und das Rheinische Judentum. Festschrift Germania Judaica, 1959–1984.* ed. Jutta Bohnke-Kollwitz. Cologne: Bachem, 1984. 445–61.

Giordano, Ralph. *Die zweite Schuld oder Von der Last, Deutscher zu sein.* Hamburg: Rasch und Röhring, 1987.

———. *Wenn Hitler den Krieg gewonnen hätte.* Hamburg: Rasch und Röhring, 1989.

———. *Wird Deutschland wider gefährlich? Mein Brief an Kanzler Kohl—Ursachen und Folgen.* Cologne: Kiepenheuer und Witsch, 1993.

Glancy, Jonathan. "The Hole in the Heart." *The Guardian* (January 27, 1999): 14.

Goerden, Elmar. "Der Andere: Fragmente einer Bühnengeschichte Shylocks im deutschen und englischen Theater des 18. und 19. Jahrhunderts." *Theatralia Judaica: Emanzipation und Antisemitismus als Moment der Theatergeschichte. Von der Lessing-Zeit bis zur Shoah.* Ed. Hans-Peter Bayerdörfer. Tübingen: Niemeyer, 1992: 129–61.

———. *Lessings Traum von Nathan der Weise. Ein Projekt.* Stuttgart: Schauspiel Staatstheater Stuttgart, Programmbuch 50, Spielzeit 1998.

Goldenbogen, Nora. "Antisemitismus und 'Säuberungen' in Sachsen (1949–1953)." In *Arbeiterbewegung und Antisemitismus: Entwicklungslinien im 20. Jahrhundert.* Ed. Mario Kessler. Bonn: Pahl-Rugenstein, 1993, 121–128.

Groehler, Olaf and Mario Kessler. *Die SED-Politik, der Antifaschismus und die Juden: In der SBZ und der frühen DDR.* Berlin: Helle Panke, 1995.

Gross, Leonard. *The Last Jews in Berlin.* New York: Simon and Schuster, 1982.

Gruber, Ruth Ellen. "Filling the Jewish Space in Europe." *International Perspectives* 35 (September 1996): 23–35.

Habe, Hans. *Aftermath.* New York: Viking, 1947.

Hage, Volker and Mathias Schreiber. *Marcel Reich-Ranicki: Ein Biographisches Porträt.* Cologne: Kiepenheuer und Witsch, 1995.

Hand, Sean, ed. *The Levinas Reader.* Oxford: Blackwell, 1989.

Hartewig, Karin. "Das Gedächtnis der Partei. Biographische und andere Bestände im Zentralen Parteiarchiv der SED in der Stiftung Archiv der Partien und Massenorganisationen der DDR im Bundesarchiv." *Jahrbuch für Kommunismusforschung.* Berlin: Akademie Verlag, 1993. 312–23.

Hartman, Geoffrey. "Learning from Survivors: Notes on the Video Archive at Yale." *Remembering for the Future: The Impact of the Holocaust on the Contemporary World.* Ed. Yehuda Bauer et al. Oxford: Pergamon, 1989. 1713–1717.

———, ed. *Holocaust Remembrance: The Shapes of Memory.* Cambridge, MA: Basil Blackwell, 1994.

Hegi, Ursula. *Stones for the River.* New York: Poseidon, 1994.

Heibert, Frank. *An Underground Life: The Memoirs of a Gay Jew in Nazi Germany.* Madison: University of Wisconsin Press, 1999.

Heidelberger-Leonard, Irene. *Ruth Klüger: weiter leben. Eine Jugend.* Munich: Oldenbourg, 1996.

Heilbut, Anthony. *Exiled in Paradise: German Refugee Artists and Intellectuals in America From the 1930s to the Present.* New York: Viking Press, 1983.

Herf, Jeffrey. "East German Communist and the Jewish Question: The Case of Paul Merker." *Journal of Contemporary History* 29 (1994): 627–61.

———. *Divided Memory: The Nazi Past in the two Germanys.* Cambridge, MA: Harvard University Press, 1997.

———. "Antisemitismus in der SED: Geheime Dokumente zum Fall Paul Merker aus SED- und MfS-Akten." *Vierteljahrshefte für Zeitgeschichte* 42 (1999): 643–50.

Heschel, Susannah, ed. *On Being a Jewish Feminist.* New York: Schocken, 1983.

"Hier Jude—Hier Lude." *Völkischer Beobachter* (November 27, 1938).

Hildebrand, Rainer. "Vorbereitungen für gesteuerten Antisemitsimus?" YIVO Archives, (Spring 1953), New York, FAD-1, Box 25.

Hirsch, Marianne. *Family Frames: Photography, Narrative, and Postmemory.* Cambridge, MA: Harvard University Press, 1997.

Hölderlin, Friedrich. *Die Trauerspiele des Sophocles.* Frankfurt am Main: Stroemfeld/Roter Stern, 1986.

Honigmann, Barbara. *Am Sonntag spielt der Rabbi Fußball.* Heidelberg: Wunderhorn, 1998.

———. *Damals, dann und danach.* Munich: Hanser, 1999.

———. *Roman von einem Kinde.* Darmstadt: Luchterhand, 1986.

———. *Eine Liebe aus Nichts.* Berlin: Rowohlt, 1991.

———. *Soharas Reise.* Reinbeck: Rowohlt, 1996.

Horowitz, Sara R. *Voicing the Void: Muteness and Memory in Holocaust Fiction.* Albany: State University of New York Press, 1997.

Howley, Frank L. *Berlin Command.* New York: Putnam, 1950.

Hutton, Oram and Andrew Rooney. *Conquerors' Peace: Report to the American Stockholders.* New York: Doubleday, 1947.

Huyssen, Andreas. "The Voids of Berlin." *Critical Inquiry* 24 (Autumn 1997): 57–81.

Hyman, Abraham S. *In Defense of the Survivors: The Letters and Documents of Oscar A. Mintzer, AJDC Legal Advisor, Germany 1945–46.* Berkeley: Judah Magnes Museum, 1999.

———. *Roman von einem Kinde.* Darmstadt: Luchterhand, 1986. *The Undefeated.* Jerusalem: Gefen, 1993.

Isenberg, Noah. "Before Kristallnacht." *The Nation* (October 19, 1998): 34–5.

———. *Between Redemption and Doom: The Strains of German-Jewish Modernism.* Lincoln: University of Nebraska Press, 1999.

———. "Scaling Daniel Libeskind's 'Architecture of Memory.'" *Forward* (January 1, 1999): 11–12.

———. "The Work of Walter Benjamin in the Age of Information: A Report on the State of Benjamin Studies at the End of the Century." *New German Critique.* 83 (Spring/Summer 2001).

Jacobmeyer, Wolfgang. "Jüdische Überlebende as Displaced Persons." *Geschichte und Gesellschaft* 9 (1983): 429–44.

Jacobs, Jack. *On Socialists and "The Jewish Question" after Marx.* New York: New York University Press, 1992.

Jacobson, Kenneth. *Embattled Selves: An Investigation into the Nature of Identity Through Oral Histories of Holocaust Survivors.* New York: The Atlantic Monthly Press, 1994.

Jäger, Lorenz. "Sag, was könnt' uns übrigbleiben? Abschied vom Mandarin: Zum Tod vons Hans Mayer, dem letzten Gelehrten mit geschichtlichem Auftrag." *Frankfurter Allgemeine Zeitung* (May 21, 2001): Feuillton, 1.

Jelinek, Elfriede. *Totenauberg: ein Stück.* Reinbek bei Hamburg: Rowohlt, 1991.

Jens, Inge, ed. *Über Hans Mayer.* Frankfurt am Main: Suhrkamp, 1977.

Jens, Walter. "Nathan der Weise und der Sicht von Auschwitz." *Kanzel und Katheder: Reden.* Munich: Kindler, 1984. 31–45.

Jessen, Jens. *Uber Marcel Reich-Ranicki: Aufsätze und Kommentare.* Munich: DTV, 1985.

"'Juden raus'—Ruf geahndet." *Süddeutsche Zeitung* (July 17, 1998).

"Jüdisches Leben" in fahrender S-Bahn. *Der Tagesspiegel.* (January 26, 2000).

K. E. "Juden in Deutschland." *Der Tagesspiegel* 39 (December 5, 1945): 3.

Kaes, Anton. "The American television series *Holocaust* is shown in West Germany." In *Yale Companion to Jewish Writing and Thought in German Culture, 1096–1996.* Ed. Sander Gilman and Jack Zipes. New Haven: Yale University Press, 1997. 783–89.

Kahn, Ludwig W. "The Changing Image of the Jew: Nathan the Wise and Shylock." In *Identity and Ethos: A Festschrift for Sol Liptzin on the Occasion of his 85th Birthday.* New York: Peter Lang, 1986. 235–52.

Kantorowicz, Alfred. *Deutsches Tagebuch II.* Berlin: A. W. Mytze, 1980.

Kaplan, Karel. "Der politische Prozess gegen R. Slánsky und Genossen." *Der Spätstalinismus und die jüdische Frage.* Ed. Leonid Luks. Cologne, Böhlau, 1998. 169–87.

Kaplan, Karel and Frantisek Svátek. "Die politischen Säuberungen in der KPC." *Terror: Stalinistische Parteisäuberungen 1936–1953.* Ed. Hermann Weber and Ulrich Mählert. Paderborn: Schöningh, 1998. 487–562.

Kaplan, Marion. *Between Dignity and Despair: Jewish Life in Nazi Germany.* New York: Oxford University Press, 1998.

Karsch, Walter. "Bekenntnis zum Theater. Rückblick auf die Berliner Spielzeit 1945/46." *Berliner Almanach* (1946): 60–76.

Kempowski, Walter. *Das Echolot: Ein kollektives Tagebuch, Januar und Februar 1943.* Munich: A. Knaur, 1993.

Kessler, Mario. "Antisemitismus in der SED 1952/53. Verdrängung der Geschichte bis ans Ende." *Utopie kreativ* 85–86 (November-December 1997): 157–70.

———. *Antisemitismus, Zionismus und Sozialismus.* Mainz: Decaton, 1993.

————. *Die SED und die Juden—zwischen Repression und Toleranz: Politische Entwicklungen bis 1967.* Berlin: Akademie Verlag, 1995.

————. *Zionismus und internationale Arbeiterbewegung 1897–1933.* Berlin: Akademie Verlag, 1994.

Kessler, Mario and Olaf Groehler. *Die SED-Politik, der Antifaschismus und die Juden: In der SBZ und der frühen DDR.* Berlin: Helle Panke, 1995.

Kiessling, Wolfgang. *Absturz in den Kalten Krieg.* Berlin: Helle Panke, 1999 (Hefte zur DDR-Geschichte, No 57).

————. *Partner im "Narrenparadies": Der Freundeskreis um Noel Field und Paul Merker.* Berlin: Dietz, 1994.

Klein, Alfred. *Unästhetische Feldzüge: Der siebenjährige Krieg gegen Hans Mayer (1956–1963).* Leipzig: Faber und Faber, 1997.

Klein, Alfred, Manfred Neuhaus, and Klaus Pezold, eds. *Hans Mayers Leipziger Jahre.* Leipzig: Rosa-Luxemburg-Stiftung Sachsen, 1997.

Klein, Gerda. *All But My Life.* New York: Hill and Wang, 1995.

Kloke, Martin W. *Israel und die deutsche Linke: Zur Geschichte eines schwierigen Verhältnisses.* Frankfurt am Main: Haag & Herchen, 1990.

Klüger, Ruth. "Missbrauch der Erinnerung: KZ Kitsch." *Von hoher und niedriger Literatur.* Göttingen: Wallstein Verlag, 1996.

————. *weiter leben. Eine Jugend.* Göttingen: Wallstein Verlag, 1992.

Knight, Robert. *"Ich bin dafür, die Sache in die Länge zu ziehen": Die Wortprotokolle der österreichischen Bundesregierung über die Entschädigung der Juden.* Vienna: Amalthea, 1988.

Koebl, Herlinde. *Jüdische Portraits: Photographien und Interviews.* Frankfurt am Main: Fischer, 1998.

Koeppen, Wolfgang. *Jacob Littners Aufzeichnungen aus einem Erdloch.* Frankfurt am Main: Jüdischer Verlag, 1992.

Kofman, Sarah. *Paroles Suffoquées.* Paris: Editions Galilée, 1987.

————. *Rue Ordener, Rue Labat.* Lincoln: University of Nebraska Press, 1996.

Koltun, Elizabeth, ed. *The Jewish Woman: New Perspectives.* New York: Schocken, 1976.

Königseder, Angelika. "Durchgangsstation Berlin: Jüdische DPs 1945–1948." *Überlebt und unterwegs: Jüdische Displaced Persons in Nachkriegsdeutschland.* Frankfurt am Main: Campus, 1997. 189–206.

————. *Flucht nach Berlin. Jüdische Displaced Persons 1945–1848.* Berlin: Metropol, 1998.

Königseder, Angelika and Juliane Wetzel. *Lebensmut im Wartesaal. Die jüdischen DPs (Displaced Persons) im Nachkriegsdeutschland.* Frankfurt am Main: Fischer Taschenbuch, 1994.

Korn, Salomon. *Geteilte Erinnerung. Beiträge zur deutsch-jüdischen Gegenwart.* Berlin: Philo, 1999.

Kortner, Fritz. *Aller Tage Abend.* Munich: Kindler, 1959.

Koselleck, Reinhart. "Nachwort." In Charlotte Beradt. *Das Dritte Reich des Traums.* Frankfurt am Main: Suhrkamp, 1994. 117–32.

Küchler, Stefan. "DDR-Geschichtsbilder: Zur Interpretation des Nationalsozialismus im Geschichtsunterricht der DDR." *International Textbook Research* 22 (2000): 31–48.

Kugelmann, Cilly. "Jewish Museums in Germany: A German-Jewish Problem." *Speaking Out: Jewish Voices from United Germany.* Ed. Susan Stern. Chicago: edition q, 1995. 243 ff.

Kwiet, Konrad and Helmut Eschwege. *Selbstbehauptung und Widerstand: Deutsche Juden im Kampf um Existenz und Menschenwürde 1933–1945.* Hamburg: Christians, 1984.

LaCapra, Dominick. *Representing the Holocaust: History, Theory, Trauma.* Ithaca: Cornell University Press, 1994.

Lackmann, Thomas. *Jewrassic Park: Wie baut man (k)ein Jüdisches Museum in Berlin.* Berlin: Philo, 2000.

Ladd, Brian. *The Ghosts of Berlin: Confronting German History in the Urban Landscape.* Chicago: University of Chicago Press, 1997.

Lander, Jeannette. *Ein Sommer in der Woche der Itke K.* Frankfurt am Main: Suhrkamp, 1971.

———. *Im Jahrhundert der Herren.* Berlin: Aufbau, 1993.

———. *Überbleibsel. Eine kleine Erotik der Küche.* Berlin: Aufbau, 1995.

Eine unterbrochene Reise. Berlin: Aufbau, 1996.

———. *Robert.* Berlin: Aufbau, 1998.

Landresberg, Alison. "America, the Holocaust, and Mass Culture of Memory: Toward a Radical Politics of Empathy." *New German Critique* 71 (Spring-Summer 1997): 63–86.

Lang, Berel. *Act and Idea in the Nazi Genocide.* Chicago: University of Chicago Press, 1990.

———. *Holocaust Representation: Art within the Limits of History and Ethics.* Baltimore: Johns Hopkins University Press, 2000.

Langer, Lawrence. *The Age of Atrocity: Death in Modern Literature.* Boston: Beacon, 1978.

———. *The Holocaust and the Literary Imagination.* New Haven: Yale University Press, 1975.

———. *Holocaust Testimonies: The Ruins of Memory.* New Haven: Yale University Press, 1991.

———. *Versions of Survival: The Holocaust and the Human Spirit.* Albany: State University of New York Press, 1982.

Lappin, Elena, ed. *Jewish Voices, German Words: Growing up Jewish in Postwar Germany & Austria.* Trans. Krishna Winston. New Haven: Catbird Press, 1994.

Lautenschäger, Rolf. "Jüdisches Museum kommt jetzt in Etappen." *Die tageszeitung* 8 (April 8, 1999).

———. "Leerstelle füllt sich wieder." *die tageszeitung* (June 15, 2000): 19.

"Lehren aus dem Prozess gegen das Verschwörerzentrum Slánsky." *Dokumente der Sozialistischen Einheitspartei Deutschlands IV.* Berlin: Dietz, 1954. 199–219.

Levi, Primo. *Moments of Reprieve.* New York: Summit Books, 1986.

Levin, Meyer. *In Search: An Autobiography.* New York: Horizon Press, 1950.

Levinas, Emmanuel. *Outside the Subject.* Stanford: Stanford University Press, 1994.

———. "Ethics as First Philosophy." *The Levinas Reader,* ed. Sean Hand. Oxford: Blackwell, 1989.

Levy, Zwi Harry. *Der "Überrest Israels" in Deutschland. The Jewish Travel Guide.* Frankfurt am Main: 1953.

Libeskind, Daniel. "Between the Lines." *radix-matrix.* Munich and New York: Prestel, 1997.

———. "Out of Line, Berlin." *radix-matrix.* Munich and New York: Prestel, 1997.

———, and Kristen Feireiss. *Erweiterung des Berlin Museums mit Abteilung Jüdisches Museum.* Berlin: Ernst & Sohn, 1992.

———. *Realisierungs Wettbewerb: Werwiterung Berlin Museum mit Abteilung Jüdisches Museum.* Berlin: Senatsverwaltung für Bau- und Wohnungswesen, 1990.

Lichtenstein, Heiner, ed. *Die Fassbinder-Kontroverse oder Das Ende der Schonzeit.* Königstein: Äthenaum, 1986.

Linden, R. Ruth. *Making Stories, Making Selves: Feminist Reflections on the Holocaust.* Columbus: Ohio State University Press, 1993.

Liss, Andrea. *Trespassing Through Shadows. Memory, Photography, and the Holocaust.* Minneapolis: University of Minnesota Press, 1998.

Loeser, Franz. *Die unglaubwürdige Gesellschaft: Quo vadis, DDR?* Cologne: Bund-Verlag, 1984.

London, Arthur. *Ich gestehe: Der Prozess um Rudolf Slánsky.* Berlin: Aufbau, 1991 (reprint of the 1970 West German edition).

Lorenz, Dagmar C. G. *Verfolgung bis zum Massenmord: Holocaust-Diskurse in deutscher Sprache aus der Sicht der Verfolgten.* New York: Peter Lang, 1992.

———. "Memory and Criticism: Ruth Klüger's 'weiter leben.'" *Women in German Yearbook* 9 (1993): 207–23.

———. *Keepers of the Motherland.* Lincoln: University of Nebraska Press, 1996.

———. "Discovering and Making Memory: Jewish Cultural Expression in Contemporary Europe." *The German Quarterly* 73 (Spring 2000): 175–78.

Lyotard, Jean-Francois. *The Differend: Phrases in Dispute.* Trans. George Van Den Abbeele. Minneapolis: University of Minnesota Press, 1988.

Maginnis, John J. *Military Government Journal, Normandy to Berlin.* Amherst: University of Massachusetts Press, 1971.

Manschot, Anke. "Ook ik heb last gehad van een Assepoestercomplex: gesprek met de Duits-joodse schrijfster Grete Weil." *Vrij Nederland* Boekenbijlage (April 13, 1985): 8–10.

Maór, Harry. *"Über den Wiederaufbau der jüdischen Gemeinden in Deutschland seit 1945."* Ph.D. University of Mainz, 1961.

Mayer, Hans. *Außenseiter.* Frankfurt am Main: Suhrkamp, 1975.

———. *Ein Deutscher auf Widerruf: Erinnerungen.* 2 vols. Frankfurt am Main: Suhrkamp, 1984.

———. *Gelebte Literatur: Frankfurter Vorlesungen.* Frankfurt am Main: Suhrkamp, 1987.

———. *Der Turm von Babel: Erinnerung an eine Deutsche Demokratische Republik.* Frankfurt am Main: Suhrkamp, 1993.

———. *Wendezeiten: Über Deutsche und Deutschland.* Frankfurt am Main: Suhrkamp, 1993.

———. *Der Widerruf: Über Deutsche und Juden.* Frankfurt am Main: Suhrkamp, 1996.

————. *Zeitgenossen.* Frankfurt am Main: Suhrkamp, 1999.

————. *Deutsche Geschichte und Deutsche Aufklärung: Gedanken auf der Wartburg.* Sonderdruck. Frankfurt am Main: Suhrkamp, 1999.

Mendes-Flohr, Paul. *German Jews: a Dual Identity.* New Haven: Yale University Press, 1999.

Merker, Paul. *Deutschland: Sein oder Nicht-Sein? Vol 2: Das Dritte Reich und sein Ende.* Mexico, D. F.: El Libro Libre, 1944.

————. "Der neue Staat des jüdischen Volkes." *Neues Deutschland* (January 24, 1948).

————. "Hilters Antisemitismus und wir." *Freies Deutschland* 1 (October 1994): 11–12.

Mertens, Lothar. *Davidstern unter Hammer und Zirkel: Die Jüdischen Gemeinden in der SBZ/DDR und ihre Behandlung durch Partei und Staat 1945–1990.* Hildesheim: Olms, 1997.

Meyers, Carol. *Discovering Eve: Ancient Israelite Women in Context.* New York: Oxford University Press, 1988.

Mitgutsch, Anna. *Abschied von Jerusalem.* Berlin: Rowohlt, 1995.

Mitscherlich, Alexander and Margarete. *The Inability to Mourn.* Trans. Beverly R. Placzek. New York: Grove Press, 1975.

Moskowitz, Moses. "The Germans and the Jews: The Postwar Report. The Enigma of German Irresponsibility." *Commentary* 2 (1946): 7–14.

Müller, Inge. *Irgendwo: noch einmal möcht ich sehn. Lyrik, Prosa, Tagebücher. Mit Beiträgen zu ihrem Werk.* ed. Ines Geipel. Berlin: Aufbau, 1996.

Murphy, Robert. *Diplomat Among Warriors.* New York: Collins, 1964. 264.

Muschamp, Herbert. "Once Again, a City Rewards the Walker." *New York Times* (April 11, 1999).

Na'aman, Shlomo. *Marxismus und Zionismus.* Gerlingen: Bleicher, 1997.

Nachama, Andreas. "Nach der Befreiung: Jüdisches Leben in Berlin 1945–1953." In *Jüdische Geschichtein Berlin. Essays und Studien.* Ed. Reinhard Rürup. Berlin: Edition Hentrich, 1995. 268–72.

Noble, Philip. "The Mystic of Lindenstrasse." *Metropolis* (January 1999).

Novick, Peter. *The Holocaust in American Life.* Boston: Houghton Mifflin, 1999.

Nussbaum, Laureen, and Uwe Meyer. "Grete Weil: unbequem, zum Denken zwingend." *Exilforschung: Ein Internationales Jahrbuch.* Band 11 "Frauen und Exil: Zwischen Anpassung und Selbstbehauptung." Ed. Krohn et al. Munich: edition text + kritik, 1993. 156–70.

"Odyssey of a Berlin Emigrant through Asia—Return of 295." *Der Telegraf* (August 22, 1947).

Oesmann, Astrid. "Nathan der Weise: Suffering Lessing's 'Erziehung.'" *The German Review* 2 (1999): 131–45.

Offe, Sabine, *Ausstellungen, Einstellungen, Entstellungen: Jüdische Museen in Deutschland und Österreich.* Berlin: Philo, 2000.

Orbach, Larry and Vivien Orbach-Smith. *Soaring Underground: A Young Fugitive's Life in Nazi Berlin.* Washington, DC: Compass Press, 1996.

Ostow, Robin. *Jews in Contemporary East Germany: The Children of Moses in the Land of Marx.* New York: St. Martin's Press, 1989.

Ozick, Cynthia. "Why I Won't Go to Germany." *Harper's* (February 1989): 16–19.

Pagis, Dan. *The Selected Poetry.* Trans. Stephen Mitchell. Berkeley: University of California Press, 1989.

Patner, Andrew. "Filling a Void." *Madison* (July-Aug. 1999): 103.

Peck, Abraham J. *Archives of the Holocaust. Volume 9, The Papers of the World Jewish Congress 1945–1950: Liberation and the Saving Remnant.* New York: Garland, 1990. 398ff.

————. "Jewish Survivors of the Holocaust in Germany: Revolutionary Vanguard or Remnants of a Destroyed People?" *Tel Aviver Jahrbuch für deutsche Geschichte* 19 (1990).

Pelinka, Anton. "Österreich und Europa: Zur Isolierung eines Landes." *Europäische Rundschau* 1 (2000): 3–8.

Perloff, Marjorie. *Wittgenstein's Ladder: Poetic Language and the Strangeness of the Ordinary.* Chicago: University of Chicago Press, 1996.

Piedmont, Ferdinand. "Unterdrückt und rehabilitiert: Zur Theatergeschichte von Lessings *Nathan der Weise* von den zwanziger Jahren bis zur Gegenwart." *Lessing Yearbook* 19 (1987): 85–94.

Pinto, Diane. "The New Jewish Europe: Challenges and Responsibilities." *European Judaism* 31 (Autumn 1998): 3–15.

Plaskow, Judith. *Standing Again at Sinai: Judaism from a Feminist Perspective.* San Francisco: Harper, 1990.

Quandt, Helen, ed. *Salz der Tränen. Zeichnungen von Ladislaus Szücs.* Düsseldorf: Mahn und Gedenkstätte, 1999.

Rahlens, Holly Jane. *Becky Bernstein Goes to Berlin.* Munich: Piper, 1996.

Rappaport, Lynn. *Jews in Germany after the Holocaust: Memory, Identity and Jewish-German Relations.* Cambridge: Cambridge University Press, 1997.

Reich-Ranicki, Marcel. *Über Ruhestörer: Juden in der deutschen Literatur.* Rev. ed. Stuttgart: Deutsche Verlags-Anstalt, 1989.

————. *Lauter Verisse.* Munich: Deutscher Taschenbuch Verlag, 1992.

————. *Der Doppelte Boden: Ein Gespräch mit Peter von Matt.* Frankfurt am Main: Fischer, 1994.

————. *Mein Leben.* Stuttgart: Deutsche Verlags-Anstalt, 1999. Translated as *The Author of Himself: The Life of Marcel Reich-Ranicki.* Trans. Ewald Osers. Princeton: Princeton University Press, 2001.

————. "Eine Lebensgeschichte, die das Jahrhundert anklagt. Freund des Gesprächs, Virtuose der Polemik: Erinnerungen an Hans Mayer." *Frankfurter Allgemeine Zeitung* (May 21, 2001): Feuillton, 1.

Reichel, Peter. *Politik mit der Erinnerung.* Munich: Hanser, 1995.

Remmler, Karen. "Im Antlitz des Anderen: Video-Interviews von Überlebenden der Shoah." In *Verfolgung und Erinnerung.* Ed. Cathy Galbin and Eva Lezzi. Potsdam: Moses Mendelssohn Zentrum, 1998. 119–34.

Reuter, Elke and Detlef Hansel. *Das kurze Leben der VVN von 1947 bis 1953.* Berlin: Edition Ost, 1997.

Riesenburger, Martin. *Das Licht verlöschte nicht. Ein Zeugnis aus der Nacht des Faschismus.* Berlin: Union Verlag, 1958.

Riess, Curt. *Berlin! Berlin! 1945–1953.* Berlin: Non Stop Bücherei, 1953.

Rischbieter, Henning, "'Nathan'—Als Märchen" *Theater Heute* 3 (1983): 24–29.

Rohloff, Joachim. *Ich bin das Volk. Martin Walser und die Berliner Republik.* Hamburg: KVV Konkret, 1999.

Rosen, Charles. *Arnold Schoenberg.* Chicago: University of Chicago Press, 1996.

Rosenberg, Leibl. "Der Onkel aus Amerika: Eine Polemik gegen die Einmischung von US-Organisationen in deutsch-jüdische Angelegenheiten." *Allgemeine Jüdische Wochenzeitung* (May 25, 2000): 1.

Rosenthal, Hans. *Zwei Leben in Deutschland.* Bergisch Gladbach: Gustav Lübbe, 1980.

Rovit, Rebecca. "Collaboration on Survival, 1933–1938: Reassessing the Role of the *Jüdischer Kulturbund.*" In *Theater in the Third Reich: The Prewar Years.* Ed. Glen W. Gadberry. Westport, CT: Greenwood, 1995. 141–56.

Rugoff, Ralph. "Cathedrals for our Times." *Financial Times* (April 24, 1999).

Rühle, Günther. "Wie zeigt man auf Wunden?" *Theater Heute* 12 (1979): 6–9.

Runge, Irene, ed. *"Ich bin kein Russe": Jüdische Zuwanderer zwischen 1989 und 1994.* Berlin: Deitz, 1995.

Ryback, Timothy. *The Last Survivor: In Search of Martin Zaidenstadt.* New York: Pantheon, 1999.

Said, Edward. "Reflections on Exile." In *Out There: Marginalization and Contemporary Cultures.* Ed. Russel Ferguson, Martha Gever, Trinh T. Minh-ha, and Cornel West. Cambridge, MA: MIT University Press, 1990. 357–66.

———. *Representations of the Intellectual.* New York: Pantheon Books, 1994.

Santner, Eric. *Stranded Objects: Mourning, Memory, and Film in Postwar Germany.* Ithaca: Cornell University Press, 1990.

Sayre, Joel. "Letter from Berlin." *The New Yorker* (July 28, 1945).

Schirrmacher, Frank, ed. *Die Walser-Bubis Debatte.* Frankfurt am Main: Suhrkamp, 1999.

Schivelbusch, Wolfgang. *In a Cold Crater: Cultural and Intellectual Life in Berlin 1945- 1948.* Berkeley: University of California Press, 1998.

Schlink, Bernard. *The Reader.* Trans. Carol Brown Janeway. New York: Pantheon Books, 1997.

Schmidt, Willi. "Rückkehr zu Nathan, dem Weisen." In *Fritz Wisen: Drei Leben für das Theater.* Ed, Jörg Gronius. Berlin: Akademie der Künste, 1990. 106–13.

Schneider, Bernhard. *Daniel Libeskind: Jewish Museum of Berlin. Between the Lines.* Munich: Prestel, 1999.

Schoeps, Julius H., Willi Jasper, and Bernhard Vogt, eds. *Ein neues Judentum in Deustschland? Fremd- und Eigenbilder der russisch-jüdischen Einwanderer.* Potsdam: Verlag für Berlin-Brandenburg, 1999.

Schorske, Carl. *Thinking with History.* Princeton: Princeton University Press, 1998.

Scholem, Gershom. "Against the Myth of the German-Jewish Dialogue." In *On Jews and Judaism: Selected Essays.* New York: Schocken, 1976. 61–4.

Schüler, Thomas. "Das Wiedergutmachungsgesetz vom 14. September 1945." *Jahrbuch für Antisemitismusforschung 2.* Frankfurt am Main: Campus, 1993. 118–38.

Schultz, Hans Jürgen, ed. *Mein Judentum.* Stuttgart: Kreuz Verlag, 1978.

Schütze, Peter. *Fritz Kortner.* Reinbek bei Hamburg: Rowohlt, 1994.

Schwab, Gustav. *Grieske Mythen en Sagen.* Trans. J. K. van den Brink. Utrecht: Het Spectrum, 1956.

Schwanitz, Dietrich. *Shylock: Von Shakespeare bis zum Nürnberger Prozeß.* Hamburg: Krämer, 1989.

———. *Das Shylock-Syndrom oder die Dramaturgie der Barbarei.* Frankfurt am Main: Eichborn, 1997.

Segal, Lore. "Memory: The Problems of Imagining the Past." In *Writing and the Holocaust.* Ed. Berel Lang. New York: Holmes & Meier, 1988. 56–65.

Seligmann, Rafael. *Israels Sicherheitspolitik.* Munich: Bernard and Graefe, 1982.

———. *Rubensteins Versteigerung.* Frankfurt am Main: Eichborn, 1990.

———. *Die jiddische Manne.* Frankfurt am Main: Eichborn, 1990.

———. *Mit beschränkter Hoffnung: Juden, Deutsche, Israelis.* Hamburg: Hoffmann und Campe, 1991.

———. "What Keeps Jews in Germany Quiet?" *Reemerging Jewish Culture in Germany: Life and Literature Since 1989.* ed. Sander L. Gilman and Karen Remmler. New York: New York University Press, 1994. 173–83.

———. *Das deutsch-jüdische Verhältnis: Bestandsaufnahme und Perspektiven.* Hannover: Rudolf von Benningsen Stiftung, 1994–1995.

———. *Der Musterjude.* Munich: Piper, 1997.

———. *Schalom meine Liebe.* Munich: DTV, 1998.

———. "Nicht in jüdischer Macht. Von der Mehrheit allein gelassen, der Selbstisolation bezichtigt—Erfahrungen im veränderten Deutschland." *Die Zeit* (November 25, 1999).

———. *Der Milchmann.* Munich: DTV, 1999.

Semprun, Jorge. *Literature or Life.* Trans. Linda Coverdale. New York: Viking, 1997.

Shandley, Robert R. ed. *Unwilling Germans? The Goldhagen Debate.* Trans. Jeremiah Riemer. Minneapolis: University of Minnesota Press, 1998.

Silbermann, Alphons. *Was ist jüdischer Geist? Zur Identität der Juden.* Zurich: Edition Interfrom, 1984.

———. *Verwandlungen. Eine Autobiographie.* Bergisch Gladbach: Lübbe, 1989.

———. *Propheten des Untergangs. Das Geschäft mit den Angsten.* Bergisch Gladbach: Lübbe, 1995.

———. *Von der Kunst der Arschkriecherei.* Reinbek bei Hamburg: Rowohlt, 1998.

Silbermann, Alphons and Herbert Sallen. *Juden in Westdeutschland. Selbstbild und Fremdbild einer Minorität.* Cologne: Verlag Wissenschaft und Politik, 1992.

Silbermann, Alphons and Manfred Stoffers. *Auschwitz: Nie davon gehört? Erinnern und Vergessen in deutschland.* Berlin: Rowohlt, 2000.

Smith, Jean Edward. *The Defense of Berlin.* Baltimore, MD: Johns Hopkins Press, 1963.

Smith, Sidonie. *A Poetics of Women's Autobiography: Marginality and the Fictions of Self-Representation.* Bloomington: Indiana University Press, 1987.

Sophocles. *Die Tragödien.* Trans. Heinrich Weinstock. Stuttgart: Kröner Verlag, 1962.

Speier, Hans. *From the Ashes of Disgrace: A Journal from Germany 1945–1955.* Amherst, MA: University of Massachusetts Press, 1981.

Stadelmaier, Gerhard. *Lessing auf der Bühne: Ein Klassiker im Theateralltag (1968-1974)*. Tübingen: Niemeyer, 1980.

———. "Lessings unmenschliche Märchenmenschlichkeit." *Theater Heute* 5 (1981): 38- 39.

———. "Satan der Weise." *Frankfurter Allgemeine Zeitung* (November 16, 1991).

———. "Tut nichts, der Jude wird verkannt." *Frankfurter Allgemeine Zeitung* (October 10, 1994).

Steiner, George. *Language and Silence*. New York: Atheneum, 1986.

Stern, Frank. *The Whitewashing of the Yellow Badge: Antisemitism and Philosemitism in Postwar Germany*. Oxford: Pergamon, 1992.

———. "Antagonistic Memories: The Post-War Survival and Alienation of Jews and Germans." *Memory and Totalitarianism: International Yearbook of Oral History and Life Stories*. Vol. I. Ed. Luisa Passerini. New York: Oxford University Press, 1992.

———. *Facing the Past: Representations of the Holocaust in German Cinema since 1945*. Washington, DC: United States Holocaust Memorial Museum, Center for Advanced Holocaust Studies, 2000.

Stern, Guy. "Barbara Honigmann: A Preliminary Assessment." In *Bridging the Abyss: Reflections on Jewish Suffering, Anti-Semitism, and Exile*. Ed. Amy Colin and Elisabeth Strenger. Munich: Fink, 1994.

Stern, Susan, ed. *Speaking Out: Jewish Voices from United Germany*. Chicago: edition q, 1995.

Swabey, Marie Collins. *Comic Laughter: A Philosophical Essay*. New Haven: Yale University Press, 1961.

Szücs, Ladislaus. *Zählappell: Als Arzt im Konzentrationslager*. Frankfurt am Main: Fischer Taschenbuch Verlag, 1995.

Tabori, George. "Ein Goi bleibt immer ein Goi . . ." *Unterammergau oder Die guten Deutschen*. Frankfurt am Main: Suhrkamp, 1981.

Tanakh: A New Translation of the Holy Scriptures According to the Hebrew Text. Philadelphia: The Jewish Publication Society, 1985.

Telushkin, Joseph. *Biblical Literacy: The Most Important People, Events, and Ideas of the Hebrew Bible*. New York: William Morrow and Company, 1997.

Timm, Angelika. *Alles umsonst? Verhandlungen zwischen der Claims Conference und der DDR über "Wiedergutmachung" und Entschädigung*. Berlin: Helle Panke, 1996.

———. "Assimilation of History: The GDR and the State of Israel." *The Jerusalem Journal of International Relations* 14 (1992): 33–47.

———. *Hammer, Zirkel, Davidstern: Das gestörte Verhältnis der DDR zu Zionismus und Staat Israel*. Bonn: Bouvier, 1997.

Traverso, Enzo. *The Marxists and the Jewish Question: The History of a Debate, 1843-1943*. Atlantic Highlands, NJ: Humanities Press, 1994.

Tress, Madeleine. "Soviet Jews in the Federal Republic of Germany: The Rebuilding of a Community." *Jewish Journal of Sociology* 37 (1995): 39–43.

Van Dis, Adriaan. "Nee seggen is de enige onverwoestbare vrijheid." *NRC Handelsblad*. Cultureel Supplement (November 12, 1982): 3.

Völker, Klaus. *Fritz Kortner: Schauspieler und Regisseur*. Berlin: Hentrich, 1993.

Wallach, Erica. *Licht um Mitternacht: Fünf Jahre in der Welt der Verfemten.* Munich: List, 1969.

Wapnewski, Peter, ed. *Betrifft Literatur: Über Marcel-Reich Ranicki.* Stuttgart: Deutsche Verlags-Anstalt, 1990.

Wegner, Judith Romney. *Chattel or Person? The Status of Women in the Mishnah.* New York: Oxford University Press, 1988.

Weigel, Gerd and Johannes Klotz, ed. *Geistige Brandstiftung? Die Walser-Bubis Debatte.* Cologne: PappyRossa, 1999.

Weigel, Sigrid. *Ingeborg Bachmann. Hinterlassenschaften unter Wahrung des Briefgeheimnisses.* Vienna: Paul Zsolnay, 1999.

Weil, Grete. *Ans Ende der Welt.* Frankfurt am Main: Fischer Taschenbuch Verlag, 1987. (1949).

———. *Tramhalte Beethovenstraat.* Frankfurt am Main: Fischer Taschenbuch Verlag, 1983 (1963).

———. *Happy, sagte der Onkel.* Frankfurt am Main: Fischer Taschenbuch Verlag, 1982 (1968).

———. *Meine Schwester Antigone.* Frankfurt am Main: Fischer Taschenbuch Verlag, 1982 (1980).

———. *Generationen.* Frankfurt am Main: Fischer Taschenbuch Verlag, 1985 (1983).

———. *Der Brautpreis.* Frankfurt am Main: Fischer Taschenbuch Verlag, 1991 (1988).

———. *Spätfolgen: Erzählungen.* Zurich: Nagel und Kimche, 1992.

Weinland, Martina and Kurt Winkler, eds. *Das Jüdische Museum im Stadtmuseum Berlin.* Berlin: Nicolai, 1997.

Weissman, Gary. "Lawrence Langer and 'The Holocaust Experience.'" *Response: A Contemporary Jewish Review* 68 (1998): 78–97.

Welker, Andrea and Tina Berger, eds. *'Ich wollte meine Tochter läge tot zu meinen Füßen und hätte die Juwelen in den Ohren': Improvisationen über Shakespeares Shylock.* Munich: Hanser, 1979.

Werkbund-Arkiv, Ed. *Bucklicht Männlein und Engel der Geschichte: Walter Benjamin, Theoretiker der Moderne.* Giessen: Annabas, 1990.

White, Hayden. "Historical Emplotment and the Problem of Truth." In *Probing the Limits of Representation: Nazism and the "Final Solution."* Ed. Saul Friedländer. Cambridge, MA: Harvard University Press, 1992.

Wilkomirski, Binjamin. *Fragments: Memories of a Childhood, 1938–1948.* New York: Schocken, 1996.

Wirth, Andrej. "Doesn't Matter." *Theater Heute* 7 (1983): 45.

Wise, Michael Z. *Capital Dilemma: Germany's Search for a New Architecture of Democracy.* New York: Princeton Architectural Press, 1998.

———. "Daniel Libeskind." *Art News* (November 1998): 135.

Wistrich, Robert S. "Fateful Trap: The German-Jewish Symbiosis." *Tikkun* 5.2 (March- April 1990): 34–38.

Wolffsohn, Michael. "Plea for an Inwardly Directed Nationalism." In *Speaking Out: Jewish Voices from United Germany.* Ed. Susan Stern. Chicago: edition q, 1995.

Wyden, David. *Stella: One Woman's True Tale of Evil, Betrayal, and Survival in the Holocaust.* New York: Simon and Schuster, 1992.

Yehudah Bauer. *Flight and Rescue: Bricha.* New York: Random House, 1970.

Young, James E. *At Memory's Edge: After-Images of the Holocaust in Contemporary Art and Architecture.* New Haven: Yale University Press, 2000.

————. *The Texture of Memory: Holocaust Memorial and Meaning.* New Haven: Yale University Press, 1993.

————. *Writing and Rewriting the Holocaust: Narrative and the Consequences of Interpretation.* Bloomington: University of Indiana Press, 1988.

Zachau, Reinhard. "Das Originalmanuskript zu Wolfgang Koeppens *Jacob Littners Aufzeichunungen aus einem Erdloch.*" *Colloquia Germanica* 32 (1999): 124ff.

Zadek, Peter. *My Way: Eine Autobiographie, 1926–1969.* Cologne: Kiepenheuer & Witsch, 1998.

Zentralwohlfahrtsstelle der Juden in Deutschland, ed. *Mitgliederstatistik der einzelnen jüdischen Gemeinden und Landesverbände in Deutschland per 1. Januar 1999.* Frankfurt am Main: 1999.

Zertal, Idith. *From Catastrophe to Power: Holocaust Survivors and the Emergence of Israel.* Berkeley: University of California Press, 1998.

Zipes, Jack. *The Operated Jew: Two Tales of Anti-Semitism.* New York: Routledge, 1991.

————. "The Contemporary German Fascination for Things Jewish: Toward a Jewish Minor Culture." In *Reemerging Jewish Culture in Germany: Life and Literature Since 1989.* Eds. Sander Gilman and Karen Remmler. New York: New York University Press, 1994. 15–45.

————. "The Negative German-Jewish Symbiosis." *Insiders and Outsiders: Jewish and Gentile Culture in Germany and Austria.* Ed. Dagmar C. G. Lorenz, and Gabriele Weinberger. Detroit: Wayne University Press, 1994. 144–54.

Zuckermann, Moshe. *Gedenken und Kulturindustrie. Ein Essay zur neuen deutschen Normalität.* Berlin: Philo, 1999.

Zuckmayer, Carl. *Als wär's ein Stuck von mir. Horen der Freundschaft.* Vienna: S. Fischer Verlag, 1966. 551–52.

INDEX

Abusch, Alexander, 144–145, 152, 193
Adass Jissroel, 50
Adelson, Leslie, 25, 214, 229
Adorno, Theodor W., , 5, 8, 18–19, 28,
    97, 176, 184–185, 189, 198
Adultery, 216–217, 229
African Americans, 253
Alexanderplatz, 160
Alienation, 92, 113, 205, 212
Aliyah, 56, 93, 146
Allgemeine Jüdische Wochenzeitung, 103,
    116, 172, 178
Allianza Nationale, 122–123, 131
Allied *Kommandatura,* 73, 93
American GIs, 72
American Jewish Distribution
    Committee (AJDC), 69, 74–76,
    89, 95, 111, 149
American Zone, 50, 68, 71, 73, 93,
    110
Americanization, 172, 178
Améry, Jean, 204, 226
Amsterdam Treaty, 120, 122
Andreas-Friedrich, Ruth, 64, 91
Anschluss, 126–127, 129, 133
Antelme, Robert, 293, 295, 298, 304
Anti-Americanism, 136
Anti-Semitism, 4–5, 7, 23, 40, 50,
    52–53, 57, 76, 79–80, 84–87,
    95, 97–98, 101, 103–111,
    113–116, 119, 122–123,
    130–132, 134, 136, 138, 141,
    143, 145, 147, 149–154, 172,
    189–190, 194, 235, 237–240,
    242–246, 251–252, 254–259,
    263–264, 266, 269–270,
    272–273, 275–276, 284, 286,
    289
Anti-Zionism, 57, 107, 147
Arafat, Yasser, 131
Archives, 58, 90, 99, 152, 154, 179,
    291, 295, 304
Arendt, Hannah, 14, 32, 98
Aryanism, 85, 114, 130
Ashkenazi Jews, 284, 287
Assmann, Aleida, 234, 241, 246, 249
Association of Germans of Jewish Faith,
    82
Association of Persecutees of National
    Socialism (VVN), 79
Association of Victims of Nazism, 142
Aufbau, 28, 153, 271, 290
Aufklärung, 198, 200
Auschwitz–Birkenau, 220
Austria, 27, 119–133, 137–140, 191,
    203–205, 225–226, 231, 255,
    277–282, 286, 290
    Catholics, 134
    Civil War, 128
    Exceptionalism ("Austro-
        chauvinism"), 119, 121, 123,
        125, 127, 129, 131, 133, 135,
        137, 139
    Fascism, 128, 131, 133
    Freedom Party (FPOe), 119–126,
        129, 131–139, 282
    Jews in, 119, 131, 204–205, 213,
        220, 226, 289
    Marxism, 130
    Nazism, 135
    People's Party (OeVP), 120, 122,
        131–135, 139, 282

Republic, 286, 133
SPOe (Social Democratic Party), 120, 129–134, 139

Bachmann, Ingeborg, 11–12, 14, 27, 194, 294
Baeck, Rabbi Leo, 52, 110
Baltic Jews, 54
Barlog, Boleslaw, 238, 247–248
Barthes, Roland, 297–298, 301, 304–305
Barzel, Amnon, 156, 160
Bauer, Fritz/Fritz Bauer Institut, 35, 42, 93
Bauer, Leo, 144, 152
Bavaria, 49, 51, 56, 110–111, 272
Bayerdörfer, Hans-Peter, 246, 249
Bebel, August, 145, 153
Beckermann, Ruth, 277–279, 281, 283–284, 290
Beck, Gad, 246, 68, 83, 93–94, 96–97
Behrens, Katja, 7, 277, 280–281, 283, 290
Belgium, 113, 120, 127, 131, 204
Belsen, 88
Bendt, Veronika, 159, 174–175
Benjamin, Walter, 11–12, 18, 157, 165–166, 175–176, 246, 249–250
Benn, Gottfried, 44
Benz, Wolfgang, 101–102, 104, 106, 108, 110, 112, 114, 116, 294
Berlin, 7–8, 13–14, 19–20, 22–24, 28–29, 35, 39, 44, 50–51, 53, 57–61, 63–86, 88–90, 92, 102, 108, 110, 128, 144, 155–157, 159, 165, 171, 173–174, 186, 192, 194, 234–235, 248, 255–257, 280
    Community, 50–51, 59–60, 75, 79, 92, 150, 158–159, 238
    Holocaust Memorial, 57, 178
    Jewish Club, 69
    Jewish Museum, 8, 58, 155, 158, 162, 168, 171, 173–174, 176,

Berlin Jews, 8, 51, 58, 64, 69, 72, 76, 81–82, 86, 88–89, 92, 155, 158–159, 162, 168, 171, 173–174, 176, 178
    Museums, 28, 57–58, 161, 175
    Republic, 19–20, 28, 245–246
Berlin Wall, 53, 128, 155, 188, 244
Berliner Almanach, 94
Berliner Forum, 175
Berliner Tageblatt, 76
Berliner Zeitung, 70, 175
Berliners, 13, 28, 64–65, 67–68, 70, 76, 86–87, 89, 92, 94, 174–175, 246
Bible (Torah, Tanakh, Old & New Testament), 108, 215–218, 230, 285
Biller, Maxim, 27, 197, 263–265, 267, 269–270, 274–276, 306
Birkenau, 78
Bitburg, 53, 127, 242, 279
Blanchot, Maurice, 293, 295
Bloch, Ernst, 184, 186–189
Blumenthal, W. Michael, 160, 170, 176–177, 179
Bodemann, Michal, 82, 92, 96–97
Böll, Heinrich, 194–195
Bolshevism, 42, 108, 125, 150
Bonn, 35, 38, 54, 105, 152–153, 248
Borneman, John, 96
Brandt, Willy, 127, 131, 196
Brecht, Bertolt, 70, 187–188
Brenner, Michael, 7, 49–50, 52, 54, 56, 58, 60–61, 92, 97, 158, 175,
Bricha Network, 68, 74–75, 93–95
British Jews, 67, 74
Broder, Henryk M., 57, 103, 116, 172, 178, 197, 247, 275, 277, 281, 289
Brother Eichmann, 36, 249
Brumlik, Micha, 57, 113, 117, 197, 226, 275
Buber, Martin, 252
Bubis, Ignatz, 39, 57, 104–105, 115
Buchenwald, 8–10, 83, 244
Büchner, Georg, 186

Budapest, 299
Bullock, Marcus, 176
Bundesarchiv, 152
Bundesländer, 244
Bundesregierung, 140
Bundesrepublik (*see* German Republic),
    116, 275, 283, 290
Bundestag, 57, 127
Burgtheater, 236, 126
Burschenschaften, 134
Busse, 67, 70, 78, 86–89, 94, 96, 98

Campe, 117, 290
Canaris, Volker, 237–238, 247–248
Canetti, Elias, 281
Canetti, Veza, 281, 289
Catholicism, 102, 106, 134, 149, 282,
    302
CDU (*see* Christian Democratic Party),
    88, 129, 139
Celan, Paul, 10–14, 27, 157, 165, 168,
    297, 303
Central Council of Jews, 52, 57, 104,
    112–113, 115
Chabad, 59
Chaluzi, Chug, 68, 94
Chancellery (*Reichs Kanslerei*), 64, 71
Charlottenburg, 68–69
Cheka, 124
Chernobyl, 288
Chirac, Jacques, 120
Christian Democratic Party (CDU),
    41, 57
Christian Germans, 24, 185
Christians, 24, 41, 57, 88, 92, 102,
    106, 130, 133, 183, 185–187,
    236, 241, 283
Churban (*see* Holocaust)
Club Seagull, 71
Club Voltaire, 290
Cohen, Hermann, 251, 260
Cohn-Bendit, Daniel, 121, 292
Cold War, 7, 71, 85, 90, 135, 260
Communism, 52, 63, 68, 70–71, 80,
    83–84, 95–96, 107–109,

141–147, 149–150, 153–154,
    185–187, 193–194, 261, 266
Communist International (Comintern),
    141, 151
Communist Party, 142, 146–147,
    186–187, 193
Communists in East Germany,
    153–154
Cosmopolitanism, 4–5, 7–8, 16–23,
    147, 173, 178, 251, 286–287
Cyclon B, 108
Czaplicka, John, 175
Czechoslovakian Communist Party, 146
Czechoslovakia, 35, 49, 77, 110, 112,
    127, 143, 146–147, 150, 231
Czernowitz, 102

Dachau, 250, 301
Darville, Helen (*see also* Helen
    Demidenko), 300
DDR (*see also* German Democratic
    Republic, GDR), 152–154
"Deconstructivist Architecture"
    exhibition, 156
Demidenko, Helen (*see also* Helen
    Darville), 15, 292–293, 296,
    300, 302, 305
Democracy, 5, 20–22, 35, 44, 52, 54,
    68, 80, 85, 88, 114, 120, 122,
    125–126, 130–133, 136–137,
    140–142, 145–146, 153, 174,
    186–188, 207
Democratic Republic, 22, 141,
    187–188, 190–191, 244, 279
Derrida, Jacques, 165, 176
Deutsch, Ernst, 70, 235–236, 238,
    246
Deutsche Juden (German Jews), 92
Deutschkron, Inge, 93
Deutschland (Germany), 60–61, 93,
    95, 97, 116–117, 145, 150,
    153–154, 186–188, 226, 228,
    251, 261, 275–276
Diary of Anne Frank, 236
Die Zeit, 189, 194, 249–250, 91, 117

Diner, Dan, 173, 179, 197, 205,
226–227, 263, 275–276, 291,
32–33, 45, 57
Dischereit, Esther, 24, 28, 103, 116,
197, 277, 280–281, 285,
288–290
Dische, Irene, 280–283
Displaced Persons (DPs), 74, 79, 95,
111
Döblin, Alfred, 44
Dos Passos, John, 64, 72, 91, 95
Dösseker, Bruno Dösseker, 300
Dreyfus (as role for stage), 258
Dritte Reich (see Third Reich)
Duras, Marguerite, 294, 296

East Berlin, 159–160, 227, 150
East Europe, 66
East Europeans, 23, 31–32, 50–55, 57,
59, 63, 68–69, 73–76, 80, 90,
92, 97, 110–113, 124, 128, 131,
146, 153, 188, 264, 268, 279
East German Jews, 149
East German PENs, 43
East Germans, 53, 142, 189
Eastern European DPs, 51, 80
Eastern European Jewish DPs, 55, 75
Eastern European Jews, 59, 76, 90,
112–113, 131, 268
Eastern Territories, 31–32
Eastern Bloc/Eastern Europe, 23,
31–32, 50–55, 57, 59, 63,
68–69, 74–76, 80, 90, 110–113,
124, 128, 131, 146, 153, 188,
264, 268, 279
Eichmann, Adolf (Eichmann Trial),
35–36, 237, 249, 279
Eisenman, Peter, 170
"Elders of Zion, Protocols of the," 146
Emigration, 9, 34, 43, 52, 54, 67, 75,
87–89, 97, 103, 107, 110, 144,
147, 168, 171, 206, 220, 235,
255, 265, 299–300
English Language, 199, 221
Erosion of Memory, 246, 289

Eroticism (Erotik), 124, 268–269, 272,
275, 290
Ethnic Distinction, 17, 53–54, 63, 73,
160, 171, 173, 205, 252, 289,
294, 306
European Commission, 120, 122
European Jewry, 23, 53, 55, 59, 65, 68,
75–76, 90, 112–113, 131, 141,
145, 203, 268, 282, 284, 287
European Union (EU), 55, 119–126,
135
Expressionism, 186, 235, 266
Ezrahi, Sidra DeKoven, 212–214, 228

Fabian, Hans Erich, 85–86, 90, 95, 97,
99
Fascism (Faschismus), 67, 72, 79, 82,
94, 121, 123, 133, 136, 142,
148, 160, 185
Fassbinder, Rainer Werner, 36, 53, 57,
104, 114, 116, 127, 190,
195–196, 233, 242–243, 245,
261
Fassbinder Scandal, 57, 190, 195, 243
Federal Republic of Germany
(FDR/FRG), 61, 101, 114, 139,
190, 196, 280, 283
Fejtö, François, 146, 153
Felman, Shoshana, 225, 232
Felstiner, John, 27
Feminism, 208, 217, 230, 280, 287
Fest, Joachim, 195, 281
Feuchtwanger, Lion, 248
Fin-de-Siècle Vienna (see Vienna)
Final Solution, 65, 114, 255, 305
Finkielkraut, Alain, 292, 302–303
First Republic, 128, 130, 136
Fischer, Barbara, 245, 247, 250, 290
Fischer, Erika, 93, 97
Fischer, Joschka, 120
Fleischmann, Lea, 278–279, 281–283,
285, 290
Free Germany (Freies Deutschland),
153, 186–187, 192
Freedom Party, 119–120, 135, 282

Freedom (Freiheit), 20, 89, 91, 94, 115, 119–120, 135, 138, 187, 198–199, 212–213, 228, 272, 280, 282, 286
Fremont, Helen, 292, 296, 302–303, 306
French Jews, 297
Freud, Siegmund, 11
Freudenheim, Tom, 177
Freund, Elisabeth, 96, 200
FRG (see Federal Republic of Germany)
Friedländer, Saul, 305
Friedrich Wilhelm I, 160
Fried, Erich, 196, 281
Friends of Austrian Labor, 130
Führer, Der (see also Hitler), 39, 42
Fürtwangler, Wilhelm, 75, 89

Galinski, Heinz, 57, 150, 159, 238
Gay Jews (see Homosexuality)
GDR (see German Democratic Republic)
Gehry, Frank, 167
Geisel, Eike, 247
Gelber, Mark, 248
Genocide, 20, 102, 104, 109–110, 114, 127, 142, 151, 208, 219, 226, 254, 263, 266, 269, 279, 282, 294–295, 298, 304–305
German Armed Forces, 22, 278
German Cinema, 94, 254
German Democracy, 20, 114
German Democratic Republic (GDR), 22–23, 25, 43, 53, 61, 67, 107, 141, 143, 147–152, 187–188, 190–191, 237, 244, 248, 277, 279, 284–285
German Enlightenment, 189, 191, 197, 199, 222
German History (Deutsche Geschichte), 93, 198, 200
German Identity, 8, 22
German Jews, 4–8, 10–11, 14–15, 18–19, 21–22, 24, 31, 36, 38, 51–53, 55–57, 59–60, 63, 67,

71–72, 75–76, 79–80, 85–90, 92, 95–97, 105, 109–114, 149, 158, 160, 165, 167, 170–173, 178, 183, 185, 191, 197, 199, 203–206, 208, 211, 219–222, 226, 228, 231, 246–247, 251, 254–255, 263–265, 268, 270, 274, 292, 300
German Culture (Kultur), 82
German Wehrmacht, 211
"Germanies," 7, 52, 97, 153, 198
Germanization, 281
Gestapo, 41, 66, 81–82, 93, 106, 204, 266
Geyer, Michael, 18, 28, 303, 306
Ghetto (see also Warsaw Ghetto), 90, 111, 114, 186, 193, 211, 239, 243, 273, 299
Gilman, Sander L., 200, 229, 249, 289
Giordano, Ralph, 35, 44, 103, 116
God, 17, 64, 69, 102, 167, 206, 217–218, 245
Goebbels, Joseph, 42, 108, 231
Goldenbogen, Nora, 143, 152
Goldene Medine, 54
Goldhagen Debate, 16, 57, 115, 128, 142, 171, 177, 244, 261, 272
Goldmann, Nahum, 99, 289
Gorbachev, Mikhail, 151
Göttingen, 61, 116, 200, 220, 247, 290
Grand Coalition, 129
Grass, Günter, 14, 193, 195
Greek Culture & Mythology, 209, 215, 219, 226
Green Party, 57, 120, 122
Grief, 32, 41, 81, 238, 295–296, 304
Guilt, 34, 83, 88, 109, 145, 236
Gulf War, Persian, 38, 285

Haiderism, 119
Haider, Jörg, 119–121, 123–126, 128–132, 134–135, 137–139, 279, 282
Hamm, Peter, 231

Haraszti, Miklos, 124
Harlan, Veit, 248
Hartewig, Karin, 152
Hebrew Bible, 216, 230
Heidegger, Martin, 10–14, 27
Heidelberg University, 53, 55, 60, 290
Heine, Heinrich, 195, 241, 249, 258, 274
Herf, Jeffrey, 97, 145, 153–154
Herz, Henriette, 82
Heschel, Susannah, 174, 230
High Holidays (Rosh Hashana & Yom Kippur), 71
Hildesheim, 154, 196, 276
Hilsenrath, Edgar, 274, 283
Hirsch, Marianne, 295, 303
Historians' Debate (*Historiker–Debatte*, *Historikerstreit*), 190, 242, 248
Hitler Youth (Hitler Jugend), 133, 269
Hitler, Adolf, 10, 16, 33, 51, 64–65, 80, 88, 106–108, 110, 114, 116, 123, 127, 142, 148, 158, 206, 209, 231, 251, 266, 272, 281, 283, 306
    Antisemitism of, 153
Hitler's Willing Executioners (*see also* Goldhagen Debate), 16, 142
Hochhuth, Rolf, 237
Hoffmann, E. T. A., 117, 157, 168, 173, 290
Hölderlin, Friedrich, 228
Holland (*see also* Netherlands), 206
Hollywood, 71, 75, 115, 235, 241, 253, 255, 257
Holocaust (Shoah, Churban, Kurban), 6–7, 12–16, 20–24, 27, 29, 50–52, 56–57, 61, 93–94, 99, 102–103, 106, 108–109, 112–115, 127–128, 142, 156–157, 159, 167–174, 176–178, 185, 190, 192, 197, 203–205, 207–208, 214, 219–226, 228, 232, 234–237, 240–242, 244–246, 249, 251, 257, 260, 263–265, 267–270, 272–285, 288–289, 291–294, 296–298, 301–306
    Discourse on (*Holocaust–Diskurse*), 81, 172, 211, 221, 224, 242
    Memorial, 20, 22, 36, 94, 102, 128, 170, 177–178, 281
    Memorial Day (Yom haShoah), 102
    Museum, 173, 177
    Representation of, 293, 305
    Survivors of, 29, 52, 94, 108, 156, 171, 280, 282
    Tower (part of Museum complex), 14, 168–169, 171, 178
Holy Ark (Ark of the Covenant), 216
Homosexuality, 93, 187, 192
Horkheimer, Max, 8, 18, 184–186, 198
Humor, 235, 264, 274–276
Hungarian Jews, 102, 196
Huyssen, Andreas, 167, 175–176

Immigration, 52–56, 60, 88, 103, 107, 112, 257, 279, 282
Integration, 44, 55–56, 60, 107, 114, 130, 160, 175, 252
Isenberg, Noah, 7–8, 13–14
Israel, 34, 36, 40, 53–54, 56, 58, 60, 94, 105, 107–109, 111–113, 129, 145–148, 151–154, 156, 168, 216–219, 230, 249, 257, 273, 278, 280, 283–284, 288, 290
    Israeli Jews, 22, 35, 38, 53, 103, 113, 117, 196, 270, 274
    Israeli-Arabs, 143
Italy, 37, 93, 131, 135, 138
    Fascism in, 123

Jaspers, Karl, 14, 32
Jenninger, Philip, 127
Jewification (Verjudung), 173
Jewish Americans, 16, 302–303
Jewish Berliners, 92
Jewish Bolshevism, 150

Jewish Committee, 58, 61
Jewish Communists, 80, 96, 143, 150
Jewish Council, 193, 206, 209, 227
Jewish Culture, 23, 25, 50, 54, 58,
    103, 111, 151, 157–158, 175,
    197, 200, 218–219, 264,
    279–280, 289
Jewish DPs, 50–52, 55, 73, 75, 90, 111
Jewish Germans (see also German Jews),
    114, 274
Jewish *Heimkehrer*, 85
Jewish Holocaust, 52, 280
Jewish *Kulturbund*, 235
Jewish Law, 216–217, 229–230
Jewish Museum (Berlin), 174, 177
Jewish Museum, 7–8, 13–14, 28, 281,
    58, 102, 155–156, 158–162,
    165, 168, 170–174, 176–179
Jewish Old Age Home, 69
Jewish Question, 141, 148, 151,
    153–154, 190, 256
Jewish Relief Unit, 74, 89
Jewish SED, 149
Jewish Socialists, 284
Jewish Survivors, 50, 52, 65, 68, 73,
    82–84, 93–94, 110–111, 142,
    221, 254, 278, 280, 282
Jewish Symbiosis, 8, 13, 31, 42, 155,
    190
Jews
    at Auschwitz, 32, 40, 108
    Deported, 291, 293
    Dutch, 212
    in Cologne, 186
    in East Germany, 61, 150
    in West Germany, 184
    Seeheim, 41–42
Judische Mitbürger, 80
Jüdischer (see also Jews, Jewish), 117,
    153, 227, 234, 247, 249, 299,
    305
Junge Juden (Young Jews), 56–57, 275

Kaes, Anton, 241, 249
Kempowski, Walter, 23

KGB, 124
Kiessling, Wolfgang, 152, 154
Kieve Skiddel, 69, 72, 80, 91, 93–94,
    96
Kirsch, Sarah, 44
Klein, Alfred, 200
Klein, Gerda, 231
Kluger, Herbert, 299–300
Klüger, Ruth, 205–206, 219–225,
    230–232
Koeppen, Wolfgang, 292, 296,
    299–301, 305
Kofman, Berek, 291, 293
Kofman, Sarah, 291–292, 297, 304
Kohl, Helmut, 105, 116, 190, 242
Kol Nidre, 82
Krakow, 102, 299
Krauss, Werner, 187, 238
Kreisky, Bruno, 131–134, 139, 281
Kristallnacht, 97, 177, 256
Kulturbund, 234–235, 247

LaCapra, Dominick, 301, 305
Ladd, Brian, 160, 175
Lander, Jeanette, 229, 280, 282, 284,
    286–288, 290
Landesarchiv Berlin, 91, 96, 99
Lang, Berel, 276, 298, 304–305
Lanzmann, Claude, 226
Lauder Foundation, 58
Lessing, Gotthold Ephraim, 71, 188,
    191, 233–234, 239, 241,
    245–248
Levinas, Emmanuel, 12, 15, 25, 28–29
Levi, Primo, 294, 296, 301
Libeskind, Daniel, 7–8, 11, 13–14, 27,
    58, 155–178
Liss, Andrea, 293, 295, 298, 303
Lubavitch Movement, 58–59

Martin-Gropius-Bau, 176
Mass Murder (Massenmord), 76, 173,
    227, 229
Master Race (see also Aryanism), 83,
    85, 114, 130

Mendelssohn, Moses, 29, 178, 191, 198
Menuhin, Yehudi, 75, 89
Mercer, Harold, 95
Merchant of Venice (Shylock), 233–234, 237–241, 243–250, 258
Mitgutsch, Anna, 281–282, 289
Mitscherlich, Margarete, 289
Moses und Aron, 157, 167
Mourning, 18, 24, 36, 41, 83, 86, 213–214, 279, 291, 293, 304
Murderers, Germans as, 35, 83, 90, 112, 114, 255, 261, 271
Muslims, 283, 304

Nachama, Andreas, 92–93, 95
Nachman, Werner, 290, 57
National Socialist Party (National Sozialistische Deutsche Arbeiter Partei/NSDAP), 98, 107–110, 127, 131–133, 137, 152
Nazi Berlin (*see also* Berlin), 83, 95
Nazi Genocide, 127, 151, 208, 226, 279, 304
Nazism 10, 16, 23, 39, 41, 44, 50, 83–84, 87–88, 111, 123–124, 126–131, 134–136, 142, 144–145, 147, 158–159, 186, 192–193, 198, 206–208, 210–213, 215, 221–222, 225, 228, 231, 237, 239, 253–257, 305
Negative Symbiosis, 5, 22, 27, 32–35, 42, 45, 173, 179, 205, 226–227, 263–265, 267, 270, 272–273, 275–276, 291
Netherlands, 205–206, 209, 228, 230
Jews in, 212
New Cosmopolitanism, 4–5, 17, 28
Nolte, Ernst, 281
Non-Jewish Germans, 7, 173, 205, 208, 255, 257, 271
Non-Jewish Majority, 101–103
Nuremberg Laws, 68
Nuremberg Trials (Nürnberger Prozess), 187, 250

Oranienburger Synagogue, 58, 158
Ossies (*see also* East Germans), 284
Oswiecim (*see also* Auschwitz), 299

Passover (Pesach), 69, 158, 298
Peck, Abraham J., 93–94, 99
Peck, Jeff, 96
Pelinka, Anton, 120, 131, 139–140
Pestalozzistrasse Synagogue, 59
Philo-Semitism, 84, 95, 101, 103, 114, 172, 238, 241, 263–264, 267, 269–270, 273, 275–276
Pogrom, 50, 68, 94, 101, 158, 178, 247
Polish Jews, 53, 58, 68, 71, 73–75, 93, 95, 235, 299, 302
Postmemory, 12–13, 24, 291–297, 299, 301–303, 305

Ranicki-Reich, Marcel, 192–193, 197
Ravensbrück, 130
Reichschrifttumskammer, 300
Reichstag, 42, 71
Renaissance, 158, 175
Representation of Jews, 71, 110
Revenge, 35, 43, 82–84, 97, 108, 236, 239
Rosenzweig, Franz, 252
Rosh Hashanah, 71
Roth, Philip, 306
Russian Jews, 22, 49–50, 53, 55
Ryback, Timothy, 292, 301, 305

Sabbath (Shabbat), 49, 59, 272, 290
Scattering (Diaspora), 54, 72, 78, 24, 295
Scheunenviertel, 23
Schlink, Bernard, 24, 28, 302, 305
Schoenberg, Arnold, 11, 13 157, 165, 167, 176
Schoeps, Julius H., 116, 171–172, 178, 227
Scholem, Gershom, 25, 32, 36, 45, 252
Schrebergärten, 66, 68, 87
Schroeder, Gerhard, 120, 124

Second World War (*see* World War II)
SED Central Party Control Commission
(*see also* ZPKK), 143
Shoah (*see* Holocaust)
Soviet Jewry, Soviet Jews, 54, 56, 61, 146
Soviet Union, (Union of Soviet
Socialist Republics/USSR), 7, 50, 53–55, 68, 90, 103, 107, 112, 132, 144, 146–147, 150
SPD, 129, 139
Spielberg, Steven, 115, 244
SS (*see also* Waffen-SS), 11, 305, 66, 83, 123–124, 132, 138
Stalin, Joseph, 22, 52, 121, 124, 141, 143, 145–147, 150–151, 153, 190
Star of David (Magen David), 157, 160, 266, 269
Stasi, 147, 149–150
Stern, Frank, 71, 92–98
Stern, Guy, 289

Tabori, George, 240, 245–250, 274
Tanakh (*see also* Hebrew Bible), 215–217, 229–230
Theresienstadt (Terezín), 35, 67–68, 78–79, 81, 110, 220, 223, 250
Third Reich (Dritte Reich), 11, 35, 65, 96, 126–127, 158, 193, 241, 247
Torah (*see also* Hebrew Bible), 218, 285
Totalitarianism, 92, 279
Traitors, 113, 265
Treblinka, 110
Tucholksy, Kurt, 183, 186, 195, 274
Turkish Germans, 25, 271, 283, 288

United Nations Relief and
Rehabilitation Administration
(UNRRA), 50, 74, 110
United States Holocaust Memorial
Museum, 94

USSR (*see* Soviet Union)
Utopia (*Utopie*), 79, 151, 186

Vergangenheitsbewältigung, 242, 279
Victims of Fascism, 67, 72, 79, 82, 142

Waffen-SS, 242
Waldheim Affair, 127, 135
Walser-Bubis Debate, 246
Walser Speech, 57, 196
Warsaw Ghetto, 71, 127, 196
Wehrmacht, 24, 57, 128, 211, 278, 283, 289
Weil, Grete, 98, 205–210, 214–215, 217–219, 222, 225, 227–230
Weimar Republic (Weimarer Republik), 5, 7–8, 17–18, 20, 78, 158, 175, 186, 259, 261
Wessies (*see also* West Germans), 284
West Berlin, 70, 85, 91, 150, 159
West Germany, 115, 151, 153–154, 190, 234, 279
West Germans, 127
Wiesenthal, Simon, 132
Wilder, Billy, 70–71, 91
Wilkomirski, Binjamin, 15, 292, 296, 298–302, 305
Wolffsohn, Michael, 22, 28, 58
Wolf, Christa, 201
Wolf, Konrad, 67, 93, 255
World Jewish Congress, 99
World War I, 99, 128, 251
World War II, 23, 104, 129, 183, 196, 254, 265, 281

Yom Kippur, 49, 82
Young, James E., 155, 173–175, 178, 226

ZPKK (SED Central Party Control
Commission), 143–144, 146, 148